CONSUMER PROTECTION IN A CIRCULAR ECONOMY

CONSUMER PROTECTION IN A CIRCULAR ECONOMY

Bert Keirsbilck
Evelyne Terryn
(eds.)

intersentia
Cambridge – Antwerp – Chicago

Intersentia Ltd
Sheraton House | Castle Park
Cambridge | CB3 0AX | United Kingdom
Tel.: +44 1223 370 170 | Fax: +44 1223 370 169
Email: mail@intersentia.co.uk
www.intersentia.com | www.intersentia.co.uk

Distribution for the UK and Ireland:
NBN International
Airport Business Centre, 10 Thornbury Road
Plymouth, PL6 7 PP
United Kingdom
Tel.: +44 1752 202 301 | Fax: +44 1752 202 331
Email: orders@nbninternational.com

Distribution for Europe and all other countries:
Intersentia Publishing nv
Groenstraat 31
2640 Mortsel
Belgium
Tel.: +32 3 680 15 50 | Fax: +32 3 658 71 21
Email: mail@intersentia.be

Distribution for the USA and Canada:
Independent Publishers Group
Order Department
814 North Franklin Street
Chicago, IL60610
USA
Tel.: +1 800 888 4741 (toll free) | Fax: +1312 337 5985
Email: orders@ipgbook.com

Consumer Protection in a Circular Economy

ISBN 978-1-78068-657-8
ISBN 978-1-78068-858-9 (pdf)
D/2019/7849/64
NUR 827

British Library Cataloguing in Publication Data. A catalogue record for this book is available from the British Library.

CONTENTS

PART I

SETTING THE SCENE

THE CIRCULAR ECONOMY ACTION PLAN: AN AGENDA FOR CHANGE!

Hugo Maria SCHALLY*

Since the early days of global and European environmental policy, there has been the tension between the aim of the protection of the environment and societies' claim to growth and prosperity. This tension began with the first world conference on the global environment in Stockholm 1972 and has been ever more clearly enunciated in the preparation of the world conference on environment and development in Rio de Janeiro 1992 (UNCED, 1992) by the so-called "Brundtland Report", where the definition of sustainable development was clearly expressed.[1] This report describes sustainable development as a development that meets the needs of the present without compromising the ability of future generations to meet their own needs. The tension is clearly present in the two key concepts mentioned. The ambition to meet present needs in connection with the need for strengthening the ability of the environment to meet future needs.

For many years the world's environment policy focused on correcting and addressing the impact of economic development, while avoiding the fundamental element of the problem in question – the fact that the resource needs generated by current pattern of production and consumption far exceed the limits of the planet. The concept of "ecological limits of the Earth " or "planetary boundaries" was formulated and published in 2009 by a team led by Johan Rockström of the Stockholm Resilience Centre.[2] The idea is that our planetary system needs to operate in a "safe space" in which society must meet its needs without sudden or irreversible environmental changes taking place.

This tension was even more in everybody's mind in the context of the global financial and economic crisis after 2008, as the need for growth and job creation policy came to the forefront. This led to further policy reflection in Europe and

* Head of unit Multilateral environmental cooperation Directorate General for the Environment European Commission.

1 Our Common Future, Report from the United Nations World Commission on Environment and Development Oxford University Press, Oxford University Press, 1987.

2 'Planetary boundaries: Guiding human development on a changing planet'. Science. 347 (6223): 1259855.

in 2011 the European Commission published a Communication on a "Roadmap to a Resource Efficient Europe".[3] Based on this roadmap, the European Resource Efficiency Platform, a group of high-level economic and environmental experts, in 2014 drafted a report, which contained a number of recommendations for implementation at the national and regional level.[4] This report was the basis for further discussion of the European Commission about how these general macroeconomic recommendations would be turned into concrete proposals, which could be implemented at the company or administrative level. These discussions took place at a time when the international community and civil society was increasingly reflecting on these issues. New civil society actors such as the Ellen McArthur Foundation also worked intensively on the idea of the transition to a circular economy. A number of studies addressed challenges and opportunities of such a transition, finally yet importantly, a landmark study undertaken in 2013.[5] These and other studies have strongly influenced the debate on circular economy.

In June 2014, the European Commission adopted an initial circular economy package.[6] This package consisted of a communication on the transition to a circular economy, together with a legislative proposal on the revision of the targets of a number of legal instruments on waste legislation as well as several communications.[7] This package was, however, subject to a political revaluation following the taking of office of the new Commission under the leadership of President Juncker. As other initiatives, it was looked at to assess to what extent it was going to contribute to the achievements of the ten priorities for the EU as established by President Juncker. After intensive discussion with the Council of Ministers, the European Parliament and relevant stakeholders, the Commission

---

3 Communication from the Commission to the European Parliament, the Council, the European Economic and Social Committee and the Committee of the Regions. Roadmap to a Resource Efficient Europe. COM 571 (2011).

4 – EREP Manifesto and policy recommendations, European Commission, 31st March 2014.

5 – Belgium's energy challenges towards THE CIRCULAR ECONOMY – economic and business rationale for an accelerated transition, Ellen Mac Arthur Foundation, 2013.

6 Towards a circular economy: A zero waste programme for Europe (COM(2014), 398 final Brussels, 2.7.2014.

7 Proposal for a is OF THE EUROPEAN PARLIAMENT AND OF THE COUNCIL amending Directives 2008/98/EC on waste, 94/62/EC on packaging and packaging waste, 1999/31/EC on the landfill of waste, on end-of-life vehicles, 2000/53/EC on 2006/66/EC batteries and accumulators and waste batteries and accumulators, and 2012/19/EU on waste electrical and electronic equipment; COM(2014), 397 final, 2014/0201 (COD); COMMUNICATION FROM THE COMMISSION TO THE EUROPEAN PARLIAMENT, THE COUNCIL, THE EUROPEAN ECONOMIC AND SOCIAL COMMITTEE AND THE COMMITTEE OF THE REGIONS ON RESOURCE EFFICIENCY OPPORTUNITIES IN THE BUILDING SECTOR; COM/2014/0445 final; Communication FROM THE COMMISSION TO THE EUROPEAN PARLIAMENT, THE COUNCIL, THE EUROPEAN ECONOMIC AND SOCIAL COMMITTEE AND THE COMMITTEE OF THE REGIONS GREEN ACTION PLAN FOR SMEs Enabling SMEs to turn environmental challenges into business opportunities; COM/2014/0440 final.

concluded that this first package fell short of its ambitions and undertook in February 2015 to present in the course of 2015 a new, more ambitious action plan.

Following intensive work, on 2nd December 2015 the European Commission adopted a new EU action plan for the transition to a circular economy.[8] This plan has the objective of promoting the transition to a circular economy in Europe. In such a new circular economy, resources would be used in a more sustainable way and their value would be kept in the economic cycle as long as technically and economically possible. This Action Plan included proposals for the revision of the European waste legislation as well as a list of 54 measures affecting the whole life cycle of products and materials. This plan was developed in line with the priorities of the European Commission and is a key contribution to the EU's growth and jobs agenda.

The Circular Economy Action Plan aims to trigger a development in Europe, a move away from a linear economy model, which is very resource-intensive. In a world where the increase in people's needs and expectations lead to a huge increase in pressure on natural resources such as land, water, food, feed, raw materials and energy, we can no longer rely on an economic approach which is built on the principle of "take, make, use and throw away". This makes no sense, neither from an environmental, nor from an economic point of view. The transition to a circular economy will also enhance European competitiveness, as companies will have additional incentives for the development of new business models, innovative and more efficient production methods and sustainable models of consumption, while being less exposed to scarcity and price volatility of raw materials. The proposed actions are also closely linked to the EU's energy and climate policy. Moving to a circular economy therefore also supports the implementation of the Paris Climate Agreement and, within the United Nations 2030 Agenda for Sustainable Development.

The circular economy therefore is not only responding to an environmental necessity, it is a roadmap for a fundamental change of the economic and social model of our society. The circular economy is the only model that makes sense in the long term to our European society and economy. Europe has less natural

---

8 Closing the loop – An EU action plan for the Circular Economy. Closing the loop, Brussels, 2.12.2015. COM (2015), 614 final. Proposal for a is OF THE EUROPEAN PARLIAMENT AND OF THE COUNCIL amending Directive 2008/98/EC on waste; COM/2015/0595 final – 2015/0275 (COD); Proposal for a is OF THE EUROPEAN PARLIAMENT AND OF THE COUNCIL amending Directive 94/62/EC on packaging and packaging waste; COM/2015/0596 final – 2015/0276 (COD); Proposal for a is OF THE EUROPEAN PARLIAMENT AND OF THE COUNCIL amending Directive 1999/31/EC on the landfill of waste; COM/2015/0594 final – 2015/0274 (COD); Proposal for a is OF THE EUROPEAN PARLIAMENT AND OF THE COUNCIL amending Directives 2000/53/EC on end-of-life vehicles, 2006/66/EC on batteries and accumulators and waste batteries and accumulators, and 2012/19/EU on waste electrical and electronic equipment; COM/2015/0593 final – 2015/0272 (COD).

resources than many other parts of the world and can (and will) not compete based on lower labour or resource costs. In global competition, Europe can only compete on the basis of its innovation capacity and play a leading role when natural resources are used and re-used in a smarter and more sustainable way. This approach can also help to continue to be the market leader for green technologies and approaches to stay.

The measures under the Action Plan are aimed at the whole economic cycle from the use of primary and secondary raw materials, the design, production and delivery of materials, products and services, distribution and consumption of products and services as well as, the proper disposal and recycling of materials. Finally, the creation of a fully functioning market for secondary raw materials closes the loop. The European single market provides a good legal framework for that. However, the 54 measures proposed cover only those areas, where it makes sense to act at European level.

A key part of the plan is the support for the development and marketing of products and services that are "fit for circularity". Those products are durable, easier to repair, dismantle, reuse, recycle materials more effectively and lead to a more efficient use of resources. This will be achieved through the development of technical standards, but also through better implementation of existing regulatory frameworks, such as the Eco-design directive and other directives and regulations.

The Circular Economy Action Plan identified key challenges hampering consumer engagement in the transition and proposed a series of actions to address them. These relate to the quality and reliability of the information consumers have access to, the longevity of the products and their components. The action plan also identified a clear role for public authorities using their purchasing power to support the transition.

In parallel, the follow up to the fitness check of the consumers' legislation has allowed for a better integration of consumers' protection against false environmental declarations, framing the conditions for a wider consumer engagement in the circular economy within the EU's consumer policy. Following these recent developments, further actions both at EU, national and regional level will be required for consumers to embrace the circular economy and to reap its benefits.

To enhance the reliability, comparability and accuracy of the environmental information offered to consumers and, more in general, to any stakeholder, the Commission has adopted the Product and Organisation Environmental Footprint (PEF/OEF) methods. These methods allow identifying and calculating the most relevant environmental impacts for a product, service or organisation along the supply chain. They define a benchmark to compare the environmental performance of different products belonging to the same product group. The Commission is looking at potential uses of these methods in several policy areas, such as sustainable finance, climate or product-related policies.

The Commission also concluded the fitness check of the EU Ecolabel regulation and proposed follow up actions to increase its effectiveness and uptake. As a result, the Commission is developing a strategic approach, identifying those product categories with enough uptake, reinforcing monitoring and communication activities for the EU Ecolabel including the development of criteria for financial products. The role of the EU Ecolabel in public procurement is also being emphasized, as a benchmark for environmental excellence.

Ensuring the coherence of Commission's tools and schemes to provide accurate information on the environmental performance of products as well as on options and actions to extend products lifetime is one of the objectives of a more coherent product policy framework presented with this report.

Over the past three years, the Commission has also reinforced consumers' rights against false green claims and unfair premature obsolescence of products. The revised guidance to apply and implement the Unfair Commercial Practices Directive[9] incorporates key principles such as content, presentation and documentation of environmental claims. It also clarifies the application of the Directive on unfair obsolescence practices – which will allow a better enforcement by market surveillance authorities in this area. In addition, the legislative proposals under the New Deal for Consumers[10] takes consumer protection against this type of practices a step forward. In fact, it sets stronger enforcement and better opportunities for individual and collective redress against unfair commercial practices, which will act as deterrent against false environmental claims and unfair premature obsolescence practices.

A recent Behavioural Study on Consumers' Engagement in the Circular Economy[11] showed a large willingness of consumers to engage in the circular economy despite a still low engagement in reality. It also found that the lack of information regarding product durability and reparability as well as the insufficiently developed repair markets are barriers to consumers' engagement. In order to address this gap, the Commission is supporting the repair sector through the mobilisation of funding. It is also developing a scoring system on the reparability of products for possible application under Ecodesign or Energy Labelling. Further work and initiatives will be necessary to explore possible options and benefits from making this information accessible to consumers as well as to raise awareness and consumer education.

Recent developments at national level[12] confirm the role of premature obsolescence practices as barriers for longer lasting products. To address this,

9 Directive 2005/29/EC of the European Parliament and of the Council of 11 May 2005 concerning unfair business-to-consumer commercial practices in the internal market.

10 Http://europa.eu/rapid/press-release_IP-18-3041_en.htm.

11 Https://ec.europa.eu/info/sites/info/files/ec_circular_economy_final_report_0.pdf.

12 Decision from the Italian consumer protection authorities on premature obsolescence and decision of the French government include provisions rendering "planned obsolescence" a misdemeanour (French Energy Transition Law).

the Commission has set an independent, multi-stakeholder testing programme for premature obsolescence through H2020 with a view to gather further knowledge on the nature and enabling factors of premature obsolescence practices as well as on the way to address them. Building upon the results of the project and the options and actions identified in the EU Product Policy Framework, the Commission will explore further work on this area, also taking into consideration actions put forward at national level.

Aspects relating to guarantees, such as the legal guarantee period and the reversal of the burden of proof, are also an important part of the consumption puzzle, as they can protect consumers against defective products, preventing them from being thrown away. The proposal for a Directive on the online sales of goods, presented in December 2015 as a deliverable of the Circular Economy Action Plan, was amended in 2017 to extend its scope to also cover sales of goods offline.

Despite having recognised the importance of economic instruments to better reflect environmental costs in the price of products, Member States have also highlighted the difficulties to come forward with concrete proposals. The Commission will continue supporting the exchange of information and good practices on economic instruments and incentives through programmes offering technical assistance, thematic discussions and through online exchanges via the European Circular Economy Stakeholder Platform.[13]

Public authorities are identified in the action plan as drivers of the transition. In order to help them reduce their environmental impact, set the example for other consumers, and create a market for innovative and circular goods and services, the Commission has acted on two axis. On the one hand it has published/revised EU Green Public Procurement criteria (e.g. computers and monitors, textiles, furniture, indoor cleaning services, paints and varnishes, road design, construction and maintenance, office building design, construction and maintenance), which include circular economy aspects such as durability or recyclability. To promote their uptake it has mobilised EU funding developed guidance documents[14], which gather good practices at national and regional level, and has rolled out training sessions with specific toolkits in 11 EU Member States.

Waste management also has a key role to play. Based on proposals from the European Commission, the European Parliament and the Council of Ministers have already set ambitious new targets for waste management in Europe. This new framework will serve as a basis for better and more efficient provision of secondary raw materials in Europe. It includes the development of quality standards for secondary raw materials, but also improvements in the monitoring

13 Https://circulareconomy.europa.eu/platform/.

14 ???

of the economic process in terms of the presence of substances of very high concern.

These actions shall include proposals for the sectors that are considered important for the transition to a circular economy for example, the construction sector, the bio-economy, and the raw materials sectors. At the beginning of 2018, the Commission has presented an additional comprehensive package on plastics and chemicals activities.[15]

It is clear that the Commission alone cannot drive the transition to a circular economy; the transition requires a common effort by all actors. There is a need to mobilise stakeholders at all levels, including the Member States, regional and local authorities, business and industry, academia and NGOs and civil society. The role of local and regional authorities is of the utmost importance. Initiatives of the business community and of civil society are essential conditions for the success of the Circular Economy Package. The Circular Economy package is just the beginning of the transition towards a circular economy in Europe and worldwide.

The work has only just started. As part of the 2015 package, the European Commission is committed to provide, five years after the adoption of the 2015 action plan, with a comprehensive report on the implementation. This report will provide the opportunity to take stock of developments since 2015 and to lay the foundations for further reflection on measures for the transition to a circular economy.

15 http://ec.europa.eu/environment/circular-economy/index_en.htm.

CONSUMER PROTECTION IN THE CIRCULAR ECONOMY IN EUROPE – LEGAL INITIATIVES AND CHALLENGES – THE COMMISSION'S VIEW*

Key Note Speech

Renatas MAZEIKA**

INTRODUCTION

I'm delighted to be here at this important international conference on "Consumer protection in a circular economy".

If the word "circular" is originated from the "circulation" than, for sure, it has been born here in Leuven where so many young people/students, future gainers of Circular Economy, are moving around be it on bicycles or on foot.

This is a very timely conference!

Over the last years, rising consumption around the globe has increased pressure on the environment and created greater competition for resources.

The demand for resources makes our industry and society dependent on imports and vulnerable to high prices, market volatility, and the geopolitical situations.

Many EU policies aim to address these challenges and promote a more sustainable, resource-efficient and circular economy.

Integrating the consumer perspective into this circular economy is key.

- This is linked to elements such as the optimal lifetime and durability of products, as well as the easy re-use, easy repair, upgrade, disassemble and recycling of products.

---

* [Check Against Delivery].

** Head of Unit, Consumer Policy Unit, Consumers Directorate, Directorate-General Justice and Consumers.

- It is also linked the provision of clear, credible and relevant information to consumers to allow them to make informed purchasing choices.
- It is also linked to consumer protection against misleading and unfounded green claims ("greenwashing") or planned obsolescence cases.

Is the European consumer waiting for this? Are they interested? Are they keen to contribute? I think they do!

In fact, we are currently finalising an EU wide behavioural study on consumers' engagement in the Circular Economy.

This study provides insights on consumer attitudes and behaviour concerning the durability and reparability of products. The results will provide input to possible future legal and non-legal measures on circular economy at the EU, national or at the regional level.

The preliminary findings show that:

- Consumers indicate a desire for receiving better information on durability/ reparability, because they felt that it was often difficult to find information regarding how long products will last and how easy it is to repair products.
- The most important factors influencing survey respondents' purchasing decisions were quality, price and how long products would last.
- A majority of respondents attached high importance to product durability. Among these respondents, the top reason was that durable products would save them money in the long run.
- Alas, it is not about the circular economy, it is about the household economy what the consumers do care about. But, in this case, the aims coincide. Maybe this is the way we need to approach the consumers.
- The behavioural experiment corroborated many of the findings from the consumer survey. In line with consumers' self-reported statements, the experiment found hard evidence that individuals take durability and reparability into account when purchasing products. This however was only the case when relevant information on product durability and/or reparability was shown at the moment of purchase

Overall, this study shows that we need to make sure that consumers get the right information and be given the right tools, so they are empowered, assisted and encouraged to make sustainable choices and they can easily contribute to a circular economy.

You have extensively debated the actions of the December 2015 Circular Economy Package. I'm happy to say that just over two years later, the Commission has delivered almost all the initiatives planned, and in the coming year we will put the final pieces on the table, such as the upcoming initiative to reduce Single-Use-Plastics (such as cutlery, plastic plates or plastic bottles).

Overall, we have made good progress on the waste legislation that will make Europe's waste management system the most advanced regional system in the world. The European Parliament and Council came recently to an agreement, which will update current waste management rules, including new targets for recycling, packaging and landfilling.

In November 2016, the Commission adopted an Ecodesign Working Plan for the years 2016–2019, setting out its working priorities under the ecodesign and energy labelling framework.

The working plan has a stronger focus on supporting circular economy objectives.

The Commission has committed to explore the possibility of establishing more product-specific and/or horizontal requirements in areas such as durability, reparability upgradeability, information and ease of reuse and recycling.

The implementation of the working plan is currently under way. A package of different eco-design and energy labelling product measures is under preparation, namely for refrigerators, washing machines, dishwashers, televisions and lighting, and foreseen to be adopted by the end of this year.

Gradually, in the years to come, eco-design/energy labelling product measures will include more and more circular economy aspects.

There are many other important work streams too, from synergizing our chemicals and waste policies, to financing and research, to awareness raising and consumer protection and better tracking and measurement of the progress we made.

LEGAL ISSUES

Let's look a bit also into the legal framework for the Circular Economy which is the title and purpose of my intervention.

This afternoon professor Zoll provided futuristic insights how a law could develop following societal and economic changes.

However, we are not yet there. We have currently in place the Consumer protection law of eighties and nineties and we are trying to fit for "purpose", the purpose being Circular economy. Unfortunately, it works sub-optimally. This has been demonstrated today by the speakers, who manifested their attempts and struggle to make the current rules to work for Circular Economy purposes.

Indeed, the question is whether general legal framework/consumer law facilitates "green and sustainable behaviours" of businesses.

Is there legal incentive for businesses to produce goods that are more durable? Are the sanctions deterrent enough to discourage business from intentionally misleading consumers? Is the redress system robust enough to allow consumers claim for compensation of damages if they were misled and therefore made wrong purchasing choices?

One can define a situation as a **patchwork** of different legal provisions, interpretations provided by the Commission, different courts and then uneven application across the Member States. But let's be honest. The current legal framework never meant to support the aims of the circular economy. At the moment of the conception of the Sales and Guarantees directive or the Unfair Commercial Practice Directive (UCPD) the notion of the Circular Economy/ Green Economy barely existed.

Let's take an example, the Unfair Commercial Practices Directive protects consumers against misleading and aggressive commercial practices. It tells what is not allowed or considered to be wrong-doing. It is based on principles rather than on very precise regulation. It does not tell explicitly to business what, how and when to do.

In the area of environmental claims the UCPD does not provide specific rules. It does, however, allow competent national authorities and national courts to perform a case-by-case assessment of whether a claim is misleading either in its content or in the way it is presented to consumers, taking into account its impact on the average consumer's purchasing decisions.

How does it work in practice? In some countries, for example Sweden, where the culture of the green economy, sustainable consumption is in zenith, it works very well from the legal point of view. It gives ammunition to the consumer protection and environmental authorities to enter into dialogue with the traders and to request to change practices and remedy situation. In other, even if transposed nationally, it is difficult to apply and would not be a strong weapon to attack the rough trader, because in their legal traditions, there is no such understanding as "principles based". The rules must be clear and unambiguous.

In December 2017, national consumer protection enforcement authorities held their first workshop on the issue of misleading green claims under the Unfair Commercial Practices Directive. The authorities in general agreed that it would be important to investigate the issue of misleading green claims further, but then one had to acknowledge there is a lack of legal, environmental expertise and binding, explicit rules to act.

Another good example is planned/premature obsolescence and the durability of products, which are very important topics for the circular economy.

Planned obsolescence is a policy of deliberately planning or designing a product with a limited useful life, so it will become obsolete or non-functional after a certain period.

The consequences of planned obsolescence can hit consumers hard in the wallet. In addition, it can also have negative impacts on our environment and on fair competition. Overall, it goes against the objectives of a sustainable, low carbon, resource efficient, competitive and circular economy.

In some countries such as France there is a binding provision in law banning such practices and imposing severe sanctions.

In the case of the European law, this maybe could be considered as a breach of the UCPD in case a trader failed to inform the consumer that a product has been designed with a limited lifetime and if this omission likely caused the average consumer to take a transactional decision that he would not have taken otherwise. There is plenty of "ifs" and "maybe". In order to decide whether this is the case, competent national courts and authorities need to perform an assessment on a case-by-case basis. Is this good enough to fight planned obsolescence?

Furthermore, it is said that the consumers can be entitled to remedies (repair, replacement, price reduction or contract termination) if the planned obsolescence constitutes a lack of conformity under the Consumer Sales and Guarantees Directive (CSGD). But the legal guarantee is only 2 years in majority of the EU countries and then there is a burden of proof clause, which puts onus on the consumers after 6 months.

The Commission adopted in October 2017, an amended proposal on sales of goods, which will replace the CSGD once approved by the co-legislators and is expected to provide an incentive to produce higher quality and more durable products.

In particular, the Commission has proposed to extend the time period for the reversal of the burden of proof from six months to two years. This would make it easier for consumers to exercise its rights. Fair enough, but this proposal is not meant for the Circular Economy. The aims are everything but circular economy.

Nevertheless, it could encourage the business to produce more durable goods. In addition to the burden of proof, one could also consider whether the extension of the legal guarantee period or introduction of the manufactures commercial guarantee would not provide further incentives and mount pressure onto the manufactures. This proposal is currently under negotiation with co-legislators and may be subject to further changes.

NEW DEAL FOR CONSUMERS

Against this background, the Commission on 11 April 2018 adopted two legislative proposals under the "New Deal for Consumers" title that aim at better enforcement of EU consumer protection legislation, including the rules against unfair commercial practices. Once again, these changes were not conceived with the Circular Economy in mind, but it might have a positive effect in this regard.

Specifically, the Commission has proposed to: (1) provide the victims of unfair commercial practices with a right to individual remedies, (2) to introduce a new European collective redress right for when groups of consumers have suffered harm and (3) to strengthen the penalties available to national enforcement authorities in case of widespread infringements that affect consumers in several EU Member States.

When approved by the co-legislators, this legislation will better protect consumers and will likely deter traders from engaging in unfair commercial practices such as planned obsolescence, misleading and unfounded environmental claims or unfair practices such in the Diesel Gate. To increase the deterrent effect of penalties, the maximum possible fine for such widespread infringements should be at least 4% of the trader's annual turnover in the Member State concerned.

Then we proposed Directive on representative actions. This is a great step towards improving the enforcement of consumer law. It will allow consumer organisations, independent public bodies and other relevant entities designated by the Member States, such as environment protection organisations to concretely act for the protection of consumer rights.

The consumers having faced a problem within the EU, whether domestically or cross-border, did not follow it up despite feeling it would have been legitimate to do so. Among the main reasons for not acting were perceived unlikelihood of obtaining redress, previous experience of complaining unsuccessfully, uncertainty about consumer rights, not knowing where or how to complain and psychological reluctance.

We propose a principle-based instrument that respects subsidiarity and national legal traditions. It leaves to the Member States necessary autonomy as to the specific solutions, while making sure that the main features of the mechanism are common across the EU.

These main features are based on the existing 2009 Injunctions Directive: As it is the case now, in order to seek injunction orders, for stopping or prohibiting an infringement, the qualified entities won't need to obtain the mandate of the individual consumers concerned or provide proof of their actual loss.

The novelty is that qualified entities will be also able to seek collective redress in the name and on behalf of a group if individual consumers concerned by an infringement. The way how the individual consumers will be involved in the proceedings (opt-in/opt-out) will depend of the choice made by each Member State.

Still the proposal makes sure that across the Union a consumer organisation could initiate the representative action for consumer redress and be the party to the proceedings with all relevant procedural rights. In several Member State such a concept is already in place, in others it will be the real ground breaking.

Importantly, the proposal provides for a procedural mechanism, which does not affect the rules establishing substantive rights of consumers to contractual and non-contractual remedies. Therefore, the redress measures ordered within the representative action could cover the right to compensation for damages, contract termination, reimbursement, replacement, repair or price reduction, as appropriate and as available under EU law or relevant national law.

The proposed Directive on representative actions will also contribute to the effective enforcement of environmental protection, whenever the "collective interests of consumers" are harmed. The Annex I to the proposal contains a list of EU instruments which are covered by its scope, and it includes instruments like the Ecodesign Directive and the Ecolabel Regulation. The scope of the proposal covers instruments which provide for rules on the direct commercial relationships between traders and consumers, such as traders' obligations regarding consumer information.

This proposal was by some law professors already hailed as the best piece of the legislation that the EU has ever proposed. According to them, it will contribute to give to EU a human face and also contribute to creating/cementing the trust among the citizens.

Of course, there are lot of resistance here and arguments against by businesses on the grounds of the subsidiarity, potential frivolous actions, third party funding, etc. But, who said that the good creation is without the travail?

Ladies and gentlemen,

Our demand for natural resources has reached unsustainable proportions. We, policy makers, academia, business people, consumers and citizens have no choice but to look for alternative solutions.

The transition to a more circular economy in the European Union is picking up pace. The number of initiatives to stimulate the transition are increasing, both top-down from public authorities through policy actions as well as bottom-up led by industry initiatives at company or cross-sectoral level.

They complement also other initiatives in the mobility, finance and other areas, to address climate change mitigation or to promote energy efficiency, renewable energy, clean mobility and a sustainable, ethical and fair consumption.

At EU level, the EU Action Plan for the Circular Economy, adopted in December 2015, has led to concerted policy and regulatory efforts in various sectors and areas to stimulate a more circular economy in the EU. This is extremely positive.

Our efforts to promote circular economy go also beyond the EU Action Plan from 2015. For example, earlier this week, as part of the modernisation of the EU budget, the Commission has proposed to include new sources of funding for the EU budget including "a national contribution calculated on the amount of non-recycled plastic packaging waste in each Member State (0.80 € per kilo)." This will create an incentive for Member States to reduce packaging waste and stimulate Europe's transition towards a circular economy.

However, it is clear that our economy is still far from circular, and that many initiatives are still to be taken in the years to come to allow consumers to easily benefit and contribute to the circular economy for the benefit of them and society.

We need to work on this together, to make changes that make sense for our lifestyles, for consumers, for businesses and for the planet so I very much welcome your discussions and insights you provide today.

I would like to conclude with the words of Vice-President of the European Commission, Frans Timmermans, at a recent conference:

> Being prepared to face these challenges, being ready to reap the benefits that these transformations can bring, will require going back to our foundations, rethinking traditional concepts. And that's why I believe the circular economy is about more than the economy, it's more than just plastics. It's about creating a positive attitude to the future, it's about creating a sense that our future can be more prosperous, can be better. That there is a place for everyone in the circular economy. That if Europe leads in this, Europe will also be the first who profits from this. In terms of being the first who makes this transition into an economy that will come about, whether we like it or not. So we can better shape it, we can better work together to make it happen.

Thank you.

PART II

INTERDISCIPLINARY PERSPECTIVES ON A CIRCULAR ECONOMY

TECHNOLOGY FOR CIRCULAR ECONOMY

A New Paradigm for the Way We Use Resources

Karel VAN ACKER

1. THE TECHNO-ECONOMIC DRIVERS FOR CIRCULAR ECONOMY

Our society is built on materials. Materials have been extracted and sourced easily and at low prices during the last 60 years. In fact, progress in economy has profited from cheap material resources, and technological development could flourish without concerns about the availability of the needed resources. This has led to a quasi-unlimited growth in consumption and production.

The exponential growth of consumption is very clear from the rate of extraction of resources. The extraction of metal ores e.g. has risen worldwide by 54% during the decade 2005–15, for non-metallic materials we note an increase of 67% in the same period (UNEP, 2016). It is estimated (UNEP, 2011) that the amount of materials extracted and used globally – including ores, minerals, fossil fuels and biomass – increased eightfold between 1900 and 2005. This is twice the rate of population growth. Global annual resource use reached nearly 90 billion metric tons in 2017 and may more than double by 2050 (Olivetti & Cullen, 2018). In more specific sectors, e.g. electric vehicles, PV, wind energy, the demand for less common metals such as gallium, germanium, indium, neodymium, might grow sixfold within the next 20 years (Angerer et al., 2009). Meeting this increase in resource extraction is a vast technological challenge.

Furthermore, new technologies (in ICT for example) do use a lot of different precious, rare and even toxic elements. An iPhone e.g. contains up to 49 different chemical elements, of which 9 are labelled toxic (and pose a problem for treating the discarded products), 19 are considered as 'critical raw materials' (European Commission, 2017), and 4 are so-called conflict minerals as defined by the European Union (European Union, 2017) or by section 1502 or the Dodd-Frank

Wall Street Reform and Consumer Protection Act in the US. All these elements have their function to make the phone small, smart and light.

Often, the future availability of materials for the production of consumer goods is unsure. This is more due to technological and economic factors, such as the enormous investments and time to open new mines, and the decreasing grade of ores and their accessibility, than to immediate scarcity of the ores. Geopolitics also play an important role, especially when countries have a quasi-monopoly on certain resources, such China has on rare earth metals, and on antimony for example. The European Commission issues every 3 years a list of "critical raw materials" (CRMs) (European Commission, 2017), which are materials with a combined high importance to the EU economy and high risk for their supply. Twenty-seven different chemicals are on the 2017 CRMs list of the EC, see figure 1.

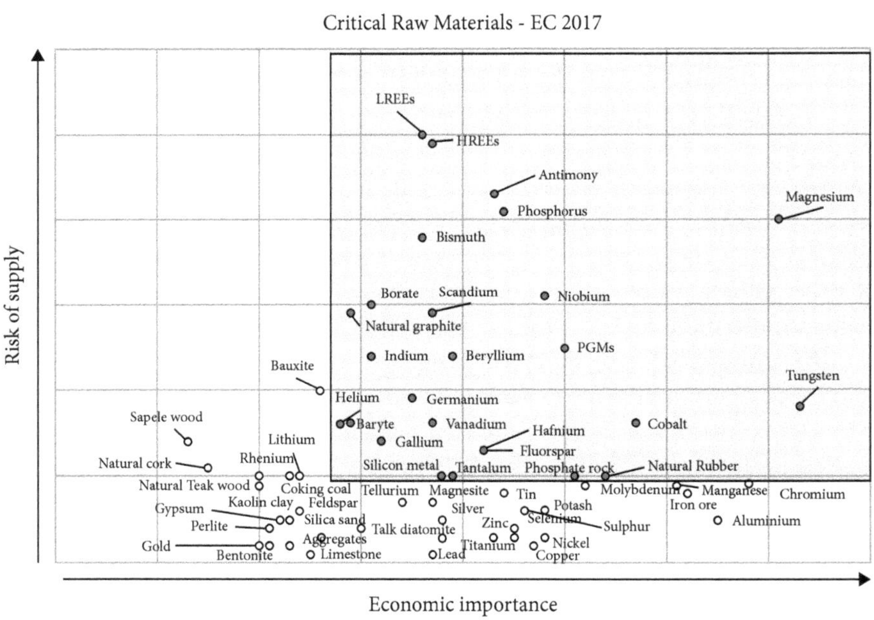

Figure 1: List of critical materials prioritized by the EU (European Commission, 2014). The critical materials are those in the upper right rectangle

Technological development of a number of consumer products has counter-intuitively yielded shorter lifetimes, also called planned obsolescence, which evidently enhances again the demand for materials. Evidence for planned obsolescence has been shown within one product category for similar products, e.g. for small consumer electronics with a decrease of 20% in lifetime between 2000 and 2006 or for printing and imaging equipment with a decrease of 11% in the same period (EEA, 2017; Wang, Huismann, Stevels, & Balde, 2013). Radical changes in technology, however, can also have a negative impact on the lifetime of products. The market introduction of flat screen TVs to replace the old CRT TVs, decreased the average lifetime from 10 to 12 years for CRT TVs to 5,6 years for flat screen TVs (Prakash, Dehoust, Gsell, Schleicher, & Stamminger, 2016). Furthermore, in 2012 60% of the TV owners replaced their TV not because of a failing screen or another failure, but just because of getting the newest type.

Next to the ever-increasing production and consumption volumes of materials due to increasing wealth and population, increasing technological complexity, and decreasing lifetime of products, we should also be aware of the impact on the environment of materials production and waste. About 25% of the worldwide greenhouse gas (GHG) emissions are directly related to the production of materials. Steel production is on its own responsible for 2,5 billion ton CO_2 emitted per year, one tenth of the worldwide industrial emissions. Steel is followed by the cement production, which emits 1,9 billion tons CO_2 per year. Materials do also have an indirect impact on greenhouse gas emission in other sectors, such as transport and heating. Lighter materials for cars can reduce the CO_2 footprint of individual transport, novel materials for batteries and electrical motors improve the e-mobility, new insulation materials enable passive house building, etc. Of course, the availability and impact of these materials have to be considered and taken care of as well.

At the end-of-life of products, still, huge amounts of materials are merely wasted, despite many efforts especially in Western Europe to recycle waste. 2,12 billion ton of waste is today landfilled worldwide, i.e. about 280 kg per person. Even in the European Union, some countries landfill more than 80% of the waste (Finland, Sweden, Romania, Greece and Bulgaria (Eurostat, 2018b)). It is estimated waste treatment globally costs 200 billion euro per year (World Bank, 2012). This cost will most probably rise up to 350 billion euro per year in 2025. This is together with the environmental problems of materials use, production and waste a very harsh downside of the way we consume today.

The take-make-waste way of production and consumption, or the linear economy, still is the prevailing practice. In the EU, the consumption of materials (for material use, not for energy) still needs 86% virgin resources (Eurostat, 2018a). At the end-of-life, only 27% of all solid wastes are recycled in some way (most often it is downcycled in a lesser quality application). This wasting linear economy is clearly not sustainable and should be transformed into a Circular Economy.

2. TECHNOLOGICAL STRATEGIES FOR CIRCULAR ECONOMY

Circular Economy (CE) refers to new technologies and business models designed to preserve wherever and at the highest level possible the value of resources and materials within the economy, to avoid waste, and to minimize the environmental impact of the resulting material cycles (Van Acker et al., 2016).

The previous paragraph summarizes the general framework of the Circular Economy. Although about 114 definitions can be found in the literature on Circular Economy (Kirchherr, Reike, & Hekkert, 2017), they all, in essence, refer to better closing material loops and preserving the value of resources. Walter Stahel, who can be considered one of the pioneers of the 'cradle-to-cradle' concept and of Circular Economy and who approaches the theme from an economic perspective, makes a clear distinction between 'Circular Economy' and 'performance economy'. The latter refers to models related to service economy and stewardship, the former to the closure of loops within a regional economy. Circular Economy in the narrow sense, therefore, relates to the effective closure of loops, a definition maintained, for example, by CSR Netherlands (MVO Nederland) and by Chatham (Preston, 2012). Walter Stahel connects a number of crucial features to the definitions of Circular Economy: (1) the 'smaller' the loop the more efficient it will be (in terms of resource consumption) and the more profitable; (2) it is crucial that the transition through a material loop is slow; (3) Circular Economy replaces energy and raw materials with labour; (4) Circular Economy manages (manufactured) stocks, rather than material flows, and its goal is the preservation of value.

In the next sections, we will give an overview of different technological strategies to realize the aims stated by the given framework of Circular Economy and the features as stated by Walter Stahel. These strategies are summarized in figure 2. Before going into further detail, note that whatever strategy is followed, the impact of the new system on resource use and the environment should be assessed with respect to its entire life cycle, since it is never obvious whether gains at one spot in the materials chain does not cause losses somewhere else.

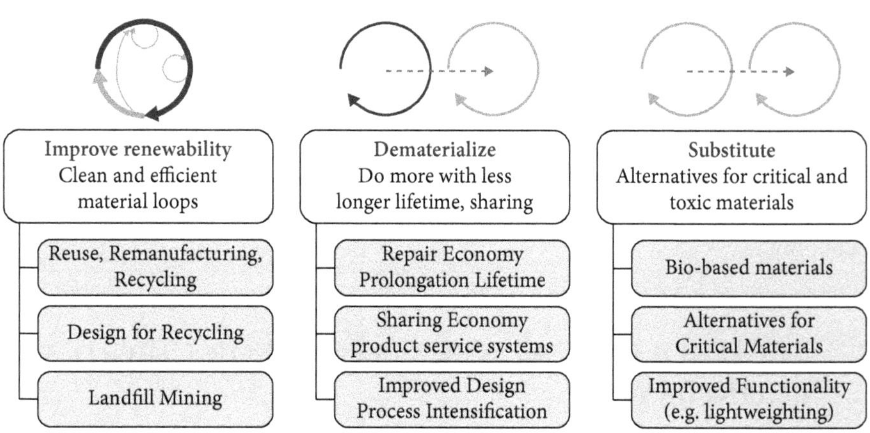

Figure 2: Schematic of different strategies to realize Circular Economy

2.1. IMPROVE RENEWABILITY

A first set of strategies is to renew materials from discarded products. The objective is to recuperate all materials at the highest quality out of waste, with the lowest impact to the environment. This often is interpreted as recycling, which is, of course, an important strategy. However, more can be done to close material circles in a clean and efficient way. It often is economically more interesting to try to recuperate or remanufacture components rather than single chemical elements, since these components have a much higher value. The total value of the individual materials extracted from a mobile phone or smartphone amounts to only 1% of the cost of the phone. The value of the components, however, could rise to one third of the total value. Even more efficient in terms of impact on resources and environment is the reuse of products whenever possible, e.g. via second-hand shops or websites. As discussed underneath, it is often quite difficult to extract and recycle materials from products in an effective way. Therefore, the design of products to enable recycling after its use actually is imperative. "Design for recycling" is crucial to better close material loops, and the recyclability of a product should at least be disclosed to consumers.

Closing material loops and recycling generally do not include the quality of the recycled materials. Targets for recycling set by legislation or directives (e.g. the ELV directive (European Commission, 2000), or the WEEE directive (European Commission, 2012)) typically are considering the weight of recycled materials only, not quality. The aim of Circular Economy should, however, be to find the optimum in qualitative recycling, remanufacturing and reuse of products.

Finally, recycling of materials out of end-of-life products is only one side of the coin. A huge amount of waste is also generated during the production phase, which also can be recovered in other application. This needs more intensified collaboration between companies, in order to find good applications for waste streams of one company into the production value chain of another company. This is called industrial symbiosis. A nice example is the use of residues from the steel industry into novel cement types (Salman, Dubois, Di Maria, Van Acker, & Van Balen, 2016).

2.2. DEMATERIALIZE

A second set of strategies are meant to realize consumer needs with less consumption of materials. The objective is to make use of every single kg of material as efficient and intensive as possible, and to do more with fewer resources.

Quite a lot of routes can be thought of for reaching this objective. A first route is to share products and make them available to other consumers during their unused time. This can be done in a very informal way, amongst neighbors e.g. sharing the lawn mower, or in a more formal way via internet platforms and third parties. Another example is car sharing. A car is on average only used for driving during 5% of its time, by on average 1,5 persons... (MacArthur, Zumwinkel, & Stuchtey, 2015) By car-pooling or car-sharing, the intensity of use of one car can increase a lot. As a matter of fact, the sharing economy has been grown a lot last years, mainly because of supporting IT technologies for the organization of the sharing. Companies also explore new business models in which they sell the service of a product instead of the product itself, e.g. pay-per-lux of Philips or the leasing of carpets by Desso.

Dematerialization can also be realized by stimulating the repair economy. Why discarding an entire mobile phone, when the screen glass has broken, while the electronics still perfectly function? The company iFixit e.g. delivers the tools and information to repair mobile phones. In this light, design for obsolescence evidently has to be reversed and consumers protected against it.

Finally, the material intensity can also be increased by design. Products can be designed such that they contain less material, or combine different functions in one single product. Most products are over-dimensioned because of conservative safety margins, or because of the use of standardized components instead of tailored made ones. 3D printing can e.g. be implemented to produce more tailored made products, with more complex and partly hollow shapes, such that less material is incorporated in the final product. Furthermore, 3D printing wastes fewer materials during production of components compared to conventional production methods such as machining.

2.3. SUBSTITUTE

Replacing scarce materials and materials with a high environmental impact by alternatives is the objective of a third set of Circular Economy strategies. Substitution hence aims at reducing the demand for scarce materials. This seems to be an obvious and purely technological strategy. When we need one of the most critical raw materials, neodymium, to produce the magnets within the motor of an e-vehicle, why not replacing this material with a less critical one? The reality often is not that simple. This material, in casu neodymium, is selected for its very specific properties. In this case, we need the neodymium for making very strong and small magnets. Alternatives are developed but often contains critical raw materials as well (in this case, samarium cobalt magnets might be an alternative, but suffers from criticality as well (Bailey, Mancheri, & Van Acker, 2017)). There might be radical new technologies under development, however, the time between inventions in a laboratory and applications typically is 10 to 15 years – hence this is a long-term and uncertain solution.

Bio-based materials often are referred to as good alternatives for fossil-based polymers, and even of construction materials. Bio-based materials are made from wood, plants, algae, etc. There certainly are interesting bio-based materials, but also here the total impact over the entire life cycle should be carefully assessed and published since not all bio-based materials have e.g. a lower CO_2 footprint than their fossil-based alternatives. Furthermore, there is a lot of confusion about how to dispose of bio-based materials. Some are biodegradable, but only in well-controlled conditions in industrial installations. For most of them, recycling is a better option with respect to Circular Economy, than just compost them, but again there are some issues of compatibility with the current plastic recycling streams (Alaerts, Augustinus, & Van Acker, 2018)

3. EXPECTED TECHNOLOGICAL INNOVATIONS FOR THE CIRCULAR ECONOMY

The strategies discussed in the previous paragraph include technological as well as economic and social aspects. In this paragraph, the expected technological innovations that support these strategies will be elaborated further.

Production and recycling technologies might be the first idea one has when thinking of new technologies for Circular Economy. There, however, is more. The rise and exponential growth of ICT and web applications have strongly stimulated Circular Economy, and will continue to become more and more important, e.g. to track and trace productions and components. The sharing economy only becomes possible because of software and apps, which make easy online reservation of cars and other products possible. The downside is the increase in data, often public data, with questions about the privacy of the consumer.

Repair economy as Circular Economy strategy is not immediately seen as technology driven, but rather depending on better regulation (e.g. guarantee periods, liability on repaired products, etc.) and better business models. However, some new technologies can underpin the growth of the repair economy. 3D printing e.g. can be instrumental in repairing components, producing spare parts that are no longer available. A new category of materials is being developed to make disassembling easier. These materials are used for connecting parts, and do fall apart under external triggers such as increased pressure or temperature, or allow for a faster manual of mechanical dismantling (Peeters, Vanegas, Dewulf, & Duflou, 2017). Another development concerns self-healing materials, e.g. self-repairing painted layers when scratched. It is evident (but often forgotten) that these new types of materials should also be recyclable themselves, another characteristic of circular products.

An initial principle for innovative technologies in a Circular Economy is foresight: recyclability must be included without compromise as a criterion from the development phase of materials. A second principle would insist that recyclability should not be restricted to the material level, but include re-usability at the component and product levels. 3D printing has already been mentioned in this paper as an example to design products with less material and to repair components. However, 3D printing designs tend to integrate more components, with a risk that repair becomes more difficult. Furthermore, 3D printing also has a 'rebound effect' when consumers are inclined to purchase more products and gadgets because they are much easier to produce than before. These examples demonstrate that innovative technologies can indeed support Circular Economy, but only when they effectively account for the principles thereof in the development process. The way in which technologies contribute to closing loops, product service systems and lifecycle extension does not only depend on the technologies themselves. Their introduction also depends on the business model behind them, the legal framework, and scientific insights into long-term effects on the environment and resource efficiency.

The bio-based economy is another unmistakable technology trend that focuses on the use of renewable and CO_2 neutral energy and materials, mainly as an alternative for fossil-based plastics (see above). A number of reports (including the EMF (Ellen MacArthur Foundation, 2012) and the UN (UNEP Earthscan, 2012)) treat cycles of biological raw materials and technological raw materials as separate, alternative loops. This distinction, however, is artificial. Biological raw materials enter the technological domain via processes that produce materials, energy carriers or food. After its use, some bio-based products can be composted, but a lot of them follow the waste management routes of conventional materials. During the use phase, a large number of products (bio-based and fossil-based) produce emissions that enter the biosphere (via waste, corrosion, exhaust gasses, etc.). These emissions have to be assimilated by the environment and not disrupt the biosphere. It shows that biosphere and technosphere are very much intermingled, and that there is no separate biological materials loop, but that materials extracted from the biosphere follow the routes of the technosphere in several phases. It also means that the Circular Economy strategies which are typical of materials in the technosphere, can and should also be considered for biological materials.

4. TECHNOLOGICAL HURDLES WITHIN THE CIRCULAR ECONOMY

While there clearly is a need for more technological development for Circular Economy, and technological development also is indispensable to bring Circular Economy further, there are also limits and hurdles. We will discuss some of them, without the aim of being exhaustive.

Technology sometimes is believed to be able to perfectly close material loops in the future. Braungart (Braungart & McDonough, 2002) even pretends that it doesn't matter how many times a loop is run through, or in other words how much we consume, as long as the loop is 100% closed. However, every loop around the circle creates dissipation and entropy, attributed to losses in quantity (physical material losses, by-products) and quality (mixing, downgrading). New materials and energy must be injected into any circular material loop, to overcome these dissipative losses. This is in line with the second law of thermodynamics, which states that entropy, which can be considered as a measure of the chaos within closed systems, always increases (Ayres, 1998).

A first consequence is that waste management systems (the keystone of closing material loops) never are perfect. A study on the recycling efficiency of the current state-of-the-art recycling of laptops (Van Eygen, De Meester, & Dewulf, 2015) shows that he total recycling chain (without taking the collection imperfection into account) yields e.g. an efficiency of 77% in case of the recuperation of gold. The metallurgical end-processing of gold is very efficient: 97% of the gold is recovered from the input to the end-processing. In the separation step before hence a lot of gold gets lost. That separation step starts with shredding the laptops into small pieces, which is a rough treatment. The recycling efficiency of other materials is even worse: 58% for silver, and only 13% of the plastics in laptops is recycled. In general, it can be said that the more materials are mixed up in the products, the more difficult it becomes to separate these materials while recycling. Pure waste streams, and products with a lower amount of different materials, which are compatible or separable, will lead to better recycling efficiencies.

A second consequence of the second law of thermodynamics is that it is impossible to obtain forever the same quality of materials after recycling. A typical example in this regard is the recycling of aluminium. In the melting phase, it is possible to add alloying elements to produce a specific type of aluminium. The removal of these elements in order to achieve a different aluminium alloy, however, is more or less impossible: economically feasible options are not available to this end at the industrial level. The result is a downcycled aluminium type, that only can be used e.g. as cast aluminium. The introduction of new, pure aluminium – highly taxing in energy terms – would be the only way to adjust the alloy. One must conclude that it is important for closing material loops that we have a sufficiently accurate knowledge of and respect for the composition of materials and that we again keep the material flows as pure as possible via waste sorting. Recycling for the same application would appear to be an appropriate and pragmatic approach. Returning to the aluminium example, this could mean that the aluminium cans collected from recycling containers might be used to produce new drinks containers, thereby guaranteeing that the addition of extraneous materials is kept to a minimum. It also is crucial to inform consumers about the quality of the recycled material, and to guarantee the quality of the recycled material for the intended use, as if e.g. done by the end-of-waste criteria the European Commission is setting up for different materials.

The better products are designed with regard to the entire material loop, the better recycling systems can be set up. Next, a well-designed recycling system – with intensive surveillance of the flow of materials and supervision of the process parameters employed – is crucial to optimize recycling efficiencies and recycling quality. It is evident that a better knowledge of materials within products, the way they are designed and combined, a better knowledge of the possibilities of recycling, remanufacturing and repair technologies is needed for promoting the Circular Economy. Material passports, in which this information about materials in products is gathered and released in a controlled way to the relevant stakeholders, could be very instrumental to facilitate the exchange of knowledge and information. Such a passport would contain instructions and data concerning composition, recycling potential, repair etc. of the material or product. A system of material passports should be compatible with the protection of intellectual property, e.g. by working with central databases with clear access rules, as is already the case in the food and health sectors. However, there is no legal framework yet for such a material passports, except for some specific cases (e.g. the demolition inventory (sloopinventaris) installed by the Flemish government for non-residential buildings larger than 1000 m^3)

Finally, it can't be stressed enough that technological development is necessary for the further emergence of Circular Economy, but certainly is not sufficient. Circular Economy is a very transdisciplinary concept, in which innovative business models, consumer interaction, legislation and economic stimuli are equally relevant. For example, technologies can enable the sharing economy, but a clear legal framework for liabilities and an innovative business model to share the benefits amongst the stakeholders is needed as well. Furthermore, actions should be undertaken to avoid rebound effects of consumers shifting from public transport to shared cars, or using the saved budget for plane travels to exotic holiday destinations e.g.

5. CONCLUDING REMARKS

Technology is often considered as the driver for Circular Economy. Indeed, most strategies followed to realize the Circular Economy do need innovative technologies and are at least partly depending on technologies. There still is a huge need for further technological developments, for recycling and separating materials, for substitution, as well as for the repair and sharing economy. Circular economy will however not succeed with technology only; especially consumers also play a crucial role in Circular Economy as part of the product loops. To make Circular Economy a success there is a need for more intensive and better interactions between consumer and producer. Both at the side of consumers and producers, incentives for sorting, recycling, refurbishing, repairing, sharing etc. are needed. The government can play an intermediary role in there. Amongst others, standardization, quality, liability, ... of recycled, repaired, resold and shared goods should be better regulated. Another issue is the availability of good data of material streams and of product composition, recyclability, and repairability, for which a material passport could be very instrumental. Furthermore, increasing the lifetime of products also is an important strategy for the Circular Economy, which again needs other business models and regulation to protect consumers and producers. Finally, sharing economy gains interest from consumers, supported by new ICT platforms, but here protection of consumers almost is a blank page.

REFERENCES

Alaerts, L., Augustinus, M., & Van Acker, K. (2018). Impact of Bio-Based Plastics on Current Recycling of Plastics. *Sustainability, 10*(5).

Angerer, G., Erdmann, L., Marscheider-Weidemann, F., Scharp, M., Lüllmann, A., Handke, V., & Marwede, M. (2009). Rohstoffe für Zukunftstechnologien: Einfluss des branchenspezifischen Rohstoffbedarfs in rohstoffintensiven Zukunftstechnologien auf die zukünftige Rohstoffnachfrage: Fraunhofer IRB Verlag, Stuttgart.

Ayres, R. U. (1998). Eco-thermodynamics: economics and the second law. *Ecological Economics, 26*(2), 189–209.

Bailey, G., Mancheri, N., & Van Acker, K. (2017). Sustainability of Permanent Rare Earth Magnet Motors in (H)EV Industry. *Journal of Sustainable Metallurgy*, 1–16. doi: 10.1007/s40831-017-0118-4.

Braungart, M., & McDonough, W. (2002). *Cradle to cradle: Remaking the Way We Make Things*. New York: North Point Press.

EEA. (2017). Circular by design – Products in the circular economy. EEA Report 6/2017. Copenhagen: EEA.

European Commission. (2000). Directive 2000/53/EC of the European Parliament and of the Council of 18 September 2000 on end-of life vehicles. *Official Journal of the European Communities*.

European Commission. (2012). Directive 2012/19/EU of the European Parliament and of the Council of 4 July 2012 on waste electrical and electronic equipment (WEEE) (recast). *Official Journal of the European Communities*.

European Commission. (2014). Report on critical raw materials for the EU, Report of the Ad hoc Working Group on defining critical raw materials. Brussels.

European Commission. (2017). Study on the review of the list of Critical Raw Materials. Brussels.

European Union. (2017). Regulation (EU) 2017/821 of the European Parliament and of the Council of 17 May 2017 laying down supply chain due diligence obligations for

Union importers of tin, tantalum and tungsten, their ores, and gold originating from conflict-affected and high-risk areas.

Eurostat. (2018a). Material Flow Diagrams. Retrieved 30 July 2018, from http://ec.europa.eu/eurostat/web/circular-economy/material-flow-diagram.

Eurostat. (2018b). Waste statistics. Retrieved 30 July 2018, from http://ec.europa.eu/eurostat/statistics-explained/index.php/Waste_statistics.

Kirchherr, J., Reike, D., & Hekkert, M. (2017). Conceptualizing the circular economy: An analysis of 114 definitions. *Resources, Conservation and Recycling, 127,* 221–232.

MacArthur, E., Zumwinkel, K., & Stuchtey, M. (2015). Growth within: a circular economy vision for a competitive Europe. *Ellen MacArthur Foundation.*

Olivetti, E. A., & Cullen, J. M. (2018). Toward a sustainable materials system. *Science, 360*(6396), 1396–1398. doi: 10.1126/science.aat6821.

Peeters, J. R., Vanegas, P., Dewulf, W., & Duflou, J. R. (2017). Economic and environmental evaluation of design for active disassembly. *Journal of Cleaner Production, 140,* 1182–1193.

Prakash, S., Dehoust, G., Gsell, M., Schleicher, T., & Stamminger, R. (2016). Einfluss der Nutzungsdauer von Produkten auf ihre Umweltwirkung: Schaffung einer Informationsgrundlage und Entwicklung von Strategien gegen „Obsoleszenz". *Dessau-Roßlau: UBA Texte, 11,* 2016.

Preston, F. (2012). A global redesign? Shaping the circular economy. *Energy, Environment and Resource Governance. London: Chatham House.*

Salman, M., Dubois, M., Di Maria, A., Van Acker, K., & Van Balen, K. (2016). Construction Materials from Stainless Steel Slags: Technical Aspects, Environmental Benefits, and Economic Opportunities. *Journal of Industrial Ecology, 20*(4), 854–866. doi: 10.1111/jiec.12314.

UNEP. (2011). *Decoupling natural resource use and environmental impacts from economic growth. A Report of the Working Group on Decoupling to the International Resource Panel.*

UNEP. (2016). Global Material Flows and Resource Productivity. An Assessment Study of the UNEP International Resource Panel. Paris: United Nations Environment Programme.

UNEP Earthscan. (2012). Global environmental outlook 5. *United Nations Environment Programme.*

Van Acker, K., Allacker, K., Bachus, K., Biedenkopf, K., Binnemans, K., Dewulf, W., ... Muchez, P. (2016). Circular Economy.

Van Eygen, E., De Meester, S., & Dewulf, J. (2015). Raw materials savings by urban mining: the case of desktop and laptop computers in Belgium. Leuven: policy research centre sustainable materials management.

Wang, F., Huismann, J., Stevels, A., & Balde, C. (2013). Enhancing E-waste estimates: Improving data quality by multivariate input-output analysis. *Waste management, 33*(11), 2397–2407.

World Bank. (2012). What a waste, A Global Review of Solid Waste Management *Urban Development Series.* Washington: World Bank.

CIRCULAR ECONOMY, AN ECONOMIST'S PERSPECTIVE

Johan Eyckmans*

1. INTRODUCTION: FROM A LINEAR TOWARDS A MORE CIRCULAR ECONOMY

The traditional economic model for many products can be labelled as linear in the sense that virgin materials are sourced by producers to make consumption goods or durables goods.[1] After their useful life, these goods, and all the materials embodied in them, are discarded and end up in incineration plants, in landfills or are just dumped somewhere in the natural environment. Not only the goods themselves, but also their packaging often gives rise to a lot of waste, think of PET water bottles or beer and soft drink cans. Especially in the consumer goods category, the linear model in combination with mass production was long (and often still is) the dominant business model. The blue arrows in the left-hand side of Figure 1 depict the one-way flow of materials in the linear economy model. In contrast, in a more circular economy as depicted in the right-hand side of Figure 1, less materials end up in landfills and incineration because they are recycled. An even more circular economy strategy is to extend the lifetime of products (and or their components) by means of repair, reuse and remanufacturing (green arrows in Figure 1). In a more circular economy, less virgin material needs to be extracted and less material end up in landfills, incineration because of reuse, remanufacturing and recycling.

* KU Leuven, Faculty of Economics and Business.

1 Durable goods are goods that do not wear out quickly, typically a lifetime of at least three years is used to distinguish them from consumables. Examples of durable goods are cars, household appliances, electronics etc. Consumables can be used only once or repeatedly but their useful live does not exceed three years. Examples are food and drinks, many items of clothing, personal products etc.

Figure 1: from a linear towards a more circular economy

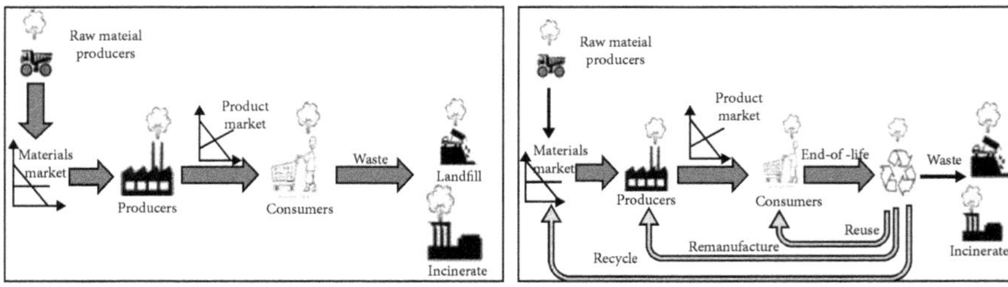

Linear economy More circular economy

Source: own drawing

In many cases, a more circular economy way of production and consumption is beneficial from the point of view of society. Especially if environmental impacts (depicted by clouds in Figure 1) of recycled materials are less than that of virgin material extraction, a shift away from the linear model reduces the negative environmental impact throughout the product's life cycle. For example, producing aluminium from scrap can be up to 90% less energy intensive than producing aluminium from the virgin resource bauxite (Hall, 2014). Clearly, if energy is produced with little or no renewable sources, the virgin material route will be causing much more damage to the environment. And apart from energy efficiency, there are also other big differences in direct environmental impacts between the virgin and recycled production route for aluminium, think of the impact of large-scale open-pit mining, mining residues, red-mud lakes and chemicals used in the production and refining of virgin aluminium. Also, if the environmental impacts of waste disposal or incineration are large, more circular economy ways of producing and consuming are better for society. Think of one-way plastic bags used as packaging which often end up in our waterways and, ultimately, in the oceans (the so-called plastic soup problem) as an example. The dispersed nature of the plastic pollution in combination with the long lifetime of plastics makes it very costly or even impossible to clean up the plastic soup (Eriksen et al. 2014).

Not only environmental impacts at all stages of the life cycle of products are causing concern. Also, many policy makers (see for example European Commission 2015) and scientists are worried about the possible exhaustion of non-renewable resources (for example metal ores, building materials like sand, gravel etc.) and overexploitation of renewable resources (for example timber wood, natural fibres like cotton, fish stocks etc.). This concern has led many to advocate a more careful use of these resources and a more circular economy model can often contribute to that as schematically illustrated in Figure 1.

If there are sufficient reasons to move from a linear towards a more circular economy, the next question is whether the stakeholders in the supply chain of products face sufficient incentives to alter their behaviour. For example, are consumers motivated to spend effort to sort their waste? Do market prices for recycled materials provide sufficient incentives for recyclers to extract valuable materials out of the waste streams? What parameters influence the choice of companies for a sales rather than a rental or leasing business model? Do designers of goods have a reason to take into account ease of disassembly and recycling of their products when they reach their end-of-life stage? It is definitely challenging to align all stakeholders' interests, and even more to align them to the interests of society at large.

In this text, we want to contribute a few arguments and insights from economics in the debate on circular economy. In particular, we will first discuss in section two reasons for public authorities to intervene in favour of a more circular economy. Different forms of market failure will be reviewed in the context of materials and product supply chains. In section 3 we will then turn to possible policy interventions and section 4 deals with business models and briefly discusses the importance of the legal environment. Section 5 concludes.

2. WHY INTERVENE?

After a short digression on the methodology of economic analysis, I will deal with different arguments for public intervention: resource scarcity, environmental externalities, asymmetric information and finally, technological and innovation externalities.

2.1. A SHORT DIGRESSION ON THE ECONOMISTS' METHODOLOGY

From the introduction above, government intervention appears to be necessary to reduce the dependency of the European and Flemish economy on often pricy and scarce raw materials and to curb negative environmental impacts of linear economy business models. While this line of reasoning seems logical, reality is much more complex because the numerous actors in the lifecycle of products (suppliers of raw materials, manufacturers, consumers, waste processors, government) make decisions on a daily basis that determine the demand for materials and final disposal of residues and waste. These decisions are often expressed in markets like the global raw material markets, markets for waste and secondary materials, repair and second-hand markets etc. So understanding why and how authorities should intervene requires a thorough insight in the (mal)functioning of these interconnected markets. That is what the discipline of economics can contribute in the debate. But clearly, economic arguments alone are not enough to decide on the right course of action. It is a genuinely interdisciplinary exercise that requires contributions from material engineers, environmental scientists, behavioural scientists and, as will be argued later, legal scholars.

The question 'why intervene' cannot be answered without first exploring the question of society's desired situation in relation to material consumption. In other words, what is the desired rhythm of extraction, the ideal degree of recyclability and material intensity of a product? This is a normative question and answering it requires unavoidably some value judgements. We will have to, for example, determine the relative value we attach to negative environmental effects at home and abroad associated with the different stages in the lifecycle of given materials, to the profits of manufacturers and producers of material resources, to the capacity of future generations to have equal access to materials and to the damages they will suffer from current generations' waste generation etc. Economists determine the ideal desired situation by solving an optimization problem whereby the objective function is a so-called social welfare function. This function consists of the benefits present and future consumers enjoy of consuming goods and services in the broadest sense and the long-term profits that businesses generate throughout the produce lifecycle. But also, the social welfare function accounts for the environmental damage caused in the various stages in the lifecycle of a product. A detailed discussion of the normative assumptions on which such a welfare function is based would take us far beyond the scope of the present paper. We should note nevertheless that the consequences for the quality of the environment and for future generations clearly have a place within this framework. In addition to the goal objective function, there are evident technological and ecological limitations, such as the state and evolution of manufacturing technologies, the finite nature of non-renewable resources, the limited regenerative capacity of renewable resources and the limited capacity of natural ecosystems to absorb waste streams.

Once we have a clear idea of the desired situation for society as a whole, we can then ask ourselves whether the internal powers of markets generate enough incentive among the various actors to operate in line with social interest. This is the descriptive part of the analysis. Given the prevailing prices and policy instruments, what choices do consumers and producers make regarding consumption, waste disposal, production, recycling etc.? If the outcome of the descriptive analysis differs from the one of the normative analysis, then we have a convincing argument for active government intervention. This is, in a rapidly changing global environment, by necessity an iterative process.

2.2. SCARCITY AND EXHAUSTION

Arguments about increasing scarcity and looming exhaustion of materials are often referring to **reserves-to-production ratios**, RP-ratios in the sequel. This ratio divides the total amount of known reserves by the annual production and the resulting number can be interpreted as how many years it takes before the resource is exhausted given the current production rate. For example, if there is 100 million tons of a given resource and annual production amounts to 20 million tons, then the RP-ratio is 100 divided by 20, i.e. 5. So at the current production rate of 20 million tons, it takes 5 years before the reserves are exhausted. Several publications provide lists of materials and their respective RP ratios and use them as arguments to illustrate that the world might be running out soon of some critical materials.

Figure 2: RP ratios for selected energy and metals

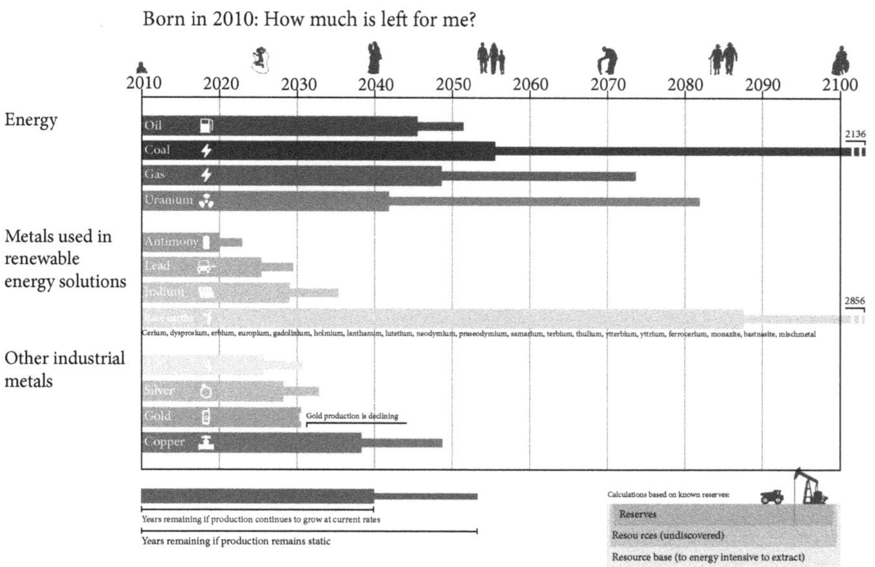

Source: adapted from infographic retrieved from http://vlaanderen-circulair.be/nl/kennis/infografieken/detail-2/how-much-is-left-en

This infographic shows for example that for indium, used in photovoltaic systems, known reserves would last for about 25 years at current production rates (narrow bar), and about 20 years taking into account expected growth rates of production (wide bar). However, estimates of RP ratios are highly volatile because both the numerator (reserves) and denominator (annual production) are fluctuating. It is obvious that annual production fluctuates over time reflecting economic business cycles and, changes in demand for the material over time. Also, in a growing market, it makes more sense to use estimated future production than current the production volume. But, perhaps more surprising, reserves' estimates change over time. Reserves are defined as the total amount of the material that can be economically extracted given current technology.[2] As technologies advance, and as higher material prices give strong incentives to increase exploration for new, so far undiscovered resources, the total amount of reserves can increase over time, even when annual production eats away part of the reserves annually. A typical example is shown below in Figure 3. It shows that reserves, annual production and the resulting RP ratio for copper. A striking observation is that global reserves have increased from about 100 million tons in the 1950ies to close to 700 million tons recently. For more than 60 years, the RP ratio for copper fluctuates around 40 years. Similar observations have been made for fossil fuel reserves (see for example British Petroleum 2017). The conclusion is that RP ratios are unreliable indicators of resource scarcity and that they typically underestimate the remaining available quantities of a material. The reason for that is that the RP ratios do not account for changing economic and technological conditions.

Figure 3: global reserves, production and RP ratios for copper

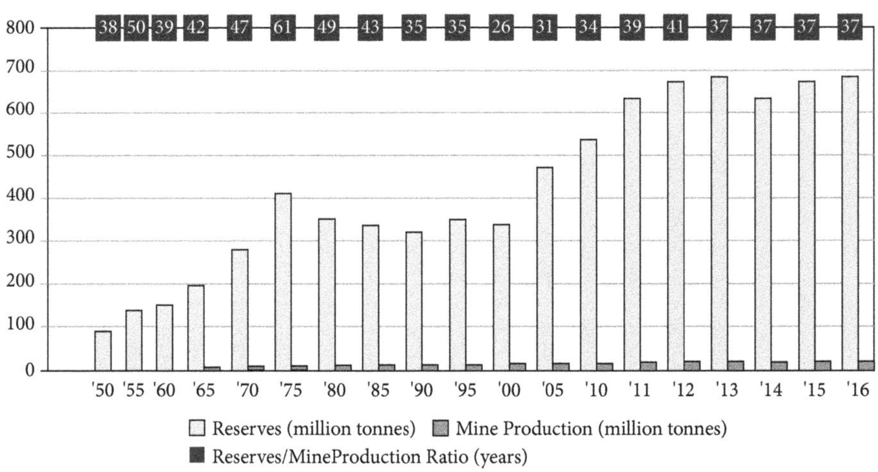

Source: graphic retrieved from: http://copperalliance.org/about-copper/long-term-availability/

What alternative indicators could better reflect scarcity? **Real prices** of materials are perhaps a natural candidate as economic theory suggests that in a competitive market setting prices reflect scarcity. Figure 4 shows the evolution of the real price (corrected for inflation) of a basket of different metals and minerals over more than 50 year. Between 1960 and 2000, there was a gradual decrease in the price of these materials. Between 2002 and 2010 however, prices went

2 Reserves are to be distinguished from resources which refers to all the known and unknown, i.e. yet to be discovered, deposits of the material. In contrast to reserves, the concept of resources does not refer to economic or technological conditions that would make it possible to extract the material.

up steeply and fluctuated strongly afterwards. The reason behind the so-called "super cycle" in commodities in the 2000s was the strong and unprecedented growth of the Chinese economy. As China became the powerhouse of the global economy, its demand for materials grew exponentially ad put upward pressure on commodity prices. Whether the resulting price increase is a reflection of scarcity is far from certain. Short-term frictions in the supply chain of materials can cause strong price movements but does not necessarily indicate an increase in scarcity, let alone a looming exhaustion of the reserves. In addition, many materials' markets are characterized by high concentration and market power. It is well known in economics that in such circumstances, prices are not a proper reflection of scarcity as dominant suppliers try to manipulate the market price upward by artificially restricting supply. The apparent scarcity of the material is then no indication of geological scarcity but rather of strategic behaviour by the suppliers.

Figure 4: The World Bank metals and minerals price index

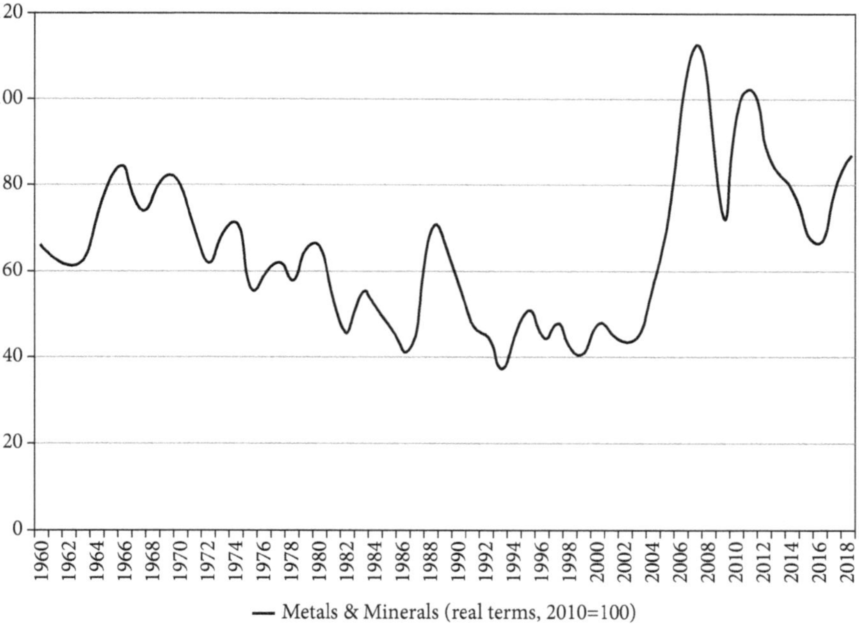

Source: own calculations based on data by The World Bank (2018), statistics for metals and minerals (aluminium, copper, iron ore, lead, nickel, tin and zinc, with respective weights 26.7, 38.4, 18.9, 1.8, 8.1, 2.1, 4.1) in real terms (2010=100).

Hotelling (1931) introduced an approach to model scarcity for non-renewable resources like oil, metal ores or minerals. His seminal model is the starting point for resource economists to think about scarcity in the long run. First, we will consider the descriptive analysis, i.e. we will analyse how owners of a scarce non-renewable resource will distribute production over time. In order to do so, we will assume in first instance that there are many resource owners that interact on a competitive material market. Hence, they are all price takes unable to influence with their supply behaviour the equilibrium market price. In a subsequent paragraph, we will relax this assumption.

Assume that you own a mine that contains a valuable non-renewable resource and that you know the total amount of material it contains. In every period of time, you should decide how much material you will extract and bring to the market. A tonne of material extracted today will yield a net profit of $p_t - c = R_t$, today's price minus the cost of extraction. For later reference, we will call this net profit the resource rent. If, on the other hand, you decide to keep this tonne of material in the ground and extract it only next year, the corresponding profit next year will be $p_{t+1} - c = R_{t+1}$. The decision to extract today or tomorrow will therefore depend on the comparison of the resource rent in both periods, taking into account discounting, i.e. the fact that companies, and their shareholders in particular, prefer profits sooner than later.

In particular, if $R_t > R_{t+1} / [1+i]$, then a profit maximizing mine owner will want to extract today. If the inequality holds with opposite sign, he would prefer waiting until next year. The argument now goes that in a competitive market equilibrium, it should hold that $R_t = R_{t+1} / [1+i]$. Indeed, if we would assume that $R_t > R_{t+1} / [1+i]$, then all mine owners would produce more in period t and less in period t+1. This would drive down the price and the rent in period t and the opposite in period t+1. Hence, a price correction would rebalance the inequality towards equality. A similar argument can be made in the case if $R_t < R_{t+1} / [1+i]$. Mine owners would now postpone production and the resulting scarcity in period t would increase the price and rent whereas the higher supply in period t+1 would lead to lower prices and rents. Again, prices would change as to restore equality. Given that neither of the two cases described before can be a stable market outcome, the only situation that is compatible with market equilibrium is one in which the relationship holds with equality.

Note that the equality can be rewritten such that: $[R_{t+1} - R_t] / R_t = i$. Hence, the percentage rate of change of the resource rent is exactly equal to the interest rate. This is the fundamental result of the descriptive analysis by HOTELLING (1931). In a competitive market, resource rents will increase over time at the rate of interest. Intuitively: if mine owners are more impatient (i.e. are characterized by a high discount or interest rate), the resource will be extracted and depleted faster, leading to faster growth in resource prices and rents. In other words, the evolution of returns and, as a result, market prices, will clearly reflect increasing scarcity over time, even without government intervention.

HOTELLING (1931) went on to examine what is for society the preferred rate of extraction of a non-renewable resource. He showed that a similar condition should hold along the socially optimal extraction path: resource rents should increase at the social rate of discount. The question whether the competitive market outcome is socially desirable then reduces to the question whether private mine owners (and their shareholders) have the same rate of time preference as society. If private and social time preferences were to coincide then private mine owners would opt for a production rhythm in line with what society desires. But there is reason to believe that private producers are less patient than society as a whole. As a result, and in the absence of government intervention, the market-driven extraction rate is most likely too high and justifies active intervention by policy makers to spread the available reserves over a longer time horizon than if it were left to market forces only.

We observed above that in a private raw materials market, extraction over time will be cut back by the extractors. Supply will thus diminish and this will lead in the case of constant or increasing demand to increasing prices in order to restore market balance in each period. In other words, the evolution of returns and, as a result, market prices, will clearly reflect increasing scarcity over time, even without government intervention. And this increasing raw materials price will give a correct signal to consumers that the goods they are consuming carry a high opportunity cost. Demand will decrease in the face of high prices and, at the same time, alternatives will become relatively more attractive and R&D into substitutes more interesting etc. High raw resources prices will also be an incentive to waste processors to collect more and to strive for a higher recycling percentage. In other words, increasing prices through time will stimulate the transition to a more circular economy with higher material efficiency, lower production losses, more recycling etc. It is clear, therefore, that an internal dynamic exists in the market which reflects increasing scarcity in market prices. Nevertheless, as we observed above, we cannot be certain whether this happens to a sufficient degree when the private discount rate that owners of raw materials employ is higher than the social time preference. In reality, we also observe significant material price fluctuations (see Figure 4) which can make can make investing in CE a risky business, although in the long term, such investments will help to increase companies' capacity to weather such volatility.

The seminal contribution by Hotelling (1931) has triggered lots of new research and extensions of the model. For example, the literature has studied extensions of the basic model in which extraction costs increase with cumulative extraction (because one has to dig deeper or one has to use ore with a lower concentration of the material for example) and models in which resource companies endogenously invest in exploration activities to find new reserves. Reviewing this literature is beyond the scope of this paper, we refer the interested reader to Conrad (1988) for example.

An extension of the model deserving more attention is the case in which the resource market is not competitive but dominated by price taking producers. This case was treated already by Hotelling (1931) and is particularly relevant because many raw materials markets are dominated by a limited number of producers who exercise an influence on prices by their strategic supply behaviour. The general intuition is that strategic suppliers will try to limit the material's supply to the market as to make the commodity scarcer. This leads to higher prices and therefore higher mark-ups (difference between price and marginal production cost) and ultimately higher profits and rents for the resource owners. The self-constraint implies that the total quantity of the material is spread out over a longer time horizon compared to a competitive market scenario. At first sight this might be thought of as desirable from the point of view as society because the strategic supply behaviour alleviates the exhaustion problem. However, this gain has to be compared to the traditional welfare cost of monopoly and oligopoly markets. The higher prices for the material make it less attractive to use it in production and there are situations in which this is clearly undesirable. Take for example the market for rare earth metals, which are used in permanent magnets for wind turbines, in electronic components and in energy efficient LED lamps. Up to 90% of the supply on the world market presently stems from China (Binnemans et al., 2013). In 2010, the Chinese introduced export limitations (since found to be illegal by the World Trade Organization) which reduced supplies and sent prices soaring. Neodymium (Nd) was traded in 2009 for roughly 20$/kg (oxide), but the price had risen in 2011 to more than 350$/kg. The fact that producers try to drive up prices and their resulting sales revenues by limiting production is a classical source of welfare loss in the economy. Products are sold for more than is desired, consumers are disadvantaged, and part of the market demand is not met. In the case of rare earth metals, the welfare costs are substantial because the high price of critical elements has the effect of driving up the price of many environmentally friendly technologies (wind turbines, LED lamps), thereby slowing their penetration of the market. The market power of China and the resultant inflation of prices for rare earth metals has the effect of decelerating the transition to a low-carbon economy. This welfare cost has to be weighted carefully against the advantage of a longer time horizon before the material's reserves are exhausted.

From the Hotelling model, we can conclude that in theory, the resource rent, i.e. the difference between marginal production cost and sales price, is a good indicator for scarcity. As the resource is running out, the rent will continue to increase. However, in practice the resource rent is hard to estimate. First the marginal production cost is not directly observed and is private information of the resource extraction companies. Secondly, the resource prices often fluctuates strongly in the short run in response to shocks in production and refining capacity, logistic problems etc. Thirdly, as described earlier, strategic behaviour by oligopolistic suppliers might cause resource rents to be higher than in the competitive benchmark case. For all of these reasons, using the resource rent as a measure of scarcity is not a very practical solution.

2.3. ENVIRONMENTAL EXTERNALITIES CALL FOR PUBLIC INTERVENTION

It is well known that competitive market prices will never reflect the social costs of environmental pollution in the production, consumption and waste phase of a product without government intervention. This is a classic example of what economists call a **market failure**. Given that the uncorrected market prices only reflect the private production costs and not the extra social costs of, for example, environmental pollution, goods that have a high environmental impact tend to be too cheap and are over-consumed. The market mechanism leads therefore to a socially undesirable situation. The presence of negative environmental externalities is a clear reason for government to intervene by introducing anti-pollution taxes, for example, or by setting up a system of tradable emissions rights, or by using other policy instruments to steer the market.

This requires us, of course, to observe the environmental effects of goods and the materials they contain throughout their entire lifecycle on the basis, for example, of a Life Cycle Assessment (LCA) or Input-Output (IO) models. Goods do not only cause environmental externalities when they are produced, when they are used and when they are discarded at their end-of-life. As was shown in Figure 1, they also can create externalities upstream in the supply chain of components and in the mining and refining of virgin materials. All of the relevant stages have to be taken into account when assessing the environmental impact of a particular good. Also, the negative environmental effects of alternative routes (e.g. recycling or extending the product's lifetime) must also be carefully charted and evaluated. The environmental impact of recycling is often lower than that of new extraction and refinement for many materials because the energy employed, among other things, is drastically lower (think, for example, of aluminium). On the other hand, many recycling techniques also demand energy and employ chemicals that can be environmentally damaging. The advice here is simple: one should consider all the environmental impacts and internalise, i.e. incorporate, them in prices and leave the market actors free thereafter to choose the most appropriate techniques.[3]

A particular point of attention here is that some of the **environmental impacts** might be situated higher up in the supply and **abroad** as for example the environmental impact of mining of raw materials in Africa or South America. From a global welfare point of view, all environmental impacts should be taken into account, wherever they occur. This is in particular true for global pollution problems like greenhouse gas emissions because for climate change, the location of emissions does not matter for the environmental damage. A tonne emitted in China has a similar effect on climate change as a tonne emitted in Africa

3 Recently, the Netherlands Bureau for Economic Policy Analysis CPB has published (in Dutch) three extensive reports on market failures in resource markets, see Vollebergh et al. (2017), Romijn et al. (2018) and Mot et al. (2018).

or Europe. In reality however, we sometimes see that policy makers only take into account domestic environmental impacts.[4] But the argument also accounts for more local pollution problems like contamination of water and soil or local air pollution. Not accounting for the international externalities means that virgin raw materials enter the market too cheaply and distorts the trade-off by the goods producers between foreign virgin material and domestic recycled materials. The conclusion is that all environmental externalities embodied in the materials and components that a consumption good is made of should be taken into account when assessing the environmental externalities.

Another complication about environmental externalities is that some long-lived durable goods cause most of their environmental impact in the use phase. Think of internal combustion engine vehicles whose exhaust causes local (NO_x, particular matter) and global pollution problems (greenhouse gasses). As a result of continuous engine technology improvements (in this case improvements in the energy efficiency or mileage driven per liter of fuel), newer vintages are cleaner than older vintages. If technology advances very fast, it might be better for society to phase out older vintages faster than the normal replacement rate. These are particularly hard policy problems because they depend on uncertain factors like the pace of technology improvement. When considering to stimulate longer lifetime (via re-use, repair, remanufacturing etc.), the environmental damages caused during the use phase have to be compared carefully to the environmental damages caused in the production phase and material extraction phase.

2.4. ASYMMETRIC INFORMATION

Besides environmental externalities, many market failures are possible in the contexts of raw materials. A significant example here is **asymmetric information**, or the fact that some market players have more and better information than others. Recycled materials can serve to illustrate our point here. In spite of the fact that such materials are often comparable with respect to quality to new materials, consumers and producers are often inclined to trust new materials more than recycled materials. As a result, they are willing to pay relatively less for recycled materials. This has an impact on the recycling sector because they receive lower prices for recycled materials making sorting and recycling less cost-effective compared to using virgin materials. This might even lead to recycling activities not being able to take off. This example resemble the problem of lemons as described by Ackerlof (1970) in his famous work on asymmetric information and adverse selection. As asymmetric information might prevent

4 Recently, the US Environmental Protection Agency has revised its estimates of the social cost of carbon in the sense that it no longer takes into account climate change damages that occur outside US territory, see https://www.scientificamerican.com/article/epa-revises-the-social-cost-of-a-potent-greenhouse-gas/ for example on methane in US.

socially desirable markets from emerging, it is an example of market failure justifying intervention by policy makers. The typical remedies for tackling this type of asymmetric information problems is for the governments to invest in information campaigns, certification and labelling for recycled materials etc. In particular certification and labelling can help users of recycled materials to overcome their initial distrust and will have a positive effect on their willingness to pay (and hence the price) for recycled materials.

2.5. TECHNOLOGICAL AND INNOVATION EXTERNALITIES

Other market failures that potentially call for government intervention include R&D and knowledge externalities. Scientific knowledge has the character of a public good because its benefits are non-excludable, i.e. the benefits can accrue to everyone, also the parties that did not invest in the research efforts. Private investors therefore find it difficult to appropriate the advantages of amassing knowledge and as a result, there is a danger that less research will take place than is socially desirable. As with all public goods, also scientific knowledge is a risk of being underprovided by the market system. Protection of intellectual property rights by means of patents, licences etc. offers a partial solution here, but it is often insufficient. Moreover, the strategic use of patents by companies can sometimes slow down the innovation process rather than speed it up. We refer the interested reader to specialised literature on the economics of innovation and R&D.

We will however discuss in some detail the case of technological externalities that can occur in a product's supply chain. Take, for example, a manufacturer developing an innovative insulation material for buildings. The new insulation's superior performance is because it is made of a variety of materials that are glued together. In the innovation process, it is clearly in the best interests of the manufacturer that he is able to offer the user maximal functionality (high insulation value) at a lowest possible price for the user. Indeed, for the consumer, the lifetime cost matters when he has to decide to use the more sophisticated versus standard insulation material. A first component of that cost-benefit analysis is the difference in initial investment cost of acquiring and installing the insulation material. Most likely, the new and more performant insulation material will be more expensive than standard materials. A second element in the equation has to do with the energy bill savings that the new insulation material can generate compared to standard insulation. This is likely to be a benefit rather than a cost as the new material is characterized by higher performance. Thirdly, there might be a difference in end-of-life costs when the house is ripe for demolition in 50 years' time or so.

From the discussion above it follows clearly that the producer of insulation material has strong incentives to keep the price of the product low and to strive for maximum insulation performance. Doing so, he can more easily convince consumers to buy his material instead of competing products. But it is of less importance to the manufacturer that the material is easily recyclable when the building is demolished in, let's say, 50 years. The responsibility of the manufacturer is mostly limited to the moment he sells his product plus an additional period of guarantee. After that, the product becomes the property of the client who becomes responsible for the correct removal of construction and demolition waste. And it is not clear in advance whether the consumer will take this into account given that it is very far away in time and perhaps he no longer owns the house at that time. Moreover, the demolition cost difference compared to standard materials might be negligible.

In such a situation one can speak here of a technological externality (see Söderholm & Tilton, 2012) because the manufacturer's choice of insulation material has an unintended impact on the production possibility of another manufacturer later in the lifecycle of the product, namely the waste processor. Incentives of the insulation producer and waste processor are not necessarily well aligned. Similar externalities might arise with respect to reparability, re-use or remanufacturing of products and components. Whether or not incentives are aligned depends on the particular circumstances. For example, incentives would be well aligned if the producer of the good would be vertically integrated with the provider of repair services or with the waste processor and recycler. In that case, the joint profit of the different stages would matter and proper incentives are in place for design for reparability and recycling. From a competition policy point of view however, vertical integration in the supply chain is often looked upon with great suspicion. The mark-ups in different consecutive stages might add up (double marginalisation problem), or the exclusive relationships might hamper entry of competitors, all of which creates additional welfare costs (see Tirole 1988).

Another way to achieve better alignment of interests is when the producer remains the owner of the good and its material as in the case of a renting or leasing business model. We will come back to this in Section 4. Finally, policy instruments like extended producer responsibility (EPR) can help to align incentives, as we will discuss in the following section.

3. WHICH POLICY INSTRUMENTS AND WHERE IN THE CHAIN?[5]

In the previous section, we proposed a number of arguments that might justify government intervention in raw resources and materials markets. Where and in what way would it be best for governments to intervene? Bearing in mind the

5 This section is based on Van Acker et al. (2016).

limited scope of the present text it would be impossible to explore every potential policy instrument in detail. We will restrict ourselves therefore to a few basic principles. For a more extensive treatment of policy instruments within the framework of materials policy and recycling, we refer the interested reader to DUBOIS and EYCKMANS (2014).

A great deal of scientific environmental-economics literature has been written about the pros and cons of particular policy instruments. The following core message can be derived from this literature: when polluters use a great variety of processes and are able to push back the environmental impact and material consumption with the use of a diversity of technologies and costs, a uniform technology or emissions norm is not cost efficient. In order to minimise the total cost necessary to achieve certain environmental quality goals, it is better to require greater effort on the part of polluters who can push back their emissions at relatively lower cost. Uniform norms are unable to realize this sort of differentiation in terms of effort, while economic price instruments, such as emissions taxes and systems of tradable emission rights, can serve as an incentive to realise environmental and material consumption goals in a cost efficient manner. In addition to **static cost-efficiency**, economic policy instruments also score better in terms of **dynamic cost-efficiency**. Since polluters are confronted year after year with a price for every unit of remaining emission, this gives them the incentive to continue to invest in research and development geared towards more efficient processes etc. This dynamic incentive is not present in a policy that is based exclusively on static norms. Once the norms have been reached, polluters are not inclined to take more ambitious measures.

These concepts make it possible to evaluate the pros and cons a number of instruments. A **recycled content standard** or recyclate norm, for example, whereby the regulating authority requires that a product must contain a certain percentage of recycled material, tends to score poorly in terms of dynamic efficiency. Once a manufacturer has adapted his processes to employ enough recycled material, the incentive to go beyond the norm in the future disappears. Moreover, static efficiency can also be problematic where the product in question is differentiated and manufacturers offer slightly different variants for various different types. A uniform norm is often inappropriate in such circumstances, and differentiating the norm can be extremely complex and demand a great deal of information. Instead of a recyclate norm, environmental economists rather support the use of price based instruments such as for example a uniform **tax on virgin resource use**. Under a virgin resource tax system, all producers face an incentive to reduce virgin resource use (and hence use recyclate instead) up to the point where the marginal cost of the last unit of reduction of virgin material use equals its corresponding marginal benefit (i.e. the virgin resource tax saved). Given that all producers are confronted with the same tax rate, marginal reduction costs will be equalized which is a necessary condition for static cost efficiency.

In the context of waste management, environmental economists also advocate the use of so called **deposit refund systems**. The latter is in fact a combination of a consumption tax and a recycling subsidy. These systems have been adopted for example in Sweden, Norway and Germany for drink bottles and cans. Upon purchase of the drink, the consumer pays a bit more for the drink container. After consumption, the consumer can recover the deposit by bringing the empty container back to certified collection points in retail outlets for example. This gives an incentive to the consumer to return the drink container instead of disposing of it in the general household waste fraction or, worse still, dispose of it illegally in the street or environment (littering). Intuitively, this two-part pricing schedule solves the problem of giving sufficient incentives to avoid illegal waste dumping and littering. As the undesirable and illegal activity of littering cannot be taxed, one could think of a subsidy for proper conduct, i.e. returning drink containers, instead. But a pure subsidy for returning the empty drink cans only would be distortive. It would lower the net price of drinks and therefore stimulate consumption beyond what is desirable from a society point of view. The deposit solves this problem as it acts as a generalized tax on consumption (Fullerton and Kinnaman 1995).

An important specific instrument within the framework of waste and materials policy is so-called **extended producer responsibility** (EPR). Flanders is familiar with several examples in this regard, including the FostPlus blue bag for consumer packaging waste[6], the collection of used batteries by Bebat[7] and the Recupel[8] contribution towards recycling discarded electrical and electronic appliances. The idea behind this system is that the responsibility of the producer of the goods continues through to the waste phase and does not stop at the moment of sale. EPR systems oblige producers (or importers) to collect a fraction of the number of goods they introduce into the market and have them recycled in an adequate manner. In most instances, the system is not applied to producers individually, but is set up rather as a system of **collective extended producer responsibility**. The sector thus establishes an organisation (mostly non-profit) that organises collection and recycling on behalf of the participating members. The members finance the activities of the organisation in proportion to the volume of goods they introduce into the market. This collective form of EPR tends to be much more efficient because it can capitalize on economies of scale by establishing a single collection system and by compelling better prices from the processors of the collected materials. EPR systems are widely used in the EU and have clearly demonstrated their worth. Improvement remains possible, however, by regularly adjusting collection goals, for example, or by varying the levy according to the recyclability of the product, or by taxing the sector on the fraction of waste that has not been collected (Dubois, 2012).

---

6 Https://www.fostplus.be/en.
7 Https://www.bebat.be/en.
8 Https://www.recupel.be/en/.

An important question related to the choice of policy instruments is where they are best deployed in the lifecycle of the product or material. Is it better, for example, to tax the extraction or import of new materials at the beginning of the chain or to introduce a tax on the dumping or incineration of non-selectively collected waste at the end of the chain? From the environmental-economic perspective, the advice is clear that the instrument should be deployed as closely as possible to the negative environmental impact the government wishes to restrict. A levy on the incineration of waste with an exemption for the normal dumping levy for bottom and fly ashes produced by incinerators, for example, might stem the flow to the incinerators, but it does not provide an incentive to make much of an effort to recuperate materials from incinerator residues. A levy immediately before the undesired activity (ash dumping) thus remains necessary to provide the correct incentives to the actors involved to act in line with social interests.

We are often confronted with a variety of market failures and environmental impacts that all have to be grappled with. An important rule of thumb here is that the government would be best advised to us use as many instruments are as there are market failures it wants to correct. Should government deploy fewer instruments than the number of market failures, then compromises will have to be made and welfare costs will quickly increase (so-called **second best** policies). In the waste incineration example outlined above, an incineration levy will never succeed in realising all the goals in an adequate manner: more recycling instead of incineration, the suppression of damaging emissions from incinerators, incentives to recuperate materials from incinerator residues, a reduction in the volume of residues dumped. The single levy thus becomes a sort of average of the externalities it aims at internalising, but is never really ideal for any given externality.

We conclude this section with a warning concerning potential **interactions and negative feedback effects** of policy instruments. Take, for example, a fictitious subsidy that would give an extra advantage to the intensive recycling of materials from waste flows when compared with standard techniques. This is a price instrument and would thus appear to score well in terms of static and dynamic efficiency. It is highly probably, however, that this subsidy will reduce the total cost for the consumer (purchase, use and waste cost) in comparison with what is socially desirable. In other words, recycling is clearly the goal, but the underlying consumption activity is actually encouraged because the consumer is not sensitive to all the external social costs. It is for this reason that levies designed to discourage environmentally harmful behaviour are often preferable to subsidies for environmentally friendly behaviour. **Rebound effects** can likewise erode the efficiency of policy instruments. A materials policy that succeeds in encouraging manufacturers to use less packaging material, for example, can also lead to a reduction in consumer prices because the total cost price of the products in question is less. The lower sale price then typically leads to more demand for the product, whereby the advantage of having less packaging waste per unit of product is diminished by the increased volume of sales.

A third and final example of the unintended side effects of policy is the so-called **green paradox**, a collective term in the environmental-economic literature for unintended side effects of policy measures that reduce effectivity. The rebound effect we have just described falls under this category. The following example illustrates the concept on a much larger scale. Imagine a group of countries that use extremely large quantities of raw materials (e.g. the EU or the OECD) were to implement a highly effective policy whereby their consumption of raw materials would substantially decrease. If the effect is large enough on a global scale, reduced demand will lower the world market price for the said raw materials. The lower raw materials price would encourage other countries that do not have a vigorous materials policy to import and consume more of the raw materials in questions. The fall in global demand for the said resources would be less than expected and one might even encounter an increase in demand if the price-sensitivity of import demand is high in the countries without an effective materials policy. In the longer term, companies with intensive raw material dependence might relocate to countries and regions with a less stringent materials policy. This is known as the **leakage effect**. The same price effect might also encourage producers of non-renewable raw materials to extend their production capacity. The prospect of a materials policy that would lead to a decrease in world demand in the long term reduces the long term value of their reserves and can, as a consequence, encourage them to put as much material as they can on the market in the shortest possible time. This effect is described by Hans-Werner Sinn (Sinn, 2012) in relation to fossil energy reserves, but it applies in essence to every form of non-renewable resource.

Summarizing we can say that the general advise about policy instruments to be found in environmental economics text books also applies in case of market failures regarding circular economy. Market based instruments like taxes and tradable permits typically provide better incentives for static and dynamic cost efficiency than uniform and static standards. Also one should ideally use as many policy instruments as there are market failures to be corrected and they should be deployed as closely as possible to the stage in the supply chain where the environmental externalities arise. Specifically for the CE context are externalities downstream in the supply chain, which can be tackled by means of extended producer responsibility schemes. Also, deposit refund systems can prove valuable policy instruments to encourage proper sorting of waste and to deter illegal dumping and littering. For a more extensive treatment of policy instruments within the framework of materials policy and recycling, we refer the interested reader to Dubois and Eyckmans (2014).

4. BUSINESS MODELS

We noted before that alternative business models like renting or sharing could bring us closer to the circular economy than standard business models based on sales and private property. The basic argument runs as follows. If producers retain ownership of the equipment they rent or lease to their customers, then they also remain owner of the materials and components the equipment contains. That should give better incentives to producers for green design (i.e. design for reparability, remanufacturing, recycling etc.) in order to limit the costs of recovery and recycling once the equipment reaches its end-of-life. For that reason, many scholars have praised **"new" business models** as an important potential driver for the transition from a linear towards a more circular economy.[9] Note however that for durable goods, renting and leasing business models are not new at all. In many sectors like industrial equipment, B2B vehicles, photocopiers, ... they are widespread and they were practiced already in the 1960ies and before. See Orbach (2004) for examples on IBM, Xerox, United Shoe Machinery and others. From a competition law perspective, these lease-only techniques have frequently been condemned in court using the argument that they might hamper competition and act exclusionary.

That brings us to the crucial question which incentives private, profit maximizing companies face when choosing for a selling or renting / leasing business model for durable goods? In order to gain insight in these incentives it is worthwhile going back to a classic conjecture by Nobel Prize winner Ronald Coase (1972). The **Coase conjecture** says that a monopolist selling a durable and non-depreciating good faces competition of its own supply because consumers can wait for the price to decrease over time. A profit maximizing strategy for the monopolist would be to sell at a high price in the first period to the consumers with the highest willingness to pay, and then lower the price to serve the next group of consumers with a somewhat lower willingness to pay and so on. In this way, the monopolist would be able to price discriminate over time between different types of consumers with different willingness to pay. However, this strategy is not possible if the monopolist has no information on the consumers' willingness to pay and if high willingness-to-pay consumers are willing to wait until prices decline. The monopolist faces a commitment problem, he cannot credibly commit to keep prices high because then he would not sell in the future periods, especially when prices can be changed quickly (Orbach 2004, Tirole 1988).

But different strategies are possible to circumvent this commitment problem. We will first discuss renting or leasing as a possible strategy to circumvent the commitment problem. Part of the commitment problem stems from the fact that

---

9 We refer the reader to Tukker (2004) for a typology and examples of business models in the context of circular economy.

the units of the durable goods sold in the first period, remain in the market in subsequent periods. The monopolist hence faces a smaller "residual" demand in the second period because of the units he sold in the first period. It is as if the monopolist's first period sales create his own competition in the subsequent period. By using a renting business model instead, the monopolist has greater control over the stock of durable goods because the units are implicitly returned under leasing/renting (Tirole 1988).

In spite of its theoretical appeal, we observe that in many markets for durables, selling instead of renting and leasing business models prevail. One of the reasons for that is that for many goods, **moral hazard** problems arise. In the Coase setting, durables are assumed not to depreciate (i.e. do not lose quality) because of usage. In many real world markets however, depreciating is considerable and might be affected by the level of care consumers spend when using the durable goods. In many fixed price maintenance service contracts for cars for example, tyres are excluded and have to be paid for extra when replaced. The reason is that the lifetime of tyres depends on the driving style of the driver, which cannot be monitored or controlled by the service provider. This is an example of so-called moral hazard: the service provider cannot easily monitor the efforts spend by users to maintain the quality of the durable good. That might lead to careless use and rapid quality deterioration. If this moral hazard problem cannot be kept under control (because monitoring is too costly for example), the leasing model might lose its attractiveness compared to the standard sales business model. (Tirole 1988).

But even when he cannot lease or rent the durable good, a producer can try different strategies to (partially) circumvent the price commitment problem central to the Coase conjecture we described earlier. For instance, some monopolists try to tie the consumer by selling specific consumables that are necessary to use the durable good. By charging low prices for the durable but high prices for the consumables, the monopolist can increase its profits compared to the case in which durables and consumables would be produced in competitive market conditions. This business model is for example well known in the markets for printer-and-cartridges or **razor-and-blades** shaving tools.

Another strategy is to **limit the lifetime** of the durable good deliberately. For example by using inferior inputs (light bulbs that last only for a limited number of hours, see Slade 2006) or by issuing new releases that have more and somewhat better functionalities the producer tries to kill older versions and seduce consumers to buy a new one (software applications, smartphones, academic handbooks, ...). Note that under a leasing / renting business model, the producer of the durable goods has an incentive to strive for optimal durability, which is durability that minimizes the intertemporal production cost. Under a sales business model however, the monopolist does have an incentive to reduce the lifetime of the good below the socially optimal level. By doing so, he can limit the stock of durables in the future periods and hence reduces the competition from its own production in previous periods.

Summarizing, we can say that, if left to profit maximizing companies, the choice for a sales or renting model depends strongly on the specific nature of the product and market. Although companies in theory can make larger profits if they can rent or lease their durable products, practical considerations often prevent them from doing so in reality. If renting or leasing proves too difficult, companies often use different strategies like tying and planned obsolescence to circumvent Coase's conjecture that they would have to sell their goods at marginal cost without profit mark-up. These techniques often involve more intense use of materials and hence environmental externalities in production. The social cost of these environmental externalities have to be carefully weighed against the social cost of non-competitive market conduct in order to determine the appropriate course of action for the regulator.

Finally, we want to point out the importance of the **legal framework**, in particular with respect to more circular business models like renting, leasing or sharing. As many of these business models are relatively new, less experience has been gained by market participants in using them. That implies that they often involve substantially higher **transaction costs** than standard linear economy business models. These transaction costs often result from the constraints imposed by the existing legal framework that is still largely based on the concept of private ownership and assigning individual responsibilities. New business models like sharing and renting often require specific and non-standard contracts. Writing these contracts requires extensive legal expertise and is often more costly than traditional sales contracts for which many details and responsibilities have been filled out already by means of standard clauses in contract law. An interesting legal question is whether the current legal consumer and product law is flexible enough to accommodate the newer and more circular business models without imposing excessive transaction costs. If the answer to this question is negative, a generic legal framework should be set up to facilitate the implementation of more circular economy business models. Ideally, such a legal framework is coordinated at the supranational level of the European Union as many of the products and services are provided by multinational companies that operate in different countries.

5. CONCLUSIONS

This contribution has reviewed economic arguments in the discussion on the transition from a linear towards a more circular economy. We reviewed several reasons for public intervention including resource scarcity, environmental externalities, information asymmetries and technological and innovation externalities. For all of these reasons, public intervention can be warranted in order to reduce market failures. The extent of these different market failures depends however on the specific details and market structure throughout the product's lifecycle. We have shown for example that the presence of environmental externalities always requires corrective policy interventions. Resource scarcity on the other hand can be a reason for intervention depending on the difference between the private and social time preference rates and depending on the relative importance of the social costs of non-competitive market behaviour, resource exhaustion and environmental externalities. Regarding policy instruments we advocated the use of flexible priced based instruments over uniform standards and direct regulation like prohibitions. However, these price-based instruments should often be specifically adapted to waste and material markets as in the case of deposit refund systems or extended producer responsibility schemes. We also warned against simplistic solutions as the policy interventions at different stages of the product cycle are likely to interact and might cause unintended negative side effects like rebound effects and leakage. Finally, we reviewed motivations of companies to choose for renting and leasing business models instead of standard (and repeated) sales transactions. We used Coase's conjecture to structure the discussion and concluded that the precise details and context of the product matters crucially for the choice of business model. We also pointed to the importance of the legal framework as a determinant of transaction costs in the choice private companies make between different business models. Finally, we strongly believe that there is a strong need for more in-depth interdisciplinary research by material engineers, environmental scientists, economists and legal scholars to facilitate the transition towards a more sustainable and circular economy.

REFERENCES

Akerlof, G. A. (1970). The Market for 'Lemons': Quality Uncertainty and the Market Mechanism *Quarterly Journal of Economics*, 84 (3), 488–500.

Binnemans, K., Jones, P. T., Blanpain, B., Van Gerven, T., Yang, Y., Walton, A., & Buchert, M. (2013). Recycling of rare earths: a critical review, *Journal of Cleaner Production* 51, 1–22.

British Petroleum (2017), *BP Statistical Review of World Energy* (BP, London), retrieved from: https://www.bp.com/content/dam/bp/en/corporate/pdf/energy-economics/statistical-review-2017/bp-statistical-review-of-world-energy-2017-full-report.pdf.

Coase, R. (1972). Durability and Monopoly, *Journal of Law & Economics* 15, 143–149.

Conrad, J.M. (2010) *Resource Economics* (Cambridge University Press, Cambridge UK).

Dubois, M. (2012). Extended producer responsibility for consumer waste: the gap between economic theory and implementation. *Waste Management & Research* 30(9 suppl), 36–42.

Dubois, M. and Eyckmans, J. (2014), Economic Instruments, in: Reuter, M. and Worrell, E. (eds), *The Handbook of Recycling* (Elsevier, Amsterdam & New York), Chapter 35, 511–519.

Eriksen M, Lebreton LCM, Carson HS, Thiel M, Moore CJ, Borerro JC, et al. (2014). Plastic Pollution in the World's Oceans: More than 5 Trillion Plastic Pieces Weighing over 250,000 Tons Afloat at Sea. *PLoS ONE* 9(12): e111913. https://doi.org/10.1371/journal.pone.0111913.

European Commission (2015), *Closing the loop – An EU action plan for the Circular Economy*. COM(2015) 614/2 (European Commission, Brussels).

Fullerton, D. & Kinnaman, T.C. (1995), Garbage, Recycling and illicit burning or dumping. *Journal of Environmental Economics and Management* 29, 78–91.

Hall, C. (2014), *Materials, a very short introduction* (Oxford University Press, Oxford UK).

Hotelling, H. (1931). The economics of exhaustible resources. *The Journal of Political Economy*, 137–175.

Mot, E. et al. (2018), *Niet-hernieuwbare grondstoffen voor de circulaire economie. Een economische analyse van de werking en beperking van grondstoffenmarkten* CPB Achtergronddocument | 20 juni 2018 (Centraal Plan Bureau, Den Haag, NL) [in Dutch].

Orbach, B. (2004). The Durapolist Puzzle: Monopoly Power in Durable-Goods Market, *Yale Journal on Regulation* 21, 67–118.

Romijn, G. et al. (2018), *Circulaire economie: economie en ecologie in balans*, CPB Policy Brief | 2018/10 (Centraal Plan Bureau, Den Haag, NL) [in Dutch].

Sinn, H.-W. (2012). *The green paradox: a supply-side approach to global warming* (MIT Press, Boston, USA).

Slade, G. (2006), *Made to break, Technology and Obsolescence in America* (Harvard University Press, Cambridge, Massachusetts, USA & London, UK).

Söderholm, P., & Tilton, J. E. (2012). Material efficiency: An economic perspective. *Resources, Conservation and Recycling*, 61, 75–82.

Tirole, J. (1988), *The Theory of Industrial Organization* (MIT Press, Boston, USA).

Tukker, A. (2004). Eight types of product-service system: eight ways to sustainability? Experiences from SUSPRONET, *Business Strategy and the Environment* 13, 246–260.

Van Acker, K. et al. (2016), *Circular Economy*, KU Leuven Metaforum Position Paper° 15 (KU Leuven, Belgium).

Vollebergh, H. et al. (2017), *Fiscale vergroening, belastingverschuiving van arbeid naar grondstoffen, materialen en afval.* (Centraal Plan Bureau, Den Haag, NL) [in Dutch].

PART III

LEGAL INITIATIVES AND CHALLENGES FOR CONSUMER PROTECTION IN A CIRCULAR ECONOMY

TITLE I

EUROPEAN UNION

THE DESIGN AND PRODUCTION STAGE: ECODESIGN REQUIREMENTS

Anaïs MICHEL*

1. ECODESIGN IN THE CIRCULAR ECONOMY

1.1. THE KEY ROLE OF ECODESIGN IN THE CIRCULAR ECONOMY

It is well known that every product bears an impact on the environment during its lifecycle. This is even more true for electrical and electronic products, for which the use of rare materials and manufacturing processes of high quality are necessary. Most of the environmental impact of products is determined during the early phases of their development, and more specifically at the design stage. When designing a product, decisions are taken on the type and amount of materials to be integrated, its durability, its ease of repair and maintenance, as well as the recyclability of its components.[1] Therefore, "*once a product is put on the market, there is relatively little that can be done to improve its environmental characteristics*".[2]

Product design has considerably evolved over the last decades. Compared with the past, today's products have a more varied and sophisticated design. This evolution is evident in the case of light bulbs, where the LED technology is more energy efficient, but also made of more complex materials than halogen lamps. In addition to that, a wide array of products becomes multifunctional and technology-intensive. As a result, they are composed of an increasing number of materials and additives, with smaller amounts of each specific material. Moreover, there is a

---

* PhD student at KU Leuven (campus Brussels) and at UCL, FWO fellow and member of the Consumer, Competition & Market Institute, preparing a thesis on "Premature Obsolescence: In Search of a Refined Legal Framework" under the supervision of Prof. Dr. Bert Keirsbilck (KUL) and Prof. Dr. Yves De Cordt (UCL).

1 D. Jepsen et al., *Delivering resource-efficient products – How Ecodesign can drive a circular economy in Europe* (European Environmental Bureau 2015) p. 6.

2 Green paper of the European Commission of 7 February 2001 on Integrated Product Policy, COM(2001) 68 final, p. 3.

trend towards the miniaturisation of products, leading to components glued and integrated into the product body. Smartphones perfectly illustrate this tendency.[3]

This evolving design intensifies the negative impacts of products on the environment. Admittedly, some features of these newly designed products are eco-friendly[4], and products with multiple functions lower the quantity of resources, energy, waste and emissions during the whole product lifecycle (production and packaging, transport and distribution, use, end-of life) compared to the case where the same functions are provided by several single function products.[5] On the other hand, their complexity and multifunctionality increase their failure rate and reduce their potential for repair, reuse, remanufacture and recycling, going thus against the circular economy target.[6] Exacerbated with the current production and consumption patterns of industrialised countries and with the rapid population growth, the consequences on the environment become dramatic.

Integrating environmental considerations at the design and production phase is thus crucial to achieve the transition towards a circular economy and preserve the environment. Designing products in a smarter way can firstly prolong their first life use, by avoiding early failures and increasing the resistance of the product to wear and degradation. Extending product lifetime is the best approach to close resource loops (except for some rapidly outdated products)[7], as it allows avoiding (or at least postponing) the purchase of substitute products and all the environmental repercussions it entails.[8] Secondly, ecodesign makes products more easily reparable and upgradeable, thanks to the accessibility of components and the availability of spare parts, tools, manuals and upgrades. Finally, at the end of their lifetime, ecodesigned products can be easily reused, remanufactured and recycled, allowing the added value in products to be kept for as long as possible and minimizing waste.

---

3 European Environmental Agency (EEA), *Circular by design: Products in the circular economy* (European Union 2017), p. 16.

4 Some innovations allow for example to reduce product energy or water consumption.

5 A. Barsan et al., '*Multi-functional Products - A Way to Decrease the Products Environmental Impact*', in I. Visa and A. Duta (eds.), *Nearly Zero Energy Communities* (CSE Springer 2017) p. 711 at p. 719.

6 European Environmental Agency (EEA), *Circular by design: Products in the circular economy* (European Union 2017), p. 16.

7 See for ex., W. Dewulf, J.R. Duflou, 'The environmentally optimized lifetime: a crucial concept in life cycle engineering', in G. Seliger et al. (eds.), *Proceedings of the global conference on sustainable product development and life cycle engineering* (Berlin Uni-edition 2004) p. 59 at p. 62; I. Rüdenauer, C.O. Gensch, *Eco-efficiency analysis of washing machines. Refinement of task 4: further use versus substitution of washing machines in stock* (Oko-Institut e.V. 2005); C. Dalhammar, 'Industry attitudes towards ecodesign standards for improved resource efficiency', 123 *Journal of Cleaner Production* (2016) p. 158.

8 Ricardo-AEA, *The durability of products – Standards assessment for the circular economy under the Eco-Innovation Action Plan* (European Commission 2015) p. 3. For example, an empirical analysis showed that it was beneficial for the environment to extend car lifetime in Japan during the period 1990–2000: S. Kagawa et al., 'The economic and environmental consequences of automobile lifetime extension and fuel economy improvement: Japan's case', 20 *Economic System Research* (2008) p. 3 at p. 28.

1.2. THE NEED OF A MULTI-TIERED ECODESIGN APPROACH

Ecodesign rules do not automatically coincide with the idea of circular economy. For example, the remanufacturing of products is part of the circular economy as it reintegrates products at the end of their lifecycle into the loops. However, imposing energy requirements on products may constitute a major obstacle to the development of the market for remanufactured products. Such strategy could paradoxically result in negative repercussions for the environment. Indeed, although some remanufactured products consume a higher amount of energy during the use phase than new products, they can achieve significant energy savings and carbon emissions reduction thanks to their reduced consumption of energy in the production phase.[9] Since environmental impacts caused by products appear at each stage of their lifecycle and under different aspects, ecodesign rules must be thoughtfully conceived to effectively tackle environmental issues and to avoid contradictions with the objective of circular economy.

Irrespective of the nature of actions (regulatory or not), it is important to follow a multi-tiered approach when adopting ecodesign requirements. On the one hand, the action must apply the principle of 'product lifecycle thinking' and thus take into account the environmental damages caused during the raw material selection, the product manufacturing, packaging, transport and distribution, installation and maintenance, use and end-of-life.[10] This principle allows preventing environmental impacts to be merely transferred from one phase of the life cycle to another. For example, new cars might have reduced energy consumption at the end-use stage, but they might also be associated with increased energy consumption at the production stage.[11] On the other hand, the various environmental parameters must be taken into account, such as the consumption of materials, energy and water, emissions to air, water or soil, waste materials generated, possibilities for reuse, recycling and recovery of materials and of energy. The aforementioned example on light bulbs is relevant in this case as LED technology might lead to a reduction of energy consumption, but to an increase of waste materials. An assessment must thus be carried out to strike a balance between these (sometimes conflicting) factors. It is only with such a multi-tiered and comprehensive approach that the best ecodesign choices could be made.

9 Centre for Strategy & Evaluation Services (CSES), *Evaluation of the Ecodesign Directive (2009/125/EC) – Final Report* (European Commission 2012) p. 23.

10 It has been considered as the "*prerequisite of any sound sustainability assessment*": see W. Klöpffer, 'Life-Cycle Based Methods for Sustainable Product Development', 8 *The International Journal of Life Cycle Assessment* (2003) p. 158.

11 See S. Kagawa et al., 'The economic and environmental consequences of automobile lifetime extension and fuel economy improvement: Japan's case', 20 *Economic System Research* (2008) p. 3 at p. 28.

1.3. TO REGULATE OR NOT TO REGULATE?

Ecodesign can be stimulated by different drivers, such as a technology push, market pull and regulatory push and pull.[12] Legislative measures are not necessarily needed to obtain ecodesigned products. In some cases, the market forces in place and external factors are able to foster the shift towards ecodesign, whereas in others public intervention is required. An example of external factors is the scarcity of resources which, associated with a constant increase of material costs, could constitute an important driver for change. In absence of such factors, changes might not occur. While some producers will never be influenced by arguments of moral when dealing with business, the pro-environmental ones may also be forced to take environmentally harming decisions after having struck the balance between environmental protection and other values such as health or safety.[13] Even when producers decide to produce ecodesigned products, some obstacles remain. First of all, the efforts devoted to ecodesign are only visible years after when it comes to recycling materials. Secondly, implementing ecodesign strategies might require some costs and investments in the research and developments sector.[14] The resulting product often costs a few cents more, but this price difference may represent a great deal from the company perspective because of low margins and fierce competition in some product sectors.[15] Hence, the absence of legislation might encourage the pursuit of business-as-usual and resistance to change, except in case of ongoing or looming crises.

When market forces fail to evolve in the right direction at an acceptable speed and when little or no voluntary initiative is undertaken, legislation might be needed. Legislative measures are adopted to support or supplement voluntary initiatives aiming at ecodesigned product and a circular economy. As rightly pointed out by T. Cooper, "*the ability and willingness of industry and consumers to take actions considered necessary by public authorities will influence decisions concerning which instruments to use*".[16] Different legislative approaches are possible: either instruments that provide incentives for ecodesign, including eco-labels, taxes and charges, or a 'command-and-control approach'[17], whereby public authorities

---

12 K. Rennings, 'Redefining innovation – eco-innovation research and the contribution from ecological economics', 32 *Ecological Economics* (2000) p. 319 at p. 332.

13 E. Maitre-Ekern, 'The Choice of Regulatory Instruments for a Circular Economy', in Klaus Mathis and Bruce R. Huber (eds.), *Environmental Law and Economics* (Springer 2017) p. 313.

14 Rapport d'information de l'Assemblée Nationale du 26 octobre 2011 sur la gestion durable des matières premières minérales, n° 3880, p. 108.

15 D. Jepsen et al., *Delivering resource-efficient products – How Ecodesign can drive a circular economy in Europe* (European Environmental Bureau 2015) p. 54.

16 T. Cooper, 'Policies for longevity', in T. Cooper (ed.), *Longer lasting products: Alternatives to the throwaway society* (Gower 2010) p. 225.

17 E. Maitre-Ekern, 'The Choice of Regulatory Instruments for a Circular Economy', in Klaus Mathis and Bruce R. Huber (eds.), *Environmental Law and Economics* (Springer 2017) p. 317.

impose direct obligations on producers and use enforcement mechanisms. The latter generally takes the form of minimum mandatory requirements.

The EU has decided to follow this 'command-and-control approach' when it adopted the Ecodesign Directive.[18] This contribution will focus on this Ecodesign Directive and on the implementing measures taken on its basis. The legal framework established by these legal instruments play a key role in shaping the design and the production stage of products circulating within the EU territory. The first part of the chapter will be dedicated to describing the main provisions of the Ecodesign Directive, as well as to identifying the existing and potential future implementing measures, taking the most recent texts adopted by EU institutions and organisations into account. In the second part, this package of rules will be evaluated against the long-term target of circular economy, with the help of criteria of necessity and effectiveness.

2. THE ECODESIGN DIRECTIVE 2009/125/EC

2.1. OBJECTIVES AND LEGAL BASIS OF THE ECODESIGN DIRECTIVE

Noticing that market failures and imperfections hindered economic actors to produce and consume ecodesigned products[19], the European legislator decided to take the lead. The concept of 'Integrated Product Policy' emerged as a new EU environmental strategy, with the aim of focusing on the environmental performance of products to promote a sustainable and greener development of the market.[20] Among the rules adopted to address the issue, a package of two legislative acts, namely the current Ecodesign Directive and Energy Labelling Regulation[21], was introduced. Together, they provide the legal support to alleviate the negative impacts of products on the environment, influencing the way they are made, used and disposed. The Ecodesign Directive 'pushes' the market towards greener products by banning the worst performing ones, while the Energy Labelling Regulation 'pulls' the market towards more energy efficient products by encouraging and empowering

18 Directive 2009/125/EC of the European Parliament and of the Council of 21 October 2009 establishing a framework for the setting of ecodesign requirements for energy-related products, OJ L 285, 31.10.2009, p. 10–35 (hereafter 'Ecodesign Directive').

19 For further details on these market failures and imperfections, see Commission staff working document accompanying the Proposal for a Directive of the European Parliament and of the Council establishing a framework for the setting of ecodesign requirements for energy related products – Impact assessment, SEC(2008) 2115, p. 11.

20 See the Green paper of the European Commission of 7 February 2001 on Integrated Product Policy, COM(2001) 68 final.

21 Regulation (EU) 2017/1369 of the European Parliament and of the Council of 4 July 2017 setting a framework for energy labelling and repealing Directive 2010/30/EU, OJ L 198, 28.7.2017, p. 1–23.

consumers to buy such efficient products based on useful information.[22] Specific requirements are laid down for the selected product groups, in *implementing measures* for ecodesign and *delegated acts* for energy labelling, on the basis of a preparatory study and extensive stakeholder consultation.[23]

Surprisingly, in spite of its main environmental goal, the Ecodesign Directive was adopted on the basis of Article 95 TEC (corresponding to Article 114 TFEU), which provides for the establishment and the functioning of the internal market. Article 95(3) TEC nevertheless allows to integrate environmental protection within the objective of internal market, taking as a base a high level of protection and considering any new development based on scientific facts. This possibility of integration goes hand in hand with Article 11 TFEU, which sets out an obligation to integrate environmental protection requirements into the definition and implementation of the Union's policies and activities. The Ecodesign Directive is a good example of such combination of goals, as it is intended to ensure that products which freely move within the EU boundaries satisfy environmental and energy related requirements.[24] Adopting ecodesign requirements at the national level would indeed create barriers to trade and distortion of competition and could consequently hinder the shift towards circular economy.[25] The legal basis of the Ecodesign Directive reflects thus its importance for both the internal market and the environmental protection.

2.2. SCOPE OF THE DIRECTIVE

The Ecodesign Directive does not create direct obligations, but instead specifies criteria and general principles for the establishment of binding ecodesign requirements for specific product groups. In other words, it sets the basis while leaving room to the European Commission (EC) for the development and adoption of implementing measures. The scope of the Directive has therefore been deliberately left large. Following Article 2, the Ecodesign Directive applies to all 'energy-related products', meaning any good placed on the market and/or put into service that has an impact on energy consumption during its use. The notion covers (1) energy-using products which use, generate, transfer or measure energy (electricity, gas, fossil fuel), such as boilers, computers and industrial fans, and (2) other energy-related products, which do not use energy but have an impact on

22 Staff Working Document of the European Commission of 15 July 2015 on the Evaluation of the Energy Labelling and Ecodesign Directives, SWD(2015) 143 final, p. 3.

23 Staff Working Document of the European Commission of 15 July 2015 on the Evaluation of the Energy Labelling and Ecodesign Directives, SWD(2015) 143 final, p. 3.

24 Proposal for a Directive of the European Parliament and of the Council establishing a framework for the setting of ecodesign requirements for energy related products, COM(2008) 399 final, pp. 5-6.

25 See Recital 2 of the Ecodesign Directive.

energy consumption, such as windows, insulation material and shower heads. The scope also includes parts intended to be incorporated into energy-related products which are placed on the market and/or put into service as individual parts for end-users and of which the environmental performance can be assessed independently. Implementing measures can thus be taken on any of these products.

The scope of the Ecodesign Directive has already been the subject of numerous discussions in the past.[26] The former Ecodesign Directive 2005/32/EC[27], which was repealed by the Directive 2009/125/EC, only applied to energy-using products. The justification was that energy-using products have a particularly important impact on the environment compared to other products.[28] This narrower scope was then considered as an important restriction on the contribution of the Ecodesign rules to the EU Integrated Product Policy.[29] The recast of the directive in 2009 finally extended the scope to energy-related products, as they also have an important environmental impact and high potential for improvement. As outlined in Recital 3 of the Directive 2009/125/EC, energy-related products "*account for a large proportion of the consumption of natural resources and energy*" in the EU and require the use of rare materials and manufacturing processes of high quality. Through this extended scope, the number of energy-efficient and eco-friendly products available on the market could be expanded. Some energy-related products remain nonetheless out of the scope of the Ecodesign Directive, the main category being the means of transport for person or goods (Article 1(3)). The reason of this exclusion is that these products are already subject to a wide range of regulatory and voluntary measures that, in addition to safety and other aspects, also address environmental performance.[30]

The possibility of broadening the scope to all products, including non-energy-related products, has always been envisaged. The Ecodesign Directive explicitly refers to this option in its Article 21 and Recital 39, requesting further investigations on the appropriateness of such extension. Based on these provisions, a study was carried out in 2012.[31] It concluded that although the

---

26 See for ex. A. Remmen et al., *Expanding the scope of the EuP Directive* (TemaNord 2011).

27 Directive 2005/32/EC of the European Parliament and of the Council of 6 July 2005 establishing a framework for the setting of ecodesign requirements for energy-using products and amending Council Directive 92/42/EEC and Directives 96/57/EC and 2000/55/EC of the European Parliament and of the Council, OJ L 191, 22.7.2005, p. 29–58.

28 Proposal for a Directive of the European Parliament and of the Council on establishing a framework for the setting of Eco-design requirements for Energy-Using Products and amending Council Directive 92/42/EEC, COM(2003) 453 final, p. 2–3.

29 Proposal for a Directive of the European Parliament and of the Council establishing a framework for the setting of ecodesign requirements for energy related products, COM(2008) 399 final, p. 5.

30 For example, the environmental performance of cars is already regulated by many EU legislations. *Cfr infra*, 4.2.

31 Centre for Strategy & Evaluation Services (CSES), *Evaluation of the Ecodesign Directive (2009/125/EC) - Final Report* (European Commission 2012), especially p. 159 at p. 220.

use of Ecodesign requirements could bring substantial improvements to an important number of non-energy-related products, no extension was needed. It was considered that (1) there was still insufficient experience with the extended scope, (2) significant progress needed to be made in the implementation of the existing Ecodesign Directive prior to any possible extension, (3) a different approach was required for non-energy-related products, (4) it would be difficult to establish ecodesign requirements for such products and (5) the possibility of applying self-regulatory initiatives and local advisory services should first be examined. Therefore, although an extension of the scope remains possible, the framework Directive is so far restricted to energy-related products.

2.3. KEY PROVISION: ARTICLE 15

The main provision of the Ecodesign Directive is undoubtedly Article 15, which clearly delineates the limits within which implementing measures can be adopted. The second paragraph of Article 15 lay down criteria governing the choice of products for the adoption of implementing measures. Pursuant to it, products shall be covered by an implementing measure (or by a self-regulation)[32] if they (1) have a volume of sales that exceeds 200 000 units per year throughout the internal European market, (2) have a significant environmental impact and (3) present significant potential for improvement in environmental impact without incurring excessive costs. Concerning the third criteria to be fulfilled, consideration has to be given to the absence of other relevant EU legislation, the existence of a market failure and the disparity amongst similar products in terms of environmental performance. These criteria leave great latitude in the implementation of the Directive.[33] However, the vagueness of the terms used in this provision, especially the word "significant", has already been pointed out as problematic.[34]

When products meet the criteria enumerated in Article 15, they can be subject to ecodesign requirements through implementing measures. These can be elaborated for specific product groups or applying more horizontally across different product categories. The Ecodesign Directive is based on lifecycle thinking (Article 15(4)(a), as well as Recitals 7 and 13), meaning that the full life cycle of products – from their production to their end-of-life – has to be taken into account when adopting ecodesign requirements. The requirements are from two types, either generic or specific. As defined in Article 2(25) of the Directive, generic requirements aim at improving product environmental performance without limit values being set. They can for example oblige producers to make

---

32 *Cfr infra*, 2.6.

33 R. Malcolm, 'Ecodesign Laws and the Environmental Impact of our Consumption of Products', 23 *Journal of Environmental Law* (2011) p. 497.

34 *Cfr infra*, 3.1.

batteries easily removable from their products or to inform consumers and recyclers about the waste disposal, disassembly and recycling. These generic requirements contribute to the achievement of the information requirements enshrined in Article 14. By contrast, specific requirements set quantitative targets, for instance on minimum quantities of recycled material to be used in production or on maximum energy consumption during use (Article 2(26)). Annexes I and II provide the methodology for setting these generic and specific ecodesign requirements. It is interesting to note that products that do not fulfil the criteria set out in Article 15 could still fall under Article 11, which requires information on components and sub-assemblies.

Mandatory ecodesign requirements set the minimal thresholds that should be reached by products in order to be put on the EU market. The requirements are intended to remain flexible so that they allow for swift improvement of environmental product performance.[35] Through this approach, Ecodesign rules seek to progressively remove the worst performing products in terms of eco-efficiency from the market, without entering the difficult area of identification and selection of the very best performing products.[36] The prime rationale of the Directive is not to promote the development of new technologies, although it incidentally does so by providing the necessary framework conditions, a clear timetable and legal certainty to producers.

In addition to these minimum requirements, implementing measures identify advanced benchmarks of environmental performance of the concerned products. They correspond to the level achieved by the top performing products available on the market. Attaining such benchmarks is voluntary for industry.[37] More than giving inspiration to producers, these benchmarks can possibly become future mandatory ecodesign requirements. This clear mid-term orientation on future requirements is of particular importance for producers (and especially SMEs) as it ensures the necessary stability and reliability for product innovation. It enables producers to take long-term strategic aspects better into consideration when investigating the sustainability of their business models and product portfolio.[38] Discussions on using these best practices in legislation have already taken place. More than questioning the incentives of these advanced benchmarks for progressive firms, it was argued that weak ecodesign rules provide legitimacy to laggards. In other words, some companies would claim that their products are

---

35 Recital 17 of Ecodesign Directive.

36 D. Jepsen et al., *Delivering resource-efficient products – How Ecodesign can drive a circular economy in Europe* (European Environmental Bureau 2015) p. 55.

37 Communication from the European Commission to the European Parliament, the Council, the European Economic and Social Committee of the Regions on the Sustainable Consumption and Production and Sustainable Industrial Policy Action Plan, COM(2008) 397 final, pp. 4–5.

38 D. Jepsen et al., *Delivering resource-efficient products – How Ecodesign can drive a circular economy in Europe* (European Environmental Bureau 2015) p. 54.

sustainable for the sole reason that they comply with the requirements adopted within the framework of the Ecodesign Directive.[39] Advancing this argument, an increasing number of stakeholders seem to view stringent standards as a potential source of competitive advantage for EU industries and advocate higher mandatory thresholds based on advanced benchmarks.[40]

While the Ecodesign Directive aims at increasing the level of protection of the environment through a product-oriented approach (Article 1(2)), the environmental interest is far from being the only one taken into account. During the preparation of implementing measures, Article 15(4)(b) requires the EC to consider the impact on the environment, but also on consumers and manufacturers, including SMEs, in terms of competitiveness, innovation, market access and costs and benefits. In that regard, Article 15(5) mentions additional criteria for ecodesign requirements, namely that:

a) *there shall be no significant negative impact on the functionality of the product, from the perspective of the user;*
b) *health, safety and the environment shall not be adversely affected;*
c) *there shall be no significant negative impact on consumers in particular as regards the affordability and the life cycle cost of the product;*
d) *there shall be no significant negative impact on industry's competitiveness;*
e) *in principle, the setting of an ecodesign requirement shall not have the consequence of imposing proprietary technology on manufacturers; and*
f) *no excessive administrative burden shall be imposed on manufacturers.*

2.4. ADOPTION PROCEDURE OF IMPLEMENTING MEASURES

The adoption of implementing measures follows a specific procedure consisting of seven distinct steps. First of all, the EC establishes a working plan for the following three years with an indicative list of priority products (Article 16). The scope of the product categories to be investigated is defined, indicating whether existing product-specific measures will be reviewed or whether additional product groups will be further examined. Following the working plan, preparatory studies are carried out with the contribution of scientists. A methodology study for Ecodesign of Energy-related Products (MEErP) has been developed together with an associated ErP Ecoreport tool to provide guidance on how to assess whether and which ecodesign requirements are appropriate

---

39 A.-K. Jönbrink and H.E. Melin, *How central authorities can support ecodesign. Company perspectives.* (TemaNord 2008) p. 54.

40 C. Dalhammar et al., *Addressing resource efficiency through the Ecodesign Directive* (TemaNord 2014) p. 101.

for a given product.[41] The assessment applies a lifecycle thinking in order to cope with the multiple dimensions of environmental protection and to achieve absolute reductions of environmental damages. Based on of the preparatory studies, a draft implementing measure is submitted to consultation of stakeholders, gathering Member States' representatives and all interested parties concerned with the product group in question, such as industry, trade unions, traders, retailers, importers, environmental protection groups and consumer organisations (Article 18). The fourth step consists of an impact assessment to evaluate the environmental, economic and social impacts of the proposed implementing measure. The proposal is then subject to the vote of regulatory committee with Member States' representatives (Article 19). After the vote, the implementing measure is scrutinized by the European Parliament (EP) and the Council, before being finally adopted by the EC.

Through this procedure, the adoption of implementing measures takes on averages 4 years. The outcome of this long process consists of a regulation, directly applicable in all Member States. This implementing measure defines the type of products covered, the ecodesign requirements that apply to them, the transitional period for its implementation and the date for its evaluation and possible revision.[42] Ecodesign requirements are gradual and not retroactive (Article 15(4)(f)), which is essential from a technological and a financial point of view. They are also regularly reviewed (Article 21), so as to ensure that minimum requirements and benchmarks remain relevant with time and provide businesses with a long-term perspective of the future regulatory mandatory requirements.

2.5. COMPLIANCE AND THE ROLE OF STANDARDISATION

Once the implementing measure is adopted, every manufacturer who produces or imports and sells products within the EU boundaries has to comply with all mandatory requirements it contains. Manufacturers bear the burden of proof, meaning that they have to prove the compliance of their products with the applicable ecodesign requirements. The conformity assessment is based on self-assessment. As explained in Article 8(2) of Ecodesign Directive, implementing measures leave the choice between two procedures to assess product conformity, namely an internal design control or an appropriate management system. In this procedure, the methods used must be reliable, accurate and reproducible, take the generally recognised state of the art into account and produce results deemed to be of low uncertainty.

---

41 European Commission, *Ecodesign: your future – How ecodesign can help the environment by making products smarter* (European Union 2012) p. 3.

42 Annex VII to Ecodesign Directive.

Article 9 nonetheless enumerates cases where the product is presumed conform to the applicable ecodesign requirements. One of them concerns products for which harmonised standards developed by the European standardization bodies have been applied. These standards provide requirements and guidelines for testing and for result assessment, measurements and verification, which help producers make products conform to ecodesign requirements laid down in implementing measures.[43] The use of these standards remains voluntary. More than for the conformity assessment, standards are of utmost importance for the transition towards circular economy, as they can "*create intra-firm and inter-firm efficiencies, facilitate economies of scale in manufacturing and promote interoperability between complementary products*".[44] Another presumption provided in Article 9(3) covers products which have been awarded a European eco-label in so far as the applicable ecodesign requirements are met by the ecolabel. The presumption may be extended on a case by case basis to other ecolabels if they fulfil equivalent conditions (Article 9(4)).[45]

The compliance with ecodesign requirements can be verified by the national market surveillance authorities (Article 3). The verification is achieved either directly on the product or on the basis of the technical documentation, depending on the implementing measure (Article 15(7)). It is for the Member States to organise such control and surveillance and find the balance while controlling the design of products. Information about the results of the market surveillance is then passed on to the EC. If the product complies with the requirements, it can bear the CE marking[46] and freely move within the EU boundaries (Article 6). No restrictions are possible, except on grounds of major needs or in case of new scientific evidence as stated in Article 114(4), (5) and (6) TFEU.[47] If the product does not conform to the ecodesign requirements, it cannot be placed on the EU market (Article 7). When Member States notice that non-complying products circulate within the EU, penalties can be imposed, depending on the extent of non-compliance and on the number of units of non-complying products (Article 20).

Control and market surveillance are of utmost importance for an effective enforcement of the Ecodesign rules. As R. Malcolm asserted, "*the enforcement of the Directive and its implementing regulations and their control of products, their energy use and environmental impact, is only as good as the enforcement*

43 P. Tecchio et al., 'In search of standards to support circularity in product policies', 168 *Journal of Cleaner Production* (2017) p. 1534.

44 A. Russell, 'Standardization in History: A Review Essay with an Eye to the Future', in S. Bolin (ed.), *The Standards Edge: Future Generations* (Sheridan Press 2005) p. 249.

45 For further details, see the chapter on Ecolabel written by B. Keirsbilck in this book.

46 See Article 5 of Ecodesign Directive.

47 Recital 11 of Ecodesign Directive.

mechanisms accompanying it".[48] The fact that control and market surveillance of compliance with ecodesign requirements is organised at the national law means great variations in compliance records throughout the EU. Article 12 of the Ecodesign Directive already requires administrative cooperation and exchange of information between national market surveillance authorities. However, the EC estimates that between 10 and 25% of products covered by the directive do not satisfy the ecodesign and energy labelling requirements.[49] Some projects have been put in place to alleviate this problem, such as the Administrative Cooperation groups on ecodesign and on energy labelling, as well as the Proposal for a Regulation of the EP and of the Council on market surveillance of products.[50]

2.6. THE PLACE OF SELF-REGULATION

In addition to implementing measures, the Ecodesign Directive raises voluntary agreements and other self-regulations as another possibility to set ecodesign requirements (Article 15(1) and (3)(b), 17 and Annex VIII). This idea has also been transposed to Energy labelling rules, acknowledging voluntary energy labels such as the Green Star.[51] Self-regulations imply an agreement between different actors of the industry. In its Recital 19, the Ecodesign Directive, describes them as advantageous compared to mandatory regulations, "*as they can enable quick progress due to rapid and cost-effective implementation and allow for flexible and appropriate adaptations to technological options and market sensitivities*". More than being stakeholders (like for implementing measures), producers have the power to control the process of self-regulations and decide on their content. When the legislator is willing to introduce or adapt ecodesign requirements in a way that is not in the direct interest of producers, implementing measures might be preferable. However, it should be noted that the difference between legislation and self-regulation is more than procedural. As A.M. Bundgaard pointed out, while implementing measures intend to remove the worst performing products from the market, self-regulations strive to pull part of the market in a more environmentally sound direction.[52]

The best example to illustrate the distinction between self-regulations and implementing measures is the household washing machines. These products were

---

48 R. Malcolm, 'Ecodesign Laws and the Environmental Impact of our Consumption of Products', 23 *Journal of Environmental Law* (2011) p. 503.

49 Communication from the Commission on Ecodesign Working Plan 2016–2019, COM(2016) 773 final, p. 9.

50 Proposal for a Regulation of the European Parliament and of the Council on market surveillance of products, COM(2013) 075 final.

51 Green Star is an Australian voluntary rating system certifying building sustainability. See https://new.gbca.org.au/green-star/certification-process/.

52 A.M. Bundgaard et al., 'From energy efficiency towards resource efficiency within the Ecodesign Directive', 144 *Journal of Cleaner Production* (2017) p. 371.

firstly covered by voluntary commitments[53] and energy labelling from 1997 to 2008. It led to phase out the least efficient household washing machines and to improve their energy efficiency by 24% in the last 10 years. However, mandatory ecodesign requirements were finally adopted instead for two reasons.[54] On the one hand, there was a market failure. As over 90% of household washing machines were in the energy label's highest efficiency class, it was giving no incentive to further improve their energy efficiency. On the other hand, given the growing share of imports from non-EU based manufacturers, the EU industry association was concerned about the risk that important actors would not join voluntary agreements and wanted to prevent free-rider problems. The case of washing machines demonstrates the added value lying in mandatory ecodesign requirements.

When existing or proposed self-regulations concern product groups that are under analysis for further ecodesign requirements, the EC can recognise these self-regulations and refrain from adopting implementing measures. Self-regulations can thus be prioritised to promote ecodesigned products in some cases, if they are in line with the policy objectives of the Ecodesign Directive. The Directive nonetheless requires them to respect strict criteria established in an indicative list in Annex VIII, in addition to the basic legal requirements.[55] These criteria include the openness of the participation of third country operators; added value in terms of the improved overall environmental performance of the product; the representativeness of a large majority of the relevant economic sector; quantified and staged objectives; the involvement of civil society; a well-designed monitoring and reporting system; the cost-effectiveness of administering a self-regulatory initiative; sustainability and incentive compatibility. A recommendation for self-regulation launched by the EC provides guidelines on these criteria.[56] Through all these requirements, the EC controls and monitors self-regulations.

Although self-regulations are acknowledged by the Ecodesign Directive, opinions are still quite divergent on their appropriateness to establish ecodesign requirements.[57] On the one hand, self-regulatory measures are deemed not to set

---

53 Voluntary Commitment of the CECED of 24 September 1997 on reducing energy consumption of domestic washing machines; Voluntary Commitment II of the CECED of 31 Augustus 2002 on reducing energy consumption of domestic washing machines (2002–2008).

54 Impact assessment accompanying document to the Draft Commission Regulation implementing Directive 2009/125/EC of the European Parliament and of the Council with regard to ecodesign requirements for household washing machines, SEC(2010) 1354, pp. 6–7 and pp. 15–16.

55 As recalled in Annex VIII, self-regulatory initiatives must comply with all provisions of the Treaty (in particular internal market and competition rules), as well as with the international engagements of the Community.

56 Commission Recommendation (EU) 2016/2125 of 30 November 2016 on guidelines for self-regulation measures concluded by industry under Directive 2009/125/EC of the European Parliament and of the Council, C/2016/7770, OJ L 329, 3.12.2016, p. 109–117.

57 See for ex. the divide described in S. Rezessy, P. Bertoldi, 'Voluntary agreements in the field of energy efficiency and emission reduction: Review and analysis of experiences in the European

sufficiently specific obligations and stringent targets compared to the business-as-usual scenario and not to achieve better or quicker results than implementing measures. There is, moreover, criticism about the transparency of their adoption and establishment procedures, as well as doubts about compliance monitoring. This is generally the view shared by Member States, European organisations and NGOs.[58] According to these opponents, self-regulations are nothing more than a complement to legislation, especially when they intend to deal with issues that implementing measures cannot effectively tackle. In the words of the consumer organisation BEUC, "*self-regulatory measures should not take precedence over regulatory measures*".[59] On the other hand, some are more positive about self-regulations (including industry representatives)[60], appreciating their flexibility, their legitimacy among (competing) producers, their technicality (thanks to information dissemination), the resulting increased environmental awareness and the inducement of innovation, the lighter burden on the legislator (from an administrative, monitoring and enforcement perspective).

3. IMPLEMENTING MEASURES SUPPLEMENTING THE ECODESIGN DIRECTIVE

3.1. VARIOUS PRODUCTS WITH A FOCUS ON ENERGY EFFICIENCY REQUIREMENTS

There is currently a wide range of implementing measures that supplement the Ecodesign Directive. In total, the ecodesign framework gathers 29 ecodesign implementing measures shaping the design of various products such as computers and dishwashers, 16 delegated acts for energy labelling and 3 recognised voluntary agreements on complex set-top boxes, imaging equipment and games consoles. Around 40 standardisation mandates were issued for these product groups. The list of products covered by implementing measures, as well as the list of existing harmonised standards supporting these latter, can be consulted on the Europa website.[61] It is intriguing to note that no implementing measure was adopted on energy-related products since the scope

Union', 39 *Energy Policy* (2011) p. 7127; Centre for Strategy & Evaluation Services (CSES), *Evaluation of the Ecodesign Directive (2009/125/EC) – Final Report* (European Commission 2012) p. 148. See also E. Croci, *The Handbook of Environmental Voluntary Agreements – Design, Implementation and Evaluation Issues* (Springer 2005).

58 Centre for Strategy & Evaluation Services (CSES), *Evaluation of the Ecodesign Directive (2009/125/EC) – Final Report* (European Commission 2012) p. 148.

59 BEUC, *Greener, better, faster, stronger Ecodesign – Consumer organisations' views on the implementation and enforcement of the Ecodesign Directive* (European Union 2017) p. 8.

60 Centre for Strategy & Evaluation Services (CSES), *Evaluation of the Ecodesign Directive (2009/125/EC) – Final Report* (European Commission 2012) p. 148.

61 See http://ec.europa.eu/growth/industry/sustainability/ecodesign_en.

of the Ecodesign Directive was extended in 2009, although impact assessments concerning such products are ongoing.[62]

Despite the fact that the Ecodesign Directive and its implementing measures follow a lifecycle approach, the main focus has so far been on setting energy efficiency improvements. Through the EEB study from 2009[63], it was observed that implementing measures included a wide scope of environmental issues at an early stage of the adoption procedure, before applying only to a few selected issues, mainly energy efficiency in the use phase. Read in conjunction with the study issued by Defra in 2011[64], this study identified several reasons explaining the focus on energy efficiency. The first reason lies in the interpretation of Article 15 of the Directive, and more particularly its second paragraph requiring "a significant environmental impact" and "significant potential for improvement". It is indeed difficult to assess whether these two criteria are met when dealing with other parameters than energy, especially due to a lack of information. On the other hand, the 'significance' of energy in the use phase was overestimated.[65] Secondly, the focus on energy efficiency finds its roots in the chosen methodology and adoption procedure. Due to the absence of the necessary data, no suitable measurement methods or testing standards were available for the development of requirement relating to other environmental aspects. The fact that Ecodesign has been under the jurisdiction of DG Enterprise and DG Energy contributes to this narrow focus too.[66] A third barrier to achieve more resourceful efficiency through the Ecodesign Directive concerns the compliance with other existing instruments, such as REACH, WEEE and RoHS. The study detected a 'passing the buck strategy' through reference to other environmental legislative measures, impeding the adoption of some ecodesign requirements.

Thanks to the existing implementing measures, there have been great reductions in energy use. The first to reap the benefits from these is the environment. It was estimated that by 2020 the ecodesign framework would result in energy savings of more than the annual primary energy consumption of Italy.[67] Energy efficiency improvement contributes to the achievement of the

---

62 This is the case of windows. See Communication from the Commission on Ecodesign Working Plan 2016–2019, COM(2016) 773 final, p. 4.

63 C. Van Rossem et al., *Designing Greener Electronic Products: Building Synergies between EU Product Policy Instruments or Simply Passing the Buck?* (European Environmental Bureau 2009).

64 D. Maxwell et al., *Review of EuP Preparatory Study Evidence: Does it support development of non-energy related implementing measures?* (DEFRA 2011).

65 C. Van Rossem et al., *Designing Greener Electronic Products: Building Synergies between EU Product Policy Instruments or Simply Passing the Buck?* (European Environmental Bureau 2009), p. 24.

66 While DG Energy mainly focuses on energy consumption in the use phase, DG Enterprise primarily focuses on the production phase and the extraction of raw materials.

67 Communication from the Commission on Ecodesign Working Plan 2016–2019, COM(2016) 773 final, p. 2.

greenhouse gas emission targets, considered as a priority environmental goal by the Directive.[68] Energy efficiency improvement is also beneficial for consumers who save on their energy bills, and producers who get extra revenue.[69] Furthermore, ecodesign rules allow increasing security of supply and reducing import dependency, as highlighted in Recital 6 of the Ecodesign Directive.

Ecodesign requirements have had influence on the array of products available on the market. While products become more energy efficient, others are simply banned from the EU market. An illustrative example concerns the inefficient halogen light bulbs which were phased out in September 2018. Exceptions exist for bulbs that are difficult to replace by others or integrated into the products (like ovens).[70] These exceptions were made to empty the existing luminaire stock, to prevent undue costs on consumers and to give time to manufacturers to develop luminaires dedicated to more efficient lighting technologies (Recital 21 of the Regulation). It should also be noted that the Regulation does not apply to products that are already on the shelves in stores, nor in consumers' houses, but only to new products being offered for sale (Recital 4).

3.2. OTHER EXISTING ECODESIGN REQUIREMENTS

In addition to these energy efficiency requirements, requirements on other environmental aspects have been adopted. This type of requirements is varied, depending on the characteristics of the product concerned. There are ecodesign requirements which limit the consumption of other resources. For example, the ecodesign requirements contained in the implementing measure on domestic washing machines limits their water consumption. The implementing measure also imposes on producers to design their washing machines with the possibility for the end-users of a cycle at 20 °C.[71]

Some ecodesign requirements support directly or indirectly product durability. The first products to be concerned are vacuum cleaners. Their hose must be considered useable after 40 000 oscillations under strain[72] and

---

68 See Recital 14 of Ecodesign Directive.

69 Communication from the Commission on Ecodesign Working Plan 2016–2019, COM(2016) 773 final, p. 2.

70 Commission Regulation (EC) No 244/2009 of 18 March 2009 implementing Directive 2005/32/EC of the European Parliament and of the Council with regard to ecodesign requirements for non-directional household lamps, OJ L 76, 24.3.2009, p. 3–16.

71 See Annex I, pt 1(3) and pt 2 to Commission Regulation (EU) No 1015/2010 of 10 November 2010 implementing Directive 2009/125/EC of the European Parliament and of the Council with regard to ecodesign requirements for household washing machines, OJ L 293, 11.11.2010, p. 21–30.

72 See Annex II, pt 7 to Commission Regulation (EU) No 666/2013 of 8 July 2013 implementing Directive 2009/125/EC of the European Parliament and of the Council with regard to ecodesign requirements for vacuum cleaners, OJ L 192, 13.7.2013, p. 24–34.

operational motor lifetime of the vacuum cleaners should last a minimum of 500 hours.[73] The second category of products is lamps. Various lamp types have to meet minimum requirements for lumen maintenance, the number of switching cycles before failure, the rated lifetime as well as a maximum premature failure rate.[74] Similar ecodesign requirements have been introduced for printers, for which spare parts should be made available for a minimum time period after the end of product manufacturing (from 3 to 5 years depending on the model).[75]

Closely linked to requirements on durable design, implementing measures can also require producers to give information on lifetime. The implementing measure on lighting establishes for example an obligation to inform end-users on the nominal lifetime of lamps in hours prior to their purchase.[76] This information must be visibly displayed on the packaging and on free access websites. Such information requirements also exist for notebooks. If a notebook computer is equipped with a battery that cannot be accessed and replaced by a non-professional user, manufacturers have to provide in the technical documentation, and make available on free-access websites and on the external packaging of the notebook computer, the following information: "*The batteries in this product cannot be easily replaced by users themselves*".[77]

Finally, some ecodesign requirements focus on the recyclability of products. More than information obligation on recyclability[78], there are requirements which improve the recycling of products. One example can be drawn from the voluntary agreement on imaging equipment.[79] This self-regulation prohibits the use of non-separable connections between different materials, for example

---

73 See Annex II, pt 8 to Commission Regulation (EU) No 666/2013 of 8 July 2013 implementing Directive 2009/125/EC of the European Parliament and of the Council with regard to ecodesign requirements for vacuum cleaners, OJ L 192, 13.7.2013, p. 24–34.

74 See Annex II (2) to Commission Regulation (EC) No 244/2009 of 18 March 2009 implementing Directive 2005/32/EC of the European Parliament and of the Council with regard to ecodesign requirements for non-directional household lamps, OJ L 76, 24.3.2009, p. 3–16.

75 Industry voluntary agreement of April 2015 to improve the environmental performance of imaging equipment placed on the European market, VA v.5.2, p. 13.

76 See Annex II (3) to Commission Regulation (EC) No 244/2009 of 18 March 2009 implementing Directive 2005/32/EC of the European Parliament and of the Council with regard to ecodesign requirements for non-directional household lamps, OJ L 76, 24.3.2009, p. 3–16.

77 See Annex II pt 7.2. to Commission Regulation (EU) No 617/2013 of 26 June 2013 implementing Directive 2009/125/EC of the European Parliament and of the Council with regard to ecodesign requirements for computers and computer servers, OJ L 175, 27.6.2013, p. 13–33.

78 See for ex. Annex II (2) to Commission Regulation (EU) 2015/1095 of 5 May 2015 implementing Directive 2009/125/EC of the European Parliament and of the Council with regard to ecodesign requirements for professional refrigerated storage cabinets, blast cabinets, condensing units and process chillers, OJ L 177, 8.7.2015, p. 19–51.

79 Industry voluntary agreement of April 2015 to improve the environmental performance of imaging equipment placed on the European market, VA v.5.2, pp. 10–11.

through weld or glue, unless they are technically or legally required. Along the same line, any cartridge produced or recommended by the original equipment manufacturer for use in the product should not be designed to prevent its reuse and recycling. Another requirement on product recyclability contained in the voluntary agreement on imaging equipment consists of making information available to customers on the minimum percentage of postconsumer recycled plastic content.

3.3. RECENT INITIATIVES FROM THE EUROPEAN COMMISSION

In its Circular Economy Package from 2015[80], the EC underlined the substantial contribution of the Ecodesign Directive in the transition towards circular economy. Recognising the strong focus on energy efficiency and the missed opportunity to cover other environmental aspects, it proposed to undertake three actions concerning the production and design stage.[81] First, the EC committed to strive for more circular economy aspects in future product requirements under the Ecodesign Directive. In the Ecodesign working plan 2016–2019[82], the EC indicated that it would explore the possibility of establishing more product-specific and/or horizontal requirements in areas such as durability (e.g. minimum lifetime of products or critical components), reparability (e.g. availability of spare parts, tools and repair manuals, design for repair), upgradeability, design for disassembly (e.g. easy removal of certain components), information (e.g. marking of plastic parts) and ease of reuse and recycling (e.g. avoiding incompatible plastics) for existing and new products regulated under the Ecodesign Directive. Ecodesign requirements related to computers[83] and household refrigerators[84] are currently reviewed in that sense. In addition, research activities conducted by the Joint Research Centre of the EC are already under

80 Communication from the European Commission to the European Parliament, the Council, the European Economic and Social Committee and the Committee of the Regions on Closing the loop – An EU action plan for the circular economy, COM(2015) 614 final (hereafter 'Circular economy Package').

81 See Annex to the Circular Economy Package, as well as the Commission Report to the European Parliament, the Council, the European Economic and Social Committee and the Committee of the Regions on the implementation of the Circular Economy Action Plan, COM(2017) 33.

82 Communication from the Commission on Ecodesign Working Plan 2016–2019, COM(2016) 773 final.

83 See the inception impact assessment available at: https://ec.europa.eu/info/law/better-regulation/initiatives/ares-2018-770780_en.

84 See the inception impact assessment available at: https://ec.europa.eu/info/law/better-regulation/initiatives/ares-2018-476272_en.

way, assessing the reparability and upgradability of TVs[85] and the durability of washing machines.[86] A general approach has been developed to assess the reparability and upgradability of Energy-related products[87], together with a study on a potential scoring system to rate the ability to repair and upgrade products.[88] Within this framework, a behavioural study was conducted on consumers' engagement in the circular economy.[89] A separate track was suggested for ICT products (such as smartphones), as this product group is under rapid technological progress, leading to uncertainty about future market developments. A more in-depth assessment was proposed to evaluate the possibility of including them in future ecodesign working plans. A draft report on the assessment of material efficiency of smartphones has been issued in April 2018 and updated in May 2019.[90]

Second, the EC planned to request to European standardization organizations the development of standards on material efficiency for setting those future ecodesign requirements. The standardisation request M/543 on material efficiency requirements was submitted in 2015, with a deadline set on 31st March 2019.[91] After three years of debate and two standardisation request attempts, CEN and CENELEC created the Joint Technical Committee 10 to develop European horizontal standards related to material efficiency aspects for Ecodesign products. A series of draft standards have been developed.[92]

---

85 The second draft of the report is available at: http://susproc.jrc.ec.europa.eu/E4C/documents.html.

86 The document is available at: https://www.eceee.org/library/conference_proceedings/eceee_Summer_Studies/2017/7-appliances-products-lighting-and-ict/durability-testing-procedure-for-washing-machines-8211-approach-and-first-learnings/.

87 M. Cordella et al., 'Development of an approach for assessing the reparability and upgradability of Energy-related Products', 69 *Procedia CIRP* (2018) p. 888 at p. 892.

88 M. Cordella et al., *Analysis and development of a scoring system for repair and upgrade of products – Final report* (European Union 2019). The study may lead to a potential graphic label that will be mandatory (extension of the energy labelling) to support ecodesign requirements.

89 European Commission, *Behavioural study on consumers' engagement in the circular economy* (European Commission 2018). Following behavioural experiments, five recommendations were given, including more easily reparable products as well as more available information on product durability and reparability.

90 The second draft of the report is available at: http://susproc.jrc.ec.europa.eu/E4C/documents.html.

91 Commission Implementing Decision of 17 December 2015 on a standardisation request to the European standardisation organisations as regards ecodesign requirements on material efficiency aspects for energy-related products in support of the implementation of Directive 2009/125/EC of the European Parliament and of the Council (M/543), C(2015)9096.

92 CEN-CENELEC TC10, Definitions related to material efficiency, prEN 45550; CEN-CENELEC TC10, Guide on how to use generic material efficiency standards when writing energy related product specific standardization deliverables, prEN 45551; CEN-CENELEC TC10, General method for the assessment of the durability of energy-related products, prEN 45552; CEN-CENELEC TC10, General method for the assessment of the ability to re-manufacture energy-related products, prEN 45553; CEN-CENELEC TC10, General methods for the assessment of the ability to repair, reuse and upgrade energy-related products, prEN 45554; CEN-CENELEC TC10, General methods for assessing the recyclability

If adopted, these standards would provide definitions of parameters and methods for assessing product durability, upgradability, ability to repair, reuse and recycle, as well as documentation and/or marking on information relating to material efficiency of the product. The standards would cover all products under the scope of the Ecodesign Directive or apply to specific products if the horizontal approach is not possible.

Third, the EC pledged the establishment of ecodesign requirements for electronic displays, as required by Article 16(2)(a) of Ecodesign Directive. A Draft Regulation on electronic displays[93] was introduced in December 2016. The proposal contains several requirements related to resource efficiency, such as the prohibition to weld or glue batteries or internal power supplies.[94] Display producers are also under the obligation to provide information on their products to third parties dealing with maintenance, repair, reuse, recycling and recovery.[95] Such information must be kept available for at least 15 years and takes the form of a diagram showing the location of some components for the product disassembly or instructions on the sequence of operations needed to remove the components, with fastening techniques and the tools needed.[96]

3.4. REACTIONS TO THESE INITIATIVES

Ecodesign rules and the related actions undertaken by the EC have triggered heated comments from EU circles. The different opinions expressed by EU institutions and organisations can be grouped into five main ideas. A first topic of discussion concerns the scope of the Ecodesign Directive. Despite the impact assessment study carried out in 2012[97] which concluded that there was no need for an extension of the scope, the issue is still under debate. In its Resolution of July 2015 on resource efficiency[98], as well as in its Resolution of

---

and recoverability of energy-related products, prEN 45555; CEN-CENELEC TC10, General method for assessing the proportion of re-used components in an energy-related product, prEN 45556; CEN-CENELEC TC10, General method for assessing the proportion of recycled content in an energy-related product, prEN 45557; CEN-CENELEC TC10, General method to declare the use of critical raw materials in energy-related products, prEN 45558; CEN-CENELEC TC10, Methods for providing information relating to material efficiency aspects of energy-related products, prEN 45559.

93 Draft Commission Regulation implementing Directive 2009/125/EC of the European Parliament and of the Council with regard to ecodesign requirements for electronic displays. Available at: https://ec.europa.eu/info/law/better-regulation/initiatives/ares-2016–7108187_en.

94 See Annex III to the Draft Regulation on electronic displays.

95 See Annex IV to the Draft Regulation on electronic displays.

96 *Ibid.*

97 *Cfr supra*, 2.2.

98 European Parliament Resolution of 9 July 2015 on resource efficiency: moving towards a circular economy, (2014/2208(INI)), pt. 24.

May 2018[99], the EP asked the EC to evaluate the possibility of using the current ecodesign methodology for other product categories in addition to energy-related products and thus broadening its scope to cover all main product groups. The same idea was expressed by the EESC in its Opinion on the Circular Economy Package, where it stated that Ecodesign principles should be applied across all sectors, mainly because mobility, housing and food have been identified as being responsible for 70–80% of the adverse environmental impact.[100]

Secondly, the current focus on energy efficiency has been highly criticized. As reflected in the EESC Opinion on the Ecodesign Working Plan from 2016–2019, the need to go beyond energy considerations is frequently emphasized, so as to drive change in behaviour through the supply chains of goods and services at a pace that would permit the achievement of the Circular Economy Action Plan.[101] In that regard, the EP called on the EC to gradually include all relevant resource-efficiency features in the mandatory requirements for product design and introduce a mandatory product passport based on these requirements.[102] One of its suggestions is to assess, on the basis of a cost-benefit analysis, the possibility of establishing minimum recycled material content in new products.[103] In July 2017, the EP also proposed the establishment of 'minimum resistance criteria', which could be based on standards, and underlined the need to promote product reparability and durability through a number of measures.[104] Along the same line, the consumer associations BEUC and ANEC stressed the importance of ambitious requirements for material efficiency, including a minimum product lifetime, the availability of spare parts at reasonable cost, the availability of software updates, the limited use of hazardous chemicals and a better waste management.[105] For these new requirements, the EP emphasized the importance of having criteria well specified and defined in a clear and objective manner, while being easily measurable and achievable

---

99 European Parliament Resolution of 31 May 2018 on the implementation of the Ecodesign Directive (2009/125/EC), (2017/2087(INI)), pt. 30.

100 EESC Opinion of 27 April 2016 on the Communication from the Commission to the European Parliament, the Council, the European Economic and Social Committee and the Committee of the Regions: Closing the loop – An EU action plan for the circular economy – COM(2015) 614 final, NAT/676, pt 4.1.2.

101 EESC Opinion on the Communication from the Commission Ecodesign Working Plan 2016–2019, COM(2016) 773 final, NAT/702, pt. 1.2.

102 European Parliament Resolution of 9 July 2015 on resource efficiency: moving towards a circular economy, (2014/2208(INI)), pt. 24.

103 European Parliament Resolution of 9 July 2015 on resource efficiency: moving towards a circular economy, (2014/2208(INI)), pt. 25.

104 European Parliament Resolution of 4 July 2017 on a longer lifetime for products: benefits for consumers and companies (2016/2272(INI)).

105 BEUC, *Greener, better, faster, stronger Ecodesign – Consumer organisations' views on the implementation and enforcement of the Ecodesign Directive* (European Union 2017).

at a proportionate cost.[106] Closely linked to this lifecycle approach, the idea of horizontal requirements on, *inter alia*, durability, reparability, reusability and recyclability was also put forward.[107]

A third criticism centers on the absence of mobiles and smartphones in the indicative list of new product groups in the Ecodesign Working Plan 2016–2019. The issue was raised by BEUC, which disapproves the specific assessment planned by the EC for ICT products as it will delay the adoption of implementing measures on this product group.[108] Sharing the same opinion, the EP repeatedly highlighted that these products, which are sold in large numbers and replaced frequently, have a clear potential for improvement, not only in terms of energy efficiency, but also concerning the recycling of rare metals, product design and removable batteries.[109] In March 2018, an open letter on that issue was submitted to the EC President Juncker by Coolproducts, a coalition of environmental NGOs, with the support of over 30 stakeholders (including Ifixit and RREUSE).[110] Deploring the exploratory study on ICT products, they called for fast and efficient actions, claiming that the necessary legislative tools were already available through Ecodesign and Energy Labelling rules.

Fourthly, the enforcement of implementing measures has caused concerns, leading the EP to constantly raise the issue. In its 2015 Resolution on 'resource efficiency', it claimed that an emphasis should be given on the implementation of self-monitoring and third-party auditing to ensure that products comply with these standards.[111] The EP Report from 2018 expressed the need to tighten up coordination between the national authorities, suggesting that (1) best practices established by Member States should be shared, (2) rapid screening methods should be implemented in cooperation with industry experts to detect the products that are most likely to be non-compliant and (3) dissuasive measures should be taken to improve compliance with ecodesign

106 European Parliament Resolution of 31 May 2018 on the implementation of the Ecodesign Directive (2009/125/EC), (2017/2087(INI)), pt. 18.

107 European Parliament Resolution of 9 July 2015 on resource efficiency: moving towards a circular economy, (2014/2208(INI)), pt. 24.

108 BEUC, *Greener, better, faster, stronger Ecodesign – Consumer organisations' views on the implementation and enforcement of the Ecodesign Directive* (European Union 2017) p. 6.

109 European Parliament Report of 7 May 2018 on the implementation of the Ecodesign Directive (2009/125/EC), (2017/2087(INI)); European Parliament Resolution of 31 May 2018 on the implementation of the Ecodesign Directive (2009/125/EC), (2017/2087(INI)), pt. 28.

110 Open letter from Coolproducts of 26 March 2018 to President Juncker: Regulate smartphones through Ecodesign available at: https://static1.squarespace.com/static/57d64e6629687f1a258ec04e/t/5ab900ea758d46cbe65597d9/1522073834956/Open+Letter+to+President+Juncker+-+Regulate+smartphones+through+Ecodesign.pdf.

111 European Parliament Resolution of 9 July 2015 on resource efficiency: moving towards a circular economy, (2014/2208(INI)), pt. 24.

requirements.[112] Lastly, the EP stated, based on a study gathering interviews of stakeholders in 2017[113], that the majority of stakeholders encounter three main obstacles to full implementation of ecodesign legislation: (1) a lack of clear political support and direction; (2) a slow pace of the regulatory process and (3) an inadequate market surveillance.[114] These concerns could grow if material efficiency requirements are adopted, due to the lack of suitable methods to support enforcement of a lifecycle ecodesign approach in and beyond the EU boundaries.

Finally, there are many comments on the Draft Regulation on electronic displays, which reflect how challenging it is to adopt ecodesign requirements.[115] From the producer side, the Joint Industry Paper on Draft Ecodesign Regulation on Electronic Displays[116] and the Comments from Digitaleurope[117] neatly summarize the major controversial points. The lack of prior assessment was put forward for some products falling within the wide scope of the draft implementing measure. The broad scope was also seen as problematic since it would result in double regulation for electronic displays already covered by other implementing measures. Furthermore, the request was made to remove the resource efficiency requirement prohibiting welding and gluing as it would impede manufacturers in their ability to design products and hamper innovation. Besides, the evidence that these fastening techniques inhibit removability of components was deemed not concrete enough. These suggestions sharply contrast with the view expressed by the consumer side, as demonstrated in the document issued by BEUC.[118] The latter calls for a wider scope including integrated displays and digital photo frames, as well as for more resource efficiency requirements.

---

112 Report of the European Parliament of 7 May 2018 on the implementation of the Ecodesign Directive (2009/125/EC), (2017/2087(INI)), pp. 5–6.

113 C. Egenhofer et al., *1. Stakeholders views on the Ecodesign Directive: An assessment of the successes and shortcomings – Briefing paper* (European Union 2017).

114 Recital K of the European Parliament Resolution of 31 May 2018 on the implementation of the Ecodesign Directive (2009/125/EC), (2017/2087(INI)).

115 See all the feedbacks available at: https://ec.europa.eu/info/law/better-regulation/initiatives/ares-2016-7108187/feedback_en?p_id=8483.

116 Joint Industry Paper from Digitaleurope et al. of 3 July 2017 on Draft Ecodesign Regulation on Electronic Displays.

117 Comments from Digitaleurope of 3 February 2017 on the Draft Ecodesign Regulation on Electronic Displays.

118 BEUC, *Consumer organization views on Ecodesign and Energy Labelling for Electronic Displays* (European Union 2017).

4. EVALUATION OF THE ECODESIGN DIRECTIVE AND ITS IMPLEMENTING MEASURES

4.1. NECESSITY OF THE ECODESIGN RULES

A legal norm is necessary if there is a certain issue to address and no existing norm with the same purpose, scope and outcome. It ties in closely with the principle of subsidiarity which question whether the EU act would provide clear added value or whether similar changes could be achieved at national level. Concerning the existence of an issue to be settled, the first part of this chapter as well as the previous chapters of this book clearly described the negative consequences of massive production and consumption of products caused by the linear economy currently dominant in European countries. Without promoting ecodesigned products, the transition towards circular economy could not be achieved.[119]

In absence of the Ecodesign Directive and its implementing measures, it has been noted that market forces and external factors were not able to trigger but hindered the development of ecodesigned products. A legislative response was thus necessary to drive specific aspects of sustainability within supply chains. While other legal instruments such as information disclosure and financial incentives, or self-regulatory measures can encourage eco-efficient design solutions among producers, the Ecodesign legal framework has distinct and irreplaceable advantages.[120] First, producers have no choice but to observe the mandatory ecodesign requirements, as non-complying products could be banned from the market. Second, the Ecodesign Directive creates a level playing field where all producers (even those who export) are subject to the same rules and not necessarily put at competitive disadvantage like with taxes and charges. Consequently, unlike other EU policies in general, mandatory ecodesign requirements tend to be taken up in other jurisdictions, who want to ensure the competitiveness of their industries on the global market.[121] These extra-territorial effects constitute the third advantage of the Ecodesign Directive. Regarding the implementing measures, their necessity is assessed during the adoption process. The working plan helps deciding whether ecodesign requirements are needed for specific or all products, while the impact assessment analyses existing initiatives on the concerned products (including voluntary agreements), as well as the capacity of the market forces to address the issue.

---

119 *Cfr supra*, 1.1.

120 See from the same opinion, N. Sachs, 'Can we regulate our way to Energy Efficiency? Products standards as climate policy', 25 *Vanderbilt Law Review* (2012) p. 1631.

121 C. Dalhammar et al., *Addressing resource efficiency through the Ecodesign Directive* (TemaNord 2014) p. 94.

The necessity of adopting Ecodesign rules at the EU level is also undeniable. Establishing mandatory ecodesign requirements at the national level would have been inappropriate. Having to comply with rules differing from one Member State to another would have created financial and administrative burden for producers who would then have passed on the costs to final consumers. Moreover, it would have exacerbated the fragmentation of the legal framework promoting circular economy, obliging consumers and producers to deal with a tortuous legal maze. The Ecodesign rules thus benefit all stakeholders by preventing disparate national legislation from becoming obstacles to intra-EU trade and by enhancing product quality and environmental protection. Moreover, the wider the level playing field is, the more it influences manufacturers from outside the EU.

4.2. EFFECTIVENESS OF THE ECODESIGN RULES

A legal norm is effective if it achieves, to the best degree, the objectives or other intended effects, having regard to their substance and to their enforcement. As aforementioned in the second part of this chapter, the Ecodesign Directive was adopted on the basis of Article 95 TEC. Although this provision has as its object the establishment and functioning of the internal market, it allows taking the protection of the environment into consideration. Through this combination of objectives, the Directive aims at ensuring the eco-efficiency of products which freely move across the EU. This contributes to closing the loops of resources in our economy. Since these objectives closely relate to the interests at stake, the effectiveness will be measured against the interest of the environment, consumers and producers.

The Ecodesign rules developed at the EU level are quite effective to achieve their objectives. Through this command-and-control approach, every company willing to sell products on the EU market has to adhere to ecodesign mandatory requirements. These requirements are tested and approved by official scientific methods and specifically adapted for the products concerned, which ensure that they enhance the protection of the environment with no or limited rebound effects. Many specific groups of energy-related products are already subject to implementing measures. Further work and debate are ongoing to include other products within this legal framework, with the question of whether ecodesign rules should be extended to all products. In that regard, voluntary agreements could be used to cover certain categories of non-energy-related products. Once the product complies with these requirements, Member States cannot restrict their movement on the market, except on the basis of grounds listed in Article 36 TFEU or from mandatory requirements (*e.g.* protection of the environment).[122]

[122] These derogations are narrowly interpreted by the European Court of Justice. Moreover, the Member State must demonstrate that the measure is proportionate and suitable to reach the goal. See for ex. ECJ 20 September 1988, Case 302/86, *Commission v Denmark*.

The ecodesign legislation thus allows to fight against climate change from a product-oriented perspective and to shift towards a circular economy, while ensuring the smooth functioning of the EU internal market.

The contribution of the Ecodesign rules to the project of circular economy could be even stronger. Many ideas on future ecodesign requirements are envisaged in that sense. Admittedly, the focus on energy efficiency allowed a great reduction of the energy consumption of the covered products and ecodesign requirements on energy efficiency should still be developed. However, the greater environmental impact of products is now shifting to materials. Constant calls are being made by EU institutions and organisations and supported by studies[123] to adopt a range of non-energy in use improvements. Although it could require the development of another methodology and the adaptation of the adoption procedure, such requirements seem essential in the current environmental context. Some inspiration could be drawn from existing legislation or self-regulation in that regard. An example of inspiring legislation is the one regulating cars, which provides *inter alia* for access to repair and maintenance information, tools and relevant software to independent operators, as well as for the almost total reuse and recovery of end-of-life vehicles.[124] Although the context in the car sector was particular[125], some ideas could be transposed to household products. Some national self-regulatory measures could also serve as an inspiration, like the Austrian Durability Mark for Electrical and Electronic appliances (ONR 192102) or the German voluntary certification (The Blue Angel). To get the label, producers have to make products with a minimum average lifetime and to guarantee the availability of spare parts for a certain period of time, the open availability of a repair manual to end-

123 See for ex. D. Maxwell et al., *Review of EuP Preparatory Study Evidence: Does it support development of non-energy related implementing measures?* (DEFRA 2011); F. Ardente et al., *Review of resource efficiency and end-of-life requirements – Deliverable 1 of the project "Integration of resource efficiency and waste management criteria in the implementing measures under the Ecodesign Directive"* (European Commission 2011); BIO Intelligence Service, *Material efficiency ecodesign report and module to the methodology for the Ecodesign of energy-related products (MEErP) – Part 1: Material efficiency for Ecodesign* (European Commission 2013).

124 See Directive 2000/53/EC of the European Parliament and of the Council of 18 September 2000 on end-of life vehicles – Commission Statements, OJ L 269, 21.10.2000, p. 34–43; Regulation (EC) No 595/2009 of the European Parliament and of the Council of 18 June 2009 on type-approval of motor vehicles and engines with respect to emissions from heavy duty vehicles (Euro VI) and on access to vehicle repair and maintenance information and amending Regulation (EC) No 715/2007 and Directive 2007/46/EC and repealing Directives 80/1269/EEC, 2005/55/EC and 2005/78/EC,OJ L 188, 18.7.2009, p. 1–13; Directive 2005/64/EC of the European Parliament and of the Council of 26 October 2005 on the type-approval of motor vehicles with regard to their reusability, recyclability and recoverability and amending Council Directive 70/156/EEC, OJ L 310, 25.11.2005, p. 10–27.

125 Car legislation was originally implemented because of a lack of competitiveness on the repair market and not because of the difficulty to repair. See Deloitte, "Study on socioeconomic impacts of increased reparability – Final Report" (European Union 2016), p. 15.

consumers and accredited centers, as well as the easy removal of the battery and other consumables by the end-user. Finally, private initiatives like Ifixit, which provides a reparability rate of some devices, could give additional insight.

The adoption and enforcement procedures could also be improved and optimized, especially if new requirements on other environmental issues are introduced. So far, the four-year period could be deemed problematic, especially for products with rapid technological progress. However, the importance of designing appropriate standards and proceeding carefully and stepwise in the process should not be neglected. It is indeed sound to avoid ecodesign measures that may have large unforeseen effects, leading to setbacks.[126] C. Dalhammar even stated that the procedure, which enables good coordination between all the relevant EC services and early interaction with other stakeholders, could pave the way for other legal instruments.[127] Yet, the adoption of ecodesign requirements on the significant environmental aspects of a product should not be unduly delayed by uncertainties regarding some potential environmental damages. Concerning the enforcement of ecodesign requirements, it seems that the coordination between the national authorities could be enhanced for more effectiveness, as highlighted by the EP.[128]

While the environment is protected through the objective of the Ecodesign Directive, it is noteworthy that the other interests at stake are duly taken into consideration. In general, ecodesign legislation is beneficial for producers and consumers. On the producer side, the level playing field established by the Directive protects them from competition from low-quality and inefficient imported products. Stringent ecodesign requirements are also a potential source of competitive advantage, triggering quality products, innovation, energy and resource savings, less waste generated, lower price volatilities and supply risks[129] and new business models. By removing the most inefficient products from the market, it is quite unlikely that innovative products are directly affected. Although some requirements might increase the costs for manufacturers in the short term, it makes a good return on investment in the longer term. Yet, as the EC indicated, these requirements must remain flexible – setting efficiency targets but not prescribing technical solutions – in order to stimulate new options and adapt to technical progress.[130]

---

126 C. Dalhammar et al., *Addressing resource efficiency through the Ecodesign Directive* (TemaNord 2014) p. 25.

127 *Ibid.*, p. 16.

128 *Cfr supra*, 3.4.

129 An illustrative example is the plastic bottle where virgin plastic depends on oil price.

130 Communication from the European Commission to the European Parliament, the Council, the European Economic and Social Committee and the Committee of the Regions on Closing the loop – An EU action plan for the circular economy, COM(2015) 614 final, p. 3; CECED, *Let's close the loop through innovation & competition* (European Union 2015) pp. 1–2.

From the consumer point of view, Ecodesign rules guarantee quality products with reliable and accessible information. Admittedly, their freedom of choice is reduced by the fact that some products are phased out of the EU market.[131] However, it is still possible for consumers to choose between a variety of best performing products for their needs, including new technologies and models that were brought to the market following the adoption of ecodesign rules.[132] Furthermore, rules banning non-eco-friendly products generally generate consumer savings, at least in the long term. While consumers might feel the price difference in their wallet when purchasing ecodesigned products[133], the latter are also of better quality, more energy- and resource-efficient and with a longer lifespan. The transition from halogen lamps to LEDs aptly illustrates this point.[134]

Considering producer and consumer interests when adopting ecodesign rules is of particular importance for a smooth transition towards circular economy, which requires a close cooperation between all actors of the chain. This is done through the active participation of stakeholders during the adoption procedure of implementing measures. This involvement not only ensures the transparency and legitimacy of the rules, but also anticipates and prevents potential adverse impacts and trade-offs. Conflicts of interests are mostly avoided by the fact that implementing measures are defined in a technology independent way. If nevertheless a conflict occurs, one could say that environmental considerations should prevail as protecting the environment inherently benefits to everyone in the end.

5. CONCLUSION

The Ecodesign Directive and the framework it establishes is essential for the success of the circular economy project. It helps weaken the impacts of energy-related products on the environment, from the beginning to the end of their lifecycle. As emphasized in this contribution, such legal tool is necessary to trigger ecodesigned products throughout the whole EU territory at a desirable

131 See in that regard examples of reactions to the ban on halogen lightbulbs: https://www.theguardian.com/environment/2018/aug/23/europe-to-ban-halogen-lightbulbs (visited on 31 August 2018).

132 D. Jepsen et al., *Delivering resource-efficient products – How Ecodesign can drive a circular economy in Europe* (European Environmental Bureau 2015) p. 57.

133 There is no clear evidence that resource-related requirements lead to more costly products. Most requirements can be met with existing technical solutions, at relatively little additional cost if at all. And if requirements are implemented in a staged approach aligning re-design activities with the normal product cycle, necessary changes can be easily included in product concepts.

134 Although halogen lamps are individually cheaper than LEDs, it is "false economy" as they use far more power (five times higher) and last less long (up to ten times shorter).

speed. There are still a few issues relating to its effectiveness, as shown by the various actions and reactions from the EU institutions and organisations. Most of the comments are fully justified to improve the effectiveness of the Ecodesign rules and thus to better achieve the ambitious transition towards circular economy. Some points should warrant the most assiduous attention from the EC, including a wider range of products covered by implementing measures, more ecodesign requirements on aspects other than energy efficiency in the use phase and more effective adoption and enforcement procedures. Inspiration for the future developments of this legal framework could be derived from national schemes (see the reports from the break-out session on national initiatives in this book) or from other EU legislations (like the one on cars).

One major idea should be kept in mind when adopting and implementing ecodesign requirements: the need for a multi-tiered approach. Without considering the various environmental aspects and the different stages of the product lifecycle, ecodesign requirements could not effectively contribute to the achievement of a circular economy. In that regard, cooperation is needed between the different actors of the chain. Consumers will not be able to repair the product if it has not been designed in a reparable way. On the other hand, it would be pointless for producers to design a reparable and a durable product, which could take more efforts, energy and resource, if consumers do not buy it or take care of it but throw it away too early, without any treatment at the end of its life. While actors are required to be actively involved in this process, they gain many advantages to do so. In the long term, designing consumer goods in an eco-friendly way can lead to economic growth and to a preserved and sound environment.

Another evaluative criterion that would have shed brighter light on the effectiveness of the Ecodesign legislation is the assessment of its coherence and consistency with other legal and self-regulatory instruments. A norm is deemed consistent if it does not contradict other norms, and coherent if it establishes positive connections with them. Although the Ecodesign Directive and its implementing measures have proven to be quite effective in the production and consumption of ecodesigned products since its adoption, this effectiveness highly depends on synergies with other legal instruments and self-regulations. As highlighted by the EP, the Ecodesign Directive is '*part of a larger toolbox*'.[135] It is no alternative, but rather a complement to other rules. Even though no such analysis has been carried out in the present contribution, the following chapters of this book will bring an overview of the possible legal combinations to reach the circular economy target.

Along the same line, ecodesign mandatory requirements should also be combined with business models other than the usual consumption model of

135 European Parliament Resolution of 31 May 2018 on the implementation of the Ecodesign Directive (2009/125/EC), (2017/2087(INI)), pt. 6.

buying, possessing and disposing things. Beyond the idea of functional economy (more deeply described in one chapter of this book), there are other business models like leasing, sharing, exchanging or collective purchasing for which ecodesigned products are more suitable. Products with ecodesign are long-lasting and more easily reparable, upgradable and recyclable, allowing producers to further economy benefits and consumers to use them longer. With such business models, economic actors are thus encouraged to turn to ecodesigned products, either because they remain involved in the exploitation and final disposal of the product (producers) or because they feel responsible towards other users (consumers).

THE MARKETING STAGE: FOSTERING SUSTAINABLE CONSUMPTION CHOICES IN A "CIRCULAR" AND "FUNCTIONAL" ECONOMY

Bert KEIRSBILCK* and Sandra ROUSSEAU**

INTRODUCTION – OUTLINE – METHODOLOGY

The purpose of this chapter is to critically examine the extent to which EU consumer protection law contributes to fostering "sustainable consumption" choices in an economy that is becoming more "circular" and "functional".

It is well-known that the traditional "linear" economy (*production – consumption – waste*) exhausts natural resources.[1] Traditional business models – based on the one-off sale of products to consumers – cause huge environmental problems which are only partly mitigated by post-consumption waste management.[2] In light of the fierce criticism on the linear economy, a gradual shift towards a more "circular" economy is taking place over the past decade. One of the key elements of the circular model is "life-cycle thinking".[3] Contrary to the linear economy that requires unlimited exploitation of natural resources,

* Associate professor, CCM, Faculty of Law, KU Leuven; Dean Brussels campus. Special thanks to drs. Anaïs MICHEL for her help with collecting relevant legal materials and to drs. Elisa PAREDIS for revising the penultimate version of this chapter.

** Professor, CEDON, Faculty of Economics and Business, KU Leuven, Brussels campus.

1 See the storyline in Commission Staff Working Document, Sustainable Products in a Circular Economy – Towards an EU Product Policy Framework contributing to the Circular Economy, 4.3.2019, SWD(2019) 91 final, 3: "*Over the whole life cycle of the product, the use of resources is often suboptimal. At the end of their service life, most products are discarded and their materials not sufficiently recycled, causing valuable resources to be wasted, including critical raw materials.*"

2 See e.g. European Commission, *Roadmap to a Resource Efficient Europe*, 20.9.2011, COM(2011) 571 final.

3 N. KOBZA and A. SCHUSTER, "Building a responsible Europe – the value of circular economy", *IFAC-PapersOnLine* 2016, 111–116; A. MURRAY, K. SKENE and K. HAYNES, "The Circular Economy: An Interdisciplinary Exploration of the Concept and Application in a Global Context", *Journal of Business Ethics* 2017, 369–380.

a circular economy is based on the continuous re-use of materials and products.[4] In the 2015 *Circular Economy Action Plan*, the European Commission proposed measures covering the entire product "life-cycle" with a view to "closing the loop"[5] and to bringing benefits for both the environment and the economy.[6]

Much of this debate goes beyond EU consumer protection law, but, importantly, the Commission consistently emphasises the crucial role of consumers as enablers of the circular economy: "*The choices made by millions of consumers can support or hamper the circular economy. These choices are shaped by the information to which consumers have access, the range and prices of existing products, and the regulatory framework.*" In other words: "*The transition towards a more circular economy requires an active engagement of citizens in changing consumption patterns.*"[7] Yet, what is – and what ought to be – the role of EU consumer protection law in fostering sustainable consumption choices?

It is acknowledged that EU law essentially follows two strategies to enhance sustainability: on the one hand, instruments addressed directly to manufacturers, encouraging them to engage in sustainable production; and, on the other hand, instruments aiming to incentivise consumers to take sustainable consumption choices.[8] This chapter focuses on *sustainable consumption* only,

---

4 E. MAITRE-EKERN, "The choice of regulatory instruments for a circular economy", in K. MATHIS and B. R. HUBER (eds.), *Environmental Law and Economics*, 2016, 305–334.

5 See the storyline in Commission Staff Working Document, Sustainable Products in a Circular Economy – Towards an EU Product Policy Framework contributing to the Circular Economy, 4.3.2019, SWD(2019) 91 final, 3: "*In a circular economy, products maintain their potential to create value for as long as possible. Products have a long lifetime, due to a durable design. In case a product breaks, it is repaired. When a consumer no longer needs a product, it is passed on and reused by another consumer, or products are shared from the outset. Products that are discarded after their first technical or economical lifecycle are updated or refurbished and begin another life cycle, or if this is not possible their materials are recycled with a minimum of remaining resources ending up in energy recovery. During production and use, products consume the minimum amount of resources such as energy or water that is needed to fulfil their functions. Consumable products such as food, drinks, cosmetics and detergents are also produced with the minimum impact on resources and consumed so as to leave as little waste as possible. Emissions into the environment and impacts on the climate are minimised across the whole life cycle. As a whole this results amongst others in less use of resources, less waste, more jobs in repair and recycling sectors and monetary savings, while maintaining the services provided by products.*"

6 European Commission, *Closing the loop – An EU Action Plan for the Circular Economy*, 2.12.2015, COM(2015) 614 final, 6. See also European Commission, *Towards A Circular Economy: A Zero Waste Programme for Europe*, 2.7.2014, COM(2014) 398 final. See R. HUGHES, "The EU Circular Economy package – life cycle thinking to life cycle law?", *Procedia CIRP* 2017, 10–16; M. DUBOIS and J. EYCKMANS, "Economic Instruments", in M. REUTER and E. WORRELL (eds), *The Handbook of Recycling*, Elsevier, Amsterdam & New York, 2014, 511–519; M. DUBOIS and J. EYCKMANS, "Efficient Waste Management Policies and Strategic Behaviour with Open Borders", *Environmental and Resource Economics* 2015, 907–923.

7 See also European Commission, *Report on the implementation of the Circular Economy Action Plan*, 4.3.2019, COM(2019) 190 final, 3.

8 See also UN SDG 12 "Goal 12: Ensure sustainable consumption and production patterns", https://www.un.org/sustainabledevelopment/sustainable-consumption-production/. See also

leaving sustainable production (e.g. Ecodesign requirements for energy-related products[9] on the basis of the *Ecodesign Directive 2009/125/EC*[10] – as discussed in the next chapter) out of its scope.

Furthermore, our focus is clearly restricted to *eco-friendly* consumption (i.e. with a reduced "environmental impact"[11]) only, leaving other, non-environmental aspects of sustainability and sustainable consumption, such as social and ethical concerns (for example concerning child labour, general working conditions, animal welfare, etc.), outside of the scope of our analysis.[12] In addition, it should be noted that we focus on consumption of *movable (non-food) goods*, although there is of course plenty to say about circular real estate (see the related chapters in this volume) and the circular transition in the food sector.[13]

Finally, our focus is on eco-friendly *purchasing* behaviour, as fostered through (general) mandatory information requirements and the regulation of (voluntary) green claims and ecolabels. This implies that we will essentially disregard consumer decision-making at other crucial stages of the life-cycle of the contract, e.g. at the *performance* stage (e.g. in relation to after-sales services, choice of remedies such as repair or replacement of products) or the *post-contractual* stage (such as decisions on disposing or re-using and recycling of products).

It is often claimed that, in addition to incentivising consumers to make eco-friendly transactional decisions, stimulating the ongoing "servitisation"

UNEP, Guidelines for Providing Product Sustainability Information, 2017, available at https://www.oneplanetnetwork.org/sites/default/files/guidelines_for_providing_product_sustainability_information_10yfp_ci-scp_2017.pdf.

9 E. MAITRE-EKERN, "The choice of regulatory instruments for a circular economy", in K. MATHIS and B. R. HUBER (eds.), *Environmental Law and Economics*, 2016, 317–322, presenting this as an illustration of the "command-and-control" approach in environmental regulation and confronting this at 322–326 with the alternative "market-based approach" (with emission taxes, subsidies, and Extended Producer Responsibility ("EPR") as an example).

10 Directive 2009/125/EC of the European Parliament and of the Council of 21 October 2009 establishing a framework for the setting of ecodesign requirements for energy-related products, OJ L 285, 31.10.2009, 10–35. See also Commission Communication, Ecodesign Working Plan 2016–2019, 30.11.2016, COM(2016) 773 final.

11 For the purposes of this chapter "environmental impact" means "any change to the environment resulting from wholly or partially from a product during its life cycle".

12 See Commission Staff Working Document, Guidance on the implementation/application of directive 2005/29/EC on unfair commercial practices, SWD(2016) 163 final, available at https://eur-lex.europa.eu/legal-content/EN/TXT/PDF/?uri=CELEX:52016SC0163&from=EN, 57–58. See N. FRASELLE and M.-P. KESTEMONT, "Le marketing éthique: vecteur de responsabilité pour les entreprises et pour les consommateurs – Les codes de conduite et les labels ne sont-ils que des faire-valoir?", *REDC* 2004, 271–287; A. BECKERS, "The regulation of market communication and market behaviour: Corporate social responsibility and the Directives on unfair commercial practices and unfair contract terms", *Common Market Law Review* 2017, 475–515.

13 See e.g. A. JURGILEVICH, T. BIRGE, J. KENTALA-LEHTONEN, K. KORHONEN-KURKI, J. PIETIKÄINEN, L. SAIKKU and H. SCHÖSLER, "Transition towards circular economy in the food system", *Sustainability* 2016, 69.

of the economy[14] could also contribute to the shift to a more circular economy. "Servitisation" is commonly defined as *"the process of creating value by adding services to products"*.[15] This trend is well-known for decades in business-to-business markets ("B2B") but is now spreading to business-to-consumer markets ("B2C") as well (household appliances, furniture, fashion, cars, etc.). New, "servitised" business models entail a shift from selling products to offering "products-as-a-service" ("PaaS")[16] or – in other words – from buying products to using products ("access-based consumption").[17] The basic idea of the emerging "functional" economy is that the consumer – or rather: the user – needs a specific functionality, but not necessarily the product and the materials to realise that functionality: *"People do not want a quarter-inch drill, they want quarter inch holes"*.[18] "Servitised" manufacturers offer various types of "product-service systems" ("PSS")[19] to users and quite often these PSS are promoted as being more environmentally friendly than the traditional one-off sales of products to consumers. Thus, it is often claimed that stimulating the ongoing "servitisation" of the economy, and incentivising consumers to switch to access-based consumption (instead of ownership-based consumption), could contribute to the shift to a more circular economy.[20] Yet, as is shown below, environmental

14 See R. VANDERMERWE and J. RADA, "Servitisation of business: Adding value by adding services", *European Management Journal* 1988, 314–324; H. LIGHTFOOT; T. S. BAINES and P. SMART, "The servitisation of manufacturing: A systematic literature review of interdependent trends", *International Journal of Operations & Productions Management* 2013, 1408–1434; V. MARTINEZ, M. BASL, J. KINGSTON and S. EVANS, "Challenges in transforming manufacturing organisations into product-service providers", *Journal of Manufacturing Technology* 2010, 449–469.

15 T. S. BAINES, H. LIGHTFOOT, O. BENEDETTINI and J. KAY, "The servitisation of manufacturing: A review of literature and reflection on future challenges", *Journal of Technology Management* 2009, 556.

16 See e.g. R. OLIVA and R. KALLENBERG, "Managing the transition from products to services", *International Journal of Service Industry Management* 2003, 160–172. See also Business Innovation Observatory, *Case Study 66: Servitisation – Service and predictive maintenance contracts*, 2016.

17 See e.g. S. J. LAWSON, M. R. GLEIM, R. PERREN and J. HWANG, "Freedom from ownership: An exploration of access-based consumption", *Journal of Business Research* 2016, 2615–2623; D. FAGUNDES, "Why Less Property Is More: Inclusion, Dispossession, & Subjective Well-Being", *Iowa Law Review* 2018, 1361.

18 T. FREEMAN, "Buying quarter inch holes: public support through results", *Archival Issues* 2000, 91.

19 See e.g. F. H. BEUREN, M. G. GOMES FERREIRA and P. A. CAUCHICK MIGUEL, "Product-Service Systems: A Literature Review on Integrated Products and Services", *Journal of Cleaner Production* 2013, 222–231.

20 See e.g. also European Commission, *Closing the loop – An EU Action Plan for the Circular Economy*, 2.12.2015, COM(2015) 614 final, 7: *"Innovative forms of consumption can also support the development of the circular economy, e.g. … consuming services rather than products …"*; European Parliament Resolution of 4 July 2017 on a longer lifetime of products: benefits for consumers and companies: *"4. Notes the role of commercial strategies, such as product leasing, in the design of durable products, whereby leasing firms retain ownership of the leased units and have an incentive to remarket products and to invest in designing more durable products."*

reasons are definitely not the only reason why firms "servitise" their offers to consumers, and a servitised economy is not *per se* eco-friendly.

In order to critically examine the extent to which EU consumer protection law contributes to fostering sustainable consumption choices in an economy that is becoming more "circular" and "functional", this chapter consists of five sections. In the first section, we identify, on the basis of a limited literature overview, some of the most important factors that inhibit consumers to make sustainable consumption choices, even when they claim to have pro-environmental attitudes or when monetary benefits can be identified.

In the second section, we analyse in some detail how EU consumer protection law currently seeks to foster sustainable consumption choices through (general) mandatory information requirements and the regulation of (voluntary) green claims and ecolabels (including the EU Ecolabel). We also draw on the 2018 *Behavioural Study on Consumers' Engagement in the Circular Economy.*[21] However, we do not delve into (sector-specific) mandatory labelling requirements, such as the energy labelling requirements for energy-related products[22] on the basis of the new *Regulation (EU) 2017/1369 setting a framework for energy labelling.*

In the third part, we analyse the main advantages and disadvantages of "servitisation" both for firms and consumers and we draw on studies demonstrating that new, circular PSS and the functional economy are not necessarily more environmentally friendly than the traditional one-off sales to consumers.[23] We also look in various *behavioural* barriers that may inhibit consumers from embracing new consumption patterns and from shifting to PSS.

In the fourth part of this chapter, we identify some of the most important *legal* barriers to engage in PSS – focusing on all stages of the "life-cycle" of such product-service contracts which currently remain almost completely subject to national default law and contractual freedom.

Finally, we come to a conclusion – emphasising the co-originality and inevitable complementarity of the *environmental* and *consumer protection* agendas.

As to the methodology, this chapter is based on a descriptive and evaluative analysis of the most relevant EU legal instruments in relation to "eco-marketing".

---

21 *Behavioural Study on Consumers' Engagement in the Circular Economy*, Final Report, October 2018, available at https://ec.europa.eu/info/sites/info/files/ec_circular_economy_final_report_0.pdf

22 E. MAITRE-EKERN, "The choice of regulatory instruments for a circular economy", in K. MATHIS and B. R. HUBER (eds.), *Environmental Law and Economics*, 2016, 317–322, presenting this as an illustration of the "information" approach in environmental regulation.

23 See also M. BARTOLOMEO et al., "Eco-efficient producer services – what are they, how do they benefit customers and the environment and how likely are they to develop and be extensively utilised?", *Journal of Cleaner Production* 2003, 829–837, warning that the shift from products to services cannot be assumed to be eco-efficient and there are a number of rebound effects which need to be carefully analysed.

The descriptive legal analysis is enriched with findings from a number of non-legal studies on the barriers to make sustainable consumption choices (section 1) and/or to shift to PSS (section 3). Our descriptive legal analysis of eco-marketing in the circular economy (section 2) does not aim to be exhaustive. National and comparative legal perspectives are not taken into account. Taking the related perspective of the shift to the functional economy (section 3), we broaden the focus to encompass legal obstacles not only in the marketing stage but also in the contractual and post-contractual stage (section 4). Our evaluative analysis is rooted in the belief that the availability of accurate, targeted and easily digestible "product sustainability information" is necessary, albeit not sufficient, to foster sustainable consumption choices.[24] In addition, we believe that consumer autonomy and consumers' economic interests should be weighed against other, non-economic (public) interests, such as the promotion of the shift to a circular economy (section 5).

1. BARRIERS TO SUSTAINABLE CONSUMPTION CHOICES

Studies show that environmental concerns at the consumer-side are definitely on the rise[25], although consumers' actual behaviour may not always reflect this.[26]

Therefore, it is being emphasised at the outset of this chapter that consumers often appear to be reluctant to make sustainable consumption choices, even when they claim to have pro-environmental attitudes or when monetary benefits can be identified.[27] There is quite some non-legal literature on the barriers to sustainable consumption choices. A number of reasons have been brought forward to potentially explain the presence of this attitude-behaviour gap.

A first reason can be found in the behavioural economics literature.[28] Bounded rationality suggests that consumers are rational, but face cognitive constraints in processing information that lead to deviations from rationality in certain

---

24 See e.g. M. SCHAUB, "How to Make the Best of Mandatory Information Requirements in Consumer Law", *European Review of Private Law* 2017, 25–44.

25 L. ZHANG et al., "The influence of greenwashing perception on green purchasing decisions: the mediating role of word-of-mouth and moderating role of green concern", *Journal of Cleaner Production* 2018, 740–750.

26 M. SCHAILE, K. KLEIN and W. BÖCK, "From Bounded Morality to Consumer Social Responsibility: A Transdisciplinary Approach to Socially Responsible Consumption and Its Obstacles", *Journal of Business Ethics* 2018, 561–588.

27 A. KOLLMUSS and J. AGYEMAN, "Mind the gap: why do people act environmentally and what are the barriers to pro-environmental behavior?", *Environmental Education Research* 2002, 239–260.

28 E.g. K. GILLINGHAM et al., *Energy efficiency economics and policy, Resources for the future*, 2009, 35. See also H. GEBAUER and T. FRIEDLI, "Behavioural implications of the transition process from products to services. *Journal of Business & Industrial Marketing* 2005, 70–78.

circumstances.[29] As an example, to decide on energy consumption, consumers use simple heuristic techniques such as payback measures, where the total investment cost is divided by the future savings calculated by using the energy price today.[30]

A second reason has to do with the informational problems and behavioural failures related to the consumers' decision making processes. Possible explanations for the attitude-behaviour gap within this setting[31] include information failures, myopic behaviour, institutional disincentives, liquidity constraints, and uncertainty about future prices, which translates into uncertainty about the returns of the investment and strategic behaviour such as free riding.

A third reason concerns the observation that markets do not work perfectly; if that were the case, externalities would already be reflected in market prices and it would be much simpler to induce consumers to take sustainability aspects into due consideration.

Finally, there exists a tension between two roles that individuals typically occupy in our society: the role of consumer and that of citizen.[32] Consumers – as a classical economic concept – are assumed to be driven by self-interest and are thus not required to take social responsibilities or duties into account. Citizens, on the other hand, are assumed to be motivated by altruistic interests and to have a sense of constraint, moderation and interest in the community.[33] The assumption of individuals occupying different roles is consistent with multiple-process theories in behavioural economics according to which people use multiple decision-making programs when making choices.[34] According to these multiple-process theories, individuals' decisions typically result from the simultaneous use of distinct cognitive programs, some of which affect conscious thought processes while others are intuitive, non-conscious processes. Consequently, specific cognitive processes may become dominant in different context-specific situations, and cross-context comparisons can lead to seemingly inconsistent behaviour.[35] Empowering individuals as consumers and

---

29 H.A. SIMON, "Theories of decision-making in economics and behavioural science", *The American Economic Review* 1959, 253.

30 W. KEMPTON and L. MONTGOMERY, "Folk Quantification of Energy", *Energy* 1982, 817–827.

31 A. SANSTAD, M. HANEMANN and M. AUFFHAMMER, "End-Use Energy Efficiency in a 'Post-Carbon' California Economy: Policy Issues and Research Frontiers", *Managing greenhouse gas emissions in California*, 2006.

32 T. LANG and Y. GABRIEL, "The consumer as citizen", *Consumer Policy Review* 1995, 96–106; G. CHAMPNISS, H. N. WILSON and E. K. MACDONALD, "Why your customers' social identities matter", *Harvard Business Review* 2015, 88–96.

33 S. MCGREGOR, "Towards a rationale for integrating consumer and citizenship education", *Journal of Consumer Studies and Home Economics* 1999, 207–211.

34 E.g. C. F. CAMERER and E. FEHR, "When does "economic man" dominate social behaviour?", *Science* 2006, 47–52; A. G. SANFEY, F. LOWENSTEIN, S. M. McCLURE and J. D. COHEN, "Neuroeconomics: Cross-currents in research on decision-making", *Trends in Cognitive Sciences* 2006, 108–16.

35 J. H. ARLEN and E. L. TALLEY (eds.), *Experimental law and economics. Economic approaches to law*, Edward Elgar, 2008.

as citizens can be a core element in bridging the well-known gap between stated pro-environmental attitudes and observed unsustainable behaviours.[36] Such individual consumer-citizens would then balance their (public) duties towards their community and environment with their (private) duties towards their families and themselves.[37]

The 2018 *Behavioural Study on Consumers' Engagement in the Circular Economy* found that consumers were generally willing to engage in Circular Economy practices ("CE practices"). Yet, actual engagement was rather low. According to this Study, a reason for this low engagement in CE practices could be that consumers lack information regarding product durability and reparability as well as the lack of sufficiently developed markets (e.g. for second hand products, renting, leasing or sharing services etc.).[38]

2. CONSUMER PROTECTION IN A CIRCULAR ECONOMY: THE MARKETING STAGE

Parallel with the growing consumer awareness for the environmental impact of consumption, "green claims" are becoming omnipresent, yet so are *misleading* environmental claims ("greenwashing"). Fortunately, EU consumer protection law contributes to ensuring that product sustainability information is available on the market and that it is accurate and non-misleading.[39] As is explained below, EU law seeks to foster sustainable consumption choices mainly through (general and sector-specific) mandatory information requirements and the regulation of (voluntary) green claims and ecolabels (including the EU Ecolabel).

2.1. MANDATORY GENERAL INFORMATION REQUIREMENTS AND LABELS

In the following paragraphs, we first give an overview of the main general pre-contractual information requirements from the perspective of product

---

36 J. THOGERSON, "How may consumer policy empower consumers for sustainable lifestyles?", *Journal of Consumer Policy* 2005, 143–178.

37 A. PROTHERO, S. DOBSCHA, J. FREUND, W.E. KILBOURNE, M.G. LUCHS, L.K. OZANNE, and J. THOGERSEN, "Sustainable consumption: Opportunities for consumer research and public policy", *Journal of Public Policy and Marketing* 2011, 31–38.

38 *Behavioural Study on Consumers' Engagement in the Circular Economy*, Final Report, October 2018, available at https://ec.europa.eu/info/sites/info/files/ec_circular_economy_final_report_0.pdf. See also M. SCHAILE, K. KLEIN and W. BÖCK, "From Bounded Morality to Consumer Social Responsibility: A Transdisciplinary Approach to Socially Responsible Consumption and Its Obstacles", *Journal of Business Ethics* 2018, 561–588.

39 See from an US perspective D. A. KYSAR, "Preferences for processes: the process/product distinction and the regulation of consumer choice", *Harvard Law Review* 2004, 526–642.

sustainability. In essence, we discuss some provisions of the Unfair Commercial Practices Directive 2005/29/EU ("UCPD")[40] and of the Consumer Rights Directive 2011/83/EU ("CRD").[41] As mentioned, we delve neither into the energy labelling requirements for energy-related products following from the new *Regulation (EU) 2017/1369 setting a framework for energy labelling* nor into related issues (such as the relation between general and sector-specific information requirements or the relation between mandatory information requirements and voluntary provision of additional information).[42]

The UCPD is a framework directive that applies to all business-to-consumer commercial practices before, during and after commercial transactions in relation to products (including goods and services). The purpose of this Directive is to contribute to the proper functioning of the internal market and achieve a high level of consumer protection by approximating the laws, regulations and administrative provisions of the Member States on unfair commercial practices harming consumers' economic interests (Article 1).[43] First and foremost, the Directive sets out a blacklist of 31 practices that are *per se* illegal (Annex I). In addition, it establishes a number of general prohibitions catching unfair, misleading or aggressive practices where they have a potential material impact on the average consumer's economic behaviour.

Article 7 of the UCPD contains a general prohibition of so-called "misleading omissions". This boils down to an *indirect* duty to disclose essential information to consumers. Article 7(1) and (2) generally prohibit all commercial practices (i) that omit, hide or provide in an unclear, unintelligible, ambiguous or untimely manner (omission *sensu lato*), "*material information that the average consumer needs, according to the context, to take an informed transactional decision*", (ii) provided that this omission has a potential material impact on the average consumer's economic behaviour.

Yet, there are many "zones of penumbra" around this rather nebulous concept of "material information". The UCPD does not clearly define "material information", except for in the specific case of an "invitation to purchase", which

40 OJ L 149, 11.6.2005, 22–39.

41 OJ L 304, 22.11.2011, 64–88.

42 See e.g. CJEU, Case C-632/16, *Dyson*.

43 The UCPD is a full harmonisation directive (Article 4), which implies that Member States cannot maintain or adopt stricter national measures within the harmonised field, even where the purpose is to establish a higher level of consumer protection than the level set out in the Directive. As the UCPD does not cover national rules intended to protect interests which are not of an economic nature, the UCPD does not affect the possibility of Member States to set rules regulating commercial practices *exclusively for reasons of environmental protection*. Conversely, national rules that aim to protect the economic interest of consumers, in conjunction with other interests (such as environmental protection), do fall within its scope. See also Commission Staff Working Document, Guidance on the implementation/application of directive 2005/29/EC on unfair commercial practices, SWD(2016) 163 final, available at https://eur-lex.europa.eu/legal-content/EN/TXT/PDF/?uri=CELEX:52016SC0163&from=EN, 8–10.

is dealt with in Article 7(4) (*infra*). According to the text of the Directive, the meaning "material information" depends strongly on its use in the specific "factual context" of a case, taking into account all the "features", "circumstances" and "limitations of time and space" (see Article 7(3)) of the practice at issue. As empirical studies show that consumers are generally becoming increasingly aware of and sensitive to the environmental impact of products, it is however safe to say that information in relation to the environmental impact of products will, on many occasions, constitute "material information that the average consumer needs to take a transactional decision". Likewise, information on the durability, on reparability, on the availability and costs of spare parts, etc. can constitute "material information". Where such product sustainability information must be provided, but is not, and where this omission *sensu lato* is likely to cause the average consumer to take a different transactional decision, this constitutes a breach of Article 7.[44]

For "invitations to purchase", Article 7(4) of the UCPD regards certain pieces of information as "material". This means that traders need to provide consumers with this information if it not otherwise apparent from the context. The concept of "invitation to purchase" means "a commercial communication which indicates characteristics of the product and the price in a way appropriate to the means of the commercial communication used and thereby enables the consumer to make a purchase". Of particular relevance is that Article 7(4) of the UCPD requires to provide information in relation to "the main characteristics of the product", which again can cover many types of product sustainability information (environmental impact, durability, reparability, etc.). Failing to provide consumers with information required by Article 7(4) in the case of an

---

44 Interestingly, the UCPD Guidance document gives a number of examples in relation to omissions of information concerning the environmental impact of products. For example, under Article 7 of the UCPD, a trader who fails to inform the consumer that a product has been designed with a limited useful lifetime so that it will become obsolete or non-functional after a certain period of time ("planned obsolescence") might, according to the specific circumstances of the individual case, be considered to have omitted to provide material information. Also, omitting information that a telephone's battery (which is subject to particular wear and tear) cannot be replaced, or that the functional lifetime of a refrigerator is planned to be significantly shorter than for comparable products, could be in breach of Article 7 of the UCPD. See UCPD Guidance document, 75–76. See also Commission Staff Working Document, Sustainable Products in a Circular Economy – Towards an EU Product Policy Framework contributing to the Circular Economy, 4.3.2019, SWD(2019) 91 final, 42–43, distinguishing further types of obsolescence and announcing that national consumer protection authorities are looking, in the framework of the CPC Network, into the consumer detriment and possible enforcement options regarding unfair obsolescence following recent national developments. See also European Commission, *Report on the implementation of the Circular Economy Action Plan*, 4.3.2019, COM(2019) 190 final, 4, footnote 28, explaining that further knowledge on the nature of premature obsolescence practices as well as on how to address them will be gathered through a four-year Horizon 2020 independent testing programme running until 2023.

invitation to purchase is a misleading omission, provided that this failure is likely to cause the average consumer to take a different transactional decision.

Article 7(5) of the UCPD provides that a breach of information requirements established by EU law in relation to commercial communication (see list of sector-specific EU legislation in Annex II of the UCPD), constitutes an omission of material information. As regards to information concerning the environmental impact, reference is made to *inter alia* the *Ecodesign Directive 2009/125/EC* and the (predecessor of the) new *Energy Labelling Regulation 2017/1369* (discussed in the following chapter).

At the pre-contractual stage, the *Consumer Rights Directive 2011/83/EU* ("CRD") sets out a general pre-contractual information requirement in Article 5. The CRD applies to all B2C sales/services contracts within the meaning of Articles 2(5) and (6). Prior to the conclusion of an on-premises contract, businesses should provide information on "the main characteristics of the product", etc. Article 5 overlaps to a considerable extent with Article 7(4) of the UCPD. As Article 5 of the CRD is based on minimum harmonisation, Member States are allowed to maintain or adopt additional national information requirements (where allowed under EU law). For example, in France, manufacturers and retailers are obliged to inform consumers about the period for which spare parts will be available.[45]

All in all, the above mandatory information requirements seem to leave room for fine-tuning with a view to promoting the circular economy in a coherent manner. First of all, the UCPD Guidance document could be amended so as to clarify that "material information" within the meaning of Article 7 includes various types of product sustainability information (environmental impact, durability, reparability, availability and cost of spare parts, etc.). Secondly, the general information requirements of Article 7 of the UCPD and Article 5 of the CRD should be streamlined and integrated. In order to create a genuine level playing field throughout the Union, a full harmonisation and integration of general information requirements, including product sustainability information requirements, is needed.

It clearly follows from the above that mandatory information requirements are important as studies show that, where consumers have access to accurate and targeted product sustainability information, they will make more sustainable consumption choices.[46] Yet, access to information is necessary, but not sufficient, to foster sustainable consumption choices. Importantly, recent studies show that consumers are often overwhelmed with information and rarely search out, read or properly digest all the information available to them. Not only the content of the information, but also the form and timing of the provision of information

---

45 Article L 111-3 French Consumption Code.

46 See e.g. D. O'ROURKE and A. RINGER, "The Impact of Sustainability Information on Consumer Decision Making", *Journal of Industrial Ecology* 2015, 882–892.

are key.[47] As regards for example the option of targeted mandatory lifespan labelling[48], two interesting studies can be mentioned. A 2016 *ILLC Study on the influence of lifespan labelling on consumers* showed that lifespan labelling has an influence on purchasing decisions in favour of products with longer lifespans. Several different ways of displaying this information were tested. Differentiated analyses were performed on nine categories of product (suitcase, printer, coffee maker, vacuum cleaner, smartphone, trousers, sport shoes, television, washing machine), four label formats, ranges of purchase prices, consumers' country of residence and profile (age, gender, household income). Labels with a scale from A to G (+ 20.4%) and displaying useful lifetime (+ 14.1%) achieved better results than the other two labels (+ 11.4% for the label displaying the cost per year and + 9% for the label displaying the lifespan in years).[49] The above-mentioned 2018 *Behavioural Study on Consumers' Engagement in the Circular Economy* showed that the provision of information on durability and reparability can shift purchasing decisions towards more sustainable choices. Yet, the Study uncovered that information on durability and reparability of products was in fact difficult to find and consumers wanted to receive better information. In the behavioural experiment, the provision of such information was found to be highly effective at shifting purchasing decisions towards products with greater durability and reparability. These findings indicate that there is a large potential to close the gap between consumers' willingness to engage and their actual engagement. Evidence from the literature review, stakeholder interviews, focus groups, and experiment showed that improved information provision at the point of purchase (e.g. on EU labels, or provided by manufacturers) was effective at promoting CE behaviours amongst consumers. The Study contains several policy recommendations, which the Commission will further examine (e.g. "*Recommendation 4 – Making durability and reparability information available at the point of sale*").[50]

---

47 See e.g. D. O'ROURKE and A. RINGER, "The Impact of Sustainability Information on Consumer Decision Making", *Journal of Industrial Ecology* 2015, 882–892, showing that direct users – those who intentionally sought out sustainability information – were most strongly influenced by sustainability information and that sustainability information had, on average, no impact on non-direct users. See also e.g. E. M. TUCKER, N. J. RIFON, E. U. LEE and B. B. REECE, "Consumer Receptivity to Green Ads", *Journal of Advertising* 2012, 9–23.

48 BEUC advocates the introduction of an explicit legal obligation, for energy-related products only, to inform consumers about the expected lifetime of a product on the EU Energy Label See BEUC, *Durable goods: More sustainable products, better consumer rights*, BEUC-X-205-069, 2015, 11.

49 *ILLC Study on the influence of lifespan labelling on consumers. Final report prepared for the European Economic and Social Committee*, 2016, available at https://www.eesc.europa.eu/resources/docs/16_123_duree-dutilisation-des-produits_complet_en.pdf. See also e.g. T. COOPER, "Inadequate Life? Evidence of consumer attitudes to product obsolescence", *Journal of Consumer Policy* 2001, 421–449.

50 *Behavioural Study on Consumers' Engagement in the Circular Economy*, Final Report, October 2018, available at https://ec.europa.eu/info/sites/info/files/ec_circular_economy_final_report_0.pdf. In particular, when, respectively, durability or reparability information

2.2. THE REGULATION OF (VOLUNTARY) GREEN CLAIMS AND ECOLABELS

It should not come as a surprise that, when consumers become increasingly aware of, and sensitive to, the environmental impact of products and services, businesses are more likely to make explicit and implicit claims about this impact of their products and services. In other words, there is a lot of voluntary provision of information concerning environmental impact, durability, reparability etc., often over and above the mandatory information requirements discussed above.[51] "Green claims" (or "environmental claims") include any commercial practice of "*suggesting or otherwise creating the impression that a good or a service has a positive or no impact on the environment or is less damaging to the environment than competing goods or services*" (due to its production process, composition and design, energy consumption or pollution during use, durability, reparability, recyclability, etc.).[52] When such claims are not true or cannot be verified, they constitute "greenwashing" (misleading environmental claims).

A 2014 *Consumer market study on environmental claims for non-food products* found that environmental claims are widespread on both product packaging and in advertising and that 76% of all the products assessed in shops contained an environmental claim. Most of the environmental claims take the form of a logo, however also many textual messages as well as more implicit environmental claims (such as images and colours) were found. Consumers have a low level of understanding of green claims. 61% of consumers state that they find it difficult to understand which products are truly environmentally friendly, and 44% indicate that they do not trust this type of information. Consumers also appear unable to understand the meaning of environmental logos, and make no distinction between non-certified (self-declarations) and third party certified

---

was provided in the experiment, consumers were almost three times more likely to choose products with the highest durability on offer, and more than two times more likely to choose products with the highest reparability ratings. General CE preferences were strongest when durability and reparability information was presented together. These findings are corroborated by consumers' significant willingness-to-pay for better durability/reparability for all product categories. 'Nudges' informing consumers of the benefits and social norms of buying durable/repairable products increased the saliency of CE characteristics and triggered shifts in preferences towards more durable/repairable products. See also European Commission, *Report on the implementation of the Circular Economy Action Plan*, 4.3.2019, COM(2019) 190 final, 4. See also European Parliament Resolution of 4 July 2017 on a longer lifetime of products: benefits for consumers and companies: "*27. Calls on the Commission to improve product durability information via …*".

51 A. LEWANDOWSKA, J. WITCZAK, P. KURCZEWSKI, "Green marketing today – a mix of trust, consumer participation and life cycle thinking", *Management* 2017, 28–48.

52 Commission Staff Working Document, Guidance on the implementation/application of directive 2005/29/EC on unfair commercial practices, SWD(2016) 163 final, available at https://eur-lex.europa.eu/legal-content/EN/TXT/PDF/?uri=CELEX:52016SC0163&from=EN, 95.

labels. Almost 60% of the respondents stated that they prefer to buy a product with an environmental label, keeping all else constant. Half of the consumers also look specifically for environmental information on the packaging when purchasing a product.[53]

Already in its 2015 Action Plan for the Circular Economy, the European Commission observed that "*Faced with a profusion of labels or environmental claims, EU consumers often find it difficult to differentiate between products and to trust the information available. Green claims may not always meet legal requirements for reliability, accuracy and clarity. The Commission … is testing the Product Environmental Footprint, a methodology for measuring environmental performance, and will explore its use to measure or communicate environmental information. The voluntary EU Ecolabel identifies products that have a reduced environmental impact throughout their lifecycle. The Commission will examine how to increase its effectiveness and contribution to the circular economy.*"[54] These very issues[55] will be discussed further in the following paragraphs.

The UCPD is the main instrument to combat misleading environmental claims and "greenwashing" practices. The UCPD does not provide specific rules on environmental claims. However, the UCPD Guidance document contains a separate section dealing with environmental claims.[56]

First of all, a number of items on the UCPD's blacklist (Annex I) prove particularly relevant to environmental claims.[57] Secondly, the general prohibitions of misleading practices (Articles 6 and 7) and the specific rule on substantiation of claims (Article 12) are key in combating greenwashing. According to the UCPD Guidance document, the application of the UCPD to environmental claims can be summarised in two main principles:

---

53 *Consumer market study on environmental claims for non-food products*, available at https://ec.europa.eu/info/sites/info/files/study_on_environmetal_claims_for_non_food_products_2014_en.pdf.

54 European Commission, *Closing the loop – An EU Action Plan for the Circular Economy*, 2.12.2015, COM(2015) 614 final, 6.

55 Have a look in the ecolabel jungle via www.ecolabelindex.com/ – the largest global directory of ecolabels, currently tracking 463 ecolabels in 199 countries, and 25 industry sectors. See also J. SALZMAN, "Informing the Green Consumer – The Debate Over the Use and Abuse of Environmental Labels", *Journal of Industrial Ecology* 1997, 11–21; M. VAN AMSTEL, P. DRIESSEN and P. GLASBERGEN, "Eco-labeling and information asymmetry: a comparison of five eco-labels in the Netherlands", *Journal of Cleaner Production* 2008, 263–276; L. BOY, "Labels écologiques et alimentaires: les enjeux de la réglementation européenne", *JDE* 2013, 2–9; J. J. CZARNEZKI, K. INGEMAR JÖNSSON & K. KUH, "Crafting next generation eco-label policy", *Environmental law* 2018, 409–452.

56 Commission Staff Working Document, Guidance on the implementation/application of directive 2005/29/EC on unfair commercial practices, SWD(2016) 163 final, available at https://eur-lex.europa.eu/legal-content/EN/TXT/PDF/?uri=CELEX:52016SC0163&from=EN. See Commission Communication, Building the Single Market for Green Products – Facilitating better information on the environmental performance of products and organisations, COM(2013) 196 final, 4.3.3.

57 Guidance document, 118–120, focusing on Point Nos. 1–4 and 10 of Annex I of the UCPD.

I. Based on the general clauses of the UCPD, particularly Articles 6 and 7, traders must present their green claims in a clear, specific, accurate and unambiguous manner, to ensure that consumers are not mislead.
II. Based on Article 12 of the UCPD, traders must have the evidence to support their claims and be ready to provide it to competent enforcement authorities in an understandable way if the claim is challenged.[58]

Article 6 of the UCPD contains the general prohibition of "misleading actions". Essentially, businesses are not allowed to engage in commercial practices (such as marketing) which are misleading in the eye of the average consumer, and which are thereby likely to have a substantial impact on his economic behaviour. An environmental claim can be misleading if it "contains false information and is therefore untruthful" in relation to one of the elements listed in Article 6(1)(a) to (g), or if it "in any way, including overall presentation, deceives or is likely to deceive the average consumer, even if the information is factually correct" in relation to one of these items. The UCPD Guidance document emphasises that insights from behavioural economics show that not only the content of the information provided, but also the way the information is presented can have a significant impact on how consumers respond to it. Therefore, the misleading character of commercial practices must be assessed by taking into account the most recent findings in behavioural economics.[59]

The list of Article 6(1)(a) to (g) include elements which are of particular importance as regard the environmental impact of products, such as Article 6(1)(a) ("*the existence or nature of the product*") and (b) ("*the main characteristics of the product, such as …*"). The latter notion includes *inter alia* "*benefits, … composition, …, method and date of manufacture or provision, … fitness for purpose, usage, … the results to be expected from its use, or the results and material features of tests or checks carried out on the product*". On the basis of Article 6(1)(c) and (e), it also prohibited to mislead in relation to "*the nature of the trader's commitment …*" and "*the need for a service, part, replacement or repair*". In any event, Article 6 can only be applied, if additionally it is proven that the misleading character of the practice is likely to cause the average consumer to take a transactional decision that he would not have taken otherwise.

As a rule of thumb, environmental claims should relate to aspects that are significant in terms of the product's main environmental impacts over its lifecycle, including its supply chain, and should be clear and unambiguous regarding which aspect of the product or its life cycle they refer to. If a trader makes an environmental claim by highlighting just one of several impacts the product has on the environment, the claim could be misleading within

[58] Guidance document, 108.
[59] Guidance document, 52–53. See also CJEU, Case C-611/14, *Canal Digital Danmark*.

the meaning of Article 6 of the UCPD.[60] If businesses do not know the most significant environmental aspects of a product, they could perform a life cycle assessment ("LCA")[61], or simply refrain from making environmental claims.[62] Yet, the Commission wants to stimulate the use of green claims and therefore recently developed the *Product Environmental Footprint* ("PEF") methods as a common way of measuring "environmental performance".[63, 64] These LCA methods of excellence can enable companies to make environmental claims that are reliable, reproducible and comparable.[65] The European Commission envisages to require the use of PEF for substantiating green claims. Under such a scenario, there would be no obligation to make environmental claims on products, but if a company wishes to do so, they would need to use the PEF method to substantiate their claim.[66]

Codes of conduct may include commitments in relation to the environmental impact of a product and often involve the use of a logo, ecolabel, symbol or certificate by the code signatory generally or on the product specifically. Consumers expect code signatories to sell products which comply with that code and they expect products bearing the logo, ecolabel, etc. to meet the commitments of the code.[67] If a business has undertaken to be bound by such a code and indicates in a commercial practice that he did so (e.g. by using the code's logo), non-compliance with the code can constitute a misleading action within the meaning of Article 6(2)(b), provided that those commitments are firm and verifiable and provided that the average consumer is likely to take a different transactional decision.[68] Also, such labels must not be capable of being confused with other labels, including, for example, labels of publicly run labelling schemes or schemes of competitors; this could constitute a breach of Article 6(2)(b).

---

60 Guidance document, 111.

61 See Commission Recommendation 2013/179/EU on the use of common methods to measure and communicate the life cycle environmental performance of products and organisations.

62 Guidance document, 111.

63 For the purposes of this chapter "environmental performance" means "the result of a manufacturer's management of those characteristics of a product that cause environmental impact".

64 See also L. ZAMPORI and R. PANT, "Suggestions for updating the Product Environmental Footprint (PEF) method", EUR 29682 EN, Publications Office of the European Union, Luxembourg, 2019, ISBN 978-92-76-00654-1, doi:10.2760/424613, JRC115959, available at https://eplca.jrc.ec.europa.eu/permalink/PEF_method.pdf.

65 European Commission, *Report on the implementation of the Circular Economy Action Plan*, 4.3.2019, COM(2019) 190 final, 3. See also Commission Staff Working Document, Sustainable Products in a Circular Economy – Towards an EU Product Policy Framework contributing to the Circular Economy, 4.3.2019, SWD(2019) 91 final, 45–50.

66 Commission Staff Working Document, Sustainable Products in a Circular Economy – Towards an EU Product Policy Framework contributing to the Circular Economy, 4.3.2019, SWD(2019) 91 final, 49.

67 Guidance document, 111.

68 Guidance document, 111.

A 2012 *Study on different options for communicating environmental information for products* examines different mechanisms (as to content, form and timing) for the provision of information concerning the environmental impact of products to consumers and determines the type of ecolabel that maximises consumers' usage, understanding and ability to compare between different substitutes.[69]

Article 7 of the UCPD is also of great relevance: environmental claims can constitute "misleading omissions", if they are based on vague and general statements of environmental benefits such as 'environmentally friendly', 'green', 'nature's friend', 'ecological', 'sustainable', 'environmentally correct', 'climate friendly', or 'gentle on the environment'.[70] Such claims could be less likely to be misleading under Article 7 if they are supplemented by prominent specifications or explanatory statements on the product's environmental impact, for example by limiting the claim to specific environmental benefits.[71]

Some products may be subject to detailed and ambitious rules and achieve such an excellent environmental performance that the use of a general benefit claim (presented without further qualifications) may be justified.[72] This could be the case if a product is covered by a license to use the ecolabel of a *publicly run* ecolabel scheme (such as the Nordic Ecolabel 'the Swan', the German 'Blue Angel' or the EU Ecolabel 'the Flower') or *other robust and reputable* labelling schemes *subject to third party verification*. This could also be the case if the LCA studies of the product (e.g. on the basis of the PEF method) have proven its excellent environmental performance.[73]

Where environmental claims suggest that a product has a more positive impact on the environment or is less damaging to the environment *than competing goods or services*, they constitute "comparative advertising" within the meaning of *Directive 2006/114/EU on misleading and comparative advertising* ("MCAD"). Hence, the permissibility conditions of Article 4 will come into play.[74] For example, comparisons should refer to products within the same product category. In addition, the method used to produce the information should be the same, applied in a consistent manner (i.e. the same methodological choices and rules are applied, results are reproducible), and allow meaningful comparisons.[75]

69 BIO Intelligence service, *Study on different options for communicating environmental information for products. Final report prepared for the European Commission DG ENV*, 2012, available at http://ec.europa.eu/environment/eussd/pdf/footprint/ProductsCommunication_Final%20Report.pdf.

70 Guidance document, 110.

71 Guidance document, 112.

72 Guidance document, 113.

73 Guidance document, 113.

74 Guidance document, 120–121.

75 Guidance document, 120–121. See also Commission Communication, Building the Single Market for Green Products – Facilitating better information on the environmental performance of products and organisations, COM(2013) 196 final, 4.3.4.

Article 12 of the UCPD clarifies that any claim (including environmental claims) should be based on evidence which can be verified by the relevant competent authorities. Traders must be able to substantiate environmental claims with appropriate evidence. Consequently, claims should be based on robust, independent, verifiable and generally recognised evidence which takes into account updated scientific findings and methods.[76] In order to ensure that environmental claims are substantiated, traders should either have the evidence necessary to support their claims from the time the claims are put into use or be certain that it can be obtained and presented upon request.[77] Although a claim may be correct and relevant to a product when the claim is first made, it could become less meaningful with time. Traders should make sure that documentation for claims is up to date for as long as the claims remain in use in marketing.[78]

The 2014 *Consumer Market Study* showed that there is certainly room for improvement on enforcement of environmental claims. Proactive surveillance or inspections are rather limited and in some cases inspectors have a limited knowledge about how to correctly interpret the UCPD with reference to environmental claims.[79] In addition, we would suggest that the Guidance document could be amended so as to cover not only misleading green claims but also e.g. misleading *durability* claims.[80]

The above-mentioned voluntary EU Ecolabel identifies products that have a reduced environmental impact throughout their lifecycle. The EU Ecolabel was established in 1992. The *Ecolabel Regulation (EC) No. 66/2010* provides the basis for the current European ecolabel scheme, which aims to promote the design, production, marketing and use of products that have a reduced environmental impact (Article 3(3)) during their entire life cycle and to provide consumers with accurate, non-deceptive, science-based information on the environmental impact of products (i.e. goods and services).

The EU Ecolabel offers a reference point of environmental excellence at the EU level in a wide range of product groups. It takes a multi-criteria approach, is based on scientific evidence considering the whole life-cycle of products, is third party certified and revised regularly to follow technological evolution. The EU Ecolabel criteria that products must fulfil in order to bear the EU Ecolabel (Article 3(2)) are based on the environmental performance (Article 3(4)). They are determined on a scientific basis considering the whole life cycle of products,

---

76 Guidance document, 115.

77 Guidance document, 116.

78 Guidance document, 117.

79 *Consumer market study on environmental claims for non-food products*, available at https://ec.europa.eu/info/sites/info/files/study_on_environmetal_claims_for_non_food_products_2014_en.pdf.

80 See in the same sense BEUC, *Durable goods: More sustainable products, better consumer rights*, BEUC-X-205-069, 2015, 12.

taking into account the most significant environmental impacts, the potential to reduce environmental impacts due to durability and reusability[81], etc. (Article 6). The uptake has been very uneven, including at geographical level, ranging from zero licences to hundreds of licences.[82]

A 2017 *Fitness Check* examined the scheme in terms of its relevance, effectiveness, efficiency, coherence and EU added value.[83] The Fitness Check confirmed the useful – even if limited – role of the scheme as a voluntary instrument for businesses that facilitates the transition to a circular economy and provides information on the environmental performance of products in B2C and B2B transactions. The Fitness Check also indicates that, in order to fully exploit the potential of the scheme, efforts need to be made to enhance its uptake. Recently, the Commission launched a study for the identification of elements for a strategic approach to EU Ecolabel.[84]

3. "SERVITISATION" – TOWARDS A "FUNCTIONAL" ECONOMY

3.1. RISE OF PSS IN B2C MARKETS

As mentioned, it is often said that the ongoing "servitisation" of the economy could contribute to the shift to a more circular economy. Various types of product-service systems ('PSS') exist.[85] In product-oriented PSS, services

---

81 For instance, the new EU Ecolabel for furniture requires manufacturers to focus on durability and reparability of their products, offering extended product guarantees of at least five years, during which time they must make available spare parts. Furniture comprised of multiple components must also be designed for disassembly by unskilled labour with basic tools, making it possible for furniture owners to dispose of, reuse and recycle used products. Manufacturers must also undertake lifecycle assessments of the material components, and highlight where they may contribute to indoor air pollution. See Commission decision (EU) 2016/1332 of 28 July 2016 establishing the ecological criteria for the award of the EU Ecolabel for furniture, OJ L 210, 4.8.2016, p. 100–149.

82 Commission Staff Working Document, Sustainable Products in a Circular Economy – Towards an EU Product Policy Framework contributing to the Circular Economy, 4.3.2019, SWD(2019) 91 final, 10–11.

83 Commission Staff Working Document, Executive Summary of the Fitness Check, 30.6.2017, SWD(2017) 252 final.

84 Commission Staff Working Document, Sustainable Products in a Circular Economy – Towards an EU Product Policy Framework contributing to the Circular Economy, 4.3.2019, SWD(2019) 91 final, 11.

85 M.J. GOEDKOOP et al., *Product service systems: Ecological and economic basics. Report for Dutch Ministries of Environment (VROM) and Economic Affairs (EZ)*, 1999; O. MONT, "Clarifying the concept of product-service system", *Journal of Cleaner Production* 2002, 237–245; A. TUKKER, "Eight types of product-service system: eight ways to sustainability. Experiences from Suspronet", *Business Strategy and the Environment* 2004, 246–260; W. REIM, V. PARIDA and D. ÖRTQVIST, "Product-Service Systems (PSS) business models and tactics – a systematic literature review", *Journal of Cleaner Production* 2015, 61–75.

(maintenance, repair, ...) are added to the sale of a product (after-sales services). User-oriented PSS entail a right of use for the recipient of the product and the payment of a periodical fee. Producers retain ownership and the responsibility for the product during the entire life cycle. Result-oriented PSS guarantee the fulfilment of a specific need; e.g. when light is sold instead of light bulbs.

New, circular business models that aim to benefit the producer, the consumer and/or the environment, are on the rise.[86] Until now, the main examples of user- and result-oriented PPS come from B2B markets, such as the Rolls-Royce's "*Power-by-the-Hour*" model[87], Philips' "*Light as a Service*" model[88] or Kaer's "*Airconditioning-as-a-service*" model.[89] Other examples include the sector of office furniture.[90]

Circular business models and PSS are now also increasingly on the rise in various B2C markets.[91] In fashion, well-known examples are the "*Lease A Jeans*" formula by the Dutch company MudJeans[92] or the luxury "*Rent the Runway*" formula.[93] As to household appliances, "*Bundles*"[94] by Miele offers subscriptions for washing machines, tumble dryers and dishwashers; "*Blue Movement*"[95] by BSH (Bosh, etc.) is a competing offer on the market. Other examples includes "*HP Instant Ink*" plan[96] or the plans by IKEA for kitchens for rent.[97] Mid 2019, the electric "*Polestar 1*" will be launched (owned by the Volvo Car Group).[98] The brand's business model is based on an 2/3-year subscription formula, where the monthly fee will include everything from use (including other vehicles within the Volvo and Polestar ranges), maintenance and repair, insurance and roadside assistance to access to on-demand services such as pick-up and delivery services.

---

86 N.M. BOCKEN, I. DE PAUW, C. BAKKER and B. VAN DER GRINTEN, "Product design and business model strategies for a circular economy", *Journal of Industrial and Production Engineering* 2016, 308–320; M. B. AMOR; M. LINDAHL, P. FRANKELIUS and H. B. ABDENNEBI, "Revisiting industrial organization: Product service systems insight", *Journal of Cleaner Production* 2018, 1459–1477.

87 For airplanes, vessels, etc. See https://www.rolls-royce.com/media/press-releases/2017/24-05-2017-nor-lines-and-rr-sign-landmark-power-by-the-hour-service-agreement.aspx.

88 Www.lighting.philips.nl/systemen/aanbod-van-pakketten/winkels-en-horeca/light-as-a-servi ce-retail.

89 Https://www.kaer.com/.

90 See e.g. www.rypeoffice.com/.

91 A. TUKKER, "Product services for a resource-efficient and circular economy – a review", *Journal of cleaner production* 2015, 76–91.

92 Www.mudjeans.eu/how-lease-a-jeans-works/ Users pay a one-off subscription fee of 29 € and 12 monthly instalments of 7,50 €. After leasing their jeans for 12 months, they can decide to switch to a new pair, return them, or keep them until they are worn out.

93 Www.renttherunway.com.

94 Www.bundles.nl/en/.

95 Https://www.bluemovement.nl/.

96 Https://instantink.hpconnected.com/be/nl/l/?jumpid=ps_wwsupplies.

97 Https://www.theguardian.com/business/2019/feb/04/kitchen-for-rent-ikea-to-trial-leasing-of-furniture.

98 Www.polestar.com.

3.2. ADVANTAGES, DISADVANTAGES AND SUSTAINABILITY

Many firms are exploiting new technologies and tend to increasingly offer these types of PSS, in order to: differentiate their output; to attract new customers; to increase the stability of revenues (long-term contracts, periodical payments, residual value of the product stays with the firm, ...)[99]; to generate increased profit margins[100], to reduce costs through disintermediation ("*cutting out the middle man*", 3rd party service integration)[101]; to create competitive and marketing advantages (customised "all-in" offers); to discover direct information on use and customer satisfaction[102]; to increase customer intimacy and loyalty[103]; to make the business model more difficult to copy[104]; and/or for environmental reasons.

Hence, PSS definitely have opportunities, not only for firms, but also for their 'unburdened' customers[105]: lower entry cost; greater business responsiveness to consumer preferences and needs; continued responsibility of the provider for the product's functionality; no responsibility for maintenance and repair; no unexpected costs; access to high-end and luxury products (that would otherwise not be affordable).

New PSS are often promoted as being more environmentally friendly than the classic model of one-off sales of products to consumers. Many scholars argue that servitisation can provide an incentive for manufacturers to increase durability and reparability of products or – in other words – to prolong the "service-life" of products. Servitisation is said to lead to redesigning products and to reduce environmental impacts associated with the linear model. Scholars also argue that servitisation can provide an incentive for consumers to use products in a more efficient way.[106]

---

99 R. WISE and P. BAUMGARTNER, "Go downstream: The new profit imperative in manufacturing", *Harvard Business Review* 1999, 133–141.

100 H. GEBAUER, E. FLEISCH and T. FRIEDLI, "Overcoming the service paradox in manufacturing companies", *European Journal of Management* 2005, 14–26.

101 See e.g. F. BOSTOEN and W. DEVROE, "From sales to subscriptions in the car sector: competition law implications of servitisation and the refusal to sell to consumers", *European Competition Law Review* 2018, 411–419.

102 W. REIM, V. PARIDA and D. ÖRTQVIST, "Product-Service Systems (PSS) business models and tactics – a systematic literature review", *Journal of Cleaner Production* 2015, 68–69.

103 J. HOJNIK, "The servitisation of industry: EU law implications and challenges", *Common Market Law Review* 2016, 1590.

104 R. OLIVA and R. KALLENBERG, "Managing the transition from products to services", *International Journal of Service Industry Management* 2003, 160–172.

105 O.K. MONT, "Clarifying the concept of product-service system", *Journal of Cleaner Production* 2002, 237–245.

106 J. HOJNIK, "Ecological modernisation through servitisation: EU regulatory support for sustainable product-service systems", *RECIEL* 2018,162–175, in particular 164–166, summarising "optimistic views" (with reference to *inter alia* A. PLEBYS, E. HEISKANEN

However, other scholars rightly emphasise that servitisation is not necessarily an enabler of the circular economy. A servitised economy is not *per se* environmentally sustainable. Most of these alternative business models are motivated mainly by economic aspirations.[107] For example, in a review of eight different types of PSS, it was pointed out that the majority will result in marginal environmental improvements at best, while some (such as product lease) could even lead to less responsible user behaviour and hence to increased environmental impacts.[108] Therefore, this chapter is not based on the assumption that the provision of PSS is *per se* more eco-efficient than the classic sale of products and post-consumption waste management. The eco-friendliness of any particular PSS can and should be subject to debate. PSS business models can be an enabling factor of the circular economy, but rebound effects, such as increased demand for a service because it costs less than ownership, can arise.[109]

Although there is a huge potential for new, circular business models and PSS, not the least in B2C markets, various economic, behavioural and legal barriers to the transition "from products to services" exist at both sides of the market.[110] For now, existing economic literature has spotted a number of economic barriers for firms to shift to PSS, including: higher up-front investment costs; slower pace of returns; risk of cannibalising own traditional product sales; problems and costs related to disintermediation ("*cutting out the middle man*", 3rd party service integration); potentially higher transaction costs due to more complex contracts; need to consider the residual value of assets; need to set up a system for collecting products upon termination of the contract; exacerbated "moral hazard" problem, as the user may behave differently if he is not the owner; uncertainty about the timing at which products-as-a-service will reach the end of their technical or useful life.[111]

---

and O. MONT, "European policy approaches to promote servicising", *Journal of Cleaner Production* 2015, 117–123) as regards servitisation as a means to bolster sustainability.

107 J. HOJNIK, "Ecological modernisation through servitisation: EU regulatory support for sustainable product-service systems", *RECIEL* 2018,162–175, in particular 164–166, summarising "vigilant approaches" (with reference to *inter alia* A. P. BARQUET, J. SEIDEL, G. SELIGER and H. KOHL, "Sustainability Factors for PSS Business Models", *Procedia CIRP* 2016, 436–441) as regards servitisation as a means to bolster sustainability.

108 See A. TUKKER, "Eight types of product-service system: eight ways to sustainability. Experiences from Suspronet", *Business Strategy and the Environment* 2004, 246–260.

109 See European Environment Agency, *EEA Report 2016/2 Circular Economy in Europe – Developing the knowledge base*, 2016, 15–16; European Environment Agency, *EEA Report 2017/6 Circular by Design – Products in the circular economy*, 2017, 18–19 and 26–28.

110 O. MONT, "Clarifying the concept of product-service system", *Journal of Cleaner Production* 2002, 237–245; V. MARTINEZ, M. BASL, J. KINGSTON and S. EVANS, "Challenges in transforming manufacturing organisations into product-service providers", *Journal of Manufacturing Technology* 2010, 449–469; P. AKBAR et al., "When do materialistic consumers join commercial sharing systems", *Journal of Business Research* 2006, 4215–4224.

111 See e.g. European Environment Agency, *EEA Report 2017/6 Circular by Design – Products in the circular economy*, 2017, 18–19 and 26. See also H. GEBAUER, E. FLEISCH and T. FRIEDLI, "Overcoming the service paradox in manufacturing companies", *European Journal of Management* 2005, 14–26; H. KASTALLI and B. VAN LOOY, "Servitisation: Disentangling

Moreover, firms are confronted with behavioural barriers at the consumer-side. It is claimed that there is still a clear difference in the success of PSS between B2B and B2C markets, since consumers attach far greater value to owning the products they use and having full control over how to use them.[112] This will be topic of the next subsection.

3.3. BEHAVIOURAL BARRIERS AT THE CONSUMER-SIDE

As firms shift to PSSs, they face many challenges, due to the fact that integrating actors into PSS is not evident. One of these actors is the consumer and past research has made it clear that not all consumers are equally willing to embrace new consumption patterns and PSS.[113] A variety of *behavioural* barriers has been identified in the literature and these can be grouped according to three dimensions: namely, the consumer, product and use dimensions.

First, looking at the consumer characteristics, "service readiness", i.e. "*the inclination to embrace, and the ability to use, relevant new services*"[114], is key and can be measured through four factors: (i) optimism, (ii) innovativeness, (iii) risk perception and (iv) perceived lack of control.[115]

(i) Firstly, optimism reflects consumers' positive view of the service and the belief that the service will offer them increased flexibility and other benefits.[116]

---

the impact of service business model innovation on manufacturing firm performance", *Journal of Operations Management* 2013, 169–180.

112 See e.g. European Environment Agency, *EEA Report 2017/6 Circular by Design - Products in the circular economy*, 2017, 18–19 and 26.

113 J. F. DURGEE and G. C. O'CONNOR, "An exploration into renting as consumption behaviour", *Psychology and Marketing* 1995, 89–104; O. MONT, "Drivers and barriers for shifting towards more service-oriented businesses: Analysis of the PSS field and contributions from Sweden", *The Journal of Sustainable Product Design* 2004, 89–103; E. G. EDBRING, M. LEHNER and O. MONT, "Exploring consumer attitudes to alternative models of consumption: motivations and barriers", *Journal of Cleaner Production* 2016, 5–15; F. BARDHI and G. M. ECKHARDT, "Liquid Consumption", *Journal of Consumer Research* 2017, 582–597; K. HOBSON, N. LYNCH, D. LILLEY and G. SMALLEY, "Systems of practice and the Circular Economy: Transforming mobile phone product service systems", *Environmental Innovation and Societal Transitions* 2018, 147–157; F. NEUNHOFFER and T. TEUBNER, "Between enthusiasm and refusal: A cluster analysis on consumer types and attitudes towards peer-to-peer sharing", *Journal of Consumer Behaviour* 2018, 221–236; E. VAITTINEN, M. MARTINSUO and R. ORTT, "Business customers' readiness to adopt manufacturer's new services", *Journal of Service Theory and Practice* 2018, 52–78.

114 E. VAITTINEN, M. MARTINSUO and R. ORTT, "Business customers' readiness to adopt manufacturer's new services", *Journal of Service Theory and Practice* 2018, 52–78.

115 R. VIZE, J. COUGHLAN, A. KENNEDY and F. ELLIS-CHADWICK, "Technology readiness in a B2B online retail context: An examination of antecedents and outcomes", *Industrial Marketing Management* 2013, 909–918; E. VAITTINEN, M. MARTINSUO and R. ORTT, "Business customers' readiness to adopt manufacturer's new services", *Journal of Service Theory and Practice* 2018, 52–78.

116 R. VIZE, J. COUGHLAN, A. KENNEDY and F. ELLIS-CHADWICK, "Technology readiness in a B2B online retail context: An examination of antecedents and outcomes", *Industrial*

(ii) Secondly, innovativeness is defined to capture an individual's tendency to be a pioneer.[117] Past studies have found ambiguous results regarding the interaction between this characteristic and technology adoption.[118] Therefore, it is not clear how this will impact consumers' willingness to participate in PSS.

(iii) Thirdly, risk perceptions of consumers are influenced by the type of insurance that is available, trust in the service provider, insecurity, responsiveness of the provider, and reliability of use through, for example, guaranteed access. The relationship between the consumer and the provider as well as ease of access are often cited as key determinants for consumer satisfaction in PSS.[119] Open and trusting relations between providers and consumers are crucial.[120] Further, PSS can be seen as a way to choose those products that best satisfy consumer needs.[121] Explicitly offering consumers a chance to try out the concept and have a test run before concluding a contract can further reduce consumers' risk perceptions.[122] Risk perceptions tend to decline as consumers become more accustomed to PSS.[123]

(iv) Fourthly, perceived lack of control plays an important role when it comes to service readiness. It reflects consumers' unfamiliarity, imperfect information, and discomfort when choosing for a particular consumption

---

Marketing Management 2013, 909–918; E. VAITTINEN, M. MARTINSUO and R. ORTT, "Business customers' readiness to adopt manufacturer's new services", *Journal of Service Theory and Practice* 2018, 52–78.

117 A. PARASURAMAN, "Technology Readiness Index (TRI) a multiple-item scale to measure readiness to embrace new technologies", *Journal of Service Research* 2000, 307–320.

118 E. VAITTINEN, M. MARTINSUO and R. ORTT, "Business customers' readiness to adopt manufacturer's new services", *Journal of Service Theory and Practice* 2018, 52–78.

119 J. Z. RAJA, D. BOURNE, K. GOFFIN, M. ÇAKKOL and V. MARTINEZ, "Achieving customer satisfaction through integrated products and services: An exploratory study", *Journal of Product Innovation Management* 2013, 1128–1144; F. NEUNHOFFER and T. TEUBNER, "Between enthusiasm and refusal: A cluster analysis on consumer types and attitudes towards peer-to-peer sharing", *Journal of Consumer Behaviour* 2018, 221–236.

120 M. CATULLI, J. L. LINDLEY, N. B. REED, A. GREEN, H. HYSENI and S. KIRI, "What is mine is not yours: Further insight on what access-based consumption says about consumers", in: *Consumer Culture Theory*, Emerald Group Publishing Limited, 2013, 185–208; J. Z. RAJA et al., "Achieving customer satisfaction through integrated products and services: An exploratory study", *Journal of Product Innovation Management* 2013, 1128–1144.; E. G. EDBRING et al., "Exploring consumer attitudes to alternative models of consumption: motivations and barriers", *Journal of Cleaner Production* 2016, 5–15.

121 O. REXFELT and V. HIORT AF ORNÄS, "Consumer acceptance of product-service systems: designing for relative advantages and uncertainty reductions", *Journal of Manufacturing Technology Management* 2009, 674–699.

122 E. G. EDBRING et al., "Exploring consumer attitudes to alternative models of consumption: motivations and barriers", *Journal of Cleaner Production* 2016, 5–15; S. J. LAWSON, M. R. GLEIM, R. PERREN and J. HWANG, "Freedom from ownership: An exploration of access-based consumption", *Journal of Business Research* 2016, 2615–2623.

123 C. K. BAUMEISTER, "Access versus ownership: Consumers' reactions to an alternative consumption mode", PhD. Technische Universät München, 2014.

option. In a study of Edbring et al.[124], for example, several respondents had difficulty in imagining how renting furniture could work in practice and they felt that it was unnecessary to rent when they could buy furniture and home products. Moreover, respondents were concerned that renting might be too complicated to be practical. Discomfort reflecting a person's incapability to manipulate the technology was highlighted by Yieh et al.[125] as having a negative impact on consumers' perceived value from technology. This discomfort can lead to consumers feeling overwhelmed by it, which may cause feelings of frustration. Insecurity can reflect the consumers' distrust of technology and its ability to function properly as well as the trustworthiness of the information provided.[126] Lastly, the extent to which the product is part of the extended self is important. The more a product is perceived as part of the extended self, the more consumers have a desire to own and to personalise this product[127] and the less they will be willing to switch to access-based consumption.[128] Consumers further rely more on digital access rather than physical ownership when the item is less relevant to the self since those items tend to have less emotional value.[129]

Second, consumer perceptions towards access-based consumption and PSS also depend on the type of product.[130] Products where respondents were 'very negative' to renting or leasing were home textiles (42%), beds (38%), and kitchens (36%). Products that respondents were most favourable about renting were appliances (14%) and tables, chairs, and shelves (13%).[131] Several product-related aspects can play a role in determining these perceptions. So, in general, consumption that is associated with high levels of brand loyalty, attachment, and identification with the brand seems to be more solid and thus more likely to favour product ownership.[132] Moreover, there are claims that "products with fast

124 E. G. EDBRING et al., "Exploring consumer attitudes to alternative models of consumption: motivations and barriers", *Journal of Cleaner Production* 2016, 5–15.

125 K. YIEH, J.S. CHEN and M. B. WEI, "The effects of technology readiness on customer perceived value: An empirical analysis", *Journal of Family and Economic Issues* 2012, 177–183.

126 A. PARASURAMAN, "Technology Readiness Index (TRI) a multiple-item scale to measure readiness to embrace new technologies", *Journal of Service Research* 2000, 307–320.

127 R. MUGGE, J. P. SCHOORMANS and H. N. SCHIFFERSTEIN, "Emotional bonding with personalised products", *Journal of Engineering Design* 2009, 467–476; S. P. WALSH and K. M. WHITE, "Me, my mobile, and I: The role of self- and prototypical identity influences in the prediction of mobile phone behaviour", *Journal of Applied Social Psychology* 2007, 2405–2434.

128 F. BARDHI and G. M. ECKHARDT, "Liquid Consumption", *Journal of Consumer Research* 2017, 582–597.

129 R. W. BELK, "Extended self in a digital world", *Journal of Consumer Research* 2013, 477–500.

130 C. K. BAUMEISTER, "Access versus ownership: Consumers' reactions to an alternative consumption mode", PhD. Technische Universät München, 2014.

131 E. G. EDBRING et al., "Exploring consumer attitudes to alternative models of consumption: motivations and barriers", *Journal of Cleaner Production* 2016, 5–15.

132 F. BARDHI and G. M. ECKHARDT, "Liquid Consumption", *Journal of Consumer Research* 2017, 582–597.

innovation cycles, are more attractive for consumers to rent, but not to own".[133] This may indicate that products that require frequent maintenance and upgrades such as products with fast innovation cycles are more attractive for consumers to rent, but not to own.[134] The more polluting a production process and the more scarce the resources used in production, the more credible a shift towards new, circular business models is to consumers. Especially, consumers with pro-environment attitudes will be more likely to support this transition.[135]

Third, there are various issues related to using rather than buying products. Consumers are often sceptical when it comes to health and safety issues related to using rather than buying products.[136] Respondents fear that products are not clean after other consumers used them. For example, health and safety was found to be important concerns for consumers considering leasing baby prams.[137] Another aspect raised in interviews was the feeling of intrusiveness that people feel if a company owns their furniture or home furnishing. The widespread concerns about data security as well as privacy concerns[138] act as another barrier to adopt access-based systems. Some consumers feel they have to be more careful about products that they do not own; some are uncertain about consequences if they rent a product and it breaks.[139] Consumers are often uncertain about the rules in the event of the leased or rented product breaking or becoming damaged.[140] They fear that they will be penalised by the provider in case of damage to the product.[141] By using products repeatedly over a long period

---

133 E. G. EDBRING et al., "Exploring consumer attitudes to alternative models of consumption: motivations and barriers", *Journal of Cleaner Production* 2016, 10.

134 O. REXFELT and V. HIORT AF ORNÄS, "Consumer acceptance of product-service systems: designing for relative advantages and uncertainty reductions", *Journal of Manufacturing Technology Management* 2009, 674–699.

135 J. HAMARI, M. SJÖKLINTAND and A. UKKONEN, "The sharing economy: Why people participate in collaborative consumption", *Journal of the Association for Information Science and Technology* 2016, 2047–2059.

136 F. BARDHI and G. M. ECKHARDT, "Access-based consumption: The case of car sharing", *Journal of Consumer Research* 2012, 881–898.

137 O. MONT, C. DALHAMMAR and N. JACOBSSON, "A new business model for baby prams based on leasing and product remanufacturing", *Journal of Cleaner Production* 2006, 1509–1518.

138 F. NEUNHOFFER and T. TEUBNER, "Between enthusiasm and refusal: A cluster analysis on consumer types and attitudes towards peer-to-peer sharing", *Journal of Consumer Behaviour* 2018, 221–236.

139 F. BARDHI and G. M. ECKHARDT, "Access-based consumption: The case of car sharing", *Journal of Consumer Research* 2012, 881–898; C. K. BAUMEISTER, "Access versus ownership: Consumers' reactions to an alternative consumption mode", PhD. Technische Universät München, 2014.

140 M. CATULLI, "What uncertainty? Further insight into why consumers might be distrustful of product service systems", *Journal of Manufacturing Technology Management* 2012, 780–793.

141 C. K. BAUMEISTER, "Access versus ownership: Consumers' reactions to an alternative consumption mode", PhD. Technische Universät München, 2014; E. G. EDBRING et al., "Exploring consumer attitudes to alternative models of consumption: motivations and barriers", *Journal of Cleaner Production* 2016, 5–15.

of time, consumers form habits and routines. In general, they aim to preserve these habits and strive for consistency and status quo rather than to continuously search for and embrace new behaviours.[142] This leads to a form of passive resistance, which is mainly caused by satisfaction with the status quo. Generally, strong attitudes toward existing objects usually increase the resistance to change and may prevent consumers from being open to innovations.

4. CONSUMER PROTECTION IN A "FUNCTIONAL" ECONOMY?

Apart from, but closely related to, these behavioural barriers, users of PSS may also perceive and experience a number of *legal* barriers, in absence of a clear regulatory framework adapted to these new product-service contracts.[143]

From a legal perspective, the 'purchase' of products-as-a-service is something completely different from the traditional purchase of consumer products. First, as to the sales method, PSS are offered mostly online only. Secondly, as to the parties, product-service contracts are concluded directly between the producer and the user (disintermediation). Thirdly, as to the subject of the contract; no transfer of ownership takes place; consumers do not buy a product against payment of the total price. Instead, they subscribe to, and become recipients of, a "bundle of services" caught in a complex service contract against payment of a periodical fee or 'payment-per-use'.

Yet, traditional EU consumer protection law, and existing legal literature, is still very much focused on the traditional business model of the one-off sale of consumer goods and transfer of ownership to consumers (within the broader context of a linear, industrial economy). Despite the growing importance of the service sector in the EU, further exacerbated by the shift from a linear to a more circular, functional economy[144], the EU regulatory framework on services is quite 'lean and mean', with much more room for contractual freedom and national regulatory freedom than in the area of sales.[145] Apart from the *Services Directive 2006/123* ("SD")[146], the *E-Commerce Directive 2000/31*[147] and the new *Directive 2019/770 on certain aspects for contracts for the supply of digital content and*

142 P. PLANING, "Business model innovation in a circular economy reasons for non-acceptance of circular business models", *Open Journal of Business Model Innovation* 2015, 11.

143 See the seminal analysis of J. HOJNIK, "The servitisation of industry: EU law implications and challenges", *Common Market Law Review* 2016, 1575–1624; J. HOJNIK, "Technology neutral EU law: digital goods within the traditional goods/services distinction", *International Journal of Law and Information Technology* 2017, 25, 63–84.

144 O. MONT, "Clarifying the concept of product–service system", *Journal of Cleaner Production* 2002, 237–245.

145 With the notable exception of financial services regulation.

146 OJ L 376, 27.12.2006, 36–68.

147 OJ L 178, 17.07.2000, 1–16.

digital services[148], there is no detailed and robust regulation on the quality[149] and safety[150] of services and PSS, on the formation of product-service contracts, on the legal guarantee for services that are not in conformity with the contract[151], etc.

Prima facie at least the following legal barriers at the consumer-side for switching to PSS can be identified.

4.1. MARKETING STAGE

In the PSS marketing stage[152], it will often not be clear to what extent a particular PSS is actually eco-friendly for consumers who want to make an eco-friendly choice. Firms often make green claims about their PSS. Yet, the above-mentioned UCPD Guidance document fails to take into account the servitisation trend generally and the issue of greenwashing of PSS specifically. This should change. In addition, the EU Ecolabel regime should also strategically focus on PSS of e.g. household appliances.

In general, consumers will often experience a lack of transparency in relation to the total cost and the main characteristics of long-term and complex PSS offers; they may have to pay not only periodical fees (instalments), but also other usage components ('pay-per-use'), as well as a deposit (a traditional supplier strategy to deal with the "moral hazard" problem); additionally, users may have to pay for joined offers of ancillary products, etc. In the access-based consumption model, financial reasons are often cited as crucial factors in the decision making process. While crucial, financial impacts can act both as drivers or as barriers to engage in PSS. For instance, users with a short-term outlook feel that it is often cheaper to hire than buy the product, while users with a long-run perspective feel it is more expensive.[153] Apart from the SD, the UCPD and the CRD might prove relevant as regard the transparency of PSS offers on the market.

148 OJ L 136, 22.5.2019, 1–27.

149 Only since 2012 does the European Standardisation Regulation No. 1025/2012 of 25 October 2012 (OJ L 316, 14.11.2012, 12–33) apply to goods as well as Services (see also COM(2016) 358 final, p. 9–10 and SWD(2016), 186 final, p. 5–6). See also Article 26 of the Services Directive 2006/123 of 12 December 2006, containing a number of 'soft' provisions on the policy on the 'quality' of services.

150 General Product Safety Directive (GPSD) 2001/95/EC, OJ L 11, 15.1.2002, 4–17.

151 See further below on the limited scope of the Consumer Sales Directive 1999/44.

152 See W. REIM, V. PARIDA and D. ÖRTQVIST, "Product-Service Systems (PSS) business models and tactics – a systematic literature review", *Journal of Cleaner Production* 2015, 68–69 on PSS marketing tactic and 72–73 on sustainability tactic.

153 E. G. EDBRING et al., "Exploring consumer attitudes to alternative models of consumption: motivations and barriers", *Journal of Cleaner Production* 2016, 5–15.

4.2. CONTRACTUAL AND POST-CONTRACTUAL STAGE

Of course, PSS are not offered in a contractual void: to all such PSS, terms and conditions ('T&C') apply as part of an offer on a 'take-it-or-leave-it' basis. Offering PPS with increasing levels of complexity nonetheless requires firms to further develop their contractual and relational capabilities.[154] Servitisation makes contract drafting increasingly demanding and complex for lawyers, who have to respond to the so-called "service ladder", referring to the high level of components and their interrelation within the service provision. Nonetheless, it is possible to use largely similar contracts for each user ("mass customisation").[155] A first and quick legal analysis of some T&Cs for PSS shows for sure much creativity and innovation in contract design, yet also much legal uncertainty for the contracting parties, especially the user, in absence of a clear regulatory framework. A detailed legal analysis of T&Cs for PSS across various B2C markets is still lacking in legal literature.

Hence, users of PSS will often not know, or feel uncertain about, their contractual rights and liabilities at the *conclusion* and *performance* stages of product-service contracts, especially in cross-border situations. As mentioned, a first and quick legal analysis of some T&Cs for products-as-a-service shows much legal uncertainty, especially for the user. Most importantly, users will face legal uncertainty as to the definition of 'non-conformity' of services with the contract and the available remedies in such case. This is because the old *Consumer Sales Directive 1999/44*[156], which established the two-year legal guarantee for consumer goods and set out four remedies in case of non-conformity with the contract (repair or replacement; price reduction or rescission of contract), does not apply to services. No EU harmonisation of the legal guarantee for services was ever realised, notwithstanding certain interesting efforts to do so[157]; neither were

154 M. E. KREYE, J. K. ROEHRICH and M. A. LEWIS, "Servitising manufacturers: the impact of service complexity and contractual and relational capabilities", *Production Planning & Control* 2015, 1233–1246.

155 J. HOJNIK, "The servitisation of industry: EU law implications and challenges", *Common Market Law Review* 2016, 1605. See also W. REIM, V. PARIDA and D. ÖRTQVIST, "Product-Service Systems (PSS) business models and tactics – a systematic literature review", *Journal of Cleaner Production* 2015, 67–68 on PSS contract tactic.

156 OJ L 171, 07.07.1999, 12–16.

157 Article 6(4) of the Amended proposal for a Council Directive on unfair terms in consumer contracts (COM(92) 66 final) provided: "*The Member States shall take the necessary measures in order to ensure that the consumer is guaranteed, as purchaser under a contract for the supply of services, the right: – to be supplied with those services at the agreed time and with all due efficiency; – to have the supplier's warranty that the supplier has the requisite skill and expertise to supply the services in the manner specified in the following indent.*" This proposal for harmonisation of certain aspects of the legal guarantee for services was backed by the European Parliament, but the Council thought it more appropriate to deal with these matters separately and in greater depth and refused to include these provisions in the Directive on unfair terms (COM(93), 509 final, p. 13).

the EU rules on the legal guarantee for consumer goods extended to services, mainly because of "*the complexity and diversity of services*".[158] And even the new *Consumer Sales Directive (EU) 2019/771*[159] neither extends the legal guarantee for consumer goods to services nor establishes new rules on the legal guarantee for services.

Importantly, essential questions linked to qualification of the product-service contract (renting, hiring, leasing, ...)[160], performance, non-conformity of services, or forms of breach of contract other than non-conformity, thus remain entirely and completely subject to national default law and contractual freedom. For example, many T&Cs for products-as-a-service contain detailed rules on *how* the product should be used (e.g. "*with great care, as if it was borrowed from your close friend*"), limited warranties, conditional refunds of deposits, financial sanctions in case of damage resulting from other than "*normal use*", etc. – all offering contractual protection to the supplier against "moral hazard".

In these regards, the *Unfair Terms Directive 93/13 of 5 April 1993* ("UCTD")[161], that provides for a control mechanism of unbalanced and non-transparent B2C standard terms, comes into play. Yet, for the moment, there is no guidance on how it should be interpreted and applied in the context of these new product-service contracts in B2C relations.[162] As there is no standard set of default rights of consumers in access-based consumption models, it is particularly difficult to predict the outcome of any assessment of the unfairness of terms against the general norm of the UCTD.[163]

A quick analysis of T&C's for PSS also shows that, although firms often make green claims about the reduced environmental impact of their PSS, these T&C

158 See the Explanatory Memorandum to the Commission Proposal (COM(95), 520 final, p. 11): "*the complexity and diversity of services do not lend themselves to a simple extension to services of rules governing the sale of goods.*" See also the Green Paper (COM(93), 509 final, p. 7): "*In the context of this project and bearing in mind the subsidiarity principle, the Commission decided to concentrate on the questions raised by the sale of products, although it is aware that similar problems may arise in the domain of services. But because services are so heterogeneous they may be difficult to treat in a global manner.*"

159 OJ L 136, 22.5.2019, 28–50.

160 Many national laws offer mandatory protection to tenants of immovable property, but not to renters of movables. See in relation to Belgian law A. VAN VAERENBERGH and F. LEYMAN, ""Product als dienst" overeenkomst, een stap in de richting van de circulaire economie", *MER* 2019, 20–30.

161 OJ L 95, 21.4.1993, 29–34.

162 In B2B markets, the lack of protection of firms against unfair terms in PSS T&C's offered on a 'take-it-or-leave-it' basis will on many occasions be less of an issue, because in B2B relations contracting parties often have equivalent bargaining power. Yet, some Member States do offer B2B protection against unfair terms – going beyond the scope of the UCTD.

163 In Case C-415/11 *Aziz* the CJEU ruled that "*the concept of 'significant imbalance' to the detriment of the consumer must be assessed in the light of an analysis of the rules of national law applicable in the absence of any agreement between the parties, in order to determine whether, and if so to what extent, the contract places the consumer in a less favourable legal situation than that provided for by the national law in force.*"

often do not contain any clauses guaranteeing that, upon collection of products at the end of their technical or useful life, products will be re-used, repaired or remanufactured. Perhaps consumers with pro-environmental attitudes are willing to pay more for circular PSS, but probably only where those PSS are really circular.

In addition, users may face difficulties with the *termination* of fixed or indeterminate term product-service contracts. Questions arise concerning the timing of termination, the required notice period, the cancellation fees, conditional refunds of deposits and other 'lock-in' tactics, etc. It should be noted that in the energy sector the EU has adopted specific mandatory rules in order to protect users against (non-)contractual barriers where a user wishes to terminate an energy contract or to switch to another offer or provider[164]; this is however not the case for services generally. Termination of PSS is governed by applicable (divergent) national contract laws.

Lastly, users may face problems in case of *insolvency* of the PSS supplier, who is still the owner of the product. Users are simply creditors of the PSS supplier who possess – during a period of time – a product still owned by that supplier. The impact of preventive restructuring procedures and insolvency proceedings on product-service contracts is again a matter that will largely regulated by national (insolvency, contract and property) laws. A related issue pertains to *insolvency* of the user. In fact, the proliferation of access-based consumption could lead to new forms of consumer over-indebtedness. Indeed, a myriad of (even small) long-term subscriptions and 'private-lease' arrangements could imply financial obligations that are quite similar to those arising under credit agreements. Yet, the *Consumer Credit Directive 2008/48* ("CCD")[165] does not apply to hiring or leasing agreements where no obligation to purchase the object of the agreement is laid in the agreement. Thus, the Directive does not offer its protection to users of PSS, although the risks for consumers are similar.

The above preliminary overview of legal barriers is by no means exhaustive. Hence, there is an urgent need for a precise identification and analysis of all relevant legal and behavioural issues, especially of the application of the existing contractual liability regimes to product-service contracts in the EU and selected Member States.[166]

---

164 E.g. Electricity Directive 2009/72 of 13 July 2009, OJ L 211, 14.8.2009, 55–93.

165 OJ L 133, 22.5.2008, 66–92.

166 This research will be done by 2 PhD students of the CCM and CEDON research institutes within the framework of a C2 research grant awarded by the Research Council of the KU Leuven (Internal Funds): *Contractual rights and liabilities in circular business models* (2019–2023).

5. CONCLUSION

Consumer autonomy and freedom of contract are, and remain, fundamental. Yet, should they be unlimited, when natural resources are not? It is not a matter of fairness vis-à-vis future generations to incentivise current consumers to make sustainable consumption choices? *You can't make a horse drink, but you can bring it to the water.*

The purpose of this chapter was to critically examine the extent to which EU consumer protection law contributes to fostering eco-friendly purchasing behaviour and consumption of movable (non-food) goods in an economy that is becoming more "circular" and "functional". First, we identified some of the most important factors that inhibit consumers to make sustainable consumption choices ("attitude-behaviour gap"), including bounded rationality, informational problems and behavioural failures, externalities and the consumer / citizen divide.

Second, we looked into the provision of product sustainability information under EU consumer protection law and analysed (general) mandatory information requirements and the regulation of (voluntary) green claims and ecolabels (including the EU Ecolabel).

- Most importantly, under the UCPD, information in relation to the environmental impact of products will often be considered "material" information of which the omission constitutes a breach of Article 7. This is certainly the case when such information is mandatory by EU law. However, there is still room to fine-tune the existing general information requirements with a view to promoting the circular economy. The "zones of penumbra" of Article 7 UCPD should be resolved by clarifying the term "material information" as to encompass various types of product sustainability information (content). The information requirements of Article 7(4) UCPD and Article 5 CRD should be streamlined, integrated and fully harmonized in order to create a genuine level playing field throughout the EU. In light of various recent studies, there is also a huge untapped potential to enhance more sustainable consumer choices by improving the manner (method and timing) in which product sustainability information is provided.
- As to the regulation of (voluntary) green claims and ecolabels, we essentially described the general principles as already spelt out in the UCPD Guidance document. We also suggested that the UCPD Guidance document could deal more explicitly with misleading durability claims. In order to fully exploit the potential of the EU Ecolabel scheme, efforts need to be made to enhance its uptake.

Third, we analysed the main advantages and disadvantages of "servitisation" – often presented as an enabler of the circular economy – both for firms, consumers and the environment. We concluded that new, circular PSS are often mainly motivated by economic aspirations and that the functional economy is not necessarily more environmentally friendly than the traditional one-off sales to consumers.[167] We also identified various *behavioural* barriers that may inhibit consumers from embracing new consumption patterns and from shifting to PSS, such as their varying service readiness, negative attitudes depending on the type of products, and issues related to using instead of buying products such as feelings of intrusiveness or data security and privacy concerns.

Fourth, we identified *legal* barriers to engage in PSS in all stages of the "life-cycle" of product-service contracts. At the marketing stage, there is often a lack of transparency of PSS offers. We suggested that the servitisation trend be properly taken into account in the UCPD guidance document (especially in relation to "greenwashing" of PSS). In addition, the EU Ecolabel regime should also strategically focus on PSS of e.g. household appliances. At the contractual and performance stages, there is much uncertainty as to contractual rights and liabilities under product-service contracts which currently remain almost completely subject to national default law and contractual freedom (qualification, 'non-conformity' and performance, termination, insolvency, etc.)

Coming at the end of this chapter, we would like to emphasise the co-originality and inevitable complementarity of the *environmental* and *consumer protection* agendas.[168] We believe that the availability of accurate, targeted and easily digestible product sustainability information on the market is necessary, albeit not sufficient, to foster sustainable consumption choices. Now more than ever, environmental law and consumer protection lawyers should join forces in developing integrated sustainable production and consumption policies (SDG 12), as there is so much work to be done.[169] This also means that consumer autonomy and consumers' economic interests should not be isolated from, but weighed against, other, non-economic (public) interests, such as the

167 See also M. BARTOLOMEO et al., "Eco-efficient producer services – what are they, how do they benefit customers and the environment and how likely are they to develop and be extensively utilised?", *Journal of Cleaner Production* 2003, 829–837, warning that the shift from products to services cannot be assumed to be eco-efficient and there are a number of rebound effects which need to be carefully analysed.

168 See C. KYE, "Environmental Law and the Consumer in the European Union", *Journal of Environmental Law* 1995, 31–54. Compare T. WILHELMSSON, "Consumer Law and the Environment: From Consumer to Citizen", *Journal of Consumer Policy* 1998, 45–70.

169 See the interesting *Reflection Paper Towards a Sustainable Europe by 2030*, January 2019, available at https://ec.europa.eu/commission/sites/beta-political/files/rp_sustainable_europe_30-01_en_web.pdf, noting that notable progress has been achieved towards SDG 12, but this is also the SDG where in the global ranking the EU-27 Member States have the second lowest average score with much work still to be done.

promotion of the shift to a circular economy. Where new, circular PSS (in B2C markets) and the functional economy are rightly on the *environmental agenda* because of potential gains in terms of "closing the loop", they should also be on the *consumer protection agenda*, as our preliminary research shows that existing EU consumer protection law is certainly not fit for the rise of PSS and the functional economy. Further research will be needed to come up with policy recommendations on how EU consumer protection law could be adjusted to boost sustainable consumption choices as regards truly circular PSS in the eco-marketing stage as well as to adequately protect consumers in the contractual and post-contractual stage. Clarifying and harmonizing the contractual rights and obligations under product-service contracts can help to reduce transactions costs, with a view to making consumer participation in circular business models more likely.

A RIGHT TO REPAIR? TOWARDS SUSTAINABLE REMEDIES IN CONSUMER LAW

Evelyne TERRYN*

1. INTRODUCTION

1. Of the 16 ton goods the average European consumer uses per year, 6 ton ends as waste.[1] An important and increasing part concerns electric and electronic waste. By 2020, European consumers would produce more than 12 million ton of electric and electronic waste.[2] If we just take the mobile phone case as an example, it clearly illustrates that more can be done to reduce the waste produced: in the EU, more than 160 million mobile phones are sold yearly. In 2010 only 6 percent were being reused and 9 percent recycled. 85 percent thus ended in the landfill or was kept somewhere unused.[3]

Although there is a growing consensus that this is not sustainable[4], the mere acknowledgment will not be sufficient. Different business models are currently being developed, including circular business models that aim to keep products and materials in use and that design out waste and pollution.[5] The law, however,

---

* Full professor KU Leuven, research institute Consumer Competition Market, guest professor UHasselt. Paper also published in ERPL. Final text submitted in February 2019. The later adopted Consumer sales directive 2019/771 could only be taken into account minimally.

1 Www.ellenmacarthurfoundation.org/assets/downloads/ce100/Empowering-Repair-Final-Public1.pdf (data from 2014).

2 European Commission, ec.europa.eu/environment/waste/weee/index_en.htm.

3 Ellen Mc Arthur Foundation, In depth, mobile phones, 2012, www.ellenmacarthurfoundation.org/news/in-depth-mobile-phones.

4 Sometimes from unexpected sources cf. the encyclical *Laudato si* of pope Francis (2015): *"our industrial system, at the end of its cycle of production and consumption, has not developed the capacity to absorb and reuse waste and by-products. We have not yet managed to adopt a circular model of production capable of preserving resources for present and future generations, while limiting as much as possible the use of non-renewable resources, moderating their consumption, maximizing their efficient use, reusing and recycling them. A serious consideration of this issue would be one way of counteracting the throwaway culture which affects the entire planet, but it must be said that only limited progress has been made in this regard" (w2.vatican.va/content/francesco/en/encyclicals/documents/papa-francesco_20150524_enciclica-laudato-si.html, para. 22).*

5 See www.ellenmacarthurfoundation.org/circular-economy/concept.

also has a role to play in this transition towards more sustainable business models. Indeed, as illustrated by Eyckmans, policy instruments and thus the legal framework has an important role to play to enable and stimulate more sustainable business models and to correct market failures. Different regulatory measures are currently being taken at different levels of the production chain, both at EU and at Member State level, to enable and stimulate such models.[6] Consumer law, in its turn has a role to play in stimulating and enabling a more sustainable consumption.

2. It will be argued in this article that consumer law does currently not sufficiently take into account sustainability aims and that more can be done to reconcile the aims of consumer protection and sustainability. This article departs from the assumption that a future proof consumer law can no longer be solely focused on the economic interests of consumers, but should also endeavor sustainability in order to reconcile the aims of art. 11 TFEU (sustainable development) and 12 TFEU (consumer protection). This assumption may not be evident as consumer law has indeed traditionally focused on the protection of the economic rights of consumers and has not always taken into account the environmental impact of such rights. Indeed, *'[c]onsumers may advocate for a better environment, but they may advocate even more strongly in favour of the rights of the widest possible selection of goods at the cheapest price'*.[7]

This contribution will analyze one particular way to contribute to a more sustainable consumer law and to reconcile the aims of consumer protection and sustainability: repair. It will briefly set out why repair can contribute to a more circular economy but is not always the preferred option (section 1). It will analyze the obstacles and possibilities to obtain repair from the seller under the legal and commercial guarantee (section 2) as well as the obstacles and possibilities for do-it-yourself ('DIY') or independent repair (section 3). Section 4 analyses the role of labelling as a means to promote repair. As a conclusion, some concrete measures to promote repair are summed up.

2. REPAIR AS A MEANS TO CONTRIBUTE TO A MORE CIRCULAR ECONOMY

3. REPAIR IS MORE EFFICIENT THAN RECYCLING. Repair can be an important tool to reduce the amount of waste and to prolong the lifespan of goods, which is the aim of a more circular economy. Although repair (and re-use) is evidently

6 See the contribution of E. Maitre-Ekern, C. Dalhammar in this volume.

7 C. Kye, "Environmental Law and the Consumer in the European Union", 7 *Journal of Environmental Law* 1995, (31), 32 ff.

not to the only way to extend the lifetime of goods or to reduce waste[8], it is a far more efficient strategy than recycling.[9]Repair (and re-use) conserves energy, materials, water and moreover, the transportation costs to put a product back into use are in general lower.[10] Recycling is less efficient as it causes a loss of material and a deterioration of the quality of the materials; rare elements may moreover be entirely lost. In addition, recycling a product implies that it has to go through a secondary production stage to bring it back into a reusable form, thus requiring more material consumption than reuse.[11]

4. Complex reasons why repair is (not) chosen. Promoting repair can therefore contribute to more sustainable business models and to a more circular economy. Repair is currently however not always chosen and there are various reasons why consumers may prefer replacement over repair.[12] The price is an important factor and more specifically the ratio of the price of repair vs. to price to replace.[13] There are however also other factors, such as implicit repair costs (travel and waiting times), fashion obsolescence (products lose their appeal because new products have appeared into the market) and also the consumer's confidence that repairs are done properly will have an impact.[14] Not all of these factors are simple to overcome in a society in which consumers are used to instant gratification and in which manufacturers spend huge budgets *'to wet consumer's appetites for the most recent products with the newest design features'*.[15]

There are however also some signs of hope. First, bottom up repair initiatives in the form of repair cafés[16] and of organisations that collect and exchange repair

---

8 See e.g. the initiatives taking in the field of waste and recycling (e.g. Directive 2008/98/EC on waste; Directive 1999/31/EC on the landfill of waste; Directive 94/62/EC on packaging and packaging waste, Directive 2000/53/EC on end-of-life vehicles; Directive 2006/66/ZC on batteries and accumulators and waste batteries and accumulators; Directive 2012/19/EU on waste electrical and electronic equipment).

9 United Nations Environment Programme 2011, *Recycling of Materials: a Status Report, wedocs.unep.org/handle/20.500.11822/8702;* APSRG, *Triple Win, the social economic and environmental case for remanufacturing. A report by the All Party Sustainable Resource Group of the UK Parliament,* 2014, www.policyconnect.org.uk/apsrg/research/report-triple-win-social-economic-and-environmental-case-remanufacturing; S. Prakash, *Einfluss der Nutzungsdauer von Produkten auf ihre Umweltwirkung: Schaffung einer Informationsgrundlage und Entwicklung von Strategien gegen "Obsoleszenz"* (UBA Texte 11/2016)).

10 Www.ellenmacarthurfoundation.org/assets/downloads/ce100/Empowerng-Repair-Final-Public1.pdf, 5–6.

11 J. Mc Collough, "The disappearing repair trades", 33 *International Journal of Consumer Studies* 2009 620.

12 See extensively, J. McCollough, "Consumer discount rates and the decision to repair or replace a durable product: a sustainable consumption issue", J Econ Issues 2010, 44 (1), 183–204.

13 J. Mc Collough, *J Econ Issues* 2010, 44 (1), 198.

14 J. Mc Collough, 33 *International Journal of Consumer Studies* 2009, p 620.

15 J. Mc Collough, 33 *International Journal of Consumer Studies* 2009, p 625.

16 More than 1500 'Repair cafés' exist in the meantime: www. Repaircafe.org and repaircafe. org/nieuwe-mijlpaal-1–500-repair-cafes-wereldwijd.

information and expertise like iFixit or the Brussels Tournevie initiative[17] are growing and expanding. Second, according to a recent Belgian study, the ratio of the price of repair vs. to price to replace, an important factor in the decision, may be better than expected. The mentioned study came to the conclusion that – at least for the products investigated (vacuum cleaners and washing machines) – repair was a more economical strategy than replacement as it resulted in a lower lifecycle cost (cost *per annum*).[18] Third, a 2014 Eurobarometer illustrated that 77% of the surveyed consumers indicated that they did consider repair of broken goods before buying new goods. 39% of the consumers who eventually disposed of goods indicated that it was too difficult or too expensive to have the goods repaired.[19]

Even if the price or the price ratio is not an issue and consumers do want to choose for repair, there are indeed often still practical and legal obstacles consumers (and businesses) face when choosing repair. Overcoming such difficulties should thus have an impact on the number of consumers that opt for repair. The next sections focus on some of these difficulties. These difficulties are present when a consumer turns to the seller to claim repair of goods that are not in conformity (section 2). They may however also be present when a consumer wants to repair goods himself or wants to turn to an independent repairer (section 3).

3. REPAIR BY THE SELLER? NOT STIMULATED BY THE CONSUMER SALES DIRECTIVE

3.1. REPAIR UNDER LEGAL GUARANTEE

5. Legal remedies under the Consumer Sales Directive. The first situation we consider is the possibility to turn to the seller for repair in case a good breaks down and the defect is covered by the legal guarantee. In the EU, the Consumer Sales Directive 1999/44 deals with the remedies for non-conformity and sets out the obligations of the seller of a consumer good.[20] The – minimum harmonization – system of the directive provides for a hierarchy between the remedies. In case of non-conformity, the consumer can in the first place ask for

---

17 Www.tournevie.be 'the affordable and ecological tool library in Brussel'. The non-profit organization also has its own workshop and organizes 'tool training' courses.

18 Vito, KU Leuven, *Repairability for energy related products*, www.benelux.int/files/7915/2896/0920/FINAL_Report_Benelux.pdf, June 2018.

19 Ec.europa.eu/commfrontoffice/publicopinion/flash/fl_388_en.pdf.

20 Directive 1999/44/EG of the European Parliament and the Council of 25 May on certain aspects of the sale of consumer goods and associated guarantees, OJ L 171 7 July 1999, eur-lex.europa.eu/legal-content/EN/TXT/?uri=celex:31999L0044, p. 12 (hereinafter 'Consumer Sales Directive').

repair or replacement.[21] Only if that is not possible within a reasonable time or without significant inconvenience, the secondary remedies of price reduction and rescission come into play.[22]

6. Repair as a primary remedy, but not preferred over replacement. Although repair is thus one of the primary remedies under the system of the directive, which is a laudable choice in terms of sustainability, repair is not preferred over the alternative primary remedy of replacement by the European legislator. The choice between repair or replacement lies with the consumer in the system of the directive[23], but there is no incentive or obligation for the consumer to opt for repair instead of replacement. Even if the consumer opts for repair, the seller can refuse repair and offer replacement if repair would be 'disproportionate'. According to the directive, this will be the case if *'it imposes costs on the seller which, in comparison with the alternative remedy, are unreasonable, taking into account: the value of the goods; the significance of the lack of conformity and whether the alternative remedy could be completed without significant inconvenience to the consumer'*.[24] Environmental consequences do not seem to play any role in the balancing exercise.

A 2006 Norwegian Supreme Court case[25] mentioned by Maitre-Ekern and Dalhammar is quite interesting in this regard. In Norway consumers also have the right to choose between repair and replacement unless the chosen remedy entails *'unreasonable costs'* for the seller.[26] The case concerned the heels of boots that broke six weeks after purchase. The seller refused replacement as this would entail unreasonable costs. The Supreme Court considered this justified and explicitly referred to environmental reasons: repair was justified as it also appeared the more environmentally friendly option i.a. as there was no market for second-hand shoes in Norway.[27] Maitre-Ekern and Dalhammar point out that it remains unclear whether this judgment implies that the seller would have to offer repair in priority in a reverse situation.

---

21 Art. 3 (3) Consumer Sales Directive.

22 Art. 3 (5) Consumer Sales Directive.

23 Art. 3(3) Consumer Sales Directive; S. Jansen, "Hiërarchie der remedies in de consumentenkoop: EU vs VS", *TPR* 2017/1, 211; M.C. Bianca, "Article 3: Rights of the consumer", in M.C. Bianca en S. Grundmann (eds.), *EU Sales Directive – Commentary* (Antwerpen/ Intersentia, 2002), (149) 168; D. Staudenmayer, "The Directive on the Sale of Consumer Goods and Associated Guarantees – A milestone in the European consumer and private law", *ERPL* 2000, (547) 554; S. Stijns, "De richtlijn consumentenkoop en het Belgische recht" in J. Smits (ed.), *De richtlijn consumentenkoop in perspectief* (Den Haag: Boom Juridische Uitgevers 2003), (41) 66.

24 Art. 3 (3) Consumer Sales Directive.

25 Supreme Court Norway 17 February 2006, Rt. 2006, s 179, cited by E. Maitre-Ekern and C. Dalhammar in this volume.

26 See the contribution of E. Maitre-Ekern and C. Dalhammar in B. Keirsbilck, E. Terryn, (eds.), *Circular economy and consumer protection*.

27 Thus summarized by E. Maitre-Ekern and C. Dalhammar in B. Keirsbilck, E. Terryn, (eds.), *Circular economy and consumer protection*.

As to the situation under EU law, we are not aware of similar cases in which the environmental impact is taken into account in the balancing exercise. It would in any event be a step forward if it would be made explicit under the system of the Consumer Sales Directive that the environmental impact can also be taken into account to determine whether the remedy chosen by the consumer is 'disproportionate'.

LACK OF ACCOMPANYING MEASURES FACILITATING REPAIR. Moreover, even if the consumer chooses repair and the seller would be willing to repair the goods that are not in conformity, he might not be able to do so because the necessary spare parts are lacking. At EU level, there is a currently a lack of accompanying measures that stimulate repair, including ensuring availability of spare parts and technical manuals (see also below, nr. 14 et seq.).[28]

Certain Member States have adopted further reaching legislation.[29] In France, the '*loi Hamon*' already introduced an obligation in 2014 for producers or importers to inform professional sellers of the period during which certain spare parts would be available. The sellers then had to provide this information to the consumer and an obligation was imposed on the producer or importer to deliver spare parts (to consumers and (independent) repairers in accordance with the information provided.[30] The April 2018 "*Feuille de Route pour une économie circulaire*" proposes to impose additional information obligations from January 2020: the repairability would need to be indicated in a clear way on all electronic and electric equipment.[31]

---

28 See in detail A. MICHEL, "La Directive 1999/44/CE sur la garantie des biens de consommation: un remède efficace contre l'obsolescence programmée?", *REDC* 2018, 228. Although some ecodesign requirements were introduced for specific products such as printers, requiring the availability of spare parts during a minimum period (from 3 to 5 years), depending on the model, see A. MICHEL in this volume, footnote 66.

29 Apart from France, legislation to inform consumers about the availability of spare parts also exists in Italy and Slovenia, and legislation that obliges businesses to keep spare parts or to facilitate access to spare parts exists in Spain, Romania, Portugal, Slovenia and Greece. See Study on the costs and benefits of extending certain right under the Consumer Sales and Guarantees Directive 1999/94/EC; publications.europa.eu/en/publication-detail/-/publication/4d120ad5-deee-11e7-9749-01aa75ed71a1/language-en, p. 19–20.

30 Loi n° 2014-344 du 17 mars 2014 relative à la consommation, *JORF* n°0065 du 18 mars 2014, p. 5400, Article L111-3: "*Le fabricant ou l'importateur de biens meubles informe le vendeur professionnel de la période pendant laquelle ou de la date jusqu'à laquelle les pièces détachées indispensables à l'utilisation des biens sont disponibles sur le marché. Cette information est délivrée obligatoirement au consommateur par le vendeur de manière lisible avant la conclusion du contrat et confirmée par écrit lors de l'achat du bien. Dès lors qu'il a indiqué la période ou la date mentionnées au premier alinéa, le fabricant ou l'importateur fournit obligatoirement, dans un délai de deux mois, aux vendeurs professionnels ou aux réparateurs, agréés ou non, qui le demandent les pièces détachées indispensables à l'utilisation des biens vendus. Un décret précise les modalités et conditions d'application du présent article*".

31 Feuille de route pour une économie circulaire: 50 mesures pour une économie 100% circulaire, www.ecologique-solidaire.gouv.fr/sites/default/files/Feuille-de-route-Economie-circulaire-50-mesures-pour-economie-100-circulaire.pdf.

7. Revision of the Consumer Sales Directive – no major changes with regard to repair. The Consumer Sales Directive has been under revision since 2015. However, the directive on consumer sales 2019/771 does not provide any improvement in this regard. Although the recitals mention that '*Enabling consumers to require repair should encourage sustainable consumption and could contribute to greater durability of products*'[32], the seller can still refuse repair on the same grounds as before.

Whether the hierarchy had to be maintained under the new directive was a point of discussion. It is of course correct that the consumer is in the best position if he has a free choice of remedies, as is currently the case in some Member States[33] and as was proposed by BEUC in its position paper.[34] However, such a free choice does not take into account externalities and is hard to reconcile with sustainability goals. A sustainable consumer law therefore requires a hierarchy of remedies whereby repair would be the primary remedy. It is (at this stage) not realistic nor desirable to impose repair as the sole remedy in all circumstances. However, a clear hierarchy whereby repair would be prioritized over replacement instead of being treated as an alternative of equal merit/ value as replacement would at least have an awareness raising effect on both consumers and businesses.[35]

The Consumer Sales Directive 2019 does moreover not provide for additional information requirements concerning the repairability of goods. The recitals only mention that '*Insofar as specific durability information is indicated in any pre-contractual statement which forms part of the sales contract, the consumer should be able to rely on them as a part of the subjective requirements for conformity*'.[36] A general *obligation* to provide such durability information in order to allow the consumer to make a sustainable product choice is not provided for. The Ecolabel initiative that allows the consumer to make such a choice (see below, section 5) remains a voluntary initiative. This is regrettable since a recent Consumer Market Study[37] demonstrated that the provision of specific durability

---

32 Recital 48 Directive 2019/771 on certain aspects concerning sale of goods and repealing directive 1999/44/EC (Consumer Sales Directive 2019).

33 Greece, Portugal, Slovenia.

34 Www.beuc.eu/publications/beuc-x-2016-053_csc_beuc_position_paper_on_tangible_goods_proposal.pdf.

35 A. Michel, *REDC* 2016/2, 228. Such a clear preference for repair is moreover not completely novel. In Belgium, eg a Royal Decree of 9 July 2000 provides that the buyer of a car was entitled to repair in case of a hidden defect. In case that was technically impossible, the parties had to agree which remedy was appropriate to cure the defect. Furthermore, the guarantee also applied to repaired cars (see art. 4 Royal Decree 9 July 2000 (KB betreffende de vermelding van de essentiële gegevens en de algemene verkoopsvoorwaarden op de bestelbon voor nieuwe voertuigen, at 6.1).

36 Recital 32.

37 Consumer Market Study to support the fitness check of the Consumer Law (lot 3), European Commission DG Justice and Consumers, 2017, publications.europa.eu/en/publication-detail/-/publication/a8d7ca32-772c-11e7-b2f2-01aa75ed71a1/language-en/format-PDF. The study also showed different impacts depending on the way the information was presented.

and repairability information can indeed lead the consumer towards choosing more durable and more easily reparable products.[38]

8. Consumer Sales Directive 2019 – impact on lifespan. The original proposal to also fully harmonize the guarantee period was luckily abandoned in the final text of the Consumer Sales Directive 2019. This is to be welcomed as a fully harmonized guarantee period of 2 years would have implied that national legislation that provides for longer guarantees had to be repealed.[39] This would have been regrettable as a longer legal guarantee period has been suggested in several studies as a means to promote a longer lifespan of products.[40]

It remains moreover regrettable that a link between the Consumer Sales Directive 2019 and the specific instruments that do the most promote a longer product lifespan continues to be lacking. It appears indeed from the recitals that the European legislator does not consider the Consumer Sales Directive the most appropriate instrument to ensure longer durability of consumer goods: product specific Union legislation is considered the more appropriate approach.[41] This is a missed opportunity. A clear link between the Consumer Sales Directive and

---

38 Consumer Market Study to support the fitness check of the Consumer Law (lot 3), European Commission DG Justice and Consumers, 2017, p. 50 et seq.

39 Art. 10, 3) Consumer Sales Directive 2019: 'Member States may maintain or introduce longer time limits than those referred to in paragraphs 1 and 2'. Five Member States and two EEA countries provide for longer guarantee periods, these countries include Ireland, the UK, Sweden and Finland and the Netherlands. See for an overview K. Tonner, R. Malcolm, "How and EU lifespan guarantee model could be implemented across the EU", study for the EP, January 2017, www.europarl.europa.eu/RegData/etudes/STUD/2017/583121/IPOL_STU(2017)583121_EN.pdf, p. 19.

40 See K. Tonner, R. Malcolm, "How and EU lifespan guarantee model could be implemented across the EU", p. 54; VITO, *Repairability for energy related products*; T. Cooper, "Inadequate life? Evidence of consumer attitudes to product obsolescence", *Journal of Consumer Policy* 2004, 421–449. The Study on the costs and benefits of extending certain right under the Consumer Sales and Guarantees Directive 199/94/EC (publications.europa.eu/en/publication-detail/-/publication/4d120ad5-deee-11e7–9749–01aa75ed71a1/language-en, p. 61) only briefly mentions the potential environmental benefits of such a measure and comes easily to the conclusion that these are outweighed by the potential disadvantages in terms of lower margins, higher prices and less access to low-quality goods …

41 According to recital *(32) Ensuring longer durability of goods is important for achieving more sustainable consumption patterns and a circular economy. Similarly, keeping non-compliant products out of the Union market by strengthening market surveillance and providing the right incentives to economic operators is essential in order to increase trust in the functioning of the internal market. For those purposes, product-specific Union legislation is the most appropriate means of introducing durability and other product-related requirements in relation to specific types or groups of products, using for this purpose adapted criteria. This Directive should therefore be complementary to the objectives pursued in such Union product-specific legislation, and should include durability as an objective criterion for the assessment of conformity of goods.'* (underligning by the author). Although 'durability' was introduced in the Consumer Sales Directive 2019 as an objective criterion for the assessment of conformity, the vague definition of the term might entail that it is of little effect in the prolongation of the lifespan of products.

product specific Union legislation referred to could definitely be made.[42] The product specific EU legislation (such as the Ecodesign directive) does not provide for private law remedies in case the product related requirements are not met. Although these requirements have traditionally focused on energy efficiency, more recent ecodesign requirements also relate to product durability.[43] This is e.g. the case for vacuum cleaners (more specifically the hoses and the motor)[44], and lamps.[45] The length of the guarantee could correspond with the durability requirements imposed.[46] This is unfortunately not the case.

3.2. REFURBISHED GOODS AS A REPLACEMENT UNDER THE LEGAL GUARANTEE?

9. Replacement by refurbished goods – a second best option? It was argued above that repair is as a rule a more sustainable remedy than replacement. However, replacement by *'refurbished'* goods or *'remanufacture'* may come close to repair in terms of sustainability. Remanufacturing is the process whereby a used product is returned into the 'like-new' condition: it includes sorting, inspection, disassembly, cleaning, reprocessing and reassembly and it may involve a combination of old and new as parts which cannot be brought back to the original quality may be replaced.[47]

This practice is however not widely spread and moreover the practice is controversial in terms of consumer rights. In the US – the problem rose with regard to the terms of the commercial guarantee of Apple. A class action was started for replacing defect products with refurbished ones where this would not have been clearly indicated in the terms of the commercial guarantee.[48] In the Netherlands, the question recently rose with regard to the legal guarantee. Apple had decided to replace phones that were not in conformity with 'refurbished' ones. The consumers concerned claimed they were entitled to a new phone in

---

42 See in this sense, www.beuc.eu/publications/beuc-x-2016-053_csc_beuc_position_paper_on_tangible_goods_proposal.pdf, p. 9; See K. Tonner, R. Malcolm, "How and EU lifespan guarantee model could be implemented across the EU".

43 See the contribution of A. Michel in B. Keirsbilck, E. Terryn, (eds.), *Circular economy and consumer protection.*

44 See Annex II, point 7 and 8 Commission Regulation (EU) No 666/2013 implementing Directive 2009/125/EC with regard to ecodesign requirements for vacuum cleaners, OJ July 2013, https://eur-lex.europa.eu/legal-content/EN/TXT/?uri=celex%3A32013R0666, p. 24–34.

45 See Annex II (2) Commission Regulation (EC) No 244/2009 implementing Directive 2005/32/EC with regard to ecodesign requirements for non-directional household lamps, OJ 24 March 2009, https://eur-lex.europa.eu/legal-content/EN/TXT/?uri=CELEX%3A32009R0244, p. 3–16.

46 Www.beuc.eu/publications/beuc-x-2016-053_csc_beuc_position_paper_on_tangible_goods_proposal.pdf, p. 9.

47 Vito, *Repairability for energy related products*,p.18.

48 See Vicky Maldonado & Joanne Mc Right v Apple Case 3:16-cv-04067-WHO and the similar case of English v Apple Inc. Case No. 14-cv-01619-WHO.

case of non-conformity and not to a refurbished one.[49] The Dutch courts found in several cases that the consumers were indeed entitled to a *new* replacement good and that the seller did not comply with its obligations under the legal guarantee by replacing a defect phone by a refurbished phone.[50] Under the Consumer Sales Directive as interpreted by the European Court of Justice in the *Quelle* judgment[51], the analysis made by the Dutch courts is probably right. Although *Quelle* focused on the question whether compensation could be required from the consumer in case defect goods were replaced by new goods, the reasoning in that judgment does seem to imply that a consumer is entitled to a new good. The Court indeed held in *Quelle* that no compensation could be demanded for a replacement with new goods and that this did not imply an unjust enrichment as a replacement meant that the consumer merely receives, belatedly, what he was entitled to from the outset.[52]

The Dutch decisions are also comprehensible in terms consumer protection. Indeed, consumers are probably best of with a new phone, as the quality of the refurbished phones may not always be guaranteed.[53] However, neither the reasoning of the Dutch courts nor of the Court of Justice takes sustainability arguments into account. A compromise solution, which would however require a change of EU legislation, could therefore be to allow a seller to replace a defect product by a refurbished phone or other remanufactured good under the legal guarantee, but to oblige him to give the consumer a new (2 year) guarantee period in such case. An additional guarantee period could help to overcome the lack of trust consumer may have in refurbished phones or other remanufactured goods. Such an obligation would not be a complete novelty as, at national level, several Member States currently already provide for a new guarantee period after repair or replacement.[54]

---

49 See for a detailed analysis of these cases V. Mak and E. Lujinovic in B. Keirsbilck, E. Terryn, (eds.), *Circular economy and consumer protection.*

50 Rb Amsterdam 8 July 2016, ECLI:NL:RBAMS:2016:4197, *TvC* 2017/4, 183 case note V. Mak; Rb Amsterdam 18 April 2017, ECLI:NL:RBAMS:2017:2519. A Dutch ADR body decided in the same sense: see Geschillencommissie 30 May 2017, www.degeschillencommissie.nl/consumenten/uitsprakenoverzicht/108944/commissie-gaat-uitvan-een-gebrek-aan-het-toestel-dat-niet-door-de-consument-is-veroorzaakt.

51 ECJ 17 April 2008, C-404/06, ECLI:EU:C:2008:231, *Quelle.*

52 Para. 41.

53 A study by Test-Achats confirmed that problems may occur with refurbished phones. Half of the (18) tested refurbished Iphones, showed important defects (www.test-aankoop.be/hightech/gsms-en-smartphones/nieuws/een-op-twee-refurbished-iphones-deugt-niet, October 2016). Only 1 phone (refurbished by Apple) was flawless.

54 See Study on the costs and benefits of extending certain rights under the Consumer Sales and Guarantees Directive 1999/94/EC; publications.europa.eu/en/publication-detail/-/publication/4d120ad5-deee-11e7-9749-01aa75ed71a1/language-en, p. 14. This is more specifically the case in Austria, Croatia, Denmark (3 years for repair), Estonia, Greece. Some other countries only provide for a new guarantee period in case of replacement (Hungary, Poland, Portugal, Slovakia, Spain).

3.3. COMMERCIAL GUARANTEE TO STIMULATE REPAIR?

10. Commercial guarantees and sustainability. It could be argued that even if the legal guarantee does not sufficiently stimulate repair or, more in general a prolonged lifespan of goods, undertakings can still promote the longer lifetime of their products by offering a commercial guarantee. Indeed, such commercial guarantees can be a marketing tool to promote products with a longer expected lifespan than the legal guarantee period of two years. As Vandemaele points out in her doctoral thesis, one of the functions of a guarantee is exactly to signal the quality of a good.[55]

However, contractual freedom mostly reigns with regard to commercial guarantees and commercial guarantees are currently not necessarily used to prolong the lifespan of goods, through repair or otherwise. The current legislative framework mainly imposes information requirements. The content of a commercial guarantee remains largely unregulated. The use of commercial guarantees in a non-sustainable way may therefore be perfectly legal. Certain companies now for example offer a '*direct replace guarantee*': '*do not wait for repair, but get your new product for free immediately*'. This is a perfectly legal practice, but it is clear that this does not stimulate a sustainable consumption pattern.

Commercial guarantees are furthermore sometimes used to hinder independent repair or repair by the consumers themselves. Thus, some commercial guarantees determine that the commercial guarantee can no longer be invoked in case of repair by an independent repairer, e.g. in case a screen of a phone is repaired in an independent repair shop. Although sellers or producers may legitimately want to exclude the risk of a badly executed repair by a third party, such widely formulated clauses also hinder the development of a network of independent repair shops. As mentioned, the regulation of commercial guarantees in the Consumer Sales Directive is limited.[56] Such commercial guarantees can in any event not affect the consumer's *legal* rights, including the right to demand repair of the seller in case of non-conformity.[57] Clauses or

---

55 S. Vandemaele, Commerciële garanties PhD thesis KU Leuven, 2019, W. Boulding en A. Kirmani, "A consumer-side experimental examination of signaling theory: Do consumers perceive warranties as signals of quality?", *Journal of Consumer Research* 1993, (111) 112; B.L. Connelly, S.T. Certo, R.D. Ireland en C.R. Reutzel, "Signaling theory: a review and assessment", *Journal of Management* 2011, (39) 43; H. Li, Y. Fang, Y. Wang, K. Lim, en L. Liang, "Are all signals equal? Investigating the differential effects of online signals on the sales performance of e-marketplace sellers", *Information Technology & People* 2015, (699) 702; C. Twigg-Flesner, *Consumer Product Guarantees* (Aldershot: Ashgate 2003) 55.

56 Art. 6 Consumer Sales Directive. The regulation of commercial guarantees in the Consumer Sales Directive 2019 is slightly more elaborate but still limited. The major novelty is the liability of a producer for repair or replacement during the 'entire period of the commercial guarantee of durability' (art. 17 Consumer Sales Directive 2019). Offering such a commercial guarantee of durability remains the free choice of a producer.

57 Art. 6 (2) and 7 Consumer Sales Directive. Contractual clauses that exclude the consumer's rights under the legal guarantee if the consumer of third parties have repaired a good are in any event void (see art. 7 (1) Consumer Sales Directive).

stickers mentioning '*Warranty void if seal broken*' are therefore contrary to the provisions of the Consumer Sales Directive to the extent that they pertain to affect the consumer's legal rights. They could also be challenged as unfair under the Unfair Contract Terms Directive[58] and they could be considered misleading on the basis of the Unfair Commercial Practices Directive.[59]

However, a contractual clause that does not allow a consumer to invoke certain (additional) *contractual* rights under a commercial guarantee in case of repair by an independent repairer do not seem to be automatically void or *per se* unfair under the Unfair Contract Terms Directive. As commercial guarantees are given on a voluntary basis, it is no so evident to install an absolute prohibition for such clauses in commercial guarantees. Other measures (such as financial incentives, see below) could be used to promote repair over replacement. In addition, the suggestion by TONNER and MALCOLM in their study for the European Parliament merits consideration.[60] These authors suggest to impose an obligation on producers to provide a commercial guarantee in which the producer has to indicate the lifespan of the product concerned and in addition he must indicate whether or not he guarantees the fitness of the product during its lifespan.[61] Although their proposal mainly creates an obligation on the producer to provide additional information without a direct impact on the right to repair, such obligation could provide an additional incentive for the producer to invest

---

58 On the basis of the general norm (art. 3 Unfair Contract Terms Directive). National implementing laws may even be stricter. Thus, the Belgian Code of Economic Law provides for a black list of terms that are prohibited in all circumstances. Art. VI.83, 14° Code of Economic Law prohibits clauses that reduce or exclude the legal obligation to deliver a good in conformity with the contract.

59 In the US, the Federal Trade Commission has recently sent warning letters to a number of companies using such statements and stickers (press release 10 April 2018, www.ftc.gov/news-events/press-releases/2018/04/ftc-staff-warns-companies-it-illegal-condition-warranty-coverage). The FTC staff expressed concerns about statements that consumers must use specific parts or service providers not to avoid their warranties. The FTC considers such statements to be generally prohibited by the Magnuson-Moss Warranty Act, and in addition they may be deceptive.

60 K. TONNER, R. MALCOLM, "How and EU lifespan guarantee model could be implemented across the EU", p. 55.

61 Tonner and Malcolm propose to insert an article along the following lines into the Consumer Sales Directive: "*Article 15a Commercial guarantees for lifespan*
1. The producer of a technical product shall (1) guarantee to the consumer the fitness of the product for such foreseeable minimum lifespan, as is normal in goods of the same type, and shall indicate the duration of this lifespan, or (2) clearly indicate that he does not guarantee the fitness of the product during its lifespan.
This information shall be made available to the consumer at the time where he takes an informed transactional decision. The producer shall inform the consumer whether the guaranteed lifespan is shorter or longer than the limitation period according to Article 14. Article 15 [commercial guarantees] is applicable.
2. If the producer does not fulfil his obligations according to no. 1, he has the same obligations to the consumer as the seller."

and guarantee a longer lifespan of products. Their proposal was not taken up in the Consumer Sales Directive 2019.

4. INDEPENDENT REPAIR / DIY REPAIR?

11. Independent repair / DIY repair. It follows from the previous section that the Consumer Sales Directive does not stimulate repair by the seller as a remedy. However, even if the hierarchy of remedies under the legal guarantee would be altered and even if stricter rules on commercial guarantees would be adopted, there will always be situations in which the consumer cannot invoke any remedy as against the seller. The defect may only appear when the legal guarantee period has lapsed and it may not be covered by the legal or commercial guarantee. In such a case, the consumer still has the possibility to repair the good himself[62] or to have it repaired by an independent repairer[63], rather than opting for a replacement. This in any even the theory. In practice, a number of obstacles hinder DIY and independent repair.

These obstacles may be of a practical and/or legal nature. They include the lack of availability of spare parts or the lack of available spare parts at a reasonable price, the presence of glued parts or of other parts that hinder disassembly. Apple's patented 'pentalobe security screws' are a notorious example in this regard.[64] These 'security screws' require special screwdrivers to open the device thus hindering independent or DIY repair.

Furthermore, the lack of publicly available technical information in the form of manuals or repair information is especially problematic for electronic devices.[65] '*Reverse engineering*', i.e. dissembling an object to extract the necessary knowledge, is only a second best solution as it is costly and time-consuming, especially given the vast number of different electronic devices. In addition, intellectual property ('IP') rights are sometimes invoked by companies to prevent consumers and independent repairers from accessing their electronic devices. Some of these issues and their possible solutions are addressed in more detail below.

12. IP rights – Digital Millennium Copyright Act – the US. IP rights have thus been used in the US to prevent users and repairers from accessing devices and repairing them. The '*Digital Millennium Copyright Act*' ('DMCA')

---

62 Cf. the increasing popularity of 'Repair cafés', more than 1500 worldwide: www. Repaircafe. org and repaircafe.org/nieuwe-mijlpaal-1-500-repair-cafes-wereldwijd/.

63 Or he may of course turn to the seller to have the good repaired against payment.

64 The use of these screws is however not limited to Apple, see ifixit.org/blog/9905/bit-history-the-pentalobe/.

65 See Ellen Mc Arthur Foundation, Empowering Repair, October 2016, www.ellenmacarthur foundation.org/assets/downloads/ce100/Empowering-Repair-Final-Public1.pdf.

was adopted in 1998 to allow producers to protect digital content. The Act prohibited to circumvent technical protection measures ('TPMs') used by copyright owners to protect access to their works.[66] Although that is as such a justifiable aim, the balance between the need to protect content and the rights of access of end users for lawful uses seemed to be lost.[67] Practices that were considered legitimate beforehand (such as using 'reverse engineering' to repair digital devices), now became illegal.[68]

In the US, the far reaching limitations on the rights of end-users by the DMCA was somewhat attenuated in the US by the '*Unlocking Consumer Choice and Wireless Competition Act*' of 2014. Every three years, the US Copyright office now recommends to the Librarian of Congress that he should grant certain specific exemptions after examining whether the law bars lawful uses of the works. The increased number of exemptions to the prohibition on circumvention of access control technologies[69] does once more enable certain activities of reverse engineering that can be necessary to repair goods.[70] The complexity of the legislation and of the exemptions makes it however difficult for reverse engineers to be certain that they are engaging in non-infringing activities.[71]

The parallel European legislation that was adopted in 2001[72] did not give as far reaching rights to producers and focused rather on control of unauthorized use of copyright protected works rather than access itself.[73]

13. IP Rights – Design – trademark – copyright protection of manuals. Not only technological protection measures may make repair difficult. Manufacturers, especially in the car industry have also invoked design rights[74] to make it difficult to repair goods with replacement parts that were not made

---

66 Section 1201 Digital Millennium Copyright Act of 1998.

67 Zie A. Foroughi, M. Albin, S. Gillard, "Digital rights management: a delicate balance between protection and accessibility", *Journal of Information Science* (28) 5 2002, 389–395.

68 J.D Sullivan, T.M. Morrow, "Practicing reverse engineering in an era of growing constraints under the digital millennium copyright act and other provisions", Albany Law Journal of Science & Technology 2003, 6. See for some extreme examples in which the DMCA was used to eg. remove a blog of some hobbyists who adapted the steering system of their calculators, www.eff.org/pages/unintended-consequences-fifteen-years-under-dmca.

69 See Library of Congress, Exemption to Prohibition on Circumvention of Copyright Protection Systems for Access Control Technologies, October 2015, www.gpo.gov/fdsys/pkg/FR-2015-10-28/pdf/2015-27212.pdf.

70 P. Samuelson, "New Exemptions to Anti-Circumvention Rules", 59. *Communications of the ACM*, March 2016, no. 3.

71 P. Samuelson, 59. *Communications of the ACM*, March 2016, no. 3.

72 Art. 6 Dir. 2001/29/EC on the harmonisation of certain aspects of copyright and related rights in the information society, OJ 22 June 2001, https://eur-lex.europa.eu/legal-content/FR/TXT/?uri=celex%3A32001L0029 obliges Member States to provide adequate legal protection against the circumvention of technological measures.

73 W. Guan, 'Copyright Anti-Circumvention & Free Trade' (2018) 52 Journal of World Trade, Issue 2, pp. 257–279.

74 See eg ECJ 20 December 2017, ECLI:EU:C:2017:992, Cases C-397/16 and C-435/16, *Acacia*.

by the OEM. Although the so-called 'repair clause' in the Community Design Regulation[75] limits the possibilities to invoke Community design protection in case of repair[76], that clause does not solve all problems. National design laws which do not provide for such a clause continue to allow protection and enforcement of design rights covering spare parts.[77] The mentioned repair clause also does not apply to trademarks[78], so that it is not allowed for manufacturers of spare parts to reproduce registered trademarks on their products simply because that use of the trade mark would lead to the restoration of the original appearance of the complex product.[79]

Quite an important number of producers furthermore refuse to make repair information available. In case such information is placed online by third parties, the copyright protection of such manuals can be successfully invoked by the producers (both in the US and in the EU).[80] To the extent that *'reverse engineering'* is not prevented by other IP rights[81], this process in theory allows

---

75 Council Regulation (EC) No 6/2002 of 12 December 2001 on Community designs ('Design Regulation'), OJ 5 January 2002, https://eur-lex.europa.eu/legal-content/en/TXT/?uri=CELEX:32002R0006.

76 See art. 110 (1) Design Regulation No 6/2002 *"a Community design shall not exist for a design which constitutes a component part of a complex product [...]for the purpose of the repair of that complex product so as to restore its original appearance"* and art. 14 of the Designs Directive (Directive 98/71/EC on the legal protection of designs OJ 28.10.1998 L 289).

77 H. Hartwig, "Spare parts under European design and trade mark law" *Journal of intellectual property law & practice* 2016, vol. 11, no. 2, 121.

78 ECJ 6 October 2015, ECLI:EU:C:205:680, C-500/14, *Ford Motor v Wheeltrims*.

79 ECJ 6 October 2015,footnote 80. It is however allowed to use a trade mark to inform the public that one carries out the repair and maintenance of goods covered by that trade mark or that one is a specialist in the sale or the repair and maintenance of such goods, unless the mark is used in a way that may create to the impression that there is a commercial connection between the other undertaking and the trade mark proprietor, see ECJ 23 February 1999, ECLI:EU:C:1999:82, C-63/97, *BMW v Deenik* (para 64).

80 Www.theguardian.com/sustainable-business/copyright-law-repair-manuals-circular-economy. For the EU, see in particular ECJ 11 August 2010, ECLI:EU/C:2012:259, C-406/10, *SAS Institute Inc v World Programming Ltd*: the parts of a user manual that contain some of the elements which are the expression of the intellectual creation of the author of the work are protected by copyright.

81 Including copyright protection for software. Here, the ECJ has accepted that certain reverse engineering practices can be performed by licencees on computer programs that are copyright protected. See ECJ 2 May 2012, ECLI:EU:C:2012:59, C-406/10, *SAS Institute Inc. v World Programming*: "a person who has obtained a copy of a computer program under a licence is entitled, without the authorisation of the owner of the copyright, to observe, study or test the functioning of that program so as to determine the ideas and principles which underlie any element of the program, in the case where that person carries out acts covered by that licence and acts of loading and running necessary for the use of the computer program, and on condition that that person does not infringe the exclusive rights of the owner of the copyright in that program" (para. 62). And see for more information, P. Ciancarini, D. Russo, A. Sillitti, G. Succi, "Reverse engineering: a European IPR perspective", 2016, www.researchgate.net/publication/303773364_Reverse_engineering_a_European_IPR_perspective [accessed Feb 11 2019]. The authors point out that the exact boundaries of legal software reengineering remain subject to discussion.

independent repairers to obtain the technical information required. Reverse engineering is however time-consuming and therefore costly and the wide variety of available consumer goods makes it impossible to perform this task for all available products and models.

14. Repair legislation as a solution? Vehicles. In certain sectors, including the vehicle industry, specific legislation has been adopted to tackle this problem. Thus e.g. in the US, the state of Massachusetts adopted '*automotive repair legislation*' in 2012.[82] That legislation guarantees that independent repairers and owners have access to the same diagnostic and repair information as authorized repair providers, while respecting trade secrets. This state legislation has been the basis for a national Memorandum of Understanding committing vehicle manufacturers also in other states to comply with the requirements of the Massachusetts legislation.[83]

In the EU, Regulations 715/2007 and 595/2009 regulate access to such information.[84, 85] Article 6(1) of Regulation 715/2007 thus provides that manufactures must provide access to vehicle repair and maintenance information to independent operators '*through websites using a standardised format in a readily accessible and prompt manner, and in a manner that is non-discriminatory compared to the provision given or access granted to authorised dealers and repairers*'. They must also make training available to independent operators and authorised dealers and repairers. Although the EU regulation of access to vehicle repair and maintenance information was not in the first place inspired by sustainability goals, but rather wanted to ensure there was still competition on the lucrative after-market[86], the regulations does contribute

---

82 Malegislature.gov/Laws/GeneralLaws/PartI/TitleXV/Chapter93K; E. Schuller, "Who has the Right to Repair?", *Fleet Maintenance* 2018, Vol. 22(1), 10–12, 14, 16.

83 Www.autonews.com/article/20140125/RETAIL05/301279936/automakers-agree-to-right-to-repair-deal; see for the text of the memorandum of 15 January 2014: www.autocare.org/workarea/DownloadAsset.aspx?id=1440&gmssopc=1.

84 Regulation (EC) No 715/2007 of 20 June 2007 on type approval of motor vehicles with respect to emissions from light passenger and commercial vehicles (Euro 5 and Euro 6) and on access to vehicle repair and maintenance information, OJ 29 June 2007, https://eur-lex.europa.eu/legal-content/en/ALL/?uri=CELEX%3A32007R0715. **See also** Report from the Commission on the operation of the system of access to vehicle repair and maintenance information established by Regulation (EC) No 715/2007 on type approval of motor vehicles with respect to emissions from light passenger and commercial vehicles (Euro 5 and Euro 6) and on access to vehicle repair and maintenance information, **COM(2016) 782 final.**

85 Regulation (EC) No 595/2009 of 18 June 2009 on type-approval of motor vehicles and engines with respect to emissions from heavy duty vehicles (Euro VI) and on access to vehicle repair and maintenance information and amending Regulation (EC) No 715/2007 and Directive 2007/46/EC and repealing Directives 80/1269/EEC, 2005/55/EC and 2005/78/EC, https://eur-lex.europa.eu/legal-content/EN/ALL/?uri=CELEX%3A32009R0595.

86 2016 Commission Report on the operation of the system of access to vehicle repair and maintenance information(**footnote 86), p. 4.**

to a right to repair at competitive prices and should therefore also have environmental benefits.[87]

15. Repair legislation as a solution – digital devices? In the meantime the plea to adopt similar legislation with a far broader scope of application is getting more and more support. In the US, such *'right to repair'* bills with a broader scope of application have been proposed in several states.[88] The content of these proposals is quite similar and seems inspired by the repair legislation in the automotive industry. If we take New Hampshire as an example, the *'House Bill 1733-FN' 'Act relative to digital product repair'* would require manufacturers of digital electronic products sold after a certain date to make available to independent repair facilities and owners the same diagnostic and repair information that it makes available to its authorized repair providers and this free of charge.[89] Service parts should also be made available for product owners at reasonable prices (*'fair and reasonable terms'*). The bill furthermore enumerates a number of factors that can be taken into account to determine the *'fair and reasonable'* character of the terms.[90] It also makes clear that these obligations do not mean that traders must divulge trade secrets.[91]

It might not surprise that there is opposition against the adoption of such legislation by manufacturers. According to some manufacturers, the adoption of the mentioned regulation would pose threats in terms of safety and it would create additional risks of hacking.[92] Although security issues definitely need to be taken into account as well as the need to trade secrets[93] when adopting *'right*

87 See Study on the operation of the system of access to vehicle repair and maintenance information, 2014, publications.europa.eu/en/publication-detail/-/publication/c2c172a5-3f49-4644-b5bb-c508d7532e4a/language-en/format-PDF/source-69056993 and 2016 Commission Report on the operation of the system of access to vehicle repair and maintenance information (footnote 86), p. 3.

88 Ifixit.org/blog/8780/apple-right-to-repair/; repair.org/legislation/. Similar legislation would have been proposed in 18 states, repair.org/legislation/ (last checked 14 November 2018).

89 See legiscan.com/NH/text/HB1733/id/1657713.

90 Section 358 T: 1. V *"Fair and reasonable terms" means terms where consideration is given to relevant factors, including but not limited to:*
(a) The net cost to the authorized repair provider for similar parts obtained from manufacturers, less any discounts, rebates, or other incentive programs;
(b) The cost to the manufacturer of preparing and distributing the parts or product, excluding any research and development costs incurred in designing and implementing, upgrading, or altering the product, but including amortized capital costs for the preparation and distribution of the parts; and
(c) The price charged by other manufacturers for similar parts or products.", legiscan.com/NH/text/HB1733/id/1657713.

91 Section 358-T:7, legiscan.com/NH/text/HB1733/id/1657713.

92 See e.g. the arguments invoked by John Deere, www.theguardian.com/environment/2017/mar/06/nebraska-farmers-right-to-repair-john-deere-apple.

93 As protected by Directive 2016/943/EU on the protection of undisclosed know-how and business information (trade secrets) against their unlawful acquisition, use and disclosure OJ 15 June 2016, https://eur-lex.europa.eu/legal-content/EN/TXT/?uri=CELEX%3A32016L0943.

to repair / fair repair' legislation, this should protect not provide an unlimited justification for manufacturers to refuse independent repairers access to repair and diagnostic information.

At EU level, a draft regulation on electronic displays of 2016[94], goes somewhat in that direction as it proposes to make it obligatory for certain categories of products to make repair information available, but it has been met with fierce opposition. The adoption of such legislation definitely requires a thorough debate and careful balancing of the rights of manufacturers and users / independent repairers. But broader repair legislation as has been proposed in New Hampshire and other US states is definitely a policy tool that can stimulate the repair industry and thus more sustainable business models and that allows to not only take the interests of businesses and consumers into account but also sustainable development as furthered by art. 11 TFEU. The experience with the existing EU automotive access to repair and maintenance regulation can be used to develop 'fair repair' legislation with a broader scope of application.

16. TAX INCENTIVES FOR REPAIR. Repair could furthermore be stimulated through tax incentives.[95] Several options are can be considered, such as a differentiated levy in function of repairability; tax deductions for repair costs or a reduced VAT. In Sweden the latter two options have already been adopted: for some repairs in the home tax deductions are possible (care of clothes and home textiles; repair and maintenance of data and information technology equipment, repair and maintenance of appliances)[96] and in addition, a reduced VAT (from 25 to 12%) applies for repair of bicycles, shoes, leather clothes and household linen.

5. LABELS AND REPAIR

17. In the absence of further reaching European and national hard law initiatives, self-regulation and soft law also have a role to play. Several (eco) labels exist that can assist the consumer in making a sustainable choice when buying a product. Such labels also help businesses that want to promote their sustainable products as they have a signaling function that is similar to a commercial guarantee. In terms of promoting repair, the impact of these labels

---

94 Resolution on a longer lifetime for products: benefits for consumers and companies, www.europarl.europa.eu/news/en/press-room/20170629IPR78633/making-consumer-products-more-durable-and-easier-to-repair; https://ec.europa.eu/info/law/better-regulation/initiatives/ares-2016-7108187_en, see also www.europarl.europa.eu/sides/getDoc.do?pubRef=-//EP//TEXT+REPORT+A8-2017-0214+0+DOC+XML+V0//EN.

95 See A. MICHEL, "La Directive 1999/44/CE sur la garantie des biens de consommation: un remède efficace contre l'obsolescence programmée?", *REDC* 2016/2, 229 and see also J. EYCKMANS in B. Keirsbilck, E. Terryn, (eds.), *Circular economy and consumer protection*.

96 See the contribution of E. MAÎTRE-EKERN, and C. DALHAMMAR in B. Keirsbilck, E. Terryn, (eds.), *Circular economy and consumer protection*.

may only be limited or at least indirect as – apart from the iFixit repairability score – most of these labels take various sustainability criteria into account of which repairability may be one.

At EU level, the voluntary EU Ecolabel facilitates communication by traders on the environmentally friendly character of their goods and services (since 1992).[97] Specific criteria need to be complied with in order to use the label. Different criteria have been developed for different products. Repairability criteria (including instruction on repair, upgradability, ease of disassembly, spare parts supply) are included for some products. At this point in time, criteria have only been developed for a relatively limited number of products.[98]

At national level, several similar initiatives exist. The Blue Angel (*der Blaue Engel*) label in Germany is the ecolabel of the German federal government (since 1978). Like the EU Ecolabel, it sets standards for environmentally friendly product design[99] and aims to help consumers to make their purchasing decisions on environmental aspects.[100] Criteria are developed per product or product group.[101] For a number of product groups (but not all), criteria related to repairability[102] are imposed in order to obtain the label.[103] The Nordic Swan Ecolabel is a similar system for the Nordic countries (Denmark, Finland, Iceland, Norway and Sweden) that was established in 1989 by the Nordic Council.[104] Like the Blue Angel label, it wants to enable customers to choose the environmentally best goods and services. Depending on the product concerned, one or more criteria related to repairability need to be complied to obtain the label.[105]

Private initiatives like "iFixit" focus even more on repairability. iFixit was started in 2003 in the US and develops and shares manuals to repair consumer devices.[106] iFixit provides for repairability scores for different (mainly electronic) products.[107] Engineers disassemble and analyze the devices and award them a score between 0 and 10. A device scoring a 10 will be relatively inexpensive to repair because it is easy to disassemble and has a service manual available. Further criteria are the difficulty of opening the device, the types of fasteners and the

---

97 Regulation (EC) No 66/2010 of 25 November 2009 on the EU Ecolabel regulates the functioning of the EU Ecolabel system. It is managed by the European Commission with bodies from the Members States and other stakeholders, ec.europa.eu/environment/ecolabel/the-ecolabel-scheme.html.

98 Vito, *Repairability for energy related products*, p. 22. See also www.beuc.eu/publications/beuc-x-2017–099_sustainable_europe_whatstill_needs_to_be_done.pdf, p. 13.

99 Www.blauer-engel.de/en.

100 Www.blauer-engel.de/en/blue-angel/what-is-behind-it.

101 Www.blauer-engel.de/sites/default/files/vergabegrundlage_uebersicht_nach_branchen_en.pdf.

102 Ia ease of disassembly, spare parts supply.

103 Eg for mobile phones, pc, TV, vacuum cleaners, coffee machines. See Vito, *Repairability for energy related products*, p. 21.

104 Www.nordic-ecolabel.org/the-nordic-swan-ecolabel/.

105 See Vito, *Repairability for energy related products*, p. 22.

106 Www.ifixit.com/Info/background.

107 See eg www.ifixit.com/tablet-repairability.

complexity to replace major components. Upgradability, use of non-proprietary tools for servicing and component modularity are also taken into account.[108]

18. While these national and private initiatives are to be welcomed as they can help a consumer to make a sustainable choice and to opt for a reparable product, not all faith can be put in these soft law initiatives. The above enumeration of initiatives is not exhaustive and apart from the mentioned, trustworthy initiatives, there are also labels that do not guarantee an independent verification nor the use of relevant environmental criteria.[109] This proliferation of labels risks to confuse consumers and to undermine their confidence in these labels. 'Greenwashing' is indeed increasingly popular. International initiatives to coordinate and 'label' the different labels exists[110], but one may wonder whether the average consumer knows where to check whether the (eco)label used is indeed trustworthy and reliable. Stronger tools (hard law) are therefore needed to complement these soft law initiatives.

6. CONCLUDING REMARKS

19. 'Humans' have only (fairly) recently become 'consumers' as Trentmann has set out in his research and it was only in the 18th century that SMITH pointed out the social and psychological impulses that push people to accumulate objects and gadgets: they started looking at the objects obtained as "means of happiness", thus leaving behind the negative connotation that had accompanied obtaining frivolous things for centuries.[111] Indeed, in ancient times, consumption was essentially negatively regarded.[112] The Latin *'consumere'*, as it found its way into European languages, came to mean 'using up, wasting away, finishing'.[113]

---

108 Www.ifixit.com/tablet-repairability. See also Vito, *Repairability for energy related products*, p. 24, a qualitative scoring system would be under further development in cooperation with TU Delft.

109 The establishment of GEN (Global Ecolabelling Network), that classifies ecolabels into different categories confirms this problem and the need for set of principles to test an environmental claim. GEN classifies the different ecolabel programmes and 'type 1' ecolabels guarantee independent verification that a product complies with multiple environmental criteria whereby the entire lifecycle of a product is considered. See Annual Report GEN 2016, view.publitas.com/global-ecolabelling-network/gen-annual-report-2016/page/6–7.

110 The establishment of GEN (Global Ecolabelling Network), that classifies ecolabels into different categories confirms this problem and the need for set of principles to test an environmental claim. GEN classifies the different ecolabel programmes and 'type 1' ecolabels guarantee independent verification that a product complies with multiple environmental criteria whereby the entire lifecycle of a product is considered. See Annual Report GEN 2016, view.publitas.com/global-ecolabelling-network/gen-annual-report-2016/page/6–7.

111 See A. SMITH's 1759's *The Theory of Moral Sentiments*, as cited by F. TRENTMANN, Empire of Things: How we Became of World of Consumers (Allen Lane 2016).

112 F. TRENTMANN, Empire of Things: How we Became of World of Consumers (Allen Lane 2016)/.

113 Www.theatlantic.com/business/archive/2016/11/how-humans-became-consumers/508700/.

Considering consumption no longer as wasteful, or as ruining a community, but rather as a way to make nations richer, more civilized and stronger can be traced back to the 18th century.[114] We may now once more have entered an era in which people start to realize that consumption does not necessarily bring happiness; that it has externalities beyond the instant gratification it provides and that there are limits to the wasting that seems inherent to our current consumption patterns.

Different and more circular business models try to limit those externalities and can help to achieve a sustainable economy along the lines of Kate Raworth's alternative 'doughnut' economic model: a model that aims to ensure that everyone on earth has access to their basic needs, such as adequate food and education, while not limiting opportunities for future generations by protecting our ecosystem and taking into account the planetary boundaries.[115]

To enable and incentivize such more circular business models, regulation definitely has a role to play and this is also the case for 'traditional' consumer law. If consumer law wants to stay relevant, consumer law must not only take into account consumer protection aims but it should balance them with sustainability goals as this is in the long term interest of the consumers it aims to protect.

This contribution focused on repair as a means to prolong the lifespan of goods and comes to the conclusion that neither in the EU nor in the US, a real 'right' to repair exist. There are obstacles to repair that are both of a practical and of a legal nature. Different policy measures can however be adopted to stimulate repair. These range from the stage of production where ecodesign requirements (including reparability criteria) could be adopted for a broader range of products, to the pre-contractual stage in which additional information could be provided on reparability and availability of spare parts, over the contractual stage in which repair could be made the primary remedy. In addition, independent and DIY repair can be stimulated by imposing obligations to ensure access to repair and diagnostic information and to spare parts on similar terms as manufacturers' own repairers. Furthermore, tax incentives, both in the form of deductions for repair services or in the form of lower VAT can be considered.

Finally, awareness raising is necessary if we want consumers to play their role in achieving more sustainable / circular business models and to act once again as 'citizens' or 'humans', capable of addressing a wider range of interests rather than as consumers solely interested in their own position in the market place.[116]

---

114 F. Trentmann, Empire of Things: How we Became of World of Consumers (Allen Lane 2016).

115 K. Raworth, *Donought economics. Seven ways to think like a 21st century economist* (Penguin 2017) 373 p.

116 See J. Lewis et al, *Citizens or consumers? What the Media tell us about political participation* (Maidenhead: Open University Press 2005), cited by K. Raworth, *Donought economics*, Penguin, 2017, 102, see also pages 99–102 of the same book on the changed attitude of people when treated as 'consumers' (stronger identification with notions as wealth, status and success) rather than as 'citizens'.

FROM A PRODUCT-BASED ECONOMY TO SERVICES?

Legal Aspects of an Economy in Transition

Fryderyk ZOLL*

1. TIME FOR TRANSITION AND THE SHAPE OF PRIVATE LAW

Technology has dramatically transformed our lives. The rise of new business models based on the most recent achievements of technology challenges our legal systems as well. At the brink of the Internet, it was quite broadly accepted that the old classical private law is sufficiently neutral from a technological point of view.[1] The scale of the challenges resulting from technological development has, however, forced these assumptions to be revised.[2] The rules of private law, based on ancient Roman concepts, have become less and less able to respond to the needs of contemporary society.

Mass production, focused on the standardised needs of consumers, has also modified the approach to products.[3] Sustainability and quality are not the most important features.[4] From the perspective of producers, the short lifecycle of products is advantageous, since it forces the consumer to replace the products quite quickly.[5] Additionally, technological development results in 'moral aging'

---

* Prof. Dr. hab. Dr. h.c. (Ternopil) F. Zoll.

1 M. Giaro mentions the approach called "state-based traditionalism" (focused on questions of applicable law, but based on the assumption that the traditional legal concepts can in principle solve the issues posed by the Internet) – M. Giaro, Zawarcie umowy w trybie aukcji internetowej (The formation of the contract by the means of the Internet auction), 2014, p. 17 (the Author mentions also another theories on this matter).

2 F. Zoll, The DCFR's specific part of the law of obligations and its feasibility for the development of a modern contract law, in: D. Voinot, J. Sénéchal, vers un droit Européen des contrats spéciaux, 2012, 5, p. 107.

3 F. Zoll, At the end of the concept of a consumer?, in: J. Lazar, M. Gajdosová, Social function of law and growing wealth inequality, 2018, Typi Universitatis Tyrnaviensis, p. 87.

4 Ch. Behrends, Consequences of planned obsolescence for consumer culture and the promotional self, Essay, 2004, p. 3.

5 Look for the economic background of planned obsolescence – B. London, Ending the Depression Through Planned Obsolescence, 1932.

of products, which in turn accelerates their replacement.[6] These facts have probably influenced another phenomenon of our times – acquiring ownership has become less attractive than was the case for previous generations.[7] Customers start seeking not to acquire ownership but only to acquire access to the goods.[8] This access is usually accompanied by a wide range of services related to the goods.[9] Even if the consumer decides (and this is still quite common) to acquire ownership, they also seek to obtain sufficient services from the seller, often an option to replace the item after a certain period under more beneficial conditions and finally to be sure that the seller will take the used thing back from the owner to recycle it if the reuse of the item is no longer economically reasonable.[10]

These circumstances not only reshape the market for all participants, but also influence the legal environment. There are several legal consequences resulting from these developments. The European Union tried to influence this development by adopting the Ecodesign Directive 2009/125/EC.[11] The European Parliament and European Commission further develop this idea of a longer life span for products by tackling planned obsolescence and making repairs and spare parts more readily accessible.[12] The long-term relationship thus becomes the dominating category of contracts, instead of the relationship that extinguishes after its successful performance.[13] As a result, the sales contract, traditionally a central category of the law of obligations, inevitably loses its position. This may lead to a dramatical change in the system of most civil codes. Not only is the sales contract traditionally perceived as the most important contract, but it has also served as a model for the general scheme of non-performance.[14] Reshaping a system is not an easy task. It is moreover an

6 K. Pope, in K. Pope, Understanding planned obsolescence. Unsustainability through production, consumption and waste generation, 2017, p. 1.

7 This phenomenon of the depart from the classical form of the ownership was already identified a few decades ago – see: L. Raiser, Die Zukunft des Privatrechts, Vortrag gehalten von der Berliner Juristischen Gesellschaft, 1971, p. 30.

8 J. Papageorgiou, The Economic Impact of Access versus Ownership, An Analysis of Spotify, 2016, pp. 25 – 26.

9 P. Low, G. O. Pasadilla, Manufacturing-related Services, in: P. Low, G. O. Pasadilla, Services in Global Value Chains, 2016, p. 62.

10 T. J. de Römph, Pressing Forward – Developments in the Transitions Towards Sustainable Materials Management in the EU-Environmental Law, in: V. Mauerhofer, Legal Aspects of Sustainable Development, 2016, pp. 518 – 520.

11 Directive 2009/125/EC of the European Parliament and of the Council of 21 October 2009 establishing a framework for the setting of ecodesign requirements for energy-related products.

12 See: Official Journal of the European Union, Resolution of the European Parliament of 4 July 2017 on a longer lifetime for products: benefits for consumers and companies, 2018/C 334/06.

13 See: S. Grundmann, F. Caffagi, G. Vettori, The Contractual Basis of Long-Term Organization – The Overall Architecture, in: S. Grundmann, F. Caffagi, G. Vettori, The Organizational Contract. From Exchange to Long-Term Network Cooperation in European Contract Law, 2016, pp. 6 – 9.

14 E.g. The CESL also provides a standard set of rules on non-performance, see: F. Zoll, The binding power of the contract, Protection of performance in the system of the Common

illusion that the contract of sales, with its system-founding role, can simply be replaced by the "contract of services".[15] This category is too heterogeneous and it is extremely difficult to find an universal solution that is sufficiently abstract to allow for the development of a set of useful rules that would be generally applicable.[16]

However, the indicated change also concerns property law. The question arises how the departure from the desirability of ownership will impact property law.[17] The decreasing utility of ownership acquisition by the final user is not merely a minor change in human behaviour.[18] Systems of private law were entirely drafted under the assumption that ownership is something worthy to be acquired.[19] This general assumption has ceased to be true. This shift has several consequences, in spite of the fact that the concept of property varies immensely within the continental legal family, and of course even more outside of it.[20] It also moves the centre of gravity for the whole system. Ownership starts to be a 'static' right that is actually not transferred to the customers. Instead, the owner only grants access to it. It may be argued that this is not such a big change. Finally, the rental contract is not an invention of recent times. Regardless, the position of such contracts within the frame of the whole system has changed dramatically. We can imagine the world with self-driving cars ready for sharing[21], but the ownership will still remain in the hands of the traders who provide access to these cars.

Lawmakers built the system under the tacit assumption that the needs of the customers, and mostly theirs, will be met by the sale and the acquisition of ownership by the buyer. This development is clearly noticeable in consumer protection law. The Consumer Sales Directive, one of the most important directives in this regard, illustrates this phenomenon. This directive provides

---

European Sales Law, in: Journal of International Trade Law and Policy, Vol. 11 No. 3, 2012, p. 261.

15 On the dramatic increase in relevance of services in the modern economy see: P. Low, G. O. Pasadilla, Manufacturing-related Services, p. 2.

16 M. Artigot, i Golobardes, F. Gómez, Dissecting Long-Term Contracts: A Law and Economics Approach, in: S. Grundmann, F. Caffagi, G. Vettori, The Organizational Contract. From Exchange to Long-Term Network Cooperation in European Contract Law, 2016, p 42; F. Zoll, The DCFR's specific part of the law of obligations and its feasibility for the development of a modern contract law, in: D. Voinot, J. Sénéchal, vers un droit Européen des contrats spéciaux, 2012, chapter 5, p. 112.

17 Siehe z. B. https://www.maschinenmarkt.vogel.de/abschied-vom-eigentum-a-5621/.

18 The concept of ownership will, however, also be subject to a transformation – see E. Tjong Tjin Tai, Data ownership and consumer protection, EuCML 4/2018, pp. 137 – 138; S. van Erp: Ownership of digital assets?, EuCML 2/2016, pp. 73 – 74.

19 On traditional civil law and its affection to ownership and contract see: L. Raiser, Die Zukunft, p. 26.

20 On different concepts of ownership in different legal systems see: C v. Bar. Gemeineuropäisches Sachenrecht, 2015, pp. 499 – 506.

21 Https://www.zipcar.com/ziptopia/future-city/future-of-car-sharing-with-autonomous-wheels.

an essential system that protects consumers' reliance on the internal market.[22] Many directives apply to services. One of these, the new Package Travel Directive 2015, even provides a fully-fledged system of rules on services, confined, however, to a narrow scope of application.[23] It cannot be compared with the relevance of the Consumer Sales Directive[24] and the respective member state laws.[25] The Consumer Sales Directive has already substantively influenced private law.[26] The Package Travel Directive[27] and its predecessor have not resulted in a comparable reshaping of the system of services, although there is a certain margin for the generalisation of this directive and one may imagine designing a general legal system in relation to services on the basis of this directive, using the method adopted by the Group Acquis.[28] The more general

---

22 F. Zoll, The binding power of the contract, Protection of performance in the system of the Common European Sales Law, in: Journal of International Trade Law and Policy, Vol. 11 No. 3, 2012, p. 259.

23 R. Schulze, F. Zoll, European Contract Law, 2018, p. 96.

24 The question whether the Consumer Sales Directive covers also the contract of work (*Werkvertrag*) which actually also means a contract for services has been negatively answered by the CJEU, C-247/16, (Schottelius). L. Bertino argues that Directive 44/99 also covers ancillary service contracts – L. Bertino, Service Contracts and EU Directive 1999/44 on Consumer Sales, EuCML 5/2018, p. 216. However, this position is questionable. The question is whether the definition of sales taken from the Consumer Rights Directive can be freely "transferred" from the Consumer Rights Directive (Art. 2 no. 5, which in some ambiguous way provides an "absorptive" definition of the contract of sales). The fact that there are good arguments for extending the concept of sales in the Consumer Sales Directive is rather a *de lege ferenda* suggestion. However, a member state is free to extend the concept or apply its own doctrine applicable to mixed contracts. The ruling of the Court of Justice is controversial: if the court of the member state believes that European law is important for the case, even due to the fact that the member state has implemented the directive in an extended manner, it should answer. The matter whether the assumption of the court is correct (*i.e.* whether European law matters for the case at hand), is to be decided by the national court. The evaluation of the request for the preliminary ruling and the judgment of the Court of Justice requires further analysis. The new proposed Directive on Certain Aspects Concerning Contracts for the Sales of Goods also contains a rule that deals with the contract of sales combined with services, inserting the application of the provisions on sales in such a case – see: F. Graf v. Westphalen, Some Thoughts on the Proposed Directive on Certain Aspects Concerning Contracts for the Sales of Goods, EuCML 2/2018, p. 68.

25 Directive 1999/44/EC of the European Parliament and of the Council of 25 May 1999 on certain aspects of the sale of consumer goods and associated guarantees.

26 K. Tonner, Verbrauchsgüterkauf-Richtlinie und Europäisierung des Zivilrechts, Betriebsberater 35/1999, p. 1769; H. Micklitz, Die Verbrauchsgüterkaufrichtlinie, EuZW 16/1999, p. 490; U. Büdenbender, Die Bedeutung der Verbrauchsgüterkaufrichtlinie für das deutsche Kaufrecht nach der Schuldrechtsreform, ZEuP 1/2004, p. 37.

27 Directive (EU) 2015/2302 of the European Parliament and of the Council of 25 November 2015 on package travel and linked travel arrangements, amending Regulation (EC) No 2006/2004 and Directive 2011/83/EU of the European Parliament and of the Council and repealing Council Directive 90/314/EEC.

28 F. Zoll, The DCFR's specific part of the law of obligations and its feasibility for the development of a modern contract law, in: D. Voinot, J. Sénéchal, vers un droit Européen des contrats spéciaux, 2012, chapter 5, p. 109.

Directive on Services in the Internal Market only contains a small number of provisions that may be categorised as private law.[29]

Even so, the problem with services is of a much deeper nature. The mentioned heterogeneity of the contract of services makes it extremely difficult to create more general rules on services. Even the definition of services is not easy. The vast majority of sources defines services in a negative manner (as "not sale") or in a circular way ("services are services"). The real problem is that it is extremely difficult to apply classical rules of contract law to many kinds of services.[30]

The difficulties with envisaging general rules on services are due to the fact that the subject matter of the contract is much more difficult to define than in case of "classical" sales. This problem of services has been identified not just recently, but it was intentionally or unintentionally one of the rationales for the medieval system of handworkers' guildes. In case of services, the customer is often not able to identify whether the service has been performed correctly and in compliance with the contract. One way to alleviate this problem was the membership of a guilde, an association which not only controlled the market and restricted competition, but also contributed in securing the quality of services (and products) through the educational system, a strict hierarchy and a complaints system.

The heterogeneity of services is an important obstacle for the creation of an overarching model for the contract on services.[31] The subject matter varies immensely and the most general feature of a service contract not being a sales contract is insufficient to allow for the identification of types of parties' interests that may be elevated to a sufficiently general level. The European Commission has identified this problem while drafting the proposal for the Directive on the Supply of Digital Content[32], the title of which was expanded by the European Parliament by adding the characteristic notion of 'digital services' (a concept that cannot really be distinguished from the notion of 'digital content' – it has rather been used to reflect different intuitions and to secure a broad understanding of the scope, which is meant to also include electronically rendered services).[33] The proposal for the directive contains one quite revolutionary solution. It refrains from the contract typology seeking to find the most general and

---

29 See e.g.: F. Zoll, R. Schulze, Europäisches Vertragsrecht, 2nd Ed., Nomos 2017, §3, p. 142f., sidenotes 32–34.

30 E.g. see: F. Zoll, Das Dienstleistungsrecht im Vorschlag für ein Gemeinsames Europäisches Kaufrecht, in: H. Schulte-Nölke/F. Zoll/ N. Jansen/R. Schulze, Der Entwurf für ein optionales europäisches Kaufrecht, Sellier, München 2012, p. 283.

31 As proposed in: F. Zoll, Das Dienstleistungsrecht im Vorschlag für ein Gemeinsames Europäisches Kaufrecht, in: H. Schulte-Nölke/F. Zoll/ N. Jansen/R. Schulze, Der Entwurf für ein optionales europäisches Kaufrecht, Sellier, München 2012, p. 287.

32 COM(2015) 634 final.

33 Www.europarl.europa.eu/RegData/etudes/BRIE/2018/614707/EPRS_BRI(2018)614707_EN.pdf; See also H. Beale, Scope of application and general approach of the new rules on contracts in digital environment. Workshop for the Juris, 2016, p. 12.

overarching concepts for the rules on non-performance, adequate for the widest possible array of contractual configurations.[34] Finally, however, the rules for the envisaged directive are too close to the model of sales. The drafters of the proposal were trying to escape from the strictly contract-of-sales-based solutions of the failed proposal for the Common European Sales Law, but despite using different terminology, they have landed not very far from the CESL model.[35] The proposal for the directive is an important step, but one may doubt whether it really addresses the most practically relevant matters.

In a world of services, we also face the phenomenon that services, or even products, often result from services rendered by many suppliers that are not legally connected. This phenomenon is discernible in smart goods that are equipped with software that is updated by a supplier that did not sell the goods, or in 3D printers, where the quality of the final product (printed item) depends on many unconnected suppliers. The future and real relevance of 3D printers, however, remains uncertain. It is also an unresolved question whether the widespread nature of this technology will have an advantageous or disadvantageous impact on the environment. This depends on the legal infrastructure of 3D printers, on whether future legislation will discourage non-useful printing and whether out-of-use printed objects will be recycled. 3D printing technology shows that the development of technology and new models of satisfying the needs of customers do not necessarily mean that these new models will turn out to be more environment-friendly than their predecessors. There is always a risk that a new technology will charge ecological resources in a new, unexpected way.[36]

We also experience the multipole structure of services in case of intermediary platforms.[37] In these constellations, the final result depends on the interaction of many subjects that not necessarily depend on each other. The current phenomenon of the need for collaboration between formally independent service providers to achieve a final result that satisfies the needs of the client may require more legislative intervention.[38]

---

34 On services in the draft for the CESL see: H. W. Micklitz, N. Reich, The Commission Proposal For A "Regulation On A Common European Sales Law. Too Broad Or Not Too Broad Enough, EUI Working Paper Law 2012/04 pp. 16 – 17; F. Zoll, Das Dienstleistungsrecht im Vorschlag für ein Gemeinsames Europäisches Kaufrecht, in: H. Schulte-Nölke/F. Zoll/ N. Jansen/R. Schulze, Der Entwurf für ein optionales europäisches Kaufrecht, Sellier, München 2012, p. 280.

35 F. Zoll: The Remedies in the Proposals of the Online Sales Directive and the Directive on the Supply of Digital Content 6/2016, pp. 252 – 253.

36 Http://wyborcza.pl/Jutronauci/7,167331,24254299,druk-3d-czy-to-koniec-rewolucji.html.

37 Ch. Busch, H. Schulte-Nölke, A. Wiewiórowska-Domagalska, F. Zoll, The Rise of the Platform Economy, 3/2016, pp. 3 – 10; A New Challenge for EU Consumer Law T. Pertot/M. D'Onofrio: Platforms – Business Models and Contracts, EuCML 4/2017, pp. 170 – 172; See also T. Dodsworth: Intermediaries as Sellers – a commentary on Wathelet, EuCML 5/2017, p. 213.

38 A.de Francheschi, Uber Spain and the "Identity Crisis" of Online Platforms, EuCML 1/2018, pp. 1 – 4, Busch: Towards a "New Approach" for the Platform Ecosystem: A European Standard for Fairness in Platform-to-Business Relations, EuCML 6/2017, pp. 227 – 228.

Nevertheless, the difficult quest for addressing services with proper legislative and non-legislative measures must continue. Several legislative and non-legislative measures will be required to ensure rules on services that fit our times.

2. FEAR OF DECREASING SALES-BASED CONSUMER PROTECTION

The fact that the needs of consumers will more often be satisfied not by sales, but through different kinds of access-granting to products (like *e.g.* through consumer-owned or rented 3D printers, or through contracts theoretically granting only temporal access to products: rental contracts, leasing[39], etc.) may lead to a decrease in consumer protection. For these kinds of contracts, there is a lack of European legislation that is comparable with the Consumer Sales Directive. In case of a lack of conformity of the products, the consumer may be deprived of effective remedies against service providers and suppliers. On the other hand, the question arises whether expanding mandatory law would be a good answer to the challenges of the heterogeneous contractual structure.

There is also another challenge, even to traditional sales law. An economy based on the sustainability of products does not always meet the expectations of the consumer, if they care little about the ecological advantages of the products and rather focus on the maximalisation on of the utility features.[40] It must be considered whether the planned Directive on Consumer Sales[41], which is set to replace Directive 99/44, should find a better balance between the justified expectations of buyers and the objective ecological requirement of the goods.

The general reshaping of the system is also difficult due to the fact that the future of consumer law is uncertain.[42] The clearly defined person of 'the consumer' is becoming more obscure – it is much more difficult to attribute a clear function to the parties to a contract. Combined with the deconstruction

39 F. Zoll, The DCFR's specific part of the law of obligations and its feasibility for the development of a modern contract law, in: D. Voinot, J. Sénéchal, vers un droit Européen des contrats spéciaux, 2012, chapter 5, p. 112.

40 Busch: Towards a "New Approach" for the Platform Ecosystem: A European Standard for Fairness in Platform-to-Business Relations.

41 Amended proposal for a Directive of the European Parliament and of the Council on certain aspects concerning contracts for the online and other distance sales of goods, amending Regulation (EC) No 2006/2004 of the European Parliament and of the Council and Directive 2009/22/EC of the European Parliament and of the Council and repealing Directive 1999/44/EC of the European Parliament and of the Council, COM(2017) 637 final.

42 F. Zoll, At the end of the concept of a consumer?, in: J. Lazar, M. Gajdosová, Social function of law and growing wealth inequality, 2018, Trnava: Typi Universitatis Tyrnaviensis, p. 90.

of the easily standardised contract of sales, this process of deconstructing the notion of consumer causes a lot of uncertainty.[43]

3. STANDARDS FOR SERVICES – THE HARMONISATION OF HETEROGENEITY

Statutory law is less and less adaptable to ongoing change. Hence, even lawmakers are considering a completely new approach to the regulation of services. EU law and in particular Regulation (EU) No 1025/2012 on European standardisation try to capture the concept of technical standards and endorse their use in the area of the law on services. This development creates an alternative to the concept of legal harmonisation through "hard legislation" – directives and regulations: instead, homogeneity of the rules on services can be achieved through the development of standards that are not strictly speaking "law", but provisions that may be qualified as standard terms. However, this contractual qualification does not fully describe the phenomenon of such standards. These standards have an indirect legitimacy that stems from the merit of the expert groups adopting the standards. Notably, standards are not generally accessible to the public: a service provider who needs or wants to comply with the standards must acquire them. Compliance with the standard may not only be enforced through the reality of the market, but also directly or indirectly by law. By way of example, this could be specified in the tender in case of public procurement. Alternatively, it could play a role in the assessment of non-performance, if the standards become a measure for the legitimate expectations of clients. The standardisation of services marks quite a different path for determining the content of legal relationships that challenges the traditional theory of the sources of law of contracts.[44] Standardisation allows for a much faster reaction to the fluid reality of services and also allows for a set of rules to be provided to the growing number of services that cannot be easily classified in groups of contracts. Standardisation is therefore an answer to the dilemma of many lawmakers that attempt to propose a new law on contracts that will be more service-oriented, but face the problem of heterogeneity of services and the difficulties in drafting general rules that apply to all services. The idea of standardisation facilitates this undertaking, allowing for a more general approach to services in legal codes, as well as operable and flexible standards.

---

43 F. Zoll, At the end of the concept of a consumer?, p. 90.

44 Ch. Busch, DIN-Normen für Dienstleistungen – Das Europäische Normungskomitee produziert Musterverträge, NJW 42/2010, pp. 3061 – 3066.

4. BETWEEN HARMONISATION AND GRANULARITY – ON THE NEED FOR MORE JUDICIAL FLEXIBILITY. INEVITABLE EXPANSION OF ADR. WILL FLEXIBILITY REPLACE THE LAW?

The progress of technology and the rise of online platforms, blockchains, smart contracts and self-adapting contracts influence and will continue to influence the close future of the law on services. It may be argued that legal systems based on the clear distinction between fact and duty (*Sein und Sollen*) are collapsing. The digital architecture allows for the rise of a new way of functioning for contract law. Contracts are concluded electronically, are often self-executing and even self-adapting in case of changing circumstances. Some authors see the development of so-called "granular law" as the future of private law.[45] Granular law means an individualised law that, based on big data that allow for the profiling of clients and the development of specific rules, adjusts to the needs of the parties and the circumstances of the case. The development of granular law will lead to the disappearance of the difference between the abstract and the concrete rule or, at least, it will move the abstract rule to the level of the algorithms governing the "granular" rule that is applicable to the case at hand. It is, however, difficult to predict in which direction the law will develop and whether granular law has a future as a useful concept. In any case, we must look for solutions that consist of flexible rules adaptable to the heterogeneous world of services.

Alternative dispute resolution (ADR) mechanisms are linked to services in particular and are likely especially adjusted thereto.[46] Online platforms often include different dispute resolution systems. In practice, dispute resolution becomes privatised and based on autonomous systems that are driven by different incentives than governmental justice. The decision can be rendered *e.g.* in a bid to develop the "attractive power" of the business model. As a result, such decisions are not taken by applying the law as such. This does not mean that they are automatically unfair. The legal system does not exist in the background and serves as a reference frame for the decision-making process.

---

45 Ch. Busch, A. de Franceschi, Granular Legal Norms: Big Data and the Personalization of Private Law, (March 06, 2018). Forthcoming in Vanessa Mak, Eric Tjong Tjin Tai and Anna Berlee (eds), Research Handbook on Data Science and Law, Edward Elgar 2018. Available at SSRN: https://ssrn.com/abstract=3181914 F. Zoll, At the end of the concept of a consumer?, in: J. Lazar, M. Gajdosová, Social function of law and growing wealth inequality,2018, Trnava: Typi Universitatis Tyrnaviensis, p. 94.

46 H.Schulte-Nölke: The Brave New World of EU Consumer Law – Without Consumers, or Even Without Law? EuCML, 4/2015, p. 137; Ch. Busch/S. Reinhold: Standardisation of Online Dispute Resolution Services: Towards a More Technological Approach, p. 50; N. Creutzfeldt, Alternative Dispute Resolutions for Consumers, in: M. Stürner, F. Gascón Inchausti, R. Caponi, The Role of Consumer ADR in the Administration of Justice, 2015, p. 3.

5. THE DISAPPEARANCE OF LAW?

We are facing a time of reshaping the function of law. Technology removes the difference between the normative content of the law and its application. This phenomenon is not only restricted to services: it encompasses a vast array of legal relationships, while it cannot be denied that the majority of these relationships include a service component.[47] The legal framework of services, and maybe of contract law in general, will be (and maybe even already is) suppressed by self-regulating systems that are supported or dominated by technology. The general theory of contracts must be reconsidered and the legal system must find a way to maintain its regulatory function, ensuring that the goals that are important from the perspective of the lawmaker will be attained. Services are also a challenge from the perspective of the legislator, due to their heterogeneity, complexity and permanently changing nature. The rise of technology increases these difficulties. Service providers are less dependent on the state and its monopoly in relation to the enforcement of rights. Technology may secure self-enforcement. Moreover, the state-based rules governing the non-performance of obligations become less important than the feedback-system, which often provides the customer with much more powerful tools of pressure and reaction in case of failure to perform the obligations regarding services. This mere fact removes the attractive power of state-driven legislation.[48] The law remains in power, but loses its regulatory ability. This does not mean, however, that regulatory functions are not needed. Due to the need to move contract law into a more environment-oriented direction, regulatory tools are needed even more. Providers of technology must be charged with duties aimed at achieving the regulatory goals of the government. This may cause other threats to the liberal economy. The picture of how to regulate contractual relationships and especially services in the future remains in a very early stage of *status nascendi*.

47 As mentioned in: F. Zoll, Das Dienstleistungsrecht im Vorschlag für ein Gemeinsames Europäisches Kaufrecht, in: H. Schulte-Nölke/F. Zoll/ N. Jansen/R. Schulze, Der Entwurf für ein optionales europäisches Kaufrecht, Sellier, München 2012, p. 279.

48 H. Schulte-Nölke: The Brave New World of EU Consumer Law, p. 137.

TITLE II

NATIONAL INITIATIVES – MOVABLES

TOWARDS A CIRCULAR ECONOMY IN EU CONSUMER MARKETS

Legal Possibilities and Legal Challenges and the Dutch Example*

Vanessa MAK and Enna LUJINOVIC**

1. INTRODUCTION

The development of the circular economy is on the European Union as well as on the member states' agendas. In December 2015, the European Commission presented a 'Circular Economy Package' as part of its continuous effort to transform Europe's economy into a more sustainable one.[1] The implementation of that package was fleshed out in an action plan from the Commission that has formed the basis for a number of legislative initiatives aimed at waste management and recycling, and on specific actions in relation to eco-innovation and consumption.[2] Recently, in May 2018, the EU member states gave their seal of approval to a set of new rules based on the circular economy package.[3] At the same time, businesses are taking measures to implement production schemes that enable the reuse and return of resources with the aim of minimising environmental harm. In the Netherlands, for example, Amsterdam

---

* This contribution also appeared as an article in (2019) 8 *Journal of European Consumer and Market Law* 4-13.

** Vanessa Mak is a Professor of Private Law at Tilburg University. Enna Lujinovic is a master student at the same university. This article is based on a presentation given at the University of Leuven on 4 May 2018 as part of the conference 'Consumer Protection in a Circular Economy'. We thank the participants of the conference for their feedback, which has helped to develop the argument presented in this article.

1 See <http://ec.europa.eu/environment/circular-economy/index_en.htm>.

2 Communication from the Commission to the European Parliament, the Council, the European Economic and Social Committee and the Committee of the Regions, 'Closing the Loop – An EU Action Plan for the Circular Economy' COM(2015) 614 final. See also <http://ec.europa.eu/environment/green-growth/index_en.htm> for an overview of the areas in which actions are being taken.

3 European Comission, 'Circular Economy: New rules will make EU the global front-runner in waste management and recyclying', press release (Brussels, 22 May 2018), available at: <http://europa.eu/rapid/press-release_IP-18-3846_en.htm>.

Airport Schiphol has incorporated sustainability actions into their Corporate Responsibility strategy. One example of their strategy is an agreement with Philips for the supply of lighting in one of the airport terminals, under which rather than buying lamps, the airport buys light. Philips has the freedom to choose which luminaires to use, and to repair and take them back over time, hence expanding the lifetime of assets and materials to effectuate a circular economy.[4] Importantly, however, business activities may also conflict with sustainability goals, or even seek to circumvent them. The US Environmental Protection Agency found in 2015 that Volkswagen sold cars with a 'defeat device', which tampered with its emission controls during testing, lowering the values of carbon emissions so that they fell within EU and US environmental standards.[5] The Volkswagen scandal raised awareness of environmental aspects of consumer markets, and illustrates that regulation can fall short of protecting sustainability goals as well as consumer interests. Regulation will have to be reviewed in light of both these goals.[6] Part of such renewed sustainability policies will be the pursuit of a circular economy, in which resources are used and re-used in the most efficient manner.

The idea of a circular economy is not completely new, but it is closely connected to sustainability goals and has in that light gained renewed momentum in recent years. While definitions may include various aspects, generally speaking the term circular economy designates an economy where the value of products and materials is maintained for as long as possible. In its broadest definition, the circular economy relates to all actions that can be taken to use and reuse the earth's resources in a continuous flow to produce useful products and services.[7] Some of those actions will be aimed at the regeneration of biological resources, whereas others will be directed at restoring technical nutrients such as metals and synthetic fibers.[8] These actions implicate human activity which seeks to 'meet the needs of the present without compromising the ability of future generations to meet their own needs' or, in other words, sustainability.[9]

---

4 See <www.lighting.philips.com/cases/cases/airports/schiphol-airport> and, for other examples of sustainable projects run by Schiphol, <https://www.ellenmacarthurfoundation.org/ce100/directory/schiphol-nederland-b-v>.

5 'The Volkswagen Emissions Scandal Explained', *The Guardian* 23 September 2015.

6 See European Political Strategy Centre, 'Towards Low-Emission Mobility. Driving the Mondernisation of the EU Economy' (2016), available at https://ec.europa.eu/epsc/publications/strategic-notes/towards-low-emission-mobility_en.

7 Compare Kate Raworth, *Doughnut Economics* (Random House 2017) 220, with reference to Ken Webster, *The Circular Economy. A Wealth of Flows* (Ellen MacArthur Foundation 2015; 2nd edn 2017).

8 This is depicted in the butterfly diagram developed by the Ellen MacArthur Foundation; see <https://www.ellenmacarthurfoundation.org/circular-economy/interactive-diagram>.

9 Citing one of the most commonly accepted definitions of sustainability; see Brian R Keeble, 'The Brundtland Report: Our Common Future' (1988) 4 Medicine & War 17. See also Martin Geissdoerfer cs, 'The Circular Economy – a New Sustainability Paradigm?' (2017) 143 Journal

One might also say that a circular economy is assumed to be a precondition for sustainability.[10]

This article seeks to examine how consumer law can be used in support of the development of the circular economy. That means that its focus is on the regulation of business-to-consumer transactions (B2C), and how the legal framework for these transactions can contribute to sustainability goals. It should be noted that this perspective broadens the theoretical framework within which consumer lawyers tend to think. In that framework, the regulation of B2C relationships is seen as a balancing of party autonomy on the one hand, and consumer protection rights for the sake of the weaker party on the other.[11] Other societal goals, such as sustainability, may of course in practice overlap or interfere with that framework but the ways in which they should be integrated into consumer law have not been established.[12] Practically, at least two situations may be envisaged.[13] In some cases sustainability and consumer protection goals will coincide, e.g. in situations where consumer law aims to ensure that consumers can reasonably assess whether 'green' products are actually green, and will not be misled by advertising or product information.[14] In other cases, sustainability goals may compete with consumer protection. An example, which will be discussed below, is the question whether a trader may replace a defective mobile phone with a refurbished phone.[15] The development of the circular

of Cleaner Production 757, 766, who highlight that sustainability encompasses not only environmental protection, but also social inclusiveness and economic performance.

10 See Geissdoerfer cs (n 4) 764 and Eline van Weelden, Ruth Mugge and Conny Bakker, 'Paving the Way Towards Circular Consumption: Exploring Consumer Acceptance of Refurbished Mobile Phones in the Dutch market' (2016) 113 Journal of Cleaner Production 743, 744. See also Ellen MacArthur Foundation, 'Towards the Circular Economy. Economic and Business Rationale for an Accelerated Transition' (2013), available at: <https://www.ellenmacarthurfoundation.org/assets/downloads/publications/Ellen-MacArthur-Foundation-Towards-the-Circular-Economy-vol.1.pdf>.

11 Ewoud Hondius, 'The Notion of Consumer: European Union versus Member States' (2006) 28 Sydney Law Review 89, 93.

12 The relatively sparse literature that has engaged with the relationship between consumer law and sustainability reveals that EU policy has primarily focused on 'light touch' regimes that appeal to EU citizens to endorse sustainable lifestyles. See Jens Karsten and Lucia A Reisch, 'Sustainability Policy and the Law' (2008) 4 German Policy Studies 45, 48; Oksana Mont and Carl Dalhammar, 'Sustainable Consumption: At the Crossroads of Environmental and Consumer Policies' (2005) 8 International Journal of Sustainable Development 258.

13 For an in-depth analysis of the converging and competing aims of environmental and consumer law, see Cecelia Kye, 'Environmental Law and the Consumer in the European Union' (1995) 7 Journal of Environmental Law 31, 32 ff.

14 The EU seeks to protect consumers against false environmental claims. A stakeholder group agreed on a set of criteria for fair environmental claims in 2016, resulting in updated guidance on the application of Directive 2005/29/EC on unfair commercial practices. See <https://ec.europa.eu/info/live-work-travel-eu/consumers/unfair-treatment/unfair-treatment-policy-information_en>. The Volkswagen case has since then triggered legal action in many of the EU member states. For a series of country reports, see Journal of European Consumer and Market Law (EuCML), issues 2017/1 and 2017/2.

15 See below, section 3.2.

economy through consumer law therefore entails a broadening of the theoretical framework of consumer law, including the trade-offs that may have to be made between sustainability and consumer protection goals.[16]

Interestingly, the European Union includes both goals in its objectives, as can be seen in Article 3(3) of the Treaty on European Union (TEU). It is stipulated in that provision that the Union shall work for 'a highly competitive social market economy', which read in conjunction with other provisions in the EU Treatiesencompasses consumer protection goals, and for 'a high level of protection and improvement of the quality of the environment'. The goals are given hands and feet through Articles 11 and 12 of the Treaty on the Functioning of the European Union (TFEU) which require environmental protection and consumer protection to be integrated into the definition and implementation of the Union's policies and activities. Those requirements are repeated in Articles 37 and 38 of the EU Charter of Fundamental Rights, and the Union's goals are further elaborated in secondary legislation in the fields of consumer and environmental law. The balancing of these goals, in instances where they compete, however remains a question for the legislator or the courts to decide within the boundaries of their respective political and legal competences.

Having sketched the background against which the development of the circular economy through consumer law will be examined, the next part turns to defining to which aspects of the circular economy regulation may be directed. To demarcate the scope of the enquiry, we focus on prevalent business models in consumer markets, in which examples are drawn from experiences in the Netherlands. The Netherlands is chosen as an example due to its strong commitment to circular economy strategies in recent years, as well as the many innovative business solutions that have emerged in its jurisdiction in recent years.[17] Three aspects of these business models – durability, return, and use

---

16 Wilhemsson's view that the relationship between consumer law and environmental protection is one of conflict rather than harmony – Thomas Wilhelmsson, 'Consumer Law and the Environment: From Consumer to Citizen' (1998) 21 Journal of Consumer Policy 45 – therefore seems to have been overtaken by the rise of 'green' consumers in the new millennium. Some marketing studies have sought to identify relevant market segments for green consumers; see Arminda M Finisterra do Paço, Mário Lino Barata Raposo and Walter Leal Filho, 'Identifying the Green Consumer: A Segmentation Study' (2009) 17 Journal of Targeting, Measurement and Analysis for Marketing 17.

17 The Netherlands, other than many EU member states, has expressed a self-standing commitment to the implementation of the circular economy in a holistic and long-term strategic way. That implementation is therefore regarded as an autonomous goal, rather than as embedded in a general long-term strategy e.g. for the economy, sustainable development or energy. This means that actions are focused broadly and aim to encompass, for example, the entire value chain instead of only elements in the circular chain of production. It differs from other EU member states in this respect, but also takes a relatively long time span for achieving its circular economy policy goals: the strategic goals are aimed to be fulfilled in 2050. See Dutch Council for the Environment and Infrastructure (Rli), 'Europe Goes Circular. Outlining the Implementation of a Circular Economy in the European Area', available at <https://www.rli.nl/sites/default/files/rli_eu_goes_circular_-_eeac_working_group_on_circular_economy_def_1.pdf>, pp 9–10.

– will form the basis for an analysis of the legal trade-offs between consumer protection and sustainability in consumer law in parts III, IV and V. Part VI wraps up with a brief recapitulation of how this trade-off currently works out – as will be seen, consumer protection for now prevails – and an outlook for future regulatory action. It should be noted that while we use the Netherlands as a case study, many conclusions on the application of rules of consumer contract law may be generalised to other legal systems in Europe, in particular since relevant rules of consumer law have been subject to harmonisation.

2. THE CIRCULAR ECONOMY IN CONSUMER MARKETS

In consumer markets a range of business models can be discerned that seeks to stimulate the regenerative use of resources. Without seeking to be exhaustive, at least five business models prevail in existing markets:

- Recycling model: Recycling is considered to be one of the most established means of diverting waste from landfills and thus to contribute to a circular economy.[18] By using this model, businesses can recycle their waste and keep their products and materials in use. Recycling is seen as complementary to reuse and reduce, together referred to as the 3Rs.[19]
- Waste value model: One of the aims of the circular economy is to 'design out' waste. This means that components of products are designed by companies with the intention to fit within a biological or technical materials cycle, so that they are fit for disassembly and refurbishment. Hence, these components can be used again with minimal energy and with the highest quality retention. This model resembles recycling but it is not completely the same. The term recycling is used in relation to the complete regeneration of waste materials, whereas the waste value model can also take the form of reuse of components.[20] Further, recycling is often understood to result in a reduction of quality whilst the waste value model is aimed at retaining high product quality.[21]
- Lifespan model: Within this model the focus is on the durability of products. This means that new products are designed in ways that seek to extend the

See also Government of the Netherlands, 'A Circular Economy in the Netherlands by 2050. Government-wide Programme for a Circular Economy', available at: https://www.government.nl/documents/policy-notes/2016/09/14/a-circular-economy-in-the-netherlands-by-2050.

18 Michael Luchs cs, 'Towards a Sustainable Marketplace: Expanding Options and Benefits for Consumers' (2011) 19 Journal of Research for Consumers 1, 7.

19 Luis F Diay, 'The 3Rs as the Basis for Sustainable Waste Management: Moving Towards Zero Waste' (2012) 2.

20 Raworth (n 2) 222.

21 Ellen MacArthur Foundation (n 5) 22.

utilization period of products. Another aspect of this model that contributes to sustainability goals is that the overall usage of materials is slowed down.[22]

- Platform model: The platform model is based on the collaboration among product users and producers to share goods.[23] Platforms can facilitate the sharing of overcapacity or underutilization of resources and can thus increase productivity and decrease the waste of resources.[24] In consumer markets, examples are platforms that enable the shared use of cars or accommodation that would otherwise be unused for long periods of time.
- Product-as-service model: The product-as-service model is described as: 'a marketable set of products and services capable of jointly fulfilling a user's need.'[25] It can be offered in different varieties, sometimes as a product with additional services (e.g. maintenance or a help desk for users) or sometimes as a service with an additional product (e.g. lighting with lamps included, as in the Schiphol-Philips example in the introduction of this article). The model is seen by many as a perfect combination to both enhance competitiveness and to foster sustainability.[26]

For the analysis of sustainability and consumer protection goals it is not per se helpful to consider each business model on its own, as there are overlaps in the mechanisms that they adopt to regenerate or restore resources. It is more helpful therefore to focus on the functions that the various models have in the circular economy. From that perspective, aspects of the circular economy that are covered by these models are durability, return and shared use.[27]

Durability concerns efforts made to ensure that goods last for as long as possible before they are discarded. This is of particular importance for products in which technical nutrients are used, which cannot be regenerated, and for which the most sustainable solution is to use and restore them for as long as possible.[28] Of the five models described here, the lifespan model fits with that function.

---

22 Conny Bakker cs, 'Products that Go Round: Exploring Product Life Extension through Design' (2014) 69 Journal of Cleaner Production 10, finding that product life extension is the best strategy for refrigerators and laptops.

23 Arun Sundararajan, *The Sharing Economy* (MIT Press 2016) 26–27.

24 Ibid.

25 Mark J Goedkoop cs, 'Product Service Systems, Ecological and Economic Basics' (Report for the Dutch Ministries of the Environment (VROM) and Economic Affairs (EZ) 1999).

26 Arnold Tukker, 'Eight Types of Product-Service System: Eight Ways to Sustainability? Experiences from Suspronet' (2004) 13 Business Strategy and the Environment 246, 246.

27 These three functions are reflected also in current debates at the EU level on the implementation of the circular economy package. See e.g. European Network of the Heads of Environment Protection Agencies (EPA Network) – Interest Group on Green and Circular Economy, 'Input to the European Commission from European EPAs about Monitoring Progress of the Transition towards a Circular Economy in the European Union', discussion paper (May 2017), available at <https://www.pbl.nl/sites/default/files/cms/publicaties/PBL-2017-EPA-network-discussion-paper-monitoring-progress-of-the-circular-economy-in-the-EU_2772.pdf>, p 7, figure 4.

28 Compare the butterfly diagram, n 2.

Return concerns actions enabling consumers to return goods to the trader after having used them for a long-term period. The trader can reuse (parts of) the returned goods and turn them into new products (the waste value model and the recycling model both have this function) or sell or rent out the returned goods to new purchasers (product-as-service model). Various legal constructions can be used to support the return function, mostly through contract, although some have property law consequences.

Use is similar to the return mechanism in many respects but distinctions are that it usually involves short-term arrangements for the use of goods, and that it also includes services. Models that fit with this function are the platform model and forms of the product-as-service model, such as the Schiphol-Philips arrangement from the introduction of this article.

Each of these functions can be supported through legal mechanisms that seek to persuade businesses as well as consumers to contribute to the circular economy. At the same time, however, extant consumer rights may be challenged. In the following, we examine the legal possibilities and challenges of pursuing durability, return and use through consumer law, with specific focus on consumer contract law.

3. DURABILITY

Durability can be boosted through rules of consumer sale of goods law that aim to secure a longer lifespan for goods. Mechanisms that can be used are legal and commercial guarantees and modalities of the right to repair. In both cases, the primary reason for the introduction of these rights in legislation has been to strengthen consumer protection vis-à-vis businesses. The balancing that underlies legislative choices is therefore between the interests of consumers on the one hand and those of traders or producers on the other hand. Sustainability can be one aspect that is weighed in this balancing of interests.

Generally speaking, consumer interests reflected in European private laws include that they may hold and enforce reasonable expectations concerning the lifespan of goods, and obtain an effective remedy for non-conformity of goods for free and within a reasonable time.[29] On the business side, producers and traders have an interest in keeping the costs of remedies low, not being stuck with returned defective goods that can no longer be sold as new, and limited liability periods. The EU has laid down rules of minimum harmonisation for distance sales and other, physical consumer sales transactions.[30] In some cases

29 Harmonised rules to this effect are laid down in Directive 99/44/EC on certain aspects of the sale of consumer goods and associated guarantees [1999] OJ L171/12 (Consumer Sales Directive), Art 3.

30 Directive 2011/83/EU on consumer rights OJ L304/64 (Consumer Rights Directive) and the Consumer Sales Directive.

member states have maintained stricter consumer protection rules, e.g. with regard to the expected lifespan of goods.

These rules are part of a proposed revision through a new EU Directive on online and other sales of goods to consumers, which is envisaged to be adopted later this year.[31] That Directive may substantially affect the existing balance of rights between consumers and businesses, in particular in relation to limitation periods for invoking remedies. If the proposal goes through in its original form and fixes the time limit at two years from delivery of the goods[32] it will put pressure not only on consumer expectations concerning lifespan, but also on sustainability goals. Also if an alternative solution is adopted, the balance between consumer protection and sustainability deserves careful consideration. In addition, another proposed EU Directive on digital content contracts may introduce new rules that affect consumer expectations with regard to the availability of digital content, such as security software updates, for a reasonable time after purchase and thereby indirectly affect expectations with regard to the lifespan of goods.[33]

We will consider in more detail whether, and if so how, sustainability goals may be pursued through (i) guarantees, and (ii) the modalities of the right to repair in consumer sales law.

3.1. GUARANTEES

Consumers can under current EU laws, including the laws of the member states, invoke remedies against the seller as well as the producer of goods in case of non-conformity. The harmonised remedies against the seller are repair, replacement, price reduction and rescission of the contract.[34] National laws give consumers additional remedies, such as a right to claim damages from the seller, or a right

---

31 European Commission, Proposal for a Directive of the European Parliament and of the Council on certain aspects concerning contracts for the online and other distance sales of goods, COM(2015) 635 final. The European Parliament has published its suggested amendments, whereas the proposal has only recently been discussed in the Council on 20 June 2018. See <www.europarl.europa.eu/legislative-train/theme-connected-digital-single-market/file-jd-consumer-sale-of-goods>.

32 See Art 14 of the proposed Directive. The beginning of the time period is a little more nuanced but in most cases will be the time of delivery of the goods to the consumer or a carrier; see Art 8 of the proposed Directive.

33 European Commission, Proposal for a Directive of the European Parliament and of the Council on certain aspects concerning contracts for the supply of digital content, COM(2015) 634 final. The proposal is in the final stages of the legislative process, albeit it that negotiations are taking a long time. Trilogue negotiations have been ongoing since December 2017. See <www.europarl.europa.eu/legislative-train/theme-connected-digital-single-market/file-jd-digital-content-and-digital-services>.

34 Consumer Sales Directive, Art 3(2).

to withhold performance.[35] These remedies laid down by law are often referred to as legal guarantees.[36]

Remedies against producers mostly take the form of so-called commercial guarantees. The producer stipulates in its standard terms and conditions that the consumer has certain rights – e.g. to repair or replacement free of cost – during a fixed time after the conclusion of the contract.[37] Often this time period is set at one or two years from purchase. This arrangement has advantages, in particular because consumers can claim a remedy without having to go through troublesome steps to prove the non-conformity of the goods. After the first six months from delivery – during which the consumer benefits from a reversed burden of proof –[38] the onus is on the consumer to show that the goods were non-conforming from the time of delivery and that a defect was not caused by his or her handling of the goods. Whilst commercial guarantees therefore seem attractive, they also have a downside for the consumer. Effectively, they function as limitations of liability for the producer. After the expiration of the guarantee, many consumers believe that they cannot invoke remedies for non-conformity against the producer anymore. While that is false, since consumers can still invoke any legal rights that the applicable national law gives them[39], the practical effect in many cases is that consumers will refrain from claiming remedies.[40]

In the context of the circular economy both types of guarantees could function as mechanisms for enhancing the durability of goods. The right to repair – discussed below – can stimulate the use of goods for a longer time, instead of discarding them when they are defective. Commercial guarantees of the producer also could be designed in such a way that repair is stimulated, rather than the replacement of goods.

Vital for each guarantee, however, is the length of time during which the consumer can invoke remedies. With the 1999 Consumer Sales Directive prescribing that the minimum period for the pursuit of consumer remedies should be two years, some member states have provided for longer periods of legal guarantee.[41] The Netherlands has even refrained from setting a maximum period and takes the normal lifespan of goods as the benchmark for consumer remedies for non-conformity. Conformity relates to the reasonable expectations that a consumer may hold with regard to the purchased goods.[42] Since that

35 In the Netherlands, see Art 6:74 Dutch Civil Code (DCC) for the general provision on damages for breach of contract, and Art 6:265 DCC for termination.

36 Aneta Wiewiórowska-Domagalska, *Consumer Sales Guarantees in the European Union* (Verlag Dr Otto Schmidt 2012) 128.

37 For an analysis of the typical form of manufacturer guarantees see Christian Twigg-Flesner, *Consumer Product Guarantees* (Ashgate 2003), Chapter 2.

38 Consumer Sales Directive, Art 5(3).

39 Producers are obliged to be transparent about this; see Consumer Sales Directive, Art 6(2).

40 Wiewiórowska-Domagalska (n 12) 5–6.

41 Periods of three or five years are not uncommon. See below.

42 Art. 7:17 Dutch Civil Code; see also Consumer Sales Directive, Art 2.

includes the normal time for which a consumer could have expected the goods to be without defects, the remedies for non-conformity apply until the end of the normal lifespan of the goods. For a number of frequently sold consumer goods, such as smartphones, laptops, washing machines and coffee machines, guidelines have been developed by consumer organisations and industry as to what a normal, average lifespan amounts to.[43]

The proposed Directives on consumer sales and on digital content contracts are likely to bring changes to the legal guarantees currently applied in the EU member states, albeit that it is not settled in which respects. The question whether to limit the time during which consumers may claim remedies for non-conformity to two years for goods, laid down in Article 14 of the proposal on sale of goods, is debated and it seems unlikely that this rule goes through in its original form. The European Parliament has suggested to maintain a minimum harmonisation approach in this respect, which would allow member states to introduce or maintain longer periods during which consumer remedies may be pursued.[44] A study carried out on behalf of the European Commission as part of the Fitness Check of European consumer law[45] concludes that a favourable outcome from a cost-benefit perspective would be for time limits to be set at three or five years.[46] The Dutch option to maintain longer, undefined periods for the pursuit of remedies is deemed rather complex for a regime to be developed at the EU level.[47] Nonetheless, overall the benefits of longer time limits are emphasized and, interestingly, also defended on the basis of sustainability goals. They would lead to a reduction of waste and potentially also tackle the problem of planned obsolescence, i.e. the practice of producers to lower the quality of goods on purpose so that they break down faster and force consumers to buy new ones.[48] Whilst the compliance costs for businesses may be higher, a significant number of business respondents participating in the

---

[43] Consumentenbond, Levensduurlijst elektronica, DigitaalGids mei/juni 2016, 20–23; UNETO-VNI, Tabel met gemiddelde gebruiksduurverwachtingen, available at <https://www.uneto-vni.nl/onze-leden/waar-staan-onze-leden-voor/gebruiksduurverwachting>.

[44] European Parliament, 'Consumer Sale of Goods' (Briefing EU Legislation in Process, March 2018), available at: <www.europarl.europa.eu/RegData/etudes/BRIE/2018/614744/EPRS_BRI(2018)614744_EN.pdf>, 5.

[45] For an appraisal of the results of the Fitness Check and the New Deal for Consumers presented in April 2018, see Christian Twigg-Flesner, 'Bad Hand? The "New Deal" for EU Consumers' (May 2018), available at SSRN: <https://ssrn.com/abstract=3178952>.

[46] ICF, 'Study on the Costs and Benefits of Extending Certain Rights under the Consumer Sales and Guarantees Directive 1999/44/EC' (March 2017), available at: <http://ec.europa.eu/newsroom/just/item-detail.cfm?item_id=59332.>, 61. See also, for an evaluation of the preferred method of harmonisation and concluding in favour of a directive covering online as well as offline sales, Milieu Ltd and Europe Economics, 'Impact Assessment of Proposed Substantial EP Amendments Extending the Scope of the Commission Proposal on Online Sales of Goods to Offline Sales' (June 2017), available at: <www.europarl.europa.eu/RegData/etudes/STUD/2017/603258/EPRS_STU%282017%29603258_EN.pdf>.

[47] ICF (n 28) 61–62.

[48] European Parliament (n 26) 5. For an appraisal of ways to regulate planned obsolescence, see Eléonore Maitre-Ekern and Carl Dalhammer, 'Regulating Planned Obsolescence: A Review

study indicated that they did not think that the extension of the legal guarantee to three or five years would generate additional costs.[49] Also, there appears some willingness to introduce an obligation for businesses to keep spare parts for a minimum period of time – which would also contribute to sustainability goals – although it is hard to estimate the costs of such a rule.[50]

While it might seem that sustainability goals in the case of guarantees coincide with consumer protection since a longer time limit benefits the environment ánd gives additional rights to consumers, it should be noted that consumers may also experiences downsides from this solution. If the time limits for legal guarantees are longer, prices of goods are likely to go up to compensate for the additional costs borne by businesses in relation to consumer remedies. Further, consumer choice may diminish for consumers who are unwilling or unable to pay higher prices for goods.[51] On balance, however, the study carried out for the European Commission concludes that the extension of the time limit for legal guarantees improves consumer protection.[52]

Besides the rules on legal guarantees, the possibilities for introducing harmonised European rules concerning the lifespan of goods have also been considered in relation to commercial guarantees. Whilst there is a case to be made for the introduction of rules that oblige producers (rather than sellers) to guarantee the quality of goods for the duration of their normal lifespan[53], that idea has so far not been translated into legislation. The latest reports on the proposed EU Directive on consumers sales seem to indicate that this is a contested issue. The proposed provision on commercial guarantees, Article 15, is one of the few for which minimum harmonisation has been suggested by the European Parliament. Furthermore, that provision does not refer to the lifespan of goods but only suggests introducing a direct entitlement for consumers to demand repair or replacement from producers.[54] This possibility to pursue sustainability goals, whilst at the same time increasing consumer protection, therefore appears not to have been taken up for now. Perhaps it will be considered in the final version of the proposed consumer sales directive.[55]

---

of Legal Approaches to Increase Product Durability and Reparability in Europe' (2016) 25 Review of European, Comparative & International Environmental Law 378.

49 ICF (n 28) 62.

50 ICF (n 28) 62–63.

51 ICF (n 28) 61.

52 Ibid.

53 Centre for European Policy Studies (CEPS) and Time.lex, 'Impact Assessment of Proposed Substantial Amendments and Introducing a Commercial Lifespan Guarantee in the Proposed Online Sales and Digital Content Directives' (October 2017), available at: <https://www.ceps.eu/system/files/LifetimeGuarantee.pdf>.

54 European Parliament (n 26) 11.

55 A study commissioned by the European Parliament proposes amendments to the proposed Directive on consumer sales and the Ecodesign Directive; see Klaus Tonner and Rosalind Malcolm, 'How an EU Lifespan Guarantee Model Could be Implemented Across the European Union' (Study on behalf of the European Parliament, January 2017), available at: <www.europarl.europa.eu/RegData/etudes/STUD/2017/583121/IPOL_STU(2017)583121_EN.pdf>.

3.2. REPAIR AND REFURBISHED GOODS

The durability of goods can also be supported by giving a more prominent place to the right of repair in consumer sales law. Repair is a primary remedy for non-conformity of goods under harmonised EU consumer sales law.[56] The remedy entails that damaged goods or components are brought back to a functional and usable state[57], and hence made to comply with the reasonable expectations that the consumer was entitled to have under the contract of sale. If goods are repaired, rather than replaced, less waste will be generated and the durable use of goods will be supported.

A specific type of repair, refurbishment, can particularly contribute to sustainability policies in markets for technological products. Refurbishment can be defined as the process whereby dysfunctional goods are restored to a functional state by rebuilding or repairing major components to comply with the original contractual specification.[58] An example of a product for which refurbishment has become widely available is the Apple iPhone.[59] Refurbishment of these phones promotes sustainability as, by virtue of preserving the original energy and labour which was used to build the product, less energy is used than in case of replacement with a new phone.[60]

However, while refurbished and repaired goods contribute to sustainability goals, their success depends on consumer behaviour. That is problematic as practice shows that consumers seem to be cautious towards the modalities offered by traders and favour a new product over a repaired or refurbished one.[61] Current literature indicates that consumers' hesitance towards refurbished products is due to high perceived risks and low perceived quality of refurbished products by consumers. For example, consumers assume as a possible risk of buying refurbished phones that the phone will not work as well or might break down more quickly than a new one.[62]

Case law from the Netherlands confirms this trend in consumer behaviour. Moreover, the case law shows that the current legal framework supports the wish of consumers to obtain a new rather than a refurbished product. In 2016 and 2017 the Amsterdam district court, a court of first instance, ruled on two cases in which consumers did not accept refurbished or remanufactured items as a remedy for non-conformity. First, in 2016 the Amsterdam court had to decide whether non-conformity of a product, in this case a mobile phone, could be cured by the seller's offer of a refurbished phone or whether the consumer

---

56 Art 3 Consumer Sales Directive.
57 Bakker (n 14) 11.
58 Ibid.
59 See <https://www.apple.com/shop/browse/home/specialdeals/iphone>.
60 Van Weelden, Mugge and Bakker (n 5).
61 Ibid, 747.
62 Ibid, 746–747.

was entitled to replacement.[63] The court decided that, in accordance with Article 3 of the Consumer Sales Directive, the consumer has the right to receive a new product as a replacement, instead of a refurbished item. That decision was justified on the basis of the European Court of Justice (CJEU)'s *Quelle* judgment of 2008, in which the European Court held that, 'based on Article 3(1) of the Consumer Sales Directive, in case of a non-conformity product, a consumer does not have to pay compensation for the use of a defective good until replacement with a new good.'[64] The Amsterdam court followed the CJEU's reasoning that, if a seller does not deliver goods that are in conformity with the contract, the seller did not perform the obligations which derive from a contract and must therefore bear the consequences.[65]

While the interpretation of the *Quelle* case by the Amsterdam court is sparsely motivated, it provides a basis for a strong consumer position in case of non-conform products. In 2017 the Amsterdam court repeated its decision in a similar case about a refurbished product, in this case an iPad.[66] Both cases implicate that courts are willing to support the preference of consumers for new products that serve as a replacement. They also underline that consumer protection is put first by the courts. Nevertheless, if the line set out in these cases is followed, there is a clear conflict between sustainability goals and consumer protection. On the one hand, the interpretation of the *Quelle* judgment as dismissing replacement with refurbished goods leads to a strict protection of consumer rights; on the other hand that interpretation does very little for the stimulation of sustainable alternatives.

We believe that a better balance should be sought between consumer rights and the stimulation of sustainable alternatives. One possibility would be to submit a preliminary question to the CJEU, should a similar case comes before a national court, to inquire whether the correct interpretation of *Quelle* is indeed that Article 3 of the Consumer Sales Directive entitles consumers to replacement with a new, rather than a refurbished, good. Since the European Union is stimulating a circular economy, it would be interesting to see to whether the Court would emphasize the stimulation of the circular economy or whether it would provide a strict interpretation on the protection of consumer rights. Granted, the Court seems to have little space for maneuvering within the rules concerning the consumer's entitlement to repair and replacement at no cost laid down in Article 3 of the Consumer Sales Directive, and the interpretation given to that provision in *Quelle* and related case law of the European Court of Justice.

---

63 District Court Amsterdam 8 July 2016, ECLI:NL:RBAMS:2016:4197 (iPhone). Apple was the seller in this case, since the consumer had bought her iPhone directly through the company's website.

64 Case C-404/06 *Quelle AG v Bundesverband der Verbraucherzentralen und Verbraucherverbände* [2008] ECR I-2685, ECLI:EU:C:2008:231 (*Quelle*), para 41.

65 Ibid.

66 District Court Amsterdam 18 April 2017, ECLI:NL:RBAMS:2017:2519 (iPad).

While the Court in *Quelle* does not expressly state that the goods should be new, the fact that no discount for use may be imposed on the consumer implies that replacement should put the consumer in the position that he would (and should) have been in from the delivery of the goods under the contract. That conclusion is strengthened by the Court's motivation that the seller failed to give the consumer what he or she was entitled to expect under the contract and therefore should bear the additional costs. The Court's decision in *Messner* confirms, this time for distance sales, that consumers in principle are entitled to replacement without cost, and also without becoming liable to the trader for a discount for use of the goods.[67] Nevertheless, the decision in *Quelle* has been received somewhat critically in relation to luxury goods, and some see an opening for the Court to make an exception in the form of a 'new for old' payment on the basis of unjust enrichment if the consumer receives a new good in replacement.[68] This solution is thought acceptable even in the light of *Quelle*, as it does not concern payment for past performance but rather a payment to attenuate the prospective effect of the replacement received by the consumer.

Another possible solution could be to regulate the market for refurbished goods. Reasons for distrusting refurbishments are that the quality of refurbished goods is often dubitable, or that a consumer cannot establish that quality if the trader offers refurbished goods as a replacement. Several problems will therefore need to be addressed for regulation to work. First, there is a lack of apparent rules and standards on what refurbishment entails. Hence, the production of refurbished products leads to great variety in product quality, which in turn diminishes acceptance of refurbished goods among companies and consumers.[69] For this to improve, companies need better knowledge on what standards they would have to comply with when offering refurbished goods instead of replacements. Regulation for refurbished products could for example contribute to stimulating a production of refurbished products with equivalent quality to new goods.[70] In terms of remedying non-conformity, this could be a step towards upgrading refurbished goods to the standards of new goods, and therefore an acceptable alternative for replacement. Furthermore, research indicates that a lack of information contributes to the uncertainty experienced by consumers in relation to refurbished goods.[71] By providing information about the

---

67 Case C-489/07 *Pia Messner v Firma Stefan Krüger* [2009] ECR I-7315, ECLI:EU:C:2009:502 (*Messner*). The judgment does not, unlike *Quelle*, rule out payment for use completely, on the ground that the consumer's claim here is based on the right of withdrawal rather than non-conformity c.q. defective performance by the seller.

68 See in the Netherlands the case note of Advocate-General Mok on *Quelle* published in the official case reports *Nederlandse Jurisprudentie* 2008/382. Luxury goods such as cars lose their value quickly after purchase. Replacement of an 'old' car, used for several months, by a new car can significantly enrich the consumer.

69 Van Weelden, Mugge and Bakker (n 5) 5.

70 Ibid.

71 Ibid, 21.

refurbishment process, consumers' understanding of the concept of refurbished products may improve, including what the merits are of refurbishment and how it can contribute to a more sustainable society. We note at the same time that information is not the panacea to the problem: it only works if consumers actually receive goods of the quality that they are entitled to expect. Information may be a mechanism to convince them that this is the case. However, it only suffices if the standards for refurbished products are simultaneously established, monitored, and enforced.

In sum, existing rules of consumer sales law confirm that there is in important respects a conflict between consumer protection and sustainability goals. The contractual interests that businesses and consumers have in legal certainty with regard to the timespan within which legal or commercial guarantees apply, or with regard to obtaining conforming goods, have on balance outweighed more sustainable alternatives. Lifespan guarantees are often set at a limited time of two, three or five years. The Dutch time period based on the average lifespan of goods is an exception that is unlikely to be adopted at the EU level, and that may even disappear if the new consumer sales Directive is adopted. With regard to the conformity of goods, repair is favoured over refurbishment by consumers. Since EU consumer sales law gives consumers a free choice between repair and replacement, it lends support to this preference and therefore does little to promote sustainability. These aspects of consumer sales law may require reconsideration, either through legislation or, in case of the right to repair, through the preliminary reference procedure of the CJEU.

4. RETURN

Besides promoting durability, legal regimes may seek to promote the return of goods after a period of use as a way to contribute to the circular economy. Of the business models identified in paragraph II the most relevant for consumer markets are the waste value model, the recycling model, and the product-as-service model. The recycling model is probably the most well-known amongst consumers, as it has become omnipresent in many countries in the last decades. Biologically recyclable materials such as cardboard and paper are often collected separately by (local) governments, and businesses can be encouraged to use recyclable materials, such as paper cups, rather than plastics or other waste-creating materials. Policies to encourage such behaviour are often part of government initiatives and regulation.[72]

---

72 In the Netherlands, the recycling of raw materials is one of the primary goals of the government's strategy for the circular economy; see Government of the Netherlands, 'A Circular Economy in the Netherlands by 2050. Government-wide Programme for a Circular Economy' (n 16).

For business-to-consumer relationships the other two models are however of greater relevance. The waste value model has inspired business models in which the trader gives consumers the option to return goods after a period of use. The trader then, for example, re-sells the goods as second-hand goods or he destroys the goods so that the materials can be re-used for making new products. An example of products from a Netherlands based company are the sustainable jeans from MUD Jeans.[73]

The product-as-service model also, in certain variations, functions as a return model. An example relevant for consumers is the lease of a car. In many cases, the legal form that is used is chosen is a 'sale and lease back' contract under which ownership of the car remains with the service provider (e.g. a lease company). The provider receives the car back after the end of a contractually agreed period and can then re-use it in a sustainable manner, e.g. re-lease or re-sell it, or use the materials in other ways.

While the main legal mechanism for return schemes in general is contract, they also have relevant property law consequences. In most cases, ownership of the goods is not transferred to the consumer but remains with the trader. Alternatively, goods initially owned by the consumer may be transferred to the trader and then leased back (a sale-and-lease-back construction). Many contractual variations can exist. By illustration, we will discuss the contract and property law aspects of the two examples mentioned here already: MUD Jeans and the lease of a car.

4.1. EXAMPLE: MUD JEANS

Characteristic of return models is that the consumer obtains the goods for an indefinite period of time. In the case of the sustainable jeans, it is up to the consumer to decide whether and when he or she wants to return the jeans, provided that the consumer keeps them for at least twelve months.[74] Of course there is an incentive to return the jeans: after twelve months it is possible to exchange them for a new pair. Most consumers would not keep paying a monthly fee for a pair of jeans that has already been re-paid – which is the outcome seeing that twelve months of fees amount to almost the price of the jeans if the consumer chooses to purchase instead of lease them.[75]

In legal terms, the contract between the trader and the consumer can therefore be qualified as a lease contract. The trader continues to hold ownership of the jeans, whilst the consumer rents them and pays a monthly fee for use. That has certain advantages for the consumer, namely that he or she can call upon the

---

73 See <mudjeans.eu>.

74 See <https://mudjeans.eu/how-lease-a-jeans-works/>.

75 The fees are 7.50 EUR per month whereas a pair of jeans is offered for a price of 98 EUR.

trader for repair if the jeans get torn or otherwise damaged. MUD Jeans even states that the return of damaged jeans is welcomed, as the company aims to then reuse the materials.[76] It also means that consumer protection goals and sustainability in this case coincide. The consumer is given contractual rights that go beyond the default remedies of consumer contract law. For example, the consumer is given a right to repair free of costs, regardless of whether they caused the damage to the jeans themselves. Under Dutch contract law, as in other EU member states, the consumer would not be able to claim repair if the damage was caused by himself or through normal wear and tear.[77] The contract terms therefore give consumers protection that goes beyond the default rules of consumer contract law. At the same time, repair and reuse of waste materials contribute to sustainable solutions through the circular economy.

Since the lease contract does not have a fixed end-date, note should be taken of rules concerning long-term contracts. For business-to-consumer contracts the most relevant issue will likely be the unilateral change of conditions by the trader. Whilst most legal systems do not prohibit this, there are limitations to the types of changes that a trader can make and the conditions under which he can validly do this. The trader must for example give notice to the consumer of the changes he intends to make, with a possibility for the consumer to terminate the contract.[78]

Another problem that may arise is in relation to the enforcement of the contract. Seeing that the consumer has possession of the goods, even if the trader retains ownership, the trader loses the possibility to put pressure on the consumer if the latter does not fulfil his contractual obligations. Say, for example, that the consumer is behind with paying his monthly fees. General contract law allows the trader in that case to withhold his own performance during the time that payment is not forthcoming.[79] Practically, this is a mechanism to put pressure on the other party to perform. However, if the obligation of the trader is to make the goods available for use, as is the case here, he has no use of the right to withhold performance when the goods are already in the possession of the consumer.

In this last example, contractual mechanisms are tied to questions of possession. Other property law aspects may also be relevant in the pursuit of facilitating a circular economy, as we will now see.

---

76 See <https://mudjeans.eu/sustainable-fashion-faq/> under 'repair service'.

77 The damage can in that case not be attributed to the seller; see artt 6:74 and 6:101 of the Dutch Civil Code.

78 See Directive 1993/13/EEC on unfair terms in consumer contracts [1993] OJ L95/29 (Unfair Contract Terms Directive), Art 3(3) and Annex under 1(j) and 2(b). See also Marco Loos, 'Transparency of Unfair Terms under Unfair Contract Terms Directive and the Proposal for a Common European Sales Law' (2015) 23 European Review of Private Law 179, discussing case law of the CJEU on this matter.

79 Artt 6:52 and 6:262 of the Dutch Civil Code.

4.2. EXAMPLE: THE LEASE OF A CAR

Business models aimed at creating a possibility to return goods after long-term use in most case leave ownership of the goods with the trader. That is the case, for example, when a lease construction is used between a trader who is also producer, such as MUD Jeans, and a consumer. Some models choose a different option: sale-and-lease-back. In that case, the party that wishes to use the goods sells them, and immediately leases them back from the buyer. This construction is primarily used in business contexts as a way of raising money to finance the company's operations. Nonetheless, it may also be an option for certain consumer goods, e.g. for luxury goods that require a lot of maintenance. An example in consumer markets is the lease of a car. It is possible also, in such cases, that the original owner is the consumer's employer, who sells the car to a lease company and agrees with them that it can be rented out to the consumer under a lease contract.

An important benefit of a sale-and-lease-back construction is that the responsibilities for maintenance and repair rest on the trader or the lease company. The consumer only pays a monthly fee for use and otherwise all responsibilities rest on the trader. In relation to a car those can include not only maintenance and repair but also other responsibilities, such as taking care of taxation and insurance requirements.[80] In terms of legal protection, the same concerns are at play as with the example of the leased jeans. Most relevant is that in long-term contracts the unilateral change of terms by the trader should be monitored. From a property law perspective, the fact that the consumer is not the owner of the car also means he misses out on some rights, e.g. the right to revindicate goods if they are lost or stolen.[81]

In both examples, sustainability goals are promoted through the use of lease contracts. These contracts normally are favourable for consumers, in particular since maintenance and repair obligations rest upon the owner of the goods, i.e. in these cases the trader. There are some legal aspects to bear in mind though from a consumer protection perspective. First, the terms of the contract will have to be carefully monitored for compliance with consumer law. In particular the rules relating to long-term contracts and the unilateral change of conditions are relevant. Second, since the consumer does not own the goods, he or she does not have the strong legal position that property laws give to owners, for example to revindicate lost or stolen goods. By pursuing sustainability through lease contracts, therefore, consumers lose some of the protection of individual rights that they enjoy as owners in the 'old' economy.[82]

---

80 Many car leasing companies offer terms and conditions to this effect.

81 Compare Art 3:86 sub 1 and sub 3 of the Dutch Civil Code.

82 For an elaboration of this argument for the Netherlands, see also (in Dutch) Vanessa Mak, 'Van *ownership* naar *access*. Is toegang de nieuwe eigendom?' [2018] Ars Aequi 664.

5. USE

In the circular economy, there is a third category of business models that can be classified as 'use models'. They are aimed at facilitating the shared use of goods, often for short-term periods. Examples are bike sharing schemes such as Hello Bike in Amsterdam, car sharing schemes such as Greenwheels in the Netherlands or Zipcar in North-America, or vacation apartment rental sites like Airbnb. Another example in the Netherlands is Peerby: a platform that enables users to borrow goods from other users for a short period of time. The shared use of goods in this 'sharing economy' can in principle be considered a sustainable solution. It would entail, for example, that fewer bikes or cars are parked for a longer time without being used. Therefore also the demand for new bikes and cars should decrease. For now, that scenario seems somewhat utopian, since the market for sharing is still smaller than that for newly produced goods. Nevertheless, the trend may be different in the future. In North America it has already been noted that fewer millennials are in the possession of driver's licenses due to a desire to choose 'greener' means of transportation.[83]

Legally, there are no immediate obstacles to the shared use of goods through these business models. Nevertheless, a number of aspects of the sharing economy seem to fall within the gaps between existing rules, and may require regulation or alternative solutions. One problem is that many transactions that occur in the sharing economy are between non-professional parties, or in other words: consumer-to-consumer (C2C) contracts. The platform itself usually is not a party to the contract for the delivery of goods or services, but merely facilitates the creation of contracts between users of the platform. The rules of consumer law, which apply to business-to-consumer contracts do not cover these transactions between users, even though the contract has been concluded in a professional environment.[84] As a result, consumers who use goods rented or bought from other non-professionals do not enjoy the protection that they have if they contract with a professional trader, such a right of withdrawal or a claim to repair or replacement if goods turn out to be defective.

A second problem is that the legal classification of transactions is sometimes difficult to establish and, as a consequence, that the legal position of the parties is uncertain. If goods are offered for temporary use through a website, in particular if the transaction is between non-professional parties, it may not be clear whether the contract between the parties is a lease contract or one for usage. The legal consequences of a contract however differ between those two types. In case

83 Julie Beck, 'The Decline of the Driver's License', *The Atlantic* 22 January 2016, available at: <https://www.theatlantic.com/technology/archive/2016/01/the-decline-of-the-drivers-license/425169/>.

84 Christoph Busch, Hans Schulte-Nölke, Aneta Wiewiórowska-Domagalska, Fryderyk Zoll, 'The Rise of the Platform Economy: A New Challenge for EU Consumer Law?' (2016) 1 Journal of European Consumer and Market Law (EuCML) 3.

of usage, under Dutch law the borrower has a duty to act as a 'good user' and will only be liable for loss of the goods if that breach of contract can be attributed to him or her.[85] The lender, on the other side, can only be held liable for defects to the goods that were known to him.[86] Compared to lease contracts this is a 'light' liability regime. The lessor of goods can be held liable if goods are defective and cause harm under the condition that the breach can be attributed, if he knew *or could have known* of the defect.[87]

Third, if a user suffers harm and cannot obtain compensation from the other contracting party, they may call upon the platform operator. However, most online platforms in the EU will seek to escape liability on the basis of the host exemption laid down in Articles 14 and 15 of the E-Commerce Directive.[88] On the basis of this exemption, internet intermediaries are not under a general obligation to monitor the activities of users on their platform. They can be obliged to report illegal content and should also remove or disable access to such information[89], but that is a very limited responsibility for the intermediary. This gives rise to new regulatory issues, since it is sometimes though unjust that platforms play a pivotal role in facilitating the conclusion of contracts between consumers and suppliers, but have limited legal responsibility. For example, platforms often come across as the main service provider, since they frequently present themselves as a payment service provider and offer other modalities to users. In many cases some sort of reputation system is provided by the platform for users to inform others of their experience of the use of that platform.[90] Critics find that platforms are circumventing regulation, whilst operating as direct service providers.[91] Hence, it is thought that regulation may be required to address the liability of platforms[92] and the level of consumer protection.[93]

In some cases current regulation may already offer solutions, but the problem is to determine when. For example, in 2017 the European Court of Justice addressed the question of the legal status of online intermediaries in the platform economy its *Uber*-judgment. The Court held that the exemption laid down in Article 14 of the E-Commerce Directive does not apply to the service

---

85 Artt 7A:1781 and 7A:1782 of the Dutch Civil Code.

86 Art 7A:1790 DCC, which prescribes that the lender in that case has a duty to inform the borrower of the defect.

87 Artt 7:204 and 7:208 of the Dutch Civil Code.

88 Directive 2000/31/EC on certain legal aspects of information society services, in particular electronic commerce, in the Internal Market [2000] OJ L178/1 (E-Commerce Directive).

89 E-Commerce Directive, Artt 14 and 15.

90 See Busch cs (n 88).

91 See, e.g., Avi Asher-Schapiro, 'Against Sharing' [2014] JACOBIN https://www.jacobinmag.com/2014/09/aga inst-sharing/ (criticizing TNCs and the sharing economy generally for depressing wages and creating unfair working conditions).

92 See Vanessa Katz, 'Regulating the Sharing Economy' (2015) 4 Berkeley Technology Law Journa 1073.

93 Busch cs (n 88) 7–10.

provided by Uber.[94] The taxi service provided by Uber was regarded as forming an integral part of the overall service rather than a mere intermediary service.[95] Therefore, it was subject to applicable regulation concerning taxi services. However, until the European or national legislators introduce rules to regulate the sharing economy[96], the legal responsibilities of platforms will in many instances be marred by legal uncertainty. This means that users of goods and services in this new, mostly online economy are likely to miss out on consumer protection measures that they can benefit from in the offline economy. While this could deter consumers from participating in the sharing economy, and instead to fall back on the less sustainable option of purchasing goods rather than using them for a short time, it may well be that the effect of legal rules in this context is limited. The sharing economy's great attraction is that it makes available goods and services to consumers that were not on the market before, or not in the form in which they are offered now. The innovative nature of many initiatives in the sharing economy, therefore, is likely to overcome legal obstacles, if we give them a chance to do so.[97] In fact, the disruptive effect that some business models have on existing regulation may lead to improvements in law[98] – perhaps also contributing to sustainability goals.

6. CONCLUSION

Where do we stand with regard to consumer law and the circular economy in Europe? The analysis of three functions – durability, return, and use of goods – reveals that consumer law can in various business models be used to support the circular economy. Although we drew examples from current law and practice in the Netherlands, many of our findings might be equally applicable to other EU member states. The following observations can be made.

---

94 Case C-434/15 *Asociación Profesional Elite Taxi v Uber Systems Spain* [2017] ECLI:EU:C:2017:981 (Uber).

95 Ibid, paras 39–40.

96 The New Deal for Consumers, Art 6a, seeks to impose an obligation on online marketplaces to indicate whether a supplier is acting in a professional capacity or as a private party. The online marketplace should establish that classification on the basis of a declaration from the supplier. This provision has attracted criticism for being difficult to use in practice. See Twigg-Flesner (n 47) 12.

97 In this sense, see e.g. Christopher Koopman, Matthew Mitchell and Adam Thierer, 'The Sharing Economy and Consumer Protection Regulation: The Case for Policy Change' (2015) 8 Journal of Business, Entrepreneurship & the Law (JBEL) 2 (arguing that the sharing economy is a self-regulating market and does not require government intervention).

98 On legal improvement through disruption by platforms, see House of Lords, Select Committee on European Union, 'Online Platforms and the Digital Single Market' (10th Report of Session 2015–2016, April 2016), available at: <https://publications.parliament.uk/pa/ld201516/ldselect/ldeucom/129/12902.htm>, 90.

To prevent waste of resources and energy, the greatest contribution could come from stimulating the production of durable goods through extending the scope of legal guarantees on traders and commercial guarantees on producers. The longer the potential time period for liability for defective goods, the stronger the incentive for traders and producers to offer goods that will last for a long time. In fact, the most direct influence on durability lies with producers, rather than sellers of goods. It would therefore be worthwhile if producers were obliged to offer commercial guarantees for a longer time period, e.g. for three or five years, or even for the duration of the normal lifespan of goods. The proposed Directive on consumer sales of goods unfortunately does not seem to go that far, but if minimum harmonisation is maintained member states may still choose to introduce stricter consumer protection rules to this effect.

In relation to remedies for defective goods we see perhaps the strongest example of conflict between consumer rights and the pursuit of a circular economy. Recent case law in the Netherlands suggests that consumers are entitled to replacement of a non-conforming good with a new good and do not have to accept refurbished (i.e. repaired) goods. Whilst the cases appear to be correct in their interpretation of the current state of the law, it is regrettable that consumer law does not provide greater openings for sustainable practices such as refurbishment. In this respect, we would be in favour of a reconsideration of the *Quelle* judgment of the European Court of Justice, or of regulation of the market for refurbished goods so that higher quality standards for refurbished goods can be guaranteed.

Other models, such as the lease of clothes or other goods, either long-term or short-term, can contribute to a more sustainable use and reuse of resources. These models are facilitated by contract law and seem to work well in many instances. Nevertheless, consumer rights tend to be less strong than they are with regard to goods purchased in the 'old' economy. Concerns may arise with regard to the unilateral change of terms by the trader – and how to monitor fairness –, with regard to the possibilities to exercise property rights such as revindication of stolen goods, and with regard to liability if the counter-party of the consumer is also a non-professional party. In the sharing economy, an additional concern is that platforms may be held liable in very restrictive circumstances only, due to the host exception laid down in the E-Commerce Directive and a lack of clear rules in relation to other types of liability.

In our final assessment, however, consumer law may well in the longer run become an ally to sustainability goals. Recent years have seen an increasing interest in 'green' products and a strong push back against manufacturers who seek to circumvent regulation aimed at environmental protection, such as Volkswagen. If this trend continues, this article has shown that some low hanging fruit can easily be picked in consumer law: the durability of goods can be promoted through legal and commercial guarantees, the transparency and fairness of advertising concerning green products can be strengthened, and consumer rights in the sharing economy can be improved. Perhaps not completely incidentally, all of these issues are on the European legislature's agenda.

THE "CIRCULAR ECONOMY" – NATIONAL LEGAL INITIATIVES AND CHALLENGES CONCERNING MOVABLES – BELGIUM

Annick De Boeck*

1. INTRODUCTION

'Circular economy' means materials can be regenerated and constantly flow around a 'closed loop' system, rather than being used once and then discarded. The potential benefits of the circular economy approach are clear for businesses and the environment: the more effective use of materials means less waste and potentially lower costs. China, forerunner in the field of circular economy, adopted a national law which aims to improve resource utilization efficiency, to protect and improve the environment, and to realise sustainable development. This law applies the '3R principle' of Reduction, Reuse and Recycling.[1]

The Circular Economy is one where everything is reused and nothing is wasted. It is the antithesis of the current "build-buy-bury" model of a one-way stream of raw material to factory, to user, then landfill. A driving force of the circular economy is the pressure on natural resources, which creates an increased need for resource efficiency. The potential cost-savings involved[2] can be an attractive pull-factor, as is the benefit to company reputation. Concerns around the security of supply of raw materials, the increased demand globally for natural resources and calls for sustainability from both governments and consumers are also factors driving the calls for a circular economy. In a post-recessionary environment, with global economic growth still fragile, consumers

* Professor, KU Leuven, Faculty of Law.

1 The Circular Economy Promotion Law of the People's Republic of China, which was adopted at the 4th session of the Standing Committee of the 11th National People's Congress of the People's Republic of China on August 29, 2008, is hereby promulgated and has come into force on January 1, 2009. https://ppp.worldbank.org/public-private-partnership/library/china-circular-economy-promotion-law.

2 However, recycling is not always the cheapest alternative.

remain cautious over their spending, with conspicuous consumption being replaced by conscious consumption. Making the most of their own resources is part of this drive, with consumers increasingly open to re-use, trade-in and hiring durable goods. The continued success of auction and free-exchange websites is further evidence of this.

The circular economy is one of the trends that contribute to a 'New Consumerism'. This 'New Consumerism' sees today's consumers reassessing their priorities and increasingly asking themselves what they truly value: Why own something that I only use sporadically? Why accumulate more belongings when I could be out experiencing life? Why pay for space I don't use? Why work 9 to 5?[3]For durables, the benefits of reuse have been widely demonstrated.[4] For consumer goods -such as food and beverages or apparel and their packaging – which are short-lived and often transformed during use, the economic benefits of a circular design are more complex in origin and harder to assess.

The shift towards a circular economy will contribute to a new model of collaborative consumerism – in which consumers embrace services that enable them to access products on demand rather than owning them – and collaborative consumption models that provide more interaction between consumers, retailers, and manufacturers (e.g. performance-for-pay models, rent or leasing schemes, return and reuse). Hire and lease contracts will excessively prevail instead of sales. Value-added offerings like repair, amendment and return offer much greater customer interaction at multiple touchpoints.[5] For example Philips is developing a "pay-per-lux" model, including lightning as a service. Philips produces, installs, maintains and upgrades the lightning equipment for the customer and retains ownership of it. The customer, the building owner or the tenant, pays a service fee for a certain quality of lightning that is guaranteed by a performance contract. When the equipment reaches the end-of-life or becomes technologically dated, Philips, which still owns it, takes it back for recycling and reuse.[6]

2. THE NEED FOR REGULATION

While companies can start doing circular business in our current linear economy, only governments can tackle most of the barriers that hamper the transition towards a circular economy. In order to encourage the transition to a

---

3 Report "The New Consumerism: Redefining Ownership, Values and Priorities", www.euromonitor.com/the-new-consumerism-redefining-ownership-values-and-priorities/report.

4 Http://loadingdock.org/redo/Benefits_of_Reuse/body_benefits_of_reuse.html.

5 *Towards the circular economy. Opportunities for the consumer goods sector*, Ellen MacArthur Foundation (ed.), Rethink the future, 2013, vol. 2.

6 I. FELDMAN, R. LIFSET, T. ELLIS, W. RIFER en R.D. FELDMAN, "The Circular Economy: Regulatory and Commercial Law Implications", *Environmental Law Reporter* 2016, 46-11014.

circular economy, governments need to create the conditions that stimulate and accelerate decisions to move in this direction.

A first type of regulations should focus on limiting waste and the disposal of waste on the one hand and recovery of resources and the possibilities of reuse on the other hand. A second type of regulations is needed to facilitate the use of sharing platforms for individuals and companies as a cornerstone for the sharing economy (vehicles, material, services, personnel, etc.). Finally, consumer law should innovate all these new developments concerning a switch from product to service, the increased importance of and liability for so-called "smart goods" with embedded electronics, software and connectivity, the new type of conformity covering also durability and the remedy of repair instead of replacement.

3. STATE OF THE ART IN BELGIUM: ESPECIALLY PRIVATE INITIATIVES, BUT ALSO INCREASED GOVERNMENT ACTION

In 2014 the federal administration prepared a roadmap that laid out proposals for action for a transition towards a more circular economy, called "*Vers une Belgique Pionnière de l'Economie Circulaire/België als Voortrekker van de Circulaire Economie*".[7] Furthermore, a number of relevant plans and programmes for a circular economy have been initiated at the Federal level. Most of these encompass measures that build the enabling institutional and market environment for eco-innovative solutions. The Federal level develops 'instrumental' competences to provide support for the effective implementation or market translation of the regional objectives and initiatives (fiscal and quasi-fiscal provisions, taxation, competition rules, market structures, price regulation, etc.). Currently there are plans to set up a knowledge centre to elaborate a federal strategy and a new roadmap. In 2016, no less than 21 proposals were made by the Federal Ministry for Energy, Environment and Sustainable Development and the Federal Ministry for Work, Economy and Consumers to promote a circular economy.[8] One of the proposals concerns the presumption of non-conformity when a defect of a sold consumergood appears within 6 months after delivery of the good. This period would be extended to two years after delivery in order to strengthen the position

---

7 In application of the KB van 18 juli 2013 houdende vaststelling van de federale beleidsvisie op lange termijn inzake duurzame ontwikkeling, instauring a federal long term-policy concerning sustainable development, *BS* 8 oktober 2013.

8 *Samen de economie doen draaien dankzij de circulaire economie*, kabinet Marie Christine Marghem, Minister van Energie, Leefmilieu en duurzame ontwikkeling en kabinet Kris Peeters, Vice eerste minister, Minster van Werk, Economie en Consumenten, belast met Buitenlandse Handel.

of a consumer who bought a good with one or more defects.[9] Another initiative concerns defining criteria for the repairability of goods.[10]

3.1 WASTE – REUSE – RECYCLING

Due to its federal structure most environmental issues in Belgium are a regional competence.

The Walloon Government has put a focus on resource efficiency since the Marshall Plan 2 in 2009. In the Marshal Plan 4.0, issued on 29.05.2015, promoting circular economy is one of the five priority areas for action.

In March 2016 the regional government of Brussels also adopted a Circular Economy Regional Plan. This ambitious plan consists of 111 measures in 4 fields and is meant to be complemented every 18 months with new measures that also concern legislative barriers.[11]

The waste management and recycling sector (NACE rev. 2 – 38) and wholesale trade in waste and scrap (NACE rev. 2 – 46.77) employs approximately 12.000 people in Flanders. This is 0,5% of the Flemish employment. Moreover, the expertise and the use of recycled materials contribute to a Flemish anchoring in sectors such as metal processing and plastics production.[12]

In Flanders, another classic landfill culprit has been tackled: construction and demolition waste. Similar to cases all around the world, the Belgian construction industry produces an enormous amount of debris and demolition rubble. Most of it is dumped, unsorted in landfills, including substantial rocky fractions that are inherently valuable materials. In 2011, the Flanders regional government recognized the significant potential of recycling high quality aggregates. It therefore established a legal framework to ensure the proper management of the rocky fraction within construction and demolition waste. Additionally, the government introduced economic incentives, like higher rates for dumping debris at landfills, and imposed several restrictions regarding on the dumping of unsorted construction and demolition waste. These measures are all focused on optimising recycling rates in order to lower the pressure on natural resources, while the management system and regulations ensure high quality recycled materials. Another policy is to make it easier to recycle materials by differentiating between waste and recyclables (by-products). In 2011, the

---

9 Article 1649*quater* §4 BW.

10 *Samen de economie doen draaien dankzij de circulaire economie*, p. 35.

11 D. GOSUIN, C. FREMAULT en F. LAANAN, *Programme régionale en économie circulaire 2016–2020. Mobiliser les ressources et minimiser les richesses perdues: pour une économie régionale innovante*, be circular, be.brussels, 2016.

12 M. DUBOIS en M. CHRISTIS, *Verkennende analyse van het economisch belang van afvalbeheer, recyclage en de circulaire economie in Vlaanderen*, Steunpunt Duurzaam Materialenbeheer, Leuven, 2014, p. 2.

Flanders regional government in Belgium recognised the high potential for the recycling of good quality granulates. It therefore established a legal framework to ensure the proper management of the rocky fraction of the construction and demolition waste. The Flanders approach was very effective, because it was combined with another governmental action: the creation of a market for recycled materials through product specifications, standards and regulation.[13] This year in Veurne a new road will be built consisting 100% of recycled materials.[14]

One of the other key measures in chapter 3 of VLAREMA is the extended producer's liability for some waste materials mentioned in a list (for example cars, tires, medicines, electronic devices, batteries) the seller is obliged to take back the discarded product free of charge whenever he sells a new one to the consumer.

On 1 November 2017 the project Circular South kicked off in Antwerp. With this European project, of which EnergyVille is a partner, the city wants to stimulate the smart use of energy, water and waste in innovative ways. The Urban Innovative Action fund of the European Commission selected Circular South out of 206 project proposals. Circular South combines a series of district bound experimental initiatives that will bring into urban practice the circular economy. Spreading awareness and encouraging citizens to circular behavior is the focal point. The most sustainable district of Antwerp, New South, will play a leading role in this. The city of Antwerp is collaborating with different partners to realize these ambitions for Circular South. Together they develop new technologies to support the inhabitants as much as possible. EnergieID will make the website which contains all information about the use of energy, water and waste/materials. iMec will stimulate users to smarter use their energy, water and 'waste/materials' by sending them proposals at a right time. Digipolis makes sure the online platform, where users can check their own usage in real-time, is linked to the A-profile of the city. Ecopower, in cooperation with EnergyVille and the citizens of New South, founds a sustainable energy cooperation for which a big sustainable installation will be placed on and in several buildings to provide energy. The inhabitants are the ones to shape the project.

Belgium is Europe's most congested country in terms of delays and hours wasted in traffic jams, especially around Antwerp and Brussels. Road congestion generates higher fuel consumption and contributes to air pollution. Some measures to improve the situation were taken, such as the kilometre-charge

---

13 See **MATERIALENDECREET** and **VLAREMA:** Decreet 23 december 2011 betreffende het duurzaam beheer van materiaalkringlopen en afvalstoffen, *BS* 28 februari 2012, especially chapter 6 concerning "the transition to a circular economy", Besluit van de Vlaamse Regering 17 februari 2012 tot vaststelling van het Vlaams reglement betreffende het duurzaam beheer van materiaalkringlopen en afvalstoffen, *BS* 23 mei 2012.

14 Het Nieuwsblad, 21 december 2017.

for lorries on all Belgian roads and the extension of car-free zones or so called "low emission zones" in several cities. With a strategic plan, Brussels develops a specific approach to optimize freight traffic and reduce emissions.[15]

Regarding sustainable food, the Regional government of Brussels capital adopted a strategy entitled "Good food, towards a more sustainable food system in Brussels Capital Region" in December 2015. The main aims are local food production with respect for the environment and encouraging the innovation, raising awareness of citizens and reducing food waste.[16]

3.2 SHARING PLATFORMS

Many successful sharing concepts in relation to movables are initiated by commercial enterprises. Nevertheless, governments or local authorities have good reason to promote the use of these sorts of commercial sharing platforms through supportive policies.

The city of Antwerp is using incentives to modify consumer behaviour concerning mobility. This is the main philosophy behind implementing an urban sharing program for bikes, the so called "Velo"-system. The Velo system allows subscribers to make use of unisex bikes by taking and returning them to solar-powered docks located at strategic points throughout the city. Additional funding is organised through corporate sponsors and through the subscription fee paid by users. In order to gain access to the service, the user should register by acquiring a yearly membership via the Internet or by using a user code and password provided for short term bicycle rental. The bicycle remains the property of the service provider. The service provider reserves the right to deny the user access to the service with immediate effect in the event of non-performance by the user of one of the obligations stipulated in the terms and conditions. In that case, the service provider shall not be held liable for the non-performance of the obligations under the terms and conditions. The service provider, who is not the manufacturer of the bicycles made available under the rental program, cannot be held liable for any defects or errors in relation to the bicycle manufacturing or assembly process.[17] At the beginning of each validity period, the user gives prior consent to the service provider to charge an amount of € 150 – an amount that is kept by way of a bond – by entering his banking code. Different penalty clauses concern the case of damage or disappearance of the bicycle.

Poppy is a new car sharing platform in Antwerp with 350 environmentally friendly sharing cars (electric and CNG) according to the free-floating principle

---

15 Commission Staff Working Document. The EU Envoronmental Implemention Review Country Report- BELGIUM, COM (2017)63 final, p. 21–22.

16 Commission Staff Working Document. The EU Envoronmental Implemention Review Country Report- BELGIUM, COM (2017)63 final, p. 22–23.

17 See general conditions, www.velo-antwerpen.be.

with a mobile application.[18] The rights granted to the user under the agreement are restricted user rights and shall in no event be considered a transfer of ownership of the vehicles. A mobile application managed by Poppy enables users to receive the services from Poppy and to use the vehicles subject to the terms and conditions of the agreement to offer mobility sharing services. The recent experience shows that strict terms and conditions are needed in order to protect the property of the owner-investor against abuses and to preserve the insurability.

3.3 CONSUMER LAW CONCERNING SALES AND SERVICES: LEGAL OBSTACLES – LEGAL ANSWERS

3.3.1. Concise overview of the relevant Belgian civil law

Directive 2001/95/EC on general product safety (Product Safety Directive) is implemented in Book IX of the Economic Code. Under Article IX.2, Book IX of the Economic Code, producers and manufacturers must only place safe products on the market. The Federal Government Service Economy (FOD Economie) monitors the Belgian market, and ensures that products and services on the market meet safety requirements. There are also specific regulations for certain product groups, for example gas or electrical devices, elevators, fireworks, attractions in amusement parks and playgrounds. Products can also be subject to norms that are determined by the Bureau of Normalisation (NBN).[19] If a product (except food) does not meet the safety requirements and is a risk to consumers, the producers and distributors must inform the Central Contact Point of the Federal Government (FPS Economics) (*Centraal Meldpunt voor Producten*). Consumers and the other parties can also file a claim at the Central Contact Point. The Central Contact Point coordinates the information flow on product safety and is the Belgian contact for the RAPEX-system (the European exchange system for information on dangerous products).

Directive 85/374/EEC on product liability (Product Liability Directive) is implemented in the Product Liability Act 1991. Every user of the product is protected.

Under the Product Liability Act, a defect is defined as not meeting the safety that a party is entitled to expect, taking into account all the circumstances. It imposes strict liability. The producer can only be discharged from liability when he did not put the product into circulation, when in the circumstances, it is probable that the defect which caused the damage did not exist at the time

18 Https://poppy.be/.

19 NBN – Bureau for Standardisation is responsible for developing, publishing and selling standards in Belgium.

when the product was put into circulation by him, or that the defect occurred afterwards, when the product was not manufactured by him for sale or any form of distribution for economic purposes, nor manufactured or distributed by him in the course of his business, when the defect is due to compliance of the product with mandatory regulations issued by the public authorities, when the state of scientific and technical knowledge at the time when he put the product into circulation was not such as to enable the existence of the defect to be discovered or in the case of a manufacturer of a component, the defect is attributable to the design of the product in which the component has been fitted, or to the instructions given by the manufacturer of the product. Especially when the user takes the initiative to repair or replace the product or a part of it, he bears the risk that the producer can escape liability.

Product liability can also be incurred under Article 1382 of the Civil Code as tort liability.

The seller of the product (movables and immovables) can also be liable for hidden defects based on the articles 1641 to 1648 of the Civil Code, if the product had these defects at the time of purchase. The buyer must claim within a short period after discovery of the defect. Under article 1649*bis* of the Civil Code and other provisions on the sale of goods to consumers, the seller is responsible for defects existing at the time of delivery of the goods (movables) that become visible within two years after the date of delivery (*Article 1649quater, Civil Code*). The consumer is defined in article 1649*bis* section 2 of the Civil Code and Article I.1, 2 of the Economic Code as a natural person who acts for purposes that do not relate to his/her professional or commercial activities.

A claim for damages is also commonly based on article 1641 and following of the Civil Code. Under these provisions, a product is deemed defective when it does not meet the characteristics that a party can expect, also when it does not meet functional requirements. Although there is no strict liability under these provisions, a commercial seller cannot exclude its liability for hidden defects in the product since the seller is deemed to have known the defect. An exception is when the defect could not be discovered, given the state of scientific knowledge at the time of the sale. However, this is rarely accepted. Further, the buyer must establish that the defect was present at the time of delivery, and could not have been discovered on delivery. As to the remedy, the buyer cannot claim for a repair nor a replacement.

Liability for defects in business-to-consumer sales is regulated explicitly in article 1649*bis-quater* of the Civil Code. In these sales, the seller is liable for delivering a product that complies with the expected use of the product, public announcements (such as advertising) and the labelling. In contrast to business-to-business sales, article 1649*ter* of the Civil Code stipulates that there is a presumption (which can be rebutted by the seller) that non-compliance existed at the time of delivery, for six months from the date of delivery. The consumer has the right for a replacement product or repair of the product (as chosen by the seller). If repair or replacement is not appropriate or not provided for, the consumer can claim rescission of the contract or an appropriate price reduction. The seller or any previous seller cannot exclude this liability in consumer sales contracts. The amended proposal for a directive on certain aspects concerning contracts for the sale of goods[20] significantly raises the level of consumer protection by extending the deadline during which the presumption of non-conformity operates, to a period of two years. The European Consumer Organisation (BEUC) supported this two-year period of reversed burden of proof and also advocated a free choice of remedies for consumers instead of the hierarchy system of the CSD.[21]

The UN Convention on Contracts for the International Sale of Goods 1980 applies in Belgium. It includes the requirement for defective-free products. It therefore also forms a basis for claims for defective products in a B to B-sales relationship.

As for services, only general contract law of the Civil Code, often complemented by general terms and conditions, applies. Although freedom of contract still prevails concerning services contracts, freedom of contract is not permitted in any absolute form; Belgian law restricts and regulates freedom of contract in many ways. Most of the restrictions however concern the relation between the contracting parties and not the object of the contract (the services as such). Accordingly, the law has intervened to guide parties as to which terms they can contract on to effectively balance the inequality in their bargaining power, and ensure optimum protection for the consumer or weaker party in general, who, most times, has limited expertise in the field. Book VI of the Belgian Economic Law Code on "Market practices and consumer protection" implements the Consumer Rights Directive (2011/83/EU) and the Unfair Contract Terms Directive (93/13/EEC).

Pay-per-service unit is a type of service compensation model with payment tied to the quantity or quality of service the customer receives. It includes subcategories like pay-for-performance and pay-per-use. Product manufacturers may consider reevaluating their revenue model from single-transaction sales to a relationship-based service contract. In the pay-per-service unit model, the product manufacturer or retailer is typically responsible for installation, maintenance and take-back of the product. By tying the service price to

20 Amended proposal for a directive of the European Parliament and of the Council on certain aspects concerning contracts for the sale of goods, amending Regulation (EC) no 2006/2004 of the European Parliament and of the Council and Directive 2009/22/EC of the European Parliament and of the Council and repealing Directive 1999/44/EC of the European Parliament and of the Council, COM (2017) 637 final.

21 "Contracts for online and other distance sales of goods", February 2017, in "EU legislation in progress" briefings, p. 6, www.eprs.ep.parl.union.eu.

performance, it encourages the provider to give the best service to its customers. Some examples of pay-for-performance schemes concern lighting (pay-per-lux), tires (pay-per-kilometer), solar power (pay-per-kilowatt-hour) and office equipment (pay-per-page). It is important to establish a performance metric that aligns the service provider and receiver's objectives.[22]

As reuse, repair and remanufacturing and refurbishment are significant elements of the circular economy, future legislation should pay more attention to the aftersales market. The safety and quality of the repair could be ensured by recognising the trusted status of authorised repair networks and refurbishment or remanufacturing facilities.[23]

3.3.2. Legal challenges

1° Reinforcement of the right to know

The role of consumers in the transition to a circular economy is crucial. Access to reliable, timely and understandable information regarding the environmental characteristics of products and services can help make informed choices. For instance environmental claims, including labels, should be based on verifiable and transparent information.[24]

Nevertheless one should warn for any overload of information that might frustrate comprehension. Especially consumers are a heterogeneous group so their ability to process information poses a significant challenge to the use of pre-contractual information requirements. The notion of bounded rationality stresses the fact that consumers are able to handle only a limited amount of information.[25]

In some cases a form of preliminary quality-control of the information could also be recommendable. Traditionally, it has especially been questioned which information must be provided to the contracting party. In our opinion, we are keen that more attention should be paid to the quality of the information provided: is it correct? Is it clear and comprehensible? Is it up to date, etc.

---

22 Circular Economy, Practioner Guide: https://www.ceguide.org/.

23 See for example: *The contribution of the Digital Industry to repair, remanufacturing and refurbishment in a Circular Economy*, April 2017, p. 14, www.digitaleurope.org.

24 Council conclusions on the EU action plan for the circular economy, Press release 367/16, 20/06/2016.

25 T. WILHELMSSON and C. TWIGG-FLESNER, "Pre-contractual information duties in the acquis communautaire", *European Review of Contract Law* 2006, 452–453.

2° Risk of loss of information – increased need for information

Recovered and recycled materials may not contain hazardous chemicals. Information could get lost in the life cycle of the material.[26] Three blocks of EU legislation – chemicals[27], product[28] or waste legislation[29] – may apply, each using different terminologies triggering various rights and obligations for economic operators and consumers.[30] Under REACH[31], consumers have the right to know whether the articles they buy contain any chemicals known as "substances of very high concern" (SVHC). These are chemicals with serious and often irreversible effects on health or the environment. Those substances may occur in many everyday products, such as clothing, furniture, sports articles, shoes, bags, garden decorations, office supplies, cleaning articles, or personal care products (the list is not exhaustive).

REACH established the setting up of a so-called candidate list of "substances of very high concern", to which substances are being added regularly. A substance of very high concern can be carcinogenic, mutagenic, and toxic for reproduction, persistent, bioaccumulative and toxic in the environment). The candidate list signals to the industry that these substances will eventually be phased out of the market, and intends to encourage companies to look for safer alternatives.

Consumers can play an active role in the process by taking an interest in the safety of the products they buy. Therefore REACH introduced in article 33 the "consumer right to know". Companies are obliged to answer a consumer inquiry about the presence of a substance of very high concern in an article, within 45 days.

---

26 See case study on a flame retardant in textile after the recycling of a discarded mattress: A. BERNARD, "Chemicals in material cycles: how EU law needs adjustments for the transition to an environmentally beneficial circular economy", *Elni review* 2017,55–58, that illustrates that information on hazardous chemicals can get lost in the material cycle.

27 Regulation concerning the Registration, Evaluation, Authorisation and Restriction of Chemicals (REACH): Regulation (EC) no. 1907/2006, *OJ L*. 396 31.12.2006.

28 Directive 2001/95/EC of the European Parliament and of the Council of 3 December 2001 on general product safety, *OJ L* 011 15.01.2002 (GPSD).

29 Waste Framework Directive: Directive 2008/98/EC of the European Parliament and of the Council of 19 November 2008 on waste and repealing certain Directives *OJ L* 312 of 22.11.2008.

30 A. BERNARD, "Chemicals in material cycles: how EU law needs adjustments for the transition to an environmentally beneficial circular economy", *Elni review* 2017, 55.

31 Regulation (EC) No 1907/2006 of the European Parliament and of the Council of 18 December 2006 concerning the Registration, Evaluation, Authorisation and Restriction of Chemicals (REACH), establishing a European Chemicals Agency, amending Directive 1999/45/EC and repealing Council Regulation (EEC) No 793/93 and Commission Regulation (EC) No 1488/94 as well as Council Directive 76/769/EEC and Commission Directives 91/155/EEC, 93/67/EEC, 93/105/EC and 2000/21/EC.

The European Commission aims to place all currently known and relevant substances of very high concern (SVHC's) on the candidate list by 2020.

Producers and importers have to notify to ECHA the substances listed on the Candidate list which are present in their articles, under certain conditions: The substance is present in their relevant articles above a concentration of 0.1% weight by weight. The substance is present in these relevant articles in quantities totalling over one ton per year. The notification information can be used together with other sources (e.g. registration information) to support identification of further needs for risk management. If there are grounds for suspecting that the substance is released from the articles under normal or reasonably foreseeable conditions of use and such a release presents a risk to human health or the environment, then the producer or importer of articles may be required to submit a registration. Since the 2013 REACH Review progress can be observed as to how industry fulfils its obligations as regards substances in articles, and how this information is communicated and used. However, whilst the situation may be improving, it is still not working as well as originally envisaged. Divergence between Member States in the interpretation of the 0.1% threshold limit regarding notifications to be submitted to ECHA (Article 7(2)) and regarding communication in the supply chain and to consumers (Article 33) of REACH has been resolved by a ruling of the European Court of Justice. This provides a common basis for the harmonised implementation of the requirements related to SVHCs in articles, and for increased and coordinated enforcement activities. The amount and adequacy of information in registrations dossiers for the safe use of substances in articles is still very limited. Fewer than expected notifications to ECHA have been provided, because of: a lack of awareness; difficulties to obtain the necessary information, especially from third country suppliers; descriptions of uses in articles in registration dossiers being too broad; costs of communication for example due to complexity; a lack of methods to assess the safety of substance uses in articles (e.g. release and exposure estimation methods); a lack of methods to measure the content and release of SVHCs in articles. This limits the usefulness of such information for the identification of appropriate regulatory measures. The obligations to communicate the presence of SVHCs in articles allows operators along the supply chain to implement appropriate risk management measures as well as enabling operators and consumers to make informed purchasing decisions. This is happening, as information flows improve, but slower than foreseen reflecting perhaps the costs of managing the information flows and the need to learn from experience. Efficient functioning of supply chain communication is necessary for economic operators to implement appropriate risk management measures and to make informed purchasing decisions as well as for the ability of suppliers to respond to consumer requests. The communication requirement in Article 33 has triggered the development and potential use of information management tools by companies promoted by EU projects or activities of some Member States. However, it remains difficult for actors in the supply chain to retrieve, verify and communicate information on SVHCs in articles. The transfer of information to the consumer greatly depends on a well functioning communication in the supply chain as well as on the awareness and understanding of consumers about their "right to know". Better tracking of chemicals of concern in products would facilitate recycling and improve the uptake of secondary raw materials, as part of the Circular Economy. However, this would require transfer of information on the chemical content of end of-life articles to the waste management sector.[32]

Case studies show that information on SVHC's, for example in a mattress, does not reach the recycling company after the mattress becoming waste. The current EU legislation fails to ensure that waste operators, recyclers and manufacturers of products using recovered materials have access to information on the presence and properties of hazardous substances in recovered materials, exposing its workers, consumers and the environment to toxic chemicals.[33] Allocation of responsibilities after recycling is still unclear.

3° Poor consumer information and availability of spares

Assembly information for flat pack furniture can be challenging for some consumers, and they are rarely given guidance on how to maintain and repair furniture, in order to prolong and extend the product lifespan. The importance of not cutting off the fire label is generally not mentioned. Availability of spares is also important, e.g. to replace a broken hinge or damaged cupboard door for example, however a lack of availability of spare parts encourages the purchase of new furniture over circular consumption patterns.

4° Re-use and access over ownership

Consumers are opening up to the idea of making sharing a fundamental aspect of their consumer patterns again. Traditional ownership implies a certain level of responsibility, cost and commitment. Consumers looking for convenience and collecting as many experiences as possible want none of these things. Fractional ownership and leasing lifestyle businesses offer the possibility of perpetual upgrades to the latest and greatest, the ability to maximize the

32 COMMISSION STAFF WORKING DOCUMENT Accompanying the document COMMUNICATION FROM THE COMMISSION TO THE EUROPEAN PARLIAMENT, THE COUNCIL AND THE EUROPEAN ECONOMIC AND SOCIAL COMMITTEE Commission General Report on the operation of REACH and review of certain elements Conclusions and Actions,{COM(2018) 116 final}, 5 march 2018.

33 A. BERNARD, "Chemicals in material cycles: how EU law needs adjustments for the transition to an environmentally beneficial circular economy", *Elni review* 2017, 58.

number and variety of experiences, and allow consumers to access otherwise out-of-reach luxuries. Owning bulky, irregularly used items is both expensive and unsustainable, especially in dense urban environments where space is at a premium. With more consumers having mobile access to online systems, it becomes easier to book items whenever and wherever they are needed.[34]

Nowadays Belgium has rather rigid and incomplete legal rules for fractional ownership. Rules concerning the hire and lease of movables are not adapted to the new reality.

5° Guarantees and hierarchy of remedies for sales contracts

Starting from the requirements from the Consumer Sales and Guarantees Directive, Belgium adopted a legal guarantee regime of two years, which covers any defect that is presumed to have existed at the time of the delivery of the product and that becomes apparent within the guarantee period (*supra*; 3.3 a). On top of this legal guarantee, consumers may also be offered a commercial guarantee. When seeking a remedy for the defective product the consumer is entitled to a repair or replacement. Should it be disproportionate or impossible for the trader to provide such remedies, then the consumer is entitled to a reduction of the price or a rescission of the sales contract with refund. From a circular economy-point of view a repair – if possible – should in general prevail over the replacement of the product.[35]

4. CONCLUDING REMARKS

A circular economy favours activities that preserve more value in the form of energy, labour and materials. This means designing for durability, reuse, remanufacturing, and recycling to keep products, components, and materials circulating in the economy. Circular systems make effective use of biologically-based materials by encouraging many different uses before nutrients are returned to natural systems. A circular economy avoids the use of non-renewable resources and preserves or enhances renewable ones, for instance by returning valuable nutrients to the soil to support regeneration, or using renewable energy as opposed to relying on fossil fuels.

Legal action on different fields will have to be taken to support the transition towards a circular economy as current legislation often shows a static approach to the products or services with, for instance, an emphasis on the pre-contractual information duty. As products and services face "a longer life" in a circular

---

[34] Http://trendwatching.com/trends/11trends2011/.

[35] See the contribution of E. TERRYN, "A Right to Repair? Towards Sustainable Remedies in Consumer Law", in this book.

economy, one will have to rethink the theory on information duties as recycling and reuse require information on a continuous basis. Further, new questions arise as to liabilities for (hidden) defects: will the previous user face liability to the latter and if so, under what conditions?

A SCANDINAVIAN PERSPECTIVE ON THE ROLE OF CONSUMERS IN THE CIRCULAR ECONOMY*

Eléonore MAITRE-EKERN** and Carl DALHAMMAR***

1. INTRODUCTION

The European Union (EU) has established the need to transition towards a more circular economy as one of its policy goals.[1] The Circular Economy (CE) entails minimizing extraction of finite natural resources and designing waste out of the system. This requires improved design of products for increased durability (e.g. quality materials), reparability (disassembly and spare parts), re-use and various cascading practices (including remanufacturing and recycling). At the same time, reverse supply chains need to be established to ensure quality treatment of discarded products, and innovative business models must be put in place to replace existing ones and seize new opportunities.[2] The transition towards the CE will also depend on a number of enabling factors ranging economic incentives, infrastructure, and collaboration, and spreading information on best practice, as well as policies and regulations.[3]

The actors involved in the transition towards more sustainable production and consumption are manifold. In this paper, we explore one of the most volatile and complex of these actors: consumers. The role of consumers in the transition towards the CE is significant. They are the recipients of production output and

* This research was supported by the Research Council of Norway (Norges forskningsråd), and the Mistra REES (Resource Efficient and Effective Solutions) programme, funded by Mistra (The Swedish Foundation for Strategic Environmental Research).

** *Department of Public and International Law, University of Oslo.*

*** *International Institute for Industrial Environmental Economics (IIIEE), Lund University.*

1 Commission Communication, Closing the loop – An EU action plan for the Circular Economy, COM(2015) 614 final.

2 See e.g. Ellen MacArthur Foundation (2013), Towards the Circular Economy Vol. 2 Opportunities for the consumer goods sector.

3 Maitre-Ekern, E. (2018), Exploring the Spaceship Earth: A Circular Economy for Products, in: Maitre-Ekern, E., C. Dalhammar & H.C. Bugge. (Eds.). *Preventing environmental damage from products – Analyses of the Policy and Regulatory Framework in Europe*, Cambridge University Press.

the starting point of reverse cycles when they get rid of discarded products; and their purchasing decisions, consumption behaviours, and awareness of sustainability impacts and opportunities are crucial for the transition. Consumer roles are currently changing rapidly with the development of new consumption models, such as the Sharing Economy (SE), facilitated by the rapid expansion of digital platforms.

In the next section, we review the various and changing roles of consumers in the CE, and discuss how certain roles should be prioritised. We then examine how those roles translate into policy and law, and argue the need for a solid policy mix. We focus in particular on the policy context in Sweden and Norway, but also shortly introduce the EU policy framework. Finally, we examine some examples of concrete new CE policies, legal rules, and other business and local initiatives in Norway and Sweden. We end with the conclusions.

2. THE CIRCULAR ECONOMY OBJECTIVES AND THE ROLES OF CONSUMERS

2.1. CONSUMPTION IN THE CE

The Circular Economy (CE) is put forward as a way to overcome the current production and consumption model based on continuous growth and increasing resource throughput. For food and other biologically-based materials, this means allowing them to regenerate and provide new renewable resources for the economy. On the other hand, technical cycles shall ensure the recovery of products, components and materials in particular through re-use, repair and remanufacturing activities.[4] Transitioning to a circular economy requires us in particular to reconsider product design to prolong product lifetime and facilitate repair, re-use and other forms of recovery. At the same time, skills need to be developed to ensure that products are sorted and managed properly, and biological nutrients returned to the soil. Reverse supply networks are deemed to play an increasingly important role in a circular economic model. The shift towards the CE also requires innovative business models to replace existing ones or seize new opportunities.[5]

The success of the CE will, however, depend largely on the behaviour of end consumers. Consumption habits need to change radically from what they have been for the last half a century; from overconsumption towards more sustainable consumption, away from disposable and towards durable goods. Consumption in the CE requires buying quality rather quantity, maintaining and repairing rather than using and discarding, renting and sharing rather than owning. Consumers

4 Ellen MacArthur Foundation (2013).
5 Ellen MacArthur Foundation (2013), 74.

are however very volatile and complex market actors. Motivations behind consumer choices are manifold and may vary with time and circumstances. Environmental considerations may prompt some consumers to favour products that are (or appear) more sustainable, but even consumers who care for the environment may take harmful decisions as the result of their situation and the balancing of other social goals, notably health, housing and education.[6] The transformation towards more sustainable consumer behaviour requires notably raising awareness among consumers as well as ensuring that they have access to clear and accurate information. Moreover, whereas some consumers will always prioritise environmental considerations over other concerns (such as price or convenience), some will never be convinced to use ethics and moral arguments as guide for their purchasing decision. That is why both economics incentives and mandatory requirements need to be part of the toolkit of the policymakers to foster sustainable consumption.

2.2. WHAT ROLES FOR CONSUMERS?

Consumers are at the centre of the value chain: they are the main target of the supply chain, and the starting point of the reverse supply chain. Traditionally, consumers have been recognized in the law almost exclusively in their role as purchasers of new goods.[7] Moreover, they are seen as the weaker party in commercial transactions, the rights of which needs protecting. New forms of use and consumption, such as the Sharing Economy (SE), redefines the role and needs of the consumers, and will require law to also adapt. In official policy documents as well as research related to the CE and the SE, we can discern different roles for the actors engaging in consumption activities: depending on the context, these can be branded inter alia as 'consumers', 'users', 'peers', and so on.[8] In relation to the CE objectives, there is limited specific literature on the role of consumers in the CE.[9] In the EU Action Plan on CE, the role of

6 Maitre-Ekern, E. (2017), The Choice of Regulatory Instruments for the Circular Economy, in: Mathis K. and B. Huber (ed.), *Environmental Law and Economics*, Springer; Field B. C. & Field M. K. (2013), *Environmental economics: an introduction.* (6th ed.), McGraw-Hill.

7 And of course also services, though consumer law has traditionally struggled with providing equal rights to consumers of services as to consumers of products.

8 E.g. EU policy documents on the CE use the term 'consumer' but refers to 'users' in the context of the SE. The Ellen MacArthur Foundation uses 'consumers' in the context of biological cycles and 'users' for the technical cycles. In this paper, we use the term' consumer' to refer to any person engaging into consumption activities at large.

9 Rather, relevant literature can be found in several research fields, but seldom directly connected to consumers and the CE; for some exceptions see for instance Ferdousi, F. & Qjang, D. (2016), Implementing circular economy and its impact on Consumer ecological behaviour, *RISUS – Journal on Innovation and Sustainability*, 7 (1); Wieser, H. (2016), Beyond Planned Obsolescence: Product Lifespans and the Challenges to a Circular Economy, *GAIA – Ecological Perspectives for Science and Society*, 25 (3), 156– 160; Camacho Otero, J., Pettersen,

accurate consumer information and proper pricing is highlighted as key aspects for the consumption choices. Generally speaking, the policy documents seems to express belief that some consumers will be motivated to more sustainable consumption prices if there is relevant information, whereas many are mainly influenced through incentives, which can be provided through economic incentives or legislation (e.g. rules on consumer guarantees and laws supporting the availability of reasonably prices spare parts).

In the policy documents at the European and national levels, we can see various expectations of users in their various 'roles' that can support the objectives of the SE and the CE.

In this section, we aimed at mapping the various 'roles' and activities that can support the CE in Table 1 below. The table is only meant as a preliminary attempt at a categorization while keeping in mind that the role of consumers is currently in a state of flux and is expected to continue changing and developing.

Table 1. Examples of 'roles' for consumers in the Circular Economy.

Main role	Main potential activities/interests that can support the CE
Purchaser	- Rewarding circular business models in their purchasing decisions - Making use of product labels - Making use of product information and look for missing information - Optimizing the product choice - Purchasing re-used and second hand products as alternatives to new products - Lease instead of buy products and services - Focus on the services instead of the products - Buy durable, high quality products - Buy products for which spare parts are made available
User	- Do not replace products that work - Prolong the life of products (proper use; maintenance; updates)
Repairer	- Preference for repairs rather than buy new - Engage with own repairs when possible (do-it-yourself, DIY); communities (e.g. repair cafés) - Take part in repair workshops etc.
Seller	- Do not throw away stuff that can be sold or re-used
Sharer and collaborator	- Prioritize sharing schemes over leasing or buying - Engage with peer-to-peer (P2P) schemes that enables sharing of resources
Engaging with waste sorting and re-use	- Hand in stuff for re-use rather than recycling - Ensure waste is collected and sorted properly

I.N., Boks, C. (2017), Consumer and user acceptance in the circular economy: what are researchers missing? Proceedings from PLATE 2017, Delft Nov 2017.

2.3. A HIERARCHY OF CONSUMER BEHAVIOUR

In the EU, waste management is governed by a hierarchy according to which waste prevention is to be prioritized over preparation for re-use, followed by recycling, energy recovery, and finally landfilling.[10] This hierarchy limits the freedom of actors of the value chain for the purpose of reducing waste and promoting more sustainable management of waste. Just like the Waste Management Hierarchy (WMH), we suggest to develop a 'hierarchy of consumer behaviour' to prompt more sustainable consumption. In order to reach CE objectives, we put forward that consumers need to inter alia:

1) **Avoid** – avoid purchasing unnecessary and single use products;
2) **Maintain and repair** – maintain and repair products rather than replace or buy new ones;
3) **Share** – share products rather than buy individual ones;
4) **Lease** – rather lease high quality products instead of buying them;
5) **Buy second-hand** – purchase second-hand or remanufactured products rather than new ones;
6) **Buy quality** – purchase high quality, durable, energy efficient products rather than products of poorer quality;
7) **Recirculate** – sell products or hand them in for re-use when they are no longer wanted, rather than to recycle them (the last point is reflected in the WMH).

Similarly to the WMH, the hierarchy of consumer behaviour could not be absolute and specific circumstances would likely affect the order of priorities, notably if a second-hand product is more polluting or energy-intensive than a new one.[11]

Introducing such a hierarchy aims to indicate the priority areas for actions as well as reveal to consumers what behaviour is expected of them. It implies that law and policy have a role to play to encourage the hierarchy. This means in particular policies to promote the purchase of long-lasting, expensive high quality products that can be repaired in combination with stimulus to develop recourse to repair activities. Other policies would need to aim at encouraging second-hand purchasing and product leasing. Further and more detailed analysis about the policy mix resumes in section 3 below.

A hierarchy of behaviour would arguably oppose consumer choice and hence run up against significant constraints. For instance, it may be very difficult in practice to design policies that force everyone to share resources. A recent consumer survey in Sweden indicates that many Swedes are not very interested in sharing resources, and there are few indications that this number is growing

---

10 Cf. Directive 2008/98/EC of 19 November 2008 on waste (Waste Framework Directive), OJ L 312, 22.11.2008, p. 3, Art. 4.

11 Ibid. Art 4(2) states that deviation from the WMH can be allowed if this is a better option from a life cycle perspective.

despite the political support for the SE and all the positive media reporting on the virtues of sharing[12] (not to mention the generally pro-environment attitudes of the Swedish population). However, we know that people are much more willing to share certain products than others. Hence, measures that promote sharing could work well in certain sectors, but be of less use in others. This implies that different strategies may need to be designed for specific sectors. Then we may need an alternative route for people unwilling to share, which could include policies promoting high quality, durable products and stimulus for repairs.

3. SUSTAINABLE CONSUMPTION AND THE NEED FOR A POLICY MIX

3.1. INTRODUCING THE EUROPEAN POLICY MIX

Perez has identified the regulation of products to incentivize for durability and maintenance, and making producers responsible for the entire lifespan of their products, as key measures to encourage the circular economy and manufacturing durability, as well as stimulating the growth of a rental and maintenance economy.[13] In the last decades, the EU as well as its Member States has adopted a growing number of product regulations, and 'life cycle thinking' has an increasing importance in EU environmental law.[14]

Early product policies and laws in Europe have mainly addressed: 1) chemicals in products; 2) collection and recycling of used products, and; 3) energy efficiency of products. We now see new policies emerging that address conflict minerals and product durability. In the last couple of years, policymakers have shown growing interest in incentivizing longer product lifetimes and supporting repair services, notably through direct regulation of durability (mandatory requirements following the Ecodesign Directive), promoting the availability of spare parts (French consumer code) or longer mandated consumer warranties (EU and national rules).[15]

Table 2 gives an overview of the main product related policies in the EU and its Member States.

---

12 Aktuell Hållbarhet Direkt (Newsletter) (2018) Svenskar vill inte delta i delningsekonomin. Aktuell Hållbarhet 2018-03-07.

13 Perez, C. (2016), Capitalism, Technology and a Green Global Golden Age: The Role of History in Helping to Shape the Future, In: M. Jacobs and M. Mazzucato (Eds.) *Rethinking capitalism*. Wiley Blackwell. See also Hojnik, J. (2018), Ecological modernization through servitization: EU regulatory support for sustainable product-service systems, *Review of European, Comparative & International Environmental Law*, 1-14.

14 Dalhammar, C. (2015) The application of 'life cycle thinking' in European environmental law: theory and Practice, *Journal for European Env & Planning Law* 12: 97-127.

15 Cf. Maitre-Ekern, E. and Dalhammar, C. (2016), Regulating planned obsolescence: a review of legal approaches to increase product durability and reparability in Europe, *Review of European, Comparative & International Environmental Law (RECIEL)* 25(3), 378-394.

Table 2. Product related policies in Europe (recent policies in bold letters).

Type of environmental aspect	European Union law and policy	Examples of Member State policies
Chemical and material content	Horizontal legislation (e.g. REACH) Conflict minerals Sector oriented laws on chemical restrictions (e.g. Packaging, electronics)	Green public procurement criteria for, e.g., chemicals and conflict minerals Eco-labels Taxes on chemicals
Collection and recycling of waste products	General rules and guidelines (e.g., Waste Framework Directive) Sector oriented EPR laws (e.g. WEEE Directive[16]; Waste and Packaging Waste Directive)[17]	Waste related taxes Infrastructure for re-use and recycling Re-use parks/shops for re-used products/repair activities Mandatory re-use obligations for white goods (Spain)
Energy efficiency	Mandatory energy performance standards (MEPS) (set under the Ecodesign Directive) Mandatory energy labelling (set under the Energy Labelling Regulation)[18] Voluntary labelling (Energy Star)	Eco-labels Green public procurement criteria The use of life cycle costing (LCC) in public procurement
Durability, lifetime and reparability	*Direct incentives:* Mandatory 'lifetime'/'durability' requirements set under the Ecodesign Directive – Vacuum cleaners, lighting products Voluntary ecodesign agreement, imaging equipment *Indirect incentives:* Minimum rules on consumer guarantees	*Direct incentives:* Banning planned obsolescence (France) *Indirect incentives:* Incentivizing the provision of spare parts (France) Lower VAT on repair services National rules on longer consumer guarantees and/or changed rules for burden of proof is transferred from seller to consumer (several EU Member States) Public procurement of remanufactured furniture and computers

Source: Amended version of the table in Faure and Dalhammar 2018.[19]

---

16 Directive 2012/19/EU of 4 July 2012 on Waste Electrical and Electronic Equipment (WEEE), OJ L 197, 24.7.2012, p. 38.

17 Directive 2015/720 of 29 April 2015 amending Directive 94/62/EC as regards reducing the consumption of light weight plastic carrier bags, OJ L 115, 6.5.2015, p. 11.

18 Regulation (EU) 2017/1369 of 4 July 2017 setting a framework for energy labelling, OJ L 198, 28.7.2017, p. 1.

19 Faure, M and C. Dalhammar. (2018). Principles for the Design of a Policy Framework to Address Product Life-cycle Impacts, In: Maitre-Ekern, E., C. Dalhammar & H.C. Bugge. (Eds.). *Preventing environmental damage from products – Analyses of the Policy and Regulatory Framework in Europe*. Cambridge University Press.

These policies are quite different in nature and include mandatory requirements, as well as market-based approaches. Interestingly, some of the recent policies clearly signal that markets cannot be trusted to deliver durable products even if consumers want it, and that public interventions are needed. Governments are starting to take serious actions and question corporations they suspect of planning the premature obsolescence of their products. Following a law criminalizing the act of 'planned obsolescence', French prosecutors opened an investigation on Apple who admitted deliberately slowing down older iPhone models through software updates.[20] The judges will now have to decide on whether Apple's intention was to push consumers towards purchasing the new iPhone model or – as argued by the company – whether the aim was to preserve the battery. In any case, this is just one example of signals to the market that unsustainable business models are worn off. It is the hope that such initiatives will trigger changes in industrial practices such as product standardization activities, where product durability may become more important.

Another interesting observation regarding the laws and policies is that there is a clear tendency to regulate product design features and chemicals primarily at the EU level to avoid national regulations that may distort trade. Other policies and processes – such as incentives to trigger durability, national eco-labelling schemes, set-up of waste collection schemes, and public procurement sustainability criteria – are still adopted at the national level. This means that there will always be a need to coordinate EU and national policies to ensure a good 'policy mix' as opposed to a 'policy mess'.[21] Whereas good synergies of policies may advance the CE objectives, conflicting legislation may defeat the purpose of rules.[22] At a recent workshop in Brussels, many industries raised concerns that future EU and national laws may not be well coordinated, and that for instance rules on eco-design and consumer warranties to could lead to conflicting incentives and practices.[23]

---

[20] BBC (2018), Apple investigated by France for 'planned obsolescence', available at www.bbc.com/news/world-europe-42615378.

[21] Faure, M and C. Dalhammar (2018), Principles for the Design of a Policy Framework to Address Product Life-cycle Impacts, In: Maitre-Ekern, E., C. Dalhammar & H.C. Bugge. (Eds.), *Preventing environmental damage from products – Analyses of the Policy and Regulatory Framework in Europe*, Cambridge University Press.

[22] For example, lack of coordination between waste and chemical policies may defeat the goal of creating a market for secondary materials. See Tojo, N. and Å. Thidell (2018), Material recycling without hazardous substances – interplay of two policy streams and impacts on industry, In: Maitre-Ekern, E., C. Dalhammar & H.C. Bugge. (Eds.), *Preventing environmental damage from products – Analyses of the Policy and Regulatory Framework in Europe*, Cambridge University Press.

[23] Documentation form the workshop is available at www.eceee.org/events/eceee-seminars-and-workshops/the-ecodesign-directive-in-a-changing-policy-climate-challenges-and-opportunities/.

3.2. THE ROLE OF CONSUMPTION IN THE POLICY MIX

Changing consumption patterns requires a policy mix that addresses at the same time the product itself and the behaviour of the consumer. For example, prolonging the lifetime of consumer electronics is a very effective way to reduce life cycle impacts. However, consumer behaviour point towards ever-more frequent early discard and purchase of new appliances that cancels out the potential benefits of making more resistant and repairable items. In such a situation, an effective policy mix would need to include many components and address at the same time producers, consumers and repairers such as[24]:

- Impose ecodesign requirements to manufacturers to make durable quality products that are easy to repair and disassemble[25];
- Inform consumers about the expected lifetime and reparability of products upon purchase;
- Extend legal guarantees and place the burden of proof on producers to ensure that consumers can pursue remedies for defective products;
- Mandate producers to provide spare parts and repair tools to any repairer at reasonable costs, and ensure that competition and IP legislation may not be used to prevent repair;
- Reduce VAT for the repair sector; and/or offer tax deduction to consumers who engage in repair activities;
- Support do-it-yourself activities where people can learn to repair their stuff and prolong the lifetime (e.g. repair cafés);
- Raise consumer awareness about the environmental impacts of electronics and the environmental gains from repairs.

Currently, we are seeing a lot of 'experimentation' regarding CE related policies at national, regional and local levels. The types of policies are very different in nature from criminalization of companies' behaviour to the promotion of remanufacturing through public procurement and various initiatives to redirect materials from recycling to re-use (see section 5 below). Continuous 'policy experimentation' is likely to take place also in the coming years. These policies need to be scrutinized carefully for their potential to contribute to the CE objectives, benefit for the policy mix, as well as the opportunity to develop them at EU level.

24 Andersson, A, J. Carlestam et al. (2018), Circular Economy: Research into the Availability and Willingness to Repair Consumer Electronic Products, Report: Lund University.

25 This is crucial as it is often a malfunctioning battery that kills the whole product; making it easy to replace the battery is important.

4. THE POLICY CONTEXT IN SWEDEN AND NORWAY

4.1. THE EU AS FRAMEWORK

Both Sweden – as an EU Member States – and Norway – as member of the EEA Agreement – are bound by the legislation adopted at EU level on environmental and consumer protection. The Commission's Communications adopted in those areas, although no binding in nature, are also relevant for both countries. In particular, the EU action plan for the circular economy adopted in December 2015 had a strong impact on national policies. The Communication identified consumers as one of the driving forces in the 'transition to a more circular economy', and put forward a number of measures to foster more sustainable consumption.[26] The document emphasises is particular information disclosure as a way of shaping consumer choice, while cautioning against the damaging effects of unreliable, inaccurate and unclear environmental claims. Another important factor for influencing consumer behaviour is the economic incentive. Whether relating to the sales price or after-sale rights, incentives and other economic instruments may prove effective in promoting the purchase and availability on the market of more durable and reparable products. Measures relating to waste management also have a role to develop re-use and repair activities, and other means of reducing the amount of household waste.

Promoting sustainable consumption in the context of the CE is not confined to a single strategy and the breath of possible measures is necessarily wide. The rise of innovative forms of consumption, such as sharing or consuming services rather than products, is opening opportunities at the same time as it is creating challenges that need investigating.[27] The 2016 Communication on the Collaborative Economy cautiously puts forward the potential of sharing to 'contribute to the EU's sustainability agenda and to the transition to the circular economy'.[28] It does not, however, examine the environmental benefits nor make propositions to ensure that P2P activities support CE objectives. What the Communication puts emphasis on is the changing role of consumers, and how that affects consumer legislation. Traditionally seen as 'the weaker party requiring protection', consumers in the Collaborative Economy engage in commercial transactions with peers, who also need protecting. Since EU consumer law does not apply to those transactions, it is generally left for the Member States to regulate this issue. At present, there a great variations between

26 Commission Communication, Closing the loop – An EU action plan for the Circular Economy, COM(2015) 614 final.

27 Ibid.

28 Commission Communication, A European agenda for the collaborative economy, COM(2016) 356 final.

the national rules, and the sector regarding notably the distinction between 'peers' and professional services providers.[29]

Besides, policy decisions may take various forms – e.g. mandatory or voluntary instruments – and be adopted at different levels, not least national, regional and local. Indeed, Member States retain exclusive or shared competences to adopt legislation in decisive areas, such as taxation, waste management or – as indicated above – some areas of consumer protection.

4.2. SWEDEN: PIONEERING FOR REPAIR ACTIVITIES

Two Swedish official inquiries into the CE and the SE were published in 2017.[30] The first emanates from the Ministry of the Environment and Energy, while the Ministry of Finance wrote the second. It is clear that they have distinct focus and objective. The CE policy document advocates governmental interventions of different kinds and is accompanied with clear proposals. The Swedish governmental inquiry on the SE from 2017 however did not propose much public policy efforts to promote the SE. It stated nonetheless that consumer protection legislation and informative measures may be necessary to protect users in the SE.[31] Table 3 gives an overview of the content of both documents, and reveals the difference of approach.

Table 3. Differences in the Swedish official inquiries into the CE and SE[32]

	CE (SOU 2017:22)	SE (SOU 2017:26)
Need for governemntal interventions	Several proposals for interventions are proposed, as well as a new governmental delegation for suporting the CE.	No need for any specific interventions proposed, though it is stated that interventions to protect users may be necessary in the future.

29 Some Member States have established thresholds to differentiate between a peer offering services on an occasional basis or as a professional. Other Member States differentiate between professional and peer-to-peer services when laying down authorisation requirements. Moreover, rules may be different between the transport and the accommodation sectors. See Commission Staff Working Document, European agenda for the collaborative economy – supporting analysis, SWD(2016) 184 final.

30 Miljö- och Energidepartementet (2017), Från värdekedja till värdecykel – så får Sverige en mer cirkulär ekonomi [From value chain to value cycle – Sweden gets a more circular economy], SOU 2017:22; Finansdepartementet (2017), Delningsekonomi på användarnas villkor [Sharing Economy – on the terms of the users], SOU 2017:26.

31 SOU 2017:26.

32 Adapted from Bademo, T. (2017), Förhållandet mellan cirkulär ekonomi och delningsekonomi [The relationship between the circular economy and the sharing economy], Thesis, Lund University.

	CE (SOU 2017:22)	SE (SOU 2017:26)
Proposed policies	Several policies are proposed including tax deductions for product leasing and repairs, support to carpooling, municipal activities related to waste infrastructure, and support for a green tax reform.	No new policy proposals suggested, though flaws in the current regulatory frameworks are analysed. A potential need for advice and information activities to support users involved in peer-to-peer (P2P) transactions are discussed.
Actors in focus	Main focus on households and business-to-consumer (B2C) actors, such as car pools and repair services, and municipalities in their roles as waste service providers.	Main focus on P2P market and thus actors involved in P2P such as private persons and internet platforms for trading products, car pools, or renting out apartments etc.
Relation to social sustainability	Few discussion about social sustainability; it is however discussed in relation to convenience of carpooling, and new jobs created through stimulus to the repair sector.	Points to several positive social aspects of SE, such as the access to new networks of people, and how P2P can provide affordable solutions also to consumer groups with lower incomes.
Relation to ecological sustainability	Stresses ecological benefits such as reduced GHG emissions and lower resource use.	States that the ecological implications from the SE is hard to establish and may be both positive and negative.

4.3. NORWAY: WASTE MANAGEMENT IN FOCUS

Two policy documents are addressing the transition towards the CE in Norway: a White Paper entitled 'Waste as a Resource – waste policy and circular economy'[33]; and a Governmental Strategy on Green Competitiveness.[34] None of them shows a level of ambition that goes beyond EU's recommendations nor especially innovative means of ensuring sustainable consumption.

The White Paper takes waste policy – and in particular the hierarchy of waste management contained in the Waste Framework Directive – as a starting point. The Government then makes policy recommendations in three main areas: waste prevention, material recycling and preparation for reuse, and marine plastic litter and microplastics. With regards to the first, the White Paper mentions dematerialization, the service economy and the sharing economy as examples of ways to reduce waste without necessarily affecting living

33 Klima- og miljødepartementet (2016), Avfall som ressurs – avfallspolitikk og sirkulær økonomi [Waste as a resource – waste policy and circular economy], Meld. St. 45 (2016–2017).

34 Klima- og miljødepartementet (2017), Bedre vekst, lavere utslipp – regjeringens strategi for grønn konkurransekraft [Better growth, lower emissions – Government's strategy for green competitiveness].

standards.[35] Means of dematerializing the economy (i.e. reduction in material usage) are examined in more details for five priority sectors, namely food, textile, packaging, construction, and electrical and electronic equipment. The main recommendations from the government are to enter into dialogue with the industry. In June 2017, the government entered into an agreement with the food industry to reduce food wastage by 50% by 2030.[36] It is unclear, however, how that goal will be achieved concretely, and in particular with regard to changing consumer behaviour. Another proposition put forward in the White Paper is to pursue and develop producer responsibility schemes for packaging though it is not clear from the report how that should be done.

In addition to the lack of detailed propositions, one can also regret that the recommendations put forward by the government are not more ambitious and daring. For instance, the document could have considered measures such as phasing out certain types of products (e.g. plastic cutleries and other products made for one-time use)[37], imposing information disclosure about expected product lifetime and reparability, or promoting certain activities (such as repair) through taxation.

With regard to material recovery, Norway is not seeing much increase with a reported 38% between 2012 and 2015. Achieving the EU objective of 50% recovery from household waste by 2020 therefore calls for action. The White Paper reports that government should develop requirements for sorting and recovery of selected types of waste. It remains open what those requirements shall be.

The Governmental Strategy on Green Competitiveness recognises the importance of the need to shift towards a CE and that working towards a more efficient use of resources can strengthen green competitiveness. It does not, however, make much recommendation is this regard. The CE only accounts for a short chapter in the Strategy, which essentially incorporates the White Paper's recommendations:

- Work with the industry and waste sector to strengthen the market for secondary raw material;
- Develop rules to increase the useful and environmentally sound use of waste;
- Increase material recovery notably by expanding EPR schemes;
- Continue with the existing consumer guarantee scheme and collaborate with the EU to strengthen labelling schemes.

35 Meld. St. 45 (2016–2017), chapter 6.

36 Www.regjeringen.no/contentassets/1c911e254aa0470692bc311789a8f1cd/matsvinnavtale.pdf.

37 In its response to the White Paper, the Parliament urges the government to work towards such prohibition; Stortingsvedtak, Innst. 127 S (2017–2018), resolution nr. 498.

In February 2017, The Ministry of Finance published an official inquiry into the Sharing Economy.[38] The document does not contain any recommendations regarding the positive and negative impacts of the SE on the environment, or on how to ensure it contributes to achieving the goals of the CE. The inquiry devotes one section to consumer protection, and concludes that – pending the outcome of the 'fitness check' of consumer legislation at EU level – existing rules are sufficient and there is no need for a new regulatory framework.

With regards to hard law, the Product Control Act is worth mentioning as a prominent piece of legislation. Adopted in 1976, the Act aims at preventing damage to health and the environment through the regulation of products and the use of products.[39] It contains a general duty to act with due care and take reasonable measures to prevent or limit hazard caused by products they have influence on, such as manufacturers, importers and even users.[40] For producers, the duty of care is coupled with a duty to obtain knowledge about their products and to provide consumers with adequate and relevant information.[41] The Act also provides for the adoption by the State authorities of regulations that lay out more detailed rules for specific product groups.[42] The delegation of power is wide, and arguably could justify the adoption of far-reaching measures such as the prohibition of certain products.

5. ANALYSIS OF CHOSEN POLICIES AND LAWS FOR SUSTAINABLE CONSUMPTION

Below, we discuss some Swedish and Norwegian initiatives aimed at consumers that contribute to the CE objectives. Among the examples we find both 'older' and 'newer' examples of consumer oriented policies with implications for the CE, of quite different types. We classify them under headings related to the main consumer roles we have identified above, and following the order of our proposed hierarchy of behaviours (see section 2 above)

5.1. CONSUMERS AS MAINTAINERS AND REPAIRERS

In the Circular Economy, the circulation of products, components and materials optimizes resources utilization and prevents waste production. For technical

38 Finansdepartementet, Delingsøkonomien – muligheter og utfordringer [Sharing Economy – Opportunities and Challenges], NOU 2017:4.

39 Bugge, H. C. (2018), *Environmental Law in Norway* (3rd edition), Kluwer Law International, 64.

40 Norwegian Product Control Act (produktkontrolloven) of June 1976, nr. 79, Article 3(1).

41 Article 3(2) and (5) Product Control Act.

42 Article 4 Product Control Act.

products, the least resource intensive handling of products generally consists in keeping them in use longer through maintenance or repair. However, both activities often prove too difficult or costly for consumers in comparison to tossing aside older products to buy new ones. Most high-tech companies still make most of their profits on the sale of new products and have hence little interest in providing cheap and easy updates or enabling repairs they will not make money on.

5.1.1. Consumer guarantee

The EU Consumer Sales and Guarantees Directive establishes a minimum two-year legal guarantee for faulty consumer products.[43] In some European countries, including Norway and Sweden, the period of legal consumer guarantees have been extended beyond that minimum requirement. Following the Norwegian Consumer Law from 2002, the **legal consumer guarantee** allows consumers to request the repair or replacement of defects within a minimum period of two years, and up to five for products that have a 'significantly longer' (*vesentlig lenger*) expected lifetime.[44] Electronic equipment such as mobile phones, computers and tablets, and electrical appliances such as fridges, washing machines or vacuum cleaners, would fall within the second category.[45] A recent survey showed that a majority of Norwegian consumers are unaware of the five-year rule, and that some even confuse them with the one-year commercial guarantee offered by some retailers (e.g. for mobile phones).[46] Yet, the number of consumers complaints based on the five-year redress appears to be rising, in particular for electronic equipment (mobile phones, laptop, etc.).[47]

According to Norwegian law, within the legal guarantee period the consumer may choose between repair and replacement of the defective product unless the chosen mean would entail 'unreasonable costs' for the seller.[48] Requested to rule on the case of boots the heels of which broke six weeks after purchase, the Supreme Court supported the seller's claim that replacement would involve unreasonable costs and that offering repair should be sufficient.[49] The judgment

---

43 Directive 1999/44/EC of 25 May 1999 on certain aspects of the sale of consumer goods and associated guarantees, OJ L 171, 7.7.1999, p. 12.

44 Norwegian Consumer Sales Act [f orbrukerkjøpsloven] of June 2002, nr. 34, §27, second paragraph.

45 In 2007, the Supreme Court of Norway ruled that cell phones have an expected lifespan of 3–4 years and should hence benefit from the five-year warranty. Supreme Court [Høyesteretts] judgment of 21 September 2007, Rt. 2007 s. 1274, known as "the cell phone judgment" (mobiltelefondommen).

46 Strandbakken P. (2017), Consumer complaint deadlines and product durability: the role of law and regulation, PLATE 2017 Conference Proceedings, pp. 382–386, 384.

47 Ibid, 385.

48 §29 Consumer Sales Act.

49 Supreme Court [Høyesteretts] judgment of 17 February 2006, Rt. 2006, s. 179, known as the 'boot heel judgment' (støvletthældommen).

emphasized that repair also appeared as more environmentally friendly option, not least because the market for secondary footwear is inexistent in Norway.[50] Whether this interpretation of the law means that, in a reverse situation, the seller would have to offer repair in priority remains unclear. The judgment points towards the existence of a consumer's 'right to repair'.

In a judgment from February 2018, the District Court of Oslo dismissed the complaint by Apple that a Norwegian repairer, Huseby, was infringing **IP rights** (trademark usage)[51] by offering replacing broken iPhone screens with refurbished screens from China.[52] The refurbished screens were bearing the Apple logo, which, according to Apple, should be seen as pirated copies. One of the grounds for the court's decision, which is of particular interest for this paper, is the legitimate attempt pursed by Huseby to maintain a secondary market for unauthorized spare parts for mobile phones. One important impact of this decision is to contribute to the development of a repair market that allows consumers to access high-quality repair at low cost from local unauthorized repairers. Apple appealed the decision, but the Court of Appeal has not yet ruled on the matter.

The Swedish government has chosen to trigger repair and leasing activities through VAT and tax deductions. Using taxation to foster environmental protection is not new, but seldom progressive enough to internalise all externalities and stimulate real change. The originality of the Swedish approach comes from the fact that, unlike the Pigovian tax, which is imposed on a market activity that generates negative externalities, it is rather meant to relieve good performers from an existing tax.

The current legal framework for taxes in Sweden contains two deductions for specific repairs activities: the first concerns **repairs in the home**. The Swedish law on income tax allows deductions for some work in the home, including care of clothes and home textiles; work relating to the installation, repair and maintenance of data and information technology equipment; and repair and maintenance of appliances[53]; the second deduction aims at **some repair services**. The VAT is reduced from 25 to 12% for repairs of bicycles, shoes, leather goods, clothes and household linen.[54]

A recent official Swedish inquiry on the CE[55] proposed to introduce other tax deductions **for rental goods, second hand goods and repairs** (the so-called 'hyber' deduction). According to the legislative proposal, households would receive a tax reduction when they repair or rent consumer products or buy services to sell second-hand products. The proposed tax reduction would amount to 50 per cent of the labour cost of these services. It would reduce the tax

50 Ibid, at paragraph 33.
51 Norwegian Trademarks Act [varemerkeloven] of March 2010, nr. 8, §4.
52 Oslo District Court [Tingrett] judgment of 2 February 2018 (case 151334).
53 Swedish Income Tax Act [inkomstskattelagen] (1999:1229) Chapter 67, 13 §(Section).
54 Swedish Law on VAT [mervärdesskattelag] (1994:200) 7 Chapter, 1 §(section).
55 SOU 2017:22.

wedge for households that buy 'hyber' services. The proposal is expected to lead to ca 10 000 new jobs, and expects to reduce tax revenue with approximately SEK 0–1.8 billion (i.e. EUR 0–180 million) per year; this however depends on how many unemployed that gets employment under the scheme.[56]

Taxation can be a very useful tool to promote sustainability, but it can also become a barrier to practices supporting the CE. A **tax on chemicals in electronics** was introduced in Sweden in 2017.[57] It is charged per product and weight depending on a specified number of chemical compounds in the material.[58] For products that contain less of the taxed compounds (in weight%), the tax is reduced. Depending on the circumstances, the importer or seller is usually the party paying the tax. While the tax is pro-environment, it may have some negative effects. Firstly, it only applies in Sweden, which means that consumer may choose to import products from outside Sweden to avoid the tax.[59] Another issue is whether the tax applies to remanufactured computers; whether they should pay depends on how the rules are interpreted. Since remanufactured computers are very beneficial from an environmental perspective, the remanufacturers do not think it makes sense that they should pay.[60] The Swedish Tax Authority has however stated that tax shall only be paid once for a given product, so for future remanufacturing the tax will not have to be paid for electronics originally sold in Sweden.[61] More research on these rules are needed before the full implications are understood.

5.1.2. Re-use schemes

Keeping products in active use is an objective that some Swedish regions and municipalities have also started pursuing. In particular, they make use of **internal 're-use' schemes** for furniture, where existing furniture that is not used in one part of the municipality or region, can be an alternative to purchasing new furniture.[62] While this applies for the public sector, it can provide some support

56 The '0' in tax losses may happen if the deduction generates additional economic activities, which generate taxes.

57 Lag (2016:1067) om skatt på kemikalier i viss elektronik.

58 Examples of taxed substances are chloride and bromide compounds above a certain weight percentage.

59 Ekblom, B. 2017. '1 juli träder kemikalieskatten i kraft – så här påverkas du' [July 1, the chemical tax comes into force – here is how it affects you], available at https://pcforalla.idg.se/2.1054/1.670546/allt-om-kemikalieskatten.

60 Discussed in an editorial (SvD Näringsliv): 'Ny skatt slår mot återanvändning av it' [New tax hits IT recycling], available at www.svd.se/ny-skatt-slar-mot-ateranvandning-av-it.

61 Statement from Swedish Tax Authority: www.skatteverket.se/foretagochorganisationer/skatter/punktskatter/ kemikalieskatt/narintraderskattskyldigheten/undantagfranskattskyldighetensintrade.4.5c1163881590be297b5177e9.html.

62 Jonsson, A. (2017), Återbrukssystem för möbler i kommunal sektor. Hinder och möjligheter för cirkulära lösningar [Recycling system for furniture in the municipal sector. Obstacles and opportunities for circular solutions], Thesis: Lund University.

also to private re-use practices. There are also possibilities to share furniture between municipalities, but whether this is legally allowed is uncertain. Other legal uncertainties concerns whether municipally owned corporations can participate in the systems, and more generally whether municipalities are allowed to give away extra furniture not needed to charities etc.

5.2. CONSUMERS AS RENTERS AND SHARERS

New consumption habits have emerged recently that are particularly relevant for the CE, and in particular the shift from ownership-based to use-based consumption. In Scandinavia, as in the rest of Europe, the transport and accommodation sector in particular have seen the emergence of new business models, including Uber, Airbnb and many others, that revolutionize the market. Copenhagen, Sweden and Oslo are also among many cities that have bicycle-sharing systems.

Other interesting initiatives are developing, notably in the clothing sector with, for instance, the Swedish brand **Filippa K** that rents out its collections for 20% of the sales price.[63] The idea is that, instead of purchasing a piece of clothing that will eventually spend most of its time in a closet that item can be used repeatedly.[64] Filippa K also has a second-hand corner in their 'regular' stores for used items of their own brand.

5.3. CONSUMERS AS BUYERS

5.3.1. Second-hand

In the CE, products shall recirculate and consumers shall therefore not continually purchase new products. As a result, new businesses models are emerging, such as **ReTuna.** Located in the Swedish commune of Eskilstuna, Re-Tuna is a shopping mall where all the shops (currently 13 shops) sell reused stuff in some form or another. The products come from the municipal re-use and recycling stations. ReTuna also hosts restaurants, cafés and educational activities, as well as related activities like 'cloth swapping' for the general public. The project was initially very controversial, but the perceived success (6000 people showed up at the inauguration) has meant that most actors are very

63 Each lease lasts for four days and the costs of cleaning are included in the rental price. See www.filippa-k.com/no/filippak-world/lease/.

64 Tekie, H et al., (2014), EPR systems and new business models, Nordisk Ministerråd, available at http://urn.kb.se/resolve?urn=urn:nbn:se:norden:org:diva.

positive to the project.[65] Since ReTuna has commercial shops, there is no conflict between public and private interests related to competition, though there has been some concerns that the shops in ReTuna has primary access to re-use stuff from the municipal re-use and recycling stations, whereas other shops do not; thus the public systems favour certain actors.[66]

In Norway, a private initiative developed in remanufacturing. Established in 2013, the Norwegian company, **Norsk Ombruk**, aims at giving household electrical goods a second life. The company receives products from various sources: electrical retails stores (e.g. Elkjøp), original equipment manufacturers (EOMs, including Electrolux), and municipalities.[67] This is facilitated by the rules laid down in the EU WEEE Directive, which allows consumers to return their WEEE free of charge at distributors and retail shops.[68] The products go through a quality inspection process, which consists in sourcing those who have the greatest potential for remanufacturing, and in particular those higher-quality branded products, but also its age and condition. Those products that are deemed fit for repair or refurbishment – around 48% according to Norsk Ombruk – are kept whole and fully cleaned. The rest is taken apart in order to recover key spare parts and then sent further for recycling. Upgrades of components and performances might lead to producing remanufactured products superior to the original. After undergoing testing and cleaning, the remanufactured products are sold again to consumers for half the price of the original. Norsk Ombruk has established partnerships with various retailers like IKEA and Elkjøp.[69] These second-life products are designed to last for about 5 years and benefit from the normal legal guarantee. In 2016, the company repaired 12,331 products, including refrigerators (40%), washing machines (25%), stoves (17%), dishwashers (10%) and dryers (8%).[70]

With the expansion of P2P digital platforms, consumers buy re-use items directly from other consumers. In Norway, P2P second-hand trading has expanded in the last decade. **Finn.no**, an online second-hand market place[71] established in the early 2000s, is one of the most visited websites.[72] In 2015, it registered 1,9 million visitors per week.[73] The digital platform allows users to

---

65 Helm, P. (2016), Cirkulär ekonomi & Avfallshantering. En ny infrastruktur genom återbruk [Circular Economy & Waste Management. A new infrastructure through reuse], Thesis: Lund University.

66 This issue is not documented but has been discussed at some workshops where the authors have participated.

67 Norsk Ombruk, The Benefits Case for Remanufacturing, Report, 2017, 28.

68 Article 5 WEEE.

69 Norsk Ombruk (2017), The Benefits Case for Remanufacturing, Report, 29.

70 Ibid, 28.

71 Finn.no also offers other services, such as job and housing ads.

72 And it is only fifth after google (.no and.com), facebook and youtube; https://www.similarweb.com/top-websites/norway.

73 Finn.no: Det norske bruktmarkedet – Trender og innsikt fra 2015, http://strandlund.no/wp-content/uploads/2016/04/FINN_Rapport_Det-norske-bruktmarkedet-2015.pdf.

register and post their advertisement online for free on the website or via the mobile application. Moreover, Norwegian tax law exempts from taxation the sale of household goods or other personal property that has been used in the owner's or his family's home.[74]

5.3.2. *Qualitative consumption*

Today, consumers are continuously encouraged to indulge into consumption, and in particular of cheap, brand-new, short-lived products not least through constant advertising. One cannot surf on the Internet, watch TV, take public transportation or simply walk in the streets without being assailed by some form of publicity: advertising inserts and boards, commercial spots, or distribution of promotional materials. Several studies show that the impact of advertising on consumers is immense and may lead to overwhelming consumption impulses.[75] Children advertising is particularly problematic given the extreme vulnerability of the targets.[76]

The Nordic countries have adopted progressive restrictions on marketing, in particularly when targeting vulnerable groups.[77] Sweden **bans TV advertising to children** under the age of 12. This also includes the use of characters related to children's TV programs in commercials.[78] The Swedish case law interprets the EU and Swedish rules on advertising to children stringently.[79]

5.4. CONSUMERS AND WASTE SORTING AND RECOVERY

Preventing waste shall be the first priority, but consumers will necessarily continue to discard some products, which hence legally become waste.[80] How this 'waste' is handled and treated is significant in the CE. Consumers are at the

---

74 Skatteloven §9–3.

75 See e.g. Moore, D. and Lee S. (2012), How advertising influences consumption impulses, *Journal of Advertising* 3(41), 107–120; Hultén P. and Vansyushyn V. (2014), Promotion and shoppers' impulse purchases: the example of clothes, *Journal of consumer marketing* 2(31), 94–102.

76 Studies have notably shown the correlation between food advertising and children obesity. Andreyeva T. et al. (2011), Exposure to food advertising on television: Associations with children's fast food and soft drink consumption and obesity, *Economics & Human Biology* 3(9), 221–233.

77 Mont, O. and Dalhammar, C. (2005), Sustainable consumption: at the cross-road of environmental and consumer policies, *International Journal of Sustainable Development* 8(4), 258–279.

78 Cf. Radio- och TV-lagen (2010:696), Chapter 8, §§7–8 (sections).

79 For example, in a recent case a fine of SEK 500 000 (Euro 50 000) was charged a company who sent out direct marketing materials to 16-year olds without consent from their parents; Patent- och marknadsöverdomstolen målnr PMT 10485–16, of 21 June 2017.

80 The WFD defines waste as 'any substance or object which the holder discards or intends or is required to discard', Article 3(1) WFD.

forefront when it comes to those two crucial activities: sorting and disposing. Their knowledge about the sorting system, awareness of where to find waste recovery stations, and their willingness to engage in proper waste sorting will have an important impact on how waste is treated. For example, in 2015, representatives of Oslo commune visited thousands of households to explain how to sort waste and hand out special bins for food waste. It followed that waste sorting improved by about 40%.[81]

In various parts of Europe, there is some ongoing experimentation with infrastructure and systems for diverting waste streams from recycling (or incineration) to re-use. There are several initiatives also in Scandinavia.[82] One of them, located in Sweden, is particularly innovative in its functioning. The **Alelyckan re-use park ('kretloppspark) in Gothenburg** combines several functions including sorting and recycling, a café, and various re-use shops. Most importantly, the staff greets all visitors coming to the park for recycling purposes. They check the materials and inform the visitor that some things could be handed in for re-use instead of recycling. It is estimated that 5% of the materials are diverted from recycling to re-use, representing large environmental savings.[83] Another benefit is that the park offers employment activities for unemployed people. The main legal hurdle for the park is that as it is a municipal organization it is not supposed to make a profit, and more importantly: it is not supposed to compete with private companies.[84] This means that when there are private second hand stores close to a park, the park's activities may constitute unfair competition.

Following the Norwegian Pollution Act, a number of waste regulations have been adopted that establish waste return obligations in accordance with the principle of extended producer responsibility.[85] The most interesting and successful is the **deposit-refund system** for plastic bottles and cans. The system is operated by **Infinitum**[86], which is owned in equal share by beverage producers and the Norwegian grocery industry. The company was granted exclusive right to manage the deposit-refund system by the Norwegian Environmental Agency in 1999. Producers and importers of beverages participate voluntarily to the

81 See e.g. www.nrk.no/ostlandssendingen/oslo-folk-blir-ikke-flinkere-til-a-kildesortere-1.12380529.

82 Helm (2016).

83 Ljunggren Söderman, M, D Palm and T. Rydberg (2011), Förebygga avfall med kretsloppsparker. Analys av miljöpåverkan [Prevent waste with cycle parks. Analysis of environmental impact], IVL Swedish Environmental Research Institute.

84 Helm (2016). The rules for competition with the private sector is stated in the 3 Chapter. 27 §(section) in konkurrenslagen [Competition Act] (2008:579); the rules are open for interpretation and allows balancing the competition effects with other public interests. As far as we know there is no case law for re-use activities in Sweden.

85 Norwegian Regulation Nr. 930 of June 2004 on recovery and treatment of waste (Waste Regulation [avfallsforskriften]).

86 Previously known as Norsk Resirk, the company changed name in 2014.

system by paying a deposit to Infinitum to label their bottles and cans with the deposit symbol. Consumers pay the deposit upon purchase, which they get back when their return the empty bottles and cans to a retailer (like a store, a kiosk or a petrol station). Several retailers use reverse vending machines that read the bar code on the cans and bottles, and issues a deposit note to the customer.[87] Infinitum sends the collected bottles and cans to production facilities, which recycles cans by melting aluminium into new aluminium sheets, and cleans plastic bottles to make preforms that producers can purchase. As a result of this system, nearly all plastic bottles and cans are returned, reused and/or recycled.

Clothes collection is also operated privately in Norway. The leading organisation, **Fretex**, which is owned by the Salvation Army, has 2000 specially designed containers over the country. It also takes in deliveries through the Norwegian postal service in special packages and at some clothing stores.[88] They collected 16'620 tons of clothes in 2016. For the most part, the collected textile is re-used, some is recycled and a small amount is used for producing energy.[89] Fretex has three re-design departments, which are focusing on creating new products from used materials.[90] There are 50 second-hand Fretex stores in Norway, but the majority of collected garments (around 90%) goes to export.[91]

6. CONCLUSIONS

Consumers are deemed to play a crucial role in the transition towards the CE. From the traditional perspective where consumers were mere buyers, consumers are increasingly viewed as maintainers, repairers, users, sharer, renters and collaborators. We have attempted to categorize those roles to show the breadth of activities, and hence policies that they cover. We expect, however, that consumer roles will continue changing and developing as new and more sustainable production and consumption models emerge. With the objectives of the CE in mind, we also put forward a 'hierarchy of consumer behaviour' in the vein of the hierarchy of waste management (WMH) contained in the EU waste legislation. Following this hierarchy, consumers shall first and foremost avoid unnecessary purchases; maintain and repair products; then share and lease rather than buy; purchase second-hand or remanufactured; purchase high

87 The deposit was of NOK 1 for small bottles and NOK 2,50 for bigger bottles since it was introduced in the 1990s. In 2018, the Ministry of Environment decided to raise the deposit to respectively NOK 2 and 3 to encourage even more return of empty of beverage packaging.

88 E.g. Lindex stores.

89 Fretex puts forward the following percentages: 78% re-use; 20% recycling; 2% energy recovery. See www.fretex.no/hovedmeny/miljo/hva-blir-toyet-til.

90 See www.fretex.no/fretex-redesign/om-fretex-redesign/om-oss.

91 Fretex 2016 annual report, p. 8, available at www.fretex.no/readimage.aspx?asset=16184&down=true.

quality, durable, energy efficient products; and finally recirculate (in accordance with the WMH).

All over Europe, there is ongoing experimentation with policies and laws that support the CE in various ways. In this paper, we attempted to give an overview of Scandinavian initiatives. We found that these are quite varying in nature, and that Sweden is showing more creativity than Norway. In particular, the Swedish government is making use of its taxation powers and changing the tax structure to support repairs and second-hand activities. New infrastructure developments to support re-use practices are also on the rise. Norway, on the other hand, adopts a rather traditional approach that focuses on waste management. Prevention is, of course, the first priority and discussions are taking place to reduce material consumption. Norway also has a very successful deposit-return system for plastic bottles and cans. Moreover, extended consumer guarantee are seen as a way to foster durability and reparability of products. Both countries have also inquired into new consumption models within the SE, but without going into the environmental sustainability of such models. A number of policies are also put in place at the regional and local level; including interesting initiatives to promote re-use divert materials from recycling streams to re-use.

All these policies are part of the policy mix required to overcome barriers to sustainable practices and to support various circular business models. As these barriers are manifold – and include institutional, organisational, behavioural, technological, and market based barriers[92] – the proliferation of different policies is not really surprising, and most likely needed in order to move towards a new economic paradigm. One of the main challenges in the coming years will be to coordinate the policies at the EU, national and regional/local level, to design an appropriate policy mix, and to send clear signals to consumers and users, that it is rewarding to engage with more sustainable consumption activities.

In this paper we discussed developments in Norway and Sweden. Other countries like Netherlands and Finland have recently adopted progressive CE policies. There is an evident need for the ongoing experimentation with new policies and new modes of consumption, where countries, cities and regions can learn from each other.

92 Cf. Bastein, T., Koers, W., Dittrich, K., Becker, J., & Diaz Lopez, F. J. (2014), Business barriers to the uptake of resource efficiency measures, POLFREE project.

'SERVITIZATION' AND MOVABLES
Legal Initiatives and Challenges in Slovenia

Petra Weingerl* and Janja Hojnik**

1. INTRODUCTION: TERMINOLOGICAL AND CONCEPTUAL CHALLENGES

Slovenia, similarly to other Member States of the European Union (EU) and other developed countries, has been witnessing a decades-long decline in manufacturing together with an orientation shift of its economy towards services.[1] As a co-author of this paper argued elsewhere, the 2008 financial crisis convinced policy makers that (over)reliance on services must be balanced with manufacturing to prevent future economic crises.[2] To achieve this aim, manufacturing needs to be modernized.[3] This modernization (also called reindustrialization or industrial *renaissance*) is reflected in the so-called trend of servitization, which refers to the offering of services by manufacturing companies, in addition to the product alone, with the aim of increasing the value of the overall solution for the customer.[4] As such, servitization intrinsically falls under broader considerations of ecological modernization[5] (sometimes also referred to as eco-efficient innovation[6]), providing a formula for the interplay of ecology and economy.[7] Indeed, servitization has been very generously accepted

* DPhil, MJur (Oxon), Assistant Professor at the Faculty of Law of the University of Maribor.
** PhD, Full Professor and Jean Monnet Chair on EU law aspects of smart and sharing economy at the Faculty of Law of the University of Maribor.

1 See J Hojnik, 'Ecological modernization through servitization: EU regulatory support for sustainable product-service systems' (2018) 27 Review of European, Comparative & International Environmental Law 2 162–174; see also J Hojnik, The Servitization of Industry: EU Law Implications and Challenges (2016) 53(6) CMLRev 1575–1624. This subsection to a large extent summarises her findings presented in these articles.

2 Hojnik, 'Ecological modernization through servitization' (n 1).

3 Ibid.

4 Ibid.

5 M Jänicke, *Preventive Environmental Policy as Ecological Modernisation and Structural Policy* (IIUG 1985).

6 F Tietze and EG Hansen, 'To Own or to Use? How Product Service Systems Facilitate Eco-Innovation Behavior', 2013 Academy of Management Conference, Orlando (2013) 30.

7 Hojnik, 'Ecological modernization through servitization' (n 1).

in the domain of environmental studies. Thus, it is of tremendous importance for the stated goals of the circular economy in the EU, i.e. 'to transform our economy and make it more sustainable, contribute to climate goals and the preservation of the world's resources, create local jobs and generate competitive advantages for Europe in a world that is undergoing profound changes'.[8] However, while servitization business models could have an important impact in this respect, it is equally important not to oversimplify the relationship between servitization and sustainability.[9]

As a starting point, any discussion of challenges posed by servitization to legal scholars and practitioners in Slovenia inevitably leads to terminological issues. Hitherto, there is no adequate 'Slovene' terminology that could be used for this phenomenon. The Fran portal, a website under auspices of the Scientific Research Centre of the Slovenian Academy of Sciences and Arts, provides that an appropriate term is still to be found and suggests the word *storitvizacija* (*storitev* is a Slovene word for service) as a translation for the English counterpart 'servitization'.[10] Janja Hojnik, a co-author of this paper and a legal scholar that has pioneered the academic study of servitization in Slovenia, uses the 'Slovenianised' version of the notion 'servitization', i.e. *servitizacija*.[11] She has been discussing it at different legal symposia in Slovenia, e.g. at the conference 'Corporate Entities in the Market and European Dimensions' and at the symposium 'Medicine and Law'.

Putting the issue of the lack of proper terminology to denote servitization aside, there is also no consensus on what is actually meant by this concept. This challenge is not confined to Slovenia, as there is generally no consensus on the meaning of 'servitization'. This term was coined nearly three decades ago by two management scholars who wrote about 'the increasing offering of fuller market packages or "bundles" of customer focused combination of goods, services, support, self-service and knowledge in order to add value to core corporate offerings'.[12] Nowadays, servitization is considered as omnipresent in

8 Commission (EU), 'Communication from the Commission to the European Parliament, the Council, the European Economic and Social Committee and the Committee of the Regions on a monitoring framework for the circular economy'{SWD(2018) 17 final}.

9 Hojnik, 'Ecological modernization through servitization' (n 1). She analyses, from a regulatory vantage point, the deliberations on whether (or to what extent) servitization of the European industry can contribute to ecological modernization, in which new technology and business models lead to reduced consumption of natural resources.

10 See http://fran.si/iskanje?View=1&Query=storitvizacija. As it is stated on the *Fran* portal, it 'brings together dictionaries, Slovenian linguistic sources and portals that took shape or are currently under development at the *Fran Ramovš Institute of the Slovenian Language* at the Scientific Research Centre of the Slovenian Academy of Sciences and Arts (ZRC SAZU), as well as dictionaries that have undergone the process of retrodigitization within the Institute's framework'.

11 See fn 1.

12 Hojnik, 'Ecological modernization through servitization' (n 1), referring to S Vandermerwe and J Rada, 'Servitization of Business: Adding Value by Adding Services' (1988) 6 European Management Journal 314.

manufacturing companies in developed economies.[13] Servitization transactions may include renting cars instead of buying them, contracting services of irrigation instead of acquiring irrigation systems, or securing server capacity instead of procuring computers.[14] In addition to servitization, the 'pay-per-service-unit' business model is on the rise, where the product user does not buy the product but only the output of the product. The provision of services has turned into 'a conscious and explicit strategy', with services becoming a main differentiating factor in a totally integrated products and service offering.[15]

Servitization can be understood in its narrow sense and in a wider sense. The former concerns situations in which a supplier offers products and services (e.g. selling cars and offering consumer credit services). The latter encapsulates all possible combinations of products and services, including collaborative and sharing economy. While *'product-service bundle'* is a general description for combinations of products and services, *'product-service system (PSS)'* is a more specific scholarly concept that is describing companies offering solutions aimed at increasing market share and consumer satisfaction, but also with a parallel objective of reducing the consumption of products through alternative scenarios of product use instead of acquiring it.[16] PSS is thus strongly based on reduced environmental impact[17] and presents the philosophical basis of *access-based consumption*, promoting business models where consumers acquire consumption time with the item and are willing to pay for the use of that item rather than owning it, be it because they could otherwise not afford it or because they choose not to own due to concerns such as space limitations or the environment.[18]

As Janja Hojnik argued, there are many illustrations of the successful fusing of the supply of goods and services in practice, resulting in companies' increased profitability and employee numbers.[19] The most commonly provided service in practice is still the delivery of products, followed by the provision of spare parts

---

13 D Opresnik and M Taisch, 'The Value of Big Data in Servitization' (2015) 164 International Journal of Production Economics 174.

14 Commission (EU), Innovation for a Sustainable Future – The Eco-Innovation Action Plan (Eco-AP)' (Communication) COM (2011) 899 final (Eco-Innovation Action Plan).

15 TS Baines et al, 'The Servitization of Manufacturing: A Review of Literature and Reflection on Future Challenges' (2009) 20 Journal of Manufacturing Technology Management 556.

16 Hojnik, The Servitization of Industry: EU Law Implications and Challenges' (n 1), referring to FH Beuren and others, 'Product-Service Systems: A Literature Review on Integrated Products and Services' (2013) 47 J. of Cleaner Production 222.

17 M Goedkoop, *Product Service Systems, Ecological and Economic Basics* (Ministry of Housing, Spatial Planning and the Environment 1999); O Mont, 'Clarifying the Concept of Product–service System' (2002) 10 J. of Cleaner Production 237.

18 Hojnik, 'The Servitization of Industry: EU Law Implications and Challenges' (n 1), referring to F Durgee and G C O'Connor, 'An Exploration into Renting as Consumption Behavior' (1995) 12 Psychology and Marketing 89; F Bardhi and G Eckhardt, 'Access-Based Consumption: The Case of Car Sharing' (2012) 39 J. of Consumer Research 881.

19 The Commission refers to studies that estimate that just in Germany, further digitisation of industry is expected to bring up to 8 percent of productivity growth over ten years and lead to a 6 percent increase in employment – COM (2016) 180 final.

and consumables, and a customer helpline or support desk.[20] Additionally, one of the most archetypal examples of innovative servitization is Rolls-Royce's airplane rental model (called *Power-by-the-Hour*), while by adopting sensors that are able to monitor the airplane's engine status 24/7 (*TotalCare* programme), Rolls-Royce considerably simplified the maintenance process.[21] Moreover, Amazon is not just selling books, but offering a variety of related services, including cloud infrastructure, auto scaling and networking, and IBM has turned, with its software and consultancy growth, from a computer hardware manufacturer to a service company.[22] In this vein, numerous companies have succeeded in converting from selling goods to integrated solutions.[23]

Advocate General Szpunar referred to servitization in his opinion dealing with retail trade in goods and the Services Directive.[24] He pointed out that with the arrival of the Internet retail not only consists of merely selling a product, but also of advising, counselling and offering follow-up services and that as such, it is not an activity which is merely ancillary to a product.[25] According to him, Bristol BV, a firm wishing to establish a retail outlet for its shoe and clothing discount chain, is therefore a service provider that can rely on the provisions of the Services Directive. The Court of Justice of the EU endorsed his opinion and held that 'trade nowadays encompasses not only the legal act of sale/purchase but also an increasing range of activities or services that are closely inter-related and that are intended to induce a consumer to conclude that sale/purchase with one economic operator rather than another, to provide advice and assistance to the consumer at the time of that sale/purchase or to provide after-sales services'.[26] This may be illustrated with the prohibition of price discrimination based on nationality or residence of the purchaser, encompassed in Article 20 of the Services Directive[27] and Article 4 of the New Geo-Blocking Regulation.[28] *Does a bar sell goods or services or a combination of both? When*

---

20 B Tether and E Bascavusoglu-Moreau, 'Servitization: The Extent and Motivations for Service Provision amongst UK Manufacturers' (2012) CBS, Copenhagen 17.

21 M Christopher and L J Ryals, 'The Supply Chain Becomes the Demand Chain' (2014) 35 Journal of Business Logistics 29, 30; Editor's Note, 'Britain's Lonely High-Flier' The Economist (8 January 2009).

22 L Gerstner, *Who Says Elephants Can't Dance?: Leading an Enterprise through Dramatic Change* (Harper Business 2002).

23 C Windahl and N Lakemond, 'Integrated Solutions from a Service-Centered Perspective: Applicability and Limitations in the Capital Goods Industry' (2010) 39 Industrial Marketing Management 1278.

24 Directive 2006/123/EC of the European Parliament and of the Council of 12 December 2006 on services in the internal market, OJ L 376, 27.12.2006.

25 Joined Cases C-360/15 and C-31/16, X, Opinion of Advocate General Szpunar, ECLI:EU:C:2017:397, para. 80 and 105.

26 Joined Cases C 360/15 and C 31/16, X, ECLI:EU:C:2018:44, para. 95.

27 Directive 2006/123/EC on services in the internal market, OJ L 376, 27.12.2006, pp. 36–68.

28 Regulation (EU) 2018/302 on addressing unjustified geo-blocking and other forms of discrimination based on customers' nationality, place of residence or place of establishment within the internal market, OJ L 60I, 2.3.2018, pp. 1–15.

charging foreigners more than locals, was it the goods' or the services' part of the price that was discriminatory? The price of a product inevitably reflects not only the cost of the physical commodity but also the cost of the related services. As Stigler notes, *"stores sell more than canned beans or mink coats: it supplies also pleasant quarters, attentive salespeople, possibly generous return privileges etc., and these carry their own implicit prices".*[29] The Slovene judiciary has not dealt with this issue yet, however, the divide between goods and services is becoming increasingly blurred in all legal fields and has been posing challenges to legal scholars and businesses alike. This divide is especially important in the context of the categorization of digital goods, with implications also for consumer protection.[30]

The move towards servitization has coincided with a rising trend towards digitalization.[31] The emergence of fast and powerful ICT, like the Internet, constitutes a leading role in terms of improving existing business models and it is perceived as an important *enabler* of (innovative) servitization[32], and has been recognised as such also by the Slovenian Government in the guidelines for the preparation of the Roadmap for the transition to the circular economy.[33]

In the remainder of this chapter, an overview of innovative business solutions in Slovenia will be provided, focusing on movables. This will be followed by a sketch of challenges and legal and other initiatives dealing with servitization and a circular economy in Slovenia.

2. INNOVATIVE BUSINESS MODELS IN SLOVENIA

In the previous section, servitization in its wider sense was described as embracing all possible combinations of products and services, including the collaborative and sharing economy. This section provides an overview of the innovative business models operating or emerging in Slovenia.

There are several examples of combinations of products and services offered by retail chains to consumers and other customers in Slovenia, similarly to combinations offered in other European countries since various retail chains offer

29 G J Stigler, *The Theory of Price* (Macmillan 1987) 17. More on this in J Hojnik, 'Tell Me Where You Come from and I Will Tell You the Price: Ambiguous Expansion of Prohibited Geographical Price Discrimination in the EU' (2019) 56 CMLRev 1 1–38.

30 J Hojnik, ‚Technology neutral EU law: digital goods within the traditional goods/services distinction' (2017) 25 International journal of law and information technology 1 63.

31 C Lerch and M Gotsch, 'Digitalized Product-Service Systems in Manufacturing Firms' (2015) 58 Research Technology Management 45.

32 Hojnik, The Servitization of Industry: EU Law Implications and Challenges (n 1) fn 40 and references therein.

33 Government of the RS, 'Kažipot: predstavitev procesa', 2 April 2018, available at www.mop.gov.si/fileadmin/mop.gov.si/pageuploads/medijsko_sredisce/2018/04_April/05_Nacionalni_forum_zel.gos/Kazipot__2._4._2018__Nacionalni_forum_zelenega_gospdorstva.pdf.

more or less similar programmes across the EU. For example, OBI, a German multinational home improvement supplies retailing company, offers a possibility of buying different tools, or to simply hire tools and equipment that a consumer needs only a couple of times per year and does not find it cost-effective to buy them.

In May 2018, the Interreg Central Europe, an EU cohesion policy programme, launched a project THINGS+, with an aim to introduce service innovation into product-based manufacturing companies. Their focus is especially on SME companies to adapt their skills and successfully overcome rapid changes, following innovation and technological progress. In Slovenia, they are working with 50 SME companies at a time that take part in a pilot project over a period of 6 months. They claim that '[s]ervitisation of products through adequate human capital investment could be one of the solutions for a greater prosperity on an ever-changing market'.[34]

With regard to the sharing and collaborative economy, car sharing sector is fairly well developed in Slovenia. Different car sharing business models can be classified by the flexibility offered to users as well as the distance travelled. Avant2Go is a B2B car sharing platform which currently offers car sharing services in four Slovene towns, in the capital Ljubljana and in Maribor, Kranj and Murska Sobota, as well as at the main airport. The Ministry of Public Administration and the Ministry of Infrastructure signed a pilot agreement with Avant2Go in 2017 to introduce the possibility of sharing electric vehicles in public administration.[35] Also peer-to-peer car sharing startups have been emerging, e.g. PiPi. PiPi enables car rental in the direct vicinity of the user. This is a model where individuals provide their own car for rental by private users via a platform (carpooling). At present, they have cca. 500 users who will exchange cars, where a third signed up as car owners who would lease their car, and others as potential renters.[36] Moreover, there is a very popular peer-to-peer platform prevoz.org, where individuals offer transport in exchange for the partial coverage of expenses. This model provides solutions for longer distances as compared to traditional car sharing, which is often limited to urban areas. This is also typical for the aforementioned Avant2Go. However, in 2017, less than 50% of Slovenia's total population lived in urban areas and cities (49.63%). Thus, prevoz.org is a popular and accessible mode of transportation for numerous students and employees from rural areas. Uber, an (in)famous transportation network company headquartered in San Francisco, California, has not offered its services in Slovenia yet, though several companies offer transportation services based on similar business models (e.g. GoOpti and iGOline).

---

34 See the website available at http://interreg-central.eu/Content.Node/THINGS-.html.

35 Ministry of Public Administration, 'A Step Toward Implementing the Initiative Slovenia as a Reference Country in a Digital Europe – Sharing Electric Vehicles in Public Administration', available at www.mju.gov.si/en/media_room/news/8092/.

36 Https://www.startup.si/sl-si/novica/320/ekipa-pipi-vzpostavlja-peer-to-peer-car-sharing-za-slovenijo-.

Apart from car sharing, also bike sharing is popular in Slovenia. For example, in Ljubljana, BicikeLJ is a city bike sharing system currently offering 580 bikes. It was launched in 2011 as a private-public partnership project, with the municipality of Ljubljana being the public partner in the project. Each first hour of hire is free of charge, thus short-term rides are being incentivised. A one-year subscription to Bicike(LJ) costs only 3 € and a weekly subscription is 1 €. There are 32 BicikeLJ stations around the city, about 500 meters apart one from another, where one can hire and return a bike. Bike sharing system operates using Urbana city card – a stored-value card used on public transport services in Ljubljana, as a membership card in public libraries and can also be used as a method of payment for most of the museums, galleries, cultural events etc. In Velenje, 74 bikes are offered free of charge at 15 sharing stations provided by a sharing system BICY. In Maribor, which is the second largest city with app. 100,000 inhabitants, there are currently five bike sharing stations with electric bikes, based on a stationary model OVeNtura. They are owned by the company OVEN. The primary business activity of this company is the production of electricity from renewable sources – water and sun. Their electric bikes are charged with micro solar power stations. Besides electric bikes, users can also book 'e-tours of experience'. They plan to offer electric bike sharing also in other towns and elsewhere in the region. The municipality of Maribor has been planning to launch its own bike sharing system, starting with 12 stations and at least 120 bikes. This bike sharing system would be organised as a public-private partnership project.[37]

These innovative business and consumption models, referred to as the 'functional economy' (based on consuming services rather than buying products), contribute to a more sustainable economy.[38] It has been argued that the sharing economy may have a significant contribution to sustainable economic growth because it allows an increase in living standards and quality of life using existing resources and because it promotes less energy-intensive values than the consumer society.[39] Positive effects include reduced traffic congestion and environmental benefits. This is especially pertinent to the Slovenian situation, as the rate of motorization in Slovenia is among the highest in the EU. As the Eurostat found, in Slovenia there are 531 passenger cars per 1000 inhabitants, compared to 374 in the neighbouring Croatia.[40] Moreover, also the number of tractors is very high in Slovenia – it is claimed by some that even the highest in the world, since every 20th Slovene has its own tractor. Thus,

---

37 See its website available at www.maribor.si/dokument.aspx?id=34262.

38 European Economic and Social Committee, 'The functional economy', available at http://old.eesc.europa.eu/?i=portal.en.events-and-activities-functional-economy-model.

39 Hojnik, 'Ecological modernization through servitization' (n 1), referring to F Bonciu and AC Balgar, 'Sharing Economy as a Contributor to Sustainable Growth' (2016) 2 Romanian Journal of European Affairs 42.

40 See its website available at http://appsso.eurostat.ec.europa.eu/nui/submitViewTableAction.do.

and especially taking into account a relatively small size of an average Slovene farm, tractor sharing business models could prove helpful for increasing living standards and quality of life.

3. INITIATIVES AND CHALLENGES POSED BY SERVITIZATION IN SLOVENIA

3.1 INITIAL RELUCTANCE OF LEGAL SCHOLARS

Servitization has been only slowly included in the programmes of various legal conferences and events in Slovenia, especially in relation to the digitalization. As an illustrative example, it should be mentioned that only four years ago some Slovene senior lawyers opined that digitalisation cannot be classified as a "legal topic", and thus it should not be included in a legal conference's programme. Since today also lawyers have to admit that they cannot evade the process of digitalisation, this has proved to be an opportunity to discuss servitization to a greater extent. Consequently, hitherto, legal scholars have dealt with servitization at several legal symposia in Slovenia, for example at the conference 'Corporate Entities in the Market and European Dimensions' in 2016, at the symposium 'Medicine and Law' and at the most prestigious event, the Days of Slovenian Lawyers in 2017, where a panel covering European issues comprised two papers dealing with digitalisation. A panel at the prestigious Bled Strategic Forum 2017 was dealing with sharing economy in the tourism sector with legal aspects also being covered and the Slovenian Representation of the European Commission organised promotion events for the EU Collaborative Economy Agenda in Spring 2017. In 2018, a panel of the Days of Slovenian Lawyers dealt specifically with the sharing economy[41] and 2017 and 2018 symposiums on Law and Economics, organised by the University of Maribor Faculty of Law were dealing with legal issues of the digital economy. In September 2018, a workshop with a round table with the title 'Opportunities and challenges of the sharing economy' was organised in Ljubljana. At this event, a publication 'Sharing Economy in Europe: Opportunities and Challenges', edited by Janja Hojnik, was presented.[42] It comprises academics' and practitioners' responses to the challenges posed by the sharing economy. Thus, these issues are gradually gaining in importance among Slovenian legal scholars.

---

41 Dnevi slovenskih pravnikov, 2018, programme: available at www.dnevipravnikov.si/index.php/session/pravni-izzivi-sodelovanja-gospodarstva-v-digitalni-dobi/.

42 J Hojnik (ed), *Sharing Economy in Europe: Opportunities and Challenges* (Zavod 14 2018), available online at https://www.liberalforum.eu/wp-content/uploads/2018/11/sharingeconomy_web-1.pdf.

3.2 INITIATIVE AND CHALLENGES LINKED TO THE SHARING ECONOMY BUSINESS MODELS

At the policy level, the sharing economy is given the most attention out of all the servitization business models. The Slovene government established an interministerial working group in September 2015 with a task to prepare a legal framework for sharing economy.[43] The stated objective of this working group is to substantively examine and adopt the most appropriate measures for the necessary and proportionate regulation of the new business models, and to enable the provision of services in accordance with the law.[44] Inter alia, the tasks vested in the interministerial working group are: the identification of important areas of sharing economy; a revision of the current market access requirements and the identification of any unnecessary and disproportionate requirements which do not protect the public interest; preparing proposals for the modification of the existing legislation. These proposals should take into account:

- the distinction between profit and non-profit services and between the continuous professional provision of services and the temporary provision of services of natural persons and, consequently, to create appropriate requirements and exceptions;
- consumer protection;
- the rights of employees and self-employed;
- the contractual liability of service providers;
- the taxation regime.[45]

At first, the interministerial working group focused solely on the letting of real property aspects of sharing economy (e.g. Airbnb). Due to lack of proper regulation, many homeowners still rent out their apartments to short-term visitors on the basis of general provisions of housing legislation originally drafted with a focus on long-term tenancy relationships and not designed to regulate the area of short-term tourist accommodation.[46] Accordingly, such short-term rentals often do not comply with the special conditions the law prescribes for performing economic activity in an apartment in condominium ownership.[47] For example, the Housing Act provides that the owner may use their apartment to perform an economic activity if it does not disturb the multi-

---

43 Ministry of Economic Development and Technology, Press release published on 5 January 2017, available at www.mgrt.gov.si/si/medijsko_sredisce/novica/11194/.

44 Ibid.

45 Ibid.

46 A Vlahek and M Damjan, 'Slovenian Regulation of ShortTerm Apartment Rentals via Digital Platforms' in J Hojnik (ed), *Sharing Economy in Europe: Opportunities and Challenges* (Zavod 14 2018) 120.

47 Ibid.

apartment building's residents in their peaceful enjoyment of their dwellings, and if it does not put an excessive burden on the common areas of the apartment building (i.e. staircases, elevators, lobbies, playgrounds, parking lots etc.).[48] To this end, in principle, the apartment owner must obtain the consent of more than three-quarters of the shares of all the apartment owners, including the consent of the owners of the apartments with walls or ceilings bordering with their apartment unit.[49] Moreover, the owner has a duty to inform the building manager of their intended economy activity.[50] The Housing Act governs several other provisions that are deemed unsuitable for the sharing economy business models dealing with short-term rentals. One of the most pressing issues in this context discussed in legal scholarship is the question concerning the possibility of restricting the use of apartments by the decisions of owners in a multi-unit building is whether the owners: do owners have the right to agree on a total ban on renting?[51] Unfortunately, no real output has been produced so far by the interministerial working group to address these issues and to adopt more suitable measures in this field. One of the main challenges of this segment of sharing economy in Slovenia is the complexity of all the interests involved – e.g. the area of short-term rental of real estate to tourists falls under the competence of several departments or sectors of different ministries, while certain tasks are vested in the competence of municipalities.

Regarding movables, more specifically car sharing, the former Public Administration Minister Boris Koprivnikar used to be in favour of introducing the business model of the company Uber in Slovenia. However, when the legal threats and challenges of such business models, especially for consumers, were exposed, he stepped back and halted the progress of legislative initiatives in this field.

Despite this legislative inertia, Members of Parliament of the (then) leading political party SMC proposed a law on sharing economy in Parliament in February 2018.[52] However, it was not passed by the legislator, mainly due to its poor legislative drafting. The proposal's aim was to regulate market access for the online platforms through simple registrations, which should ensure

---

48 Article 14 of the Housing Act (Stanovanjski zakon (SZ-1)), Official Gazette of the Republic of Slovenia, No. 69/03 et seq. The same provision stipulates that such use of an apartment, i.e. the use of part of an apartment to performing an economic activity, does not change the "purpose of housing"" or the "use of housing".

49 Ibid.

50 Ibid.

51 Vlahek and Damjan, "Slovenian Regulation of ShortTerm Apartment Rentals via Digital Platforms" (n 46) 133.

52 This proposal is available at http://pisrs.si/Pis.web/pregledPredpisa?id=ZAKO7873; STA, 'SMC s predlogom zakona za ureditev spletnih platform sodelovalnega gospodarstva', 2 March 2018, available at https://krog.sta.si/2488591/smc-s-predlogom-zakona-za-ureditev-spletnih-platform-sodelovalnega-gospodarstva; see also https://www.strankasmc.si/s-spletnimi-platformami-sodelovalnega-gospodarstva-do-visje-kakovosti-zivljenja/.

transparency. Furthermore, its aim was a better exploitation of existing resources, as the sharing economy should use existing under-utilized resources. Moreover, the proposal governed the highest income to which tax exemptions apply to providers offering their products and services through the online platforms. However, the proposed act did not holistically address different aspects of the sharing economy. Importantly, while it focused on the facilitation of certain business models in the sharing economy, it failed to address issues that consumers are facing as stakeholders in the sharing economy, the taxation policy and the salient labour law aspects in this context. As aforementioned, the proposal was not endorsed by Parliament.

Despite the initial enthusiasm and motivation to prepare a policy and legal framework that would comprehensively deal with the sharing economy, the Government has later turned its focus to regulating smaller segments with the aim to limit the disruptive effect of the new business models on the competitive landscape in Slovenia and to protect all stakeholders, especially consumers and employees (including self-employed). Currently, there is a proposal of the Ministry of Infrastructure for an amendment of the Road Transport Act[53] in the pipeline.[54] It expressly deals with the sharing economy aspects, and regulates transport services offered via online platforms. Under the current legislation, any service in the field of transport can be offered solely by a service provider that fulfils all legal requirements (licensing), which is in accordance with the decision of the Court of Justice of the EU in the case of *Uber France*.[55]

The Road Transport Act does not enable the operation of new business models in the field of transport. It stipulates that the transport of one passenger can only be offered in the form of taxi transfer, since the occasional transport is intended only for a predetermined group of passengers (excursions etc.). Thus, the passenger transport services via online platforms could be carried out only as occasional services or as taxi transfer. Since occasional services are reserved for groups of passengers (excursions etc.), the only possibility left for the transport of one passenger is taxi transfer, which is regulated in detail. Taxi drivers must obtain a license at the state level, they need a local community license, a marked vehicle, and they are obliged to use a taximeter. The Ministry of Infrastructure argues in the proposal of the Road Transport Act that the current requirements are too stringent and inappropriate for the new business models. In order to facilitate new forms of passenger transport, it is therefore necessary to amend the legislation. The proposal introduces an option of "hiring a vehicle with a driver", reduces administrative barrier by abandoning the license requirement

53 Zakon o prevozih v cestnem prometu (ZPCP-2), OG of the RS No. 6/16.

54 The proposal is available at www.mzi.gov.si/fileadmin/mzi.gov.si/pageuploads/DC_splosno/ZPCP-2.pdf; see Ministry of Infrastructure, 'Novela Zakona o prevozih v cestnem prometu v javni obravnavi', 1 February 2018, available at www.mzi.gov.si/si/medijsko_sredisce/novica/8989/ (proposal).

55 Case C-320/16, *Uber France*, ECLI:EU:C:2018:221.

and taximeters, and by transferring the power to regulate this area almost entirely to the local level.[56] The proposal stipulates that the online platforms that bring together passengers and drivers must be registered in advance.[57] The Slovenian Association of Free Trade Unions vehemently objected to this proposal in February 2018, criticising it due to the significant deregulation in the field of road transport and for encouraging the insecure working arrangements.[58]

The most salient legal issue in the context of the P2P car sharing is the question of liability in the event of an accident. As there is no specific legal framework for the sharing economy yet, the owners of the aforementioned PiPi try to enhance legal certainty for this P2P business model through direct negotiations with major Slovenian insurance companies to introduce additional car insurance covering the time of renting a vehicle.[59]

3.3 INITIATIVES AND CHALLENGES IN THE FIELD OF DIGITALISATION

Since servitization is prominently linked to digitalisation, also the Government's efforts in this field should be highlighted. The Government has launched the strategy Digital Slovenia 2020 – Development strategy for the information society until 2020.[60] It 'is a commitment for a faster development of the digital society and the use of opportunities enabled by information and communication technologies and the internet for general economic and social benefits'.[61] To collectively support Slovenia's development and the implementation of the Digital Slovenia 2020 strategy, the Slovenian Digital Coalition – digitalna.si has been established, comprising stakeholders from trade and industry, science, education, public administration, public sector, local government and civil society.[62] Under the auspices of the Slovenian Digital Coalition, the Blockchain Think Tank Slovenia was launched in 2017. The then Prime Minister Miro Cerar held at its inaugural meeting: 'The think tank's activities will be focused on education and awareness-raising, the drafting of legislative proposals and solutions, and linking Slovenian knowledge and awareness with respect to Industry 4.0. Slovenia as a whole is therefore setting itself up as a blockchain-

---

56 The proposal (n 54) 3.

57 Ibid.

58 Their comments on the proposal are available at https://www.zsss.si/wp-content/uploads/2018/02/Predlogi_ZPCP_javnaRazprava_ZSSS_SDPZ_MladiPlus_13022018.pdf.

59 Available at https://www.startup.si/sl-si/novica/320/ekipa-pipi-vzpostavlja-peer-to-peer-car-sharing-za-slovenijo-.

60 Government of the RS, 'DIGITAL SLOVENIA 2020 – Development strategy for the information society until 2020', available at www.mju.gov.si/fileadmin/mju.gov.si/pageuploads/DID/Informacijska_druzba/pdf/DSI_2020_3-2016_pic1.pdf.

61 Ibid, p 6.

62 See its website available at www.digitalna.si/en/.

friendly destination, and to that end it is establishing the pillars of a national blockchain ecosystem in the area of the transfer and spread of information, the adoption of legal regulations and the promotion of a supportive environment for the development of companies working in the area of blockchain technology.'[63]

3.4 NON-LEGAL CHALLENGES

It is believed that one of the main challenges for policy makers in Slovenia is the fact that it is a small country, which hardly deals with multinational corporations' aloofness. For example, the Ministry of Economic Development and Technology wrote to Airbnb to disclose information on individuals that rent apartments through this platform in Slovenia. However, they did not receive any reply from Airbnb. Perhaps bigger countries have more bargaining power in similar situations. Therefore, it is important that the EU undertakes joint actions in this field.

3.5 INITIATIVES AND CHALLENGES LINKED TO A CIRCULAR ECONOMY

3.5.1 Legal and policy initiatives at the governmental level

Apart from servitization, there are several initiatives which show the commitment to the circular economy in Slovenia. The circular economy has found its way into the key strategic national documents, including the Slovenian Development Strategy 2030.[64] In 2017, the Government has launched an initiative to prepare the Roadmap for the transition to the circular economy.[65] In this initiative, it expressed its objective to become a regional leader (referring to Central and Eastern Europe) in the transition from the linear to the circular economy. The Roadmap itself was published in May 2018.[66]

The Roadmap is based on the well-known conceptualisation of the circular triangle, comprising circular economy, circular culture and circular change.

---

63 Speech of the PM Miro Cerar, 'Slovenia's Challenges 2020: A vision for the development and regulation of blockchain technology in modern society', 11 October 2017, available at www.vlada.si/en/prime_minister/news/a/slovenias_challenges_2020_a_vision_for_the_development_and_regulation_of_blockchain_technology_in_modern_society_1108/.

64 Government of the RS, 'Slovenian Development Strategy 2030', 12 October 2017, available at www.vlada.si/en/media_room/newsletter/slovenia_weekly/news/article/slovenian_development_strategy_2030_60466/.

65 Government of the RS, 'Izhodišča za kažipot', 30 November 2017, available at www.vlada.si/fileadmin/dokumenti/si/projekti/2016/zeleno/1711_Izhodisca_za_kazipot_PPT_1.pdf.

66 Available at www.vlada.si/fileadmin/dokumenti/si/projekti/2016/zeleno/Kazipot_prehoda_v_krozno_gospodarstvo.pdf.

Circular culture is the element of the circular triangle, which is directly based on the habits of the inhabitants, especially when they act as consumers. However, the collective rights linked to environment and individual rights of consumers are often in juxtaposition.[67] One of the more problematic rules in this context is the consumer's right to choose the remedy in the event of non-conformity of goods. Based on the Directive 1999/44 on certain aspects of the sale of consumer goods and associated guarantees (Directive 1999/44), in the case of a lack of conformity, the consumer shall be entitled to have the goods brought into conformity free of charge by repair or replacement.[68] In the case C-404/06, *Quelle*, the Court of Justice of the EU indirectly gave impetus to a conduct that favours replacement, as it ruled that a seller who has sold consumer goods which are not in conformity may not require the consumer to pay compensation for the use of those defective goods until their replacement with new goods.[69] As consumers often opt for replacement of goods, and not for repair, in practice, there are huge quantities of discarded goods, which significantly deviates from the principles of the circular economy. Although the Roadmap highlights the importance of the sustainable use of products and their reuse, it does not address the issue concerning the hierarchy of the consumer's remedies. This area is harmonised at the EU level, however, one would assume that if the 'circular' culture is to be taken seriously, the emphasis should be given to the internalisation of the circular economy principles and the encouragement of good practices.

The Government and the legislator are active also in the field of the strategy for plastics in the circular economy, to a large extent influenced by the joint action taken at the EU level. In November 2017, Members of Parliament unanimously approved the recommendation to the Government to completely ban the use of plastic bags, plastic cutlery and microplastics.[70] In 2016, Slovenia produced 19% less plastic waste than in 2015.[71]

3.5.2 *Non-governmental initiatives*

Several initiatives linked to the circular economy have been launched also at a non-governmental level. Every year, an international fair of sustainable

---

67 P Weingerl, 'Krožno gospodarstvo: premik od individualnih interesov h kolektivnim' (2018) 37 Pravna praksa 20/21 28.

68 Directive 1999/44/EC of the European Parliament and of the Council of 25 May 1999 on certain aspects of the sale of consumer goods and associated guarantees, OJ L 171, 7.7.1999, Article 3(2).

69 Case C-404/06, *Quelle*, ECLI:EU:C:2008:231.

70 STA, 'Poslanci podprli priporočilo vladi za prepoved uporabe plastičnih vrečk', 21 November 2017, available at https://www.sta.si/2452772/poslanci-podprli-priporocilo-vladi-za-prepoved-uporabe-plasticnih-vreck.

71 Government of the RS, 'Za Zemljo brez plastike', 20 April 2018, available at www.vlada.si/medijsko_sredisce/sporocila_za_javnost/sporocilo_za_javnost/article/za_zemljo_brez_plastike_61259/?tx_ttnews%5BbackPid%5D=489&cHash=1ecb2cb59b2e440e5f8f4ac6ae26a2bb.

technologies and green lifestyle (GREEN) is organised in Gornja Radgona. It presents 'concepts and products for the benefit of consumers, the environment and society: self-sustaining energy from renewable sources, natural building materials and construction, ecological and permacultural production, handicrafts and natural, home-made delicacies'.[72] In April 2018, they hosted the National Forum for Green Economy, which was co-organised by the Association of Municipalities and Towns of Slovenia. Moreover, Zero Waste Slovenia has been a member of Zero Waste Europe initiative since January 2014. They run a national network of municipalities and monitors the progress of their Zero Waste commitment. It promotes Zero Waste at the national level and establishes a platform for cooperation and business and policy integration.[73] Also the AmCham Slovenia set up the Committee for a Circular Economy and Sharing Economy.[74] This Committee drafted a proposal for the amendment of the Slovenian regulation of short-term apartment rentals via digital platforms.[75] In this proposal, they give a special recommendation as regard the regulation of the sharing economy, which should be done systematically and comprehensively. They have not published any proposal with regard to the regulation of movables thus far.

The Slovenian Tourist Agency is very active in this field. In light of the Slovenian slogan 'Green, Active, Healthy' used for tourism promotion, it promotes the label 'Slovenia Green' together with the international organisation Green Destinations as part of the Green Scheme of the Slovenian Tourism.[76] The Green Scheme encourages all service providers in tourism towards sustainable development. Each destination that wants to receive the Slovenia Green label is required to sign a green development policy as a sign of official commitment, and carry out a 7-step process including raising awareness, creating a destination profile, and collecting statistical data. Once certified, destination coordinators have to submit annual progress reports and enter a re-evaluation phase every two to three years. According to the level of sustainability that can be proven, destinations can rise up from bronze to platinum in their certification.[77] In this context, it should be mentioned that Slovenia was proclaimed the world's first green country by the Netherlands-based organisation Green Destinations, and Ljubljana was the 2016 European Green Capital.

---

72 See their website available at www.pomurski-sejem.si/index.php/en/green/catalogue-green.

73 See their website available at http://ebm.si/zw/o/zero-waste-slovenija/.

74 It has organised several events in this field, for example business breakfast under the slogan 'Green + Digital = circular. Here and now. ('Zeleno + digitalno = krožno. Tukaj in zdaj.'). See their website available at www.amcham.si/sl/zelimo-si-da-slovenija-postane-vodilna-drzava.html.

75 See their website available at www.amcham.si/sl/pobuda-za-spremembo-zakonodaje-ki-ureja-podrocje.html.

76 See their website available at www.slovenia-green.si/.

77 Commission (EU), 'Slovenia Green turns sustainable tourism into a national success model', 28 January 2018, available at https://ec.europa.eu/docsroom/documents/15851/attachments/6/translations/en/renditions/native.

4. CONCLUSION

Both servitization and digitalisation have a potential of boosting the transformation towards the circular economy. Although these phenomena put the established legal principles and rules to the test, as the latter are often ill-suited for the regulation of the new business models, there have been no legal initiatives for their comprehensive regulation in Slovenia. The initial governmental enthusiasm to systematically regulate these fields quickly vanished due to lack of political agreement. The governmental focus has turned to sectoral initiatives, so far culminating in the proposal for the amendment of the Road Transport Act. With the increased interest of legal scholars in these topics, and the lively non-governmental activity, it is hoped that the politicians will soon find the way to strike the appropriate balance between different interests at stake and to adopt suitable measures to enhance legal certainty for all the stakeholders, especially in the fields of short-term rentals and the road transport.

TITLE III

NATIONAL INITIATIVES – REAL ESTATE

BELGIAN PROPERTY LAW AND THE CIRCULAR ECONOMY

Challenges and Opportunities for Real Estate

Benjamin VERHEYE*

1. INTRODUCTION: TOWARDS FUTURE-PROOF PROPERTY LAW

1. **PROPERTY LAW FOR THE FUTURE** – The history of property law dates back thousands of years, making it one of the most ancient fields of law. As soon as the hunter-gatherer became a settled farmer, needing land to cultivate, to hold cattle on and, basically, to live on, it became important to determine which assets belonged to whom.[1] The most important of these assets was – and in some regions of the world still is –, of course, land. This historic origin, with land at its core, still determines many parts of property law. The adagium '*res mobilis, res vilis*', for instance, still resonates throughout many parts of the French-Belgian Civil Code from 1804: a movable is a vile thing and the only asset really worth regulating is land. The same is true for other principles, for instance the unity principle: what is united with the land in a durable manner is considered to form one object with that land. The objectives pursued by this principle, such as legal certainty, value preservation, etc., remain very valid, but that does not necessarily mean that these principles must still be interpreted in exactly the same way as before or that these principles are the only way to pursue those objectives. After all, society changes and the principles should change along, exactly to assure that they still pursue the same objectives in the best thinkable way.

---

* PhD Researcher, Institute for Property Law, KU Leuven. In the meantime, a more elaborated and updated Dutch version of this contribution has been accepted for publication by the Belgian *Tijdschrift voor Privaatrecht*.

1 See also: P.F. DALE and J.D. MCLAUGHLIN, *Land Information Management*, Oxford, Clarendon Press, 1988, 14, 19; H.A.L. DEKKER, *Nationale Grondboekhoudingen. Overzicht Kadastersystemen*, Leiden, Nederlandse Uitgeversmij. (NUMIJ), 1987, 1-2; G. LARSSON, *Land registration and cadastral systems*, Harlow, Longman Scientific and Technical, 1991, 9-11; S.R. SIMPSON, *Land Law and Registration*, Cambridge, Cambridge University Press, 1976, 10.

This paper concerns one major change in society that will probably – hopefully, as far as I am concerned – dominate the 21st century: the advent of the notion of 'sustainability'. The Oxford Dictionary defines sustainability as 'the ability to be maintained at a certain rate or level' and 'the avoidance of depletion of natural resources in order to maintain an ecological balance'. In the past few decades, sustainability has become ever more important as an objective that forms part of the global policy to tackle climate change and to corroborate to protect our planet for the future. One of the most interesting and promising sustainability projects that is currently sky-rocketing is, to my opinion, the idea of the Circular Economy, the essentials of which will be analysed below.

This paper will focus on the implementation of the Circular Economy in the real estate sector. After all, many Circular Economy projects are currently initiated in this sector. Of course, the real estate sector is a heavily regulated one: in almost all countries of the world a complicated real estate legal framework exists to protect important societal interests, such as public health, safety, legal certainty, etc. Some of these rules, however, appear to be difficultly reconcilable with certain Circular Economy projects. This observation raises challenging questions. Does this mean that a Circular Economy is impossible in the real estate sector? Or should we abolish some of the real estate rules that are at odds with the Circular Economy? But what happens then to the interests protected by these rules? This paper deals with these questions.

Of course, this paper has its limitations. First, it is impossible to deal with all legal norms regulating the real estate sector. This paper therefore focuses on one particular set of quintessential rules, namely property law *sensu stricto*, being the rules lying at the very basis of every system of property rights. Second, the only legal system studied is Belgian law. As a result of these limitations, the main research question in this paper is the following: "How can the idea of a Circular Economy for the real estate sector be fit into the Belgian property law framework?"

2. **Structure** – This paper consists of two large parts. It starts with a general part on Circular Economy (*cf. infra*, nr. 3 ff). In this part, the essentials of the Circular Economy are explained, mainly referring to the work of the Ellen MacArthur Foundation, that is doing excellent work in this field.

The second part of this paper analyses how Belgian property law, in particular regarding real estate, can be considered to constitute a hindrance to the development of a Circular Economy for the real estate sector (*cf. infra*, nr. 8 ff). First, some real estate initiatives implementing the idea of circularity are discussed, whereby I will focus on those initiatives that build on the service providing operationalisation of the Circular Economy (*cf. infra*, nr. 10 ff). Second, as an introduction, the concept 'immovable' in Belgian law is explained (*cf. infra*, nr. 20 ff). Third, the situation in which (leased) movables are incorporated in real estate is analysed, building on the key notion of accession (*cf. infra*, nr. 23 ff). Fourth, the leasing of movables that are put to use in real estate without being incorporated is discussed (*cf. infra*, nr. 39 ff).

Finally, all discussed issues are summarised in a brief conclusion (*cf. infra*, nr. 45 ff).

2. CIRCULAR ECONOMY: THE ESSENTIALS

3. A DEFINITION – On the website of the Ellen MacArthur Foundation, a Circular Economy is defined as follows: "Looking beyond the current "take, make and dispose" extractive industrial model, the Circular Economy is restorative and regenerative by design. Relying on system-wide innovation, it aims to redefine products and services to design waste out, while minimising negative impacts. Underpinned by a transition to renewable energy sources, the circular model builds economic, natural and social capital."[2]

In essence[3], a Circular Economy keeps material and products actively in use in a cyclic – or circular – way instead of replacing them, in order to reduce waste and pollution. As such, the idea is to redesign our linear economy with its many consumer goods to a circular one, mimicking a biological cycle. This abstract idea can best be clarified by an example. In a biological cycle, plants are eaten by small animals and small animals by larger animals, followed by those large animals dying and their waste providing nutrition to plants, after which the cycle restarts. Products in the technical cycle in a linear economy, by contrast, are made from raw materials taken from nature, that are used to create that technical product – whereby part of the raw materials are often wasted –, which is subsequently, when it is considered old or broken, replaced and disposed of. Hence: 'take, make and dispose'. The problem is, however, that those disposed products are not as easily reincorporated in nature as a dead animal, whose waste

---

2 See: https://www.ellenmacarthurfoundation.org/circular-economy (last visited on 19 March 2018). See also: E.M. FOUNDATION, *Towards the Circular Economy. Economic and business rationale for an accelerated transition*, EMF, 2013, 7.

3 See for a summary: https://www.ellenmacarthurfoundation.org/circular-economy/overview/concept (last visited on 19 March 2018). See also in general: E.M. FOUNDATION, *Towards the Circular Economy. Economic and business rationale for an accelerated transition*, EMF, 2013, 6-12, 14 ff. (on the limits of linear consumption), 22 ff. (on the move from a linear to a Circular Economy); H. PLOEGER, M. PRINS, A. STRAUB and R. VAN DEN BRINK, "Circular economy and real estate: alternatives for operational lease" in *Proceedings of the International Research Conference 2017: Shaping tomorrow's built environment*, Salford (UK), 2017, (1) 1-4; T. RAU and S. OBERHUBER, *Material matters. Het alternatief voor onze roofbouwmaatschappij*, Haarlem, Bertram + de Leeuw Uitgevers, 2017, 219 p. See specifically on the contemporary linear economy for consumer goods and possible evolution to a Circular Economy: E.M. FOUNDATION, *Towards the Circular Economy. Opportunities for the consumer goods section*, EMF, 2013, 14 ff. (linear economy), 38 ff. (Circular Economy for consumer goods); T. RAU and S. OBERHUBER, *Material matters. Het alternatief voor onze roofbouwmaatschappij*, Haarlem, Bertram + de Leeuw Uitgevers, 2017, 35 ff.

provides direct nutrition for plants or other animals. This is exactly the problem that is tackled in a Circular Economy. The core idea is to put technical goods in a cycle similar to the biological cycle. This happens by reducing the number of goods that end up as non-recyclable waste. Carefully designed goods are used by as many people as possible, maintained and repaired as much as possible and, if necessary, returned to the manufacturer who reuses them as much as possible in new products, that are put back on the market. Hence: 'make, use and return'. Thus, a Circular Economy is as restorative as possible. In addition, the Ellen MacArthur Foundation connects a Circular Economy to renewable energy, contrary to a linear economy that wastes a lot of energy, e.g. the energy that is put in products that end up as waste and the energy that is often not created from that waste.[4] Thus, in a Circular Economy, no energy is created by using products – e.g. coal or gas – that cannot be regenerated. All energy comes from renewable sources, which fits perfectly within the circular model.[5]

The proponents of a Circular Economy argue that this redesigning can happen without any negative economic effects and even generates new business opportunities (*cf. infra*, nr. 7). In general, progression towards a Circular Economy is also one of the ideas to move towards a more sustainable world: natural non-renewable resources are finite, so we must make good use of them and at the same time take care of the environment. The core ideas of a Circular Economy are not new[6]: one can mention, for instance, the tendency to develop bio-degradable materials to be used in consumer goods, the many recycling schemes, renewable energy, material use efficiency, etc.[7] However, such initiatives are to diverse and do not lead to a true change. "A change of the entire operating system seems necessary."[8]

4. Operationalisation: service providing – The above-mentioned key ideas are one thing, their operationalisation or 'bringing into reality' another. The main idea of the Ellen MacArthur Foundation is to operationalise a

---

4 See e.g.: E.M. FOUNDATION, *Towards the Circular Economy. Economic and business rationale for an accelerated transition*, EMF, 2013, 7, 16-17 (on energy use in a linear economy), 22-23 (on energy in a Circular Economy); H. PLOEGER *et al.*, "Circular economy and real estate: alternatives for operational lease" in *Proceedings of the International Research Conference 2017: Shaping tomorrow's built environment*, Salford (UK), 2017, (1) 3.

5 For a clear explanation of the essentials, watch the following short film by the Ellen MacArthur Foundation: https://www.youtube.com/watch?v=zCRKvDyyHmI.

6 For previous schools of thought, see: E.M. FOUNDATION, *Towards the Circular Economy. Economic and business rationale for an accelerated transition*, EMF, 2013, 26-29.

7 See also: E.M. FOUNDATION, *Towards the Circular Economy. Economic and business rationale for an accelerated transition*, EMF, 2013, 8.

8 E.M. FOUNDATION, *Towards the Circular Economy. Economic and business rationale for an accelerated transition*, EMF, 2013, 22. See also on the limits of current recycling initiatives: T. RAU and S. OBERHUBER, *Material matters. Het alternatief voor onze roofbouwmaatschappij*, Haarlem, Bertram + de Leeuw Uitgevers, 2017, 45-48, 117-118. RAU pleads in his entire book for a holistic approach.

Circular Economy through a so-called 'service providing model'[9]: instead of a manufacturer selling a product to a consumer, we have a manufacturer providing a service to that consumer by means of a good that is leased (*sensu lato*) to the consumer. Thus the consumer does not obtain ownership of a good, but a contract with a service provider. In addition, unlimited resources like labour become more important – someone will need to follow-up the service agreement –, whereas limited resources – the raw materials – are being used in a more rational and well-thought way.[10] In the words of the Ellen MacArthur Foundation: "durable products are leased, rented, or shared wherever possible."[11] A similar process is introduced under the name 'Turntoo-model' by RAU and OBERHUBER, who take the idea even further and argue that *all* raw materials must be offered as a service.[12] This service providing operationalisation also forms the main study object of this paper. As a synonym for service providing operationalisation, I will use the term 'lease operationalisation'.[13]

This idea is best explained by looking into a real life example. Philips, the well-known electrical tools manufacturer, has recently initiated the Philips Circular Lighting service, after an initiative by Thomas RAU.[14] In this project, Philips does not longer sell lighting tools – all kinds of lamps – to customers, but it offers them a lighting service: on a contractual basis, customers pay Philips

---

9 This operationalisation is heavily influenced by STAHELS Performance Economy. See for a very brief summary of his thoughts: E.M. FOUNDATION, *Towards the Circular Economy. Economic and business rationale for an accelerated transition*, EMF, 2013, 26-27.

10 See e.g.: E.M. FOUNDATION, *Towards the Circular Economy. Economic and business rationale for an accelerated transition*, EMF, 2013, 7-8, 14; E.M. FOUNDATION, *Towards the Circular Economy. Opportunities for the consumer goods section*, EMF, 2013, 38 ff. (specifically on consumer goods in a Circular Economy); H. PLOEGER *et al.*, "Circular economy and real estate: alternatives for operational lease" in *Proceedings of the International Research Conference 2017: Shaping tomorrow's built environment*, Salford (UK), 2017, (1) 1, 3; T. RAU and S. OBERHUBER, *Material matters. Het alternatief voor onze roofbouwmaatschappij*, Haarlem, Bertram + de Leeuw Uitgevers, 2017, 11-12 (service providing as an alternative for ownership, the so-called Turntoo-model), 85 ff.

11 E.M. FOUNDATION, *Towards the Circular Economy. Economic and business rationale for an accelerated transition*, EMF, 2013, 7.

12 See: T. RAU and S. OBERHUBER, *Material matters. Het alternatief voor onze roofbouwmaatschappij*, Haarlem, Bertram + de Leeuw Uitgevers, 2017, 12, 49 ("In het nieuwe economische model koopt de consument namelijk geen product, maar neemt hij een prestatie af."), 91 ff. See also: http://turntoo.com/ (the Turntoo model has, on 10 october 2010, lead to the creation of Turntoo, a Dutch consultancy organisation that assists companies to adapt themselves to the Circular Economy).

13 Another term used is 'servitisation'. See for instance: T. RAU and S. OBERHUBER, *Material matters. Het alternatief voor onze roofbouwmaatschappij*, Haarlem, Bertram + de Leeuw Uitgevers, 2017, 94.

14 See: www.lighting.philips.nl/systemen/circular-lighting. This project is also mentioned by: H. PLOEGER *et al.*, "Circular economy and real estate: alternatives for operational lease" in *Proceedings of the International Research Conference 2017: Shaping tomorrow's built environment*, Salford (UK), 2017, (1) 3. For the history of the project, see: T. RAU and S. OBERHUBER, *Material matters. Het alternatief voor onze roofbouwmaatschappij*, Haarlem, Bertram + de Leeuw Uitgevers, 2017, 86-89.

in return for light, but Philips remains the owner of the lighting tools, not only installing them, but also repairing and, if necessary, replacing them. Old lighting tools are subsequently reused – as a whole or in parts – or recycled. Finally, 'new' lighting tools reenter the technical cycle, without any basic materials – 'raw materials' – being needed. As the manufacturer, Philips is in the best position to organise this reuse or recycle program: it is therefore beneficial for both Philips and the consumer to tighten the reverse cycle.[15] Not only does this lead to fewer waste, it also creates an incentive for Philips to develop lighting tools with a longer life than before and more easily recyclable than before, because they bear the costs for malfunctioning lighting tools.[16]

5. **Diagram** – The following diagram, created by the Ellen MacArthur Foundation[17], summarises all this in the so-called 'value circle', also known as 'the Butterfly Model'. On the left, we can see the biological cycle and on the right the technical cycle, interpreted according to Circular Economy ideas.

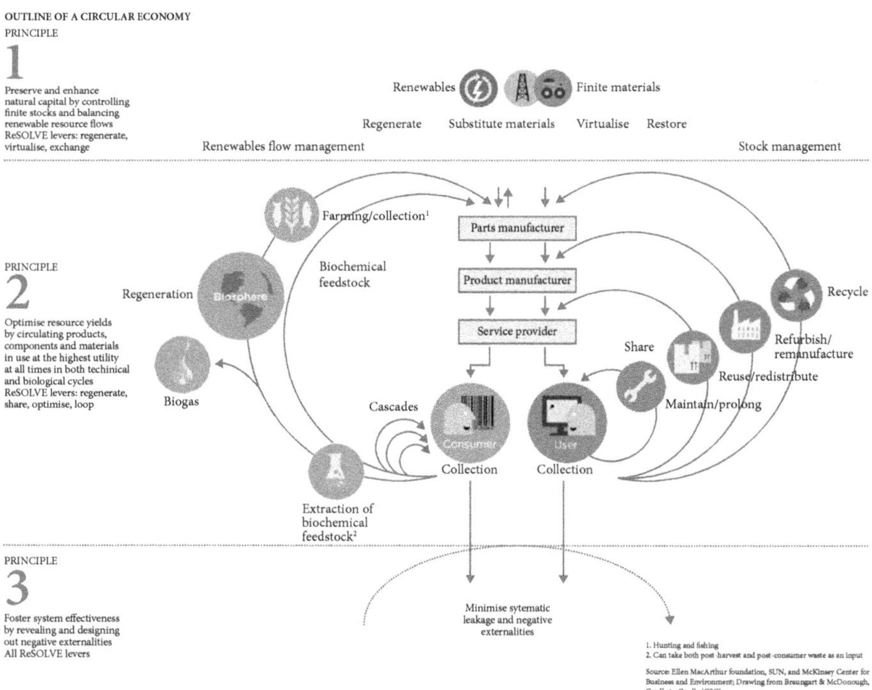

15 See also in general and for other business fields: E.M. FOUNDATION, *Towards the Circular Economy. Economic and business rationale for an accelerated transition*, EMF, 2013, 8-10.

16 This is also argued by Philips itself: see the video on www.lighting.philips.nl/systemen/circular-lighting from 1 minute onwards.

17 See: https://www.ellenmacarthurfoundation.org/circular-economy/interactive-diagram (last visited on 19 March 2018).

6. **Alternative operationalisation** – Notwithstanding the above-mentioned operationalisation, other means of implementing a Circular Economy are possible as well. Firstly, in fact, all existing recycling or anti-waste projects fit within a Circular Economy, although these initiatives are mere drops on a hot plate and are often an example of downcycling: recycling in which a lot of the original value gets lost.[18] In this respect, I think of, for instance, a recent Oxfam clothing swap fair that I saw on a poster at my university, where you can exchange the clothes that do not longer fit you for clothes from other people.[19] Another example is a Belgian website where you can sell the food that you have prepared, but not eaten.[20] Thus food waste at the consumption level is decreased.[21] A final example is the segregated collection of frying oil at Belgian communal waste centers: this segregated oil can be reused in various other industries.[22]

Secondly, other more holistic sustainability projects can also be fit into a Circular Economy. This is the case for, for instance, the sharing or platform economy ("durable products are leased, rented, or shared wherever possible.") The sharing economy, however, shows particularities that cannot be taken into account here. It needs specific research and thus falls outside the scope of this paper (also *cf. infra*, nr. 9).

7. **Advantages** – A Circular Economy creates advantages for both businesses and consumers and thus also for the economy as a whole. As to the advantage for businesses, some critics might argue that the entire Circular Economy is just philanthropy, not leading to any economic business results. However, it is soundly upheld by the Ellen MacArthur Foundation and other proponents that a Circular Economy creates new business opportunities, such as (raw) material savings, more innovation, more customer interaction and new marketing opportunities, and reduces certain risks for companies that are prominent in a linear economy, such as the risk of rising or unpredictable resource prices, supply risks, e.g. political unrest, or warranty risks.[23] Thus a Circular Economy

---

18 See also e.g.: H. PLOEGER *et al.*, "Circular economy and real estate: alternatives for operational lease" in *Proceedings of the International Research Conference 2017: Shaping tomorrow's built environment*, Salford (UK), 2017, (1) 3; T. RAU and S. OBERHUBER, *Material matters. Het alternatief voor onze roofbouwmaatschappij*, Haarlem, Bertram + de Leeuw Uitgevers, 2017, 45-48. On downcycling in the real estate sector: *cf. infra*, nr. 9.

19 See also on clothing waste and how to counter it in a Circular Economy: E.M. FOUNDATION, *Towards the Circular Economy. Opportunities for the consumer goods section*, EMF, 2013, 53-63 (the Foundation would label this Belgian example as an initiative of collaborative consumption; the main idea the Foundation has in this respect is so-called clothing-for-hire).

20 See: www.thuisafgehaald.be.

21 See also on food waste and how to counter it in a Circular Economy: E.M. FOUNDATION, *Towards the Circular Economy. Opportunities for the consumer goods section*, EMF, 2013, 41-53.

22 See also on oil recycling: E.M. FOUNDATION, *Towards the Circular Economy. Opportunities for the consumer goods section*, EMF, 2013, 44.

23 See e.g.: E.M. FOUNDATION, *Towards the Circular Economy. Economic and business rationale for an accelerated transition*, EMF, 2013, 8-9, 10-11, 14 ff. (on risks in a linear

is beneficial to businesses. Moreover, a Circular Economy is also beneficial to consumers: manufacturers are obliged to offer more personal services, customers have more choice, prices go down, etc.[24] Finally, it is beneficial to the economy as a whole, either directly, for instance by reducing waste fill costs for communities and states, or indirectly, such as higher employment rates, more future resilient growth, reduction of externalities such as environmental damage, etc.[25]

3. PROPERTY LAW HINDRANCES (?) TO A CIRCULAR ECONOMY FOR REAL ESTATE

3.1. INTRODUCTION: REAL ESTATE IN A CIRCULAR ECONOMY AND PROPERTY LAW

8. **Removing legal obstacles** – Given the fact that the change towards a Circular Economy requires that all possible subdomains of that economy implement the above-mentioned principles, the real estate sector must of course also be engaged in this project. This sector, however, knows some particular challenges: real estate requires high initial investments, has a long service life, knows limited possibilities for re-use, etc.[26] One particularly interesting challenge is that real estate and the building sector are objects of many legal rules: construction law, environmental law, health protection law, etc.[27] This paper focuses on one particular domain of law, which is probably the most basic domain for real estate: property law. Most of the afore-mentioned rules stem from a time in which sustainability was hardly an issue, let alone an issue in property law. In that respect, proponents of a Circular Economy could consider – and effectively consider – some of these rules a constraint on the development of a Circular Economy. In the words of the Ellen MacArthur Foundation: "the

economy), 71-75; T. RAU and S. OBERHUBER, *Material matters. Het alternatief voor onze roofbouwmaatschappij*, Haarlem, Bertram + de Leeuw Uitgevers, 2017, 43-45 (risk of increasing sources prices), 96-97.

24 See e.g.: E.M. FOUNDATION, *Towards the Circular Economy. Economic and business rationale for an accelerated transition*, EMF, 2013, 8-9, 11, 75-76.

25 See e.g.: E.M. FOUNDATION, *Towards the Circular Economy. Economic and business rationale for an accelerated transition*, EMF, 2013, 8-9, 9-10, 66-70 See particularly on advantages of a Circular Economy for consumer goods: E.M. FOUNDATION, *Towards the Circular Economy. Opportunities for the consumer goods section*, EMF, 2013, 82 ff.

26 See: H. PLOEGER *et al.*, "Circular economy and real estate: alternatives for operational lease" in *Proceedings of the International Research Conference 2017: Shaping tomorrow's built environment*, Salford (UK), 2017, (1) 4.

27 See also: W. DEBACKER and S. MANSHOVE, "D1 Synthesis of the State-of-the-Art. Key Barriers and Opportunities for Materials Passports and Reversible Building Design in the current system", *Building as Material Banks* 2016, (1) 24; H. PLOEGER *et al.*, "Circular economy and real estate: alternatives for operational lease" in *Proceedings of the International Research Conference 2017: Shaping tomorrow's built environment*, Salford (UK), 2017, (1) 4.

obstacles [to the full development of a Circular Economy] remain daunting. [...] Some of these barriers may fade on their own, with time. Others could require specific new frameworks – in terms of corporate governance, cross-industry collaboration, technology, **or regulation.** [own bold]"[28]

However, some of these obstacles, particularly in (property) law, might in fact be – for property law: are – rules that are based on principles that protect other interests than the interests strived for by a Circular Economy – in essence: sustainability –, such as third party rights or legal certainty. Of course, sustainability is undoubtedly an interest that deserves protection. Nevertheless, to my opinion, the interests protected by 'classical' property law cannot be simply left unprotected in favour of sustainability. After all, it is the task of the law to create a justifiable balance of interests in all matters. It is therefore important to consciously think about this balance and study how various interests might be brought in harmony with each other. This idea constitutes the rule of thumb that will be followed in this paper. Thus, I also hope to corroborate to the sound development of a Circular Economy for the real estate sector.

9. Real estate in a Circular Economy – Sustainability is already an issue in the real estate sector. Many architects, contractors, project developers, etc., are already implementing sustainability measures and concepts in their day-to-day operations. Noteworthy, for instance, are the various real estate sustainability assessment and certification methods that exist in many countries: BREEAM (Building Research Establishment Environmental Assessment Method)[29], DGNB (Deutsche Gesellschaft für Nachhaltiges Bauen)[30], LEED (Leadership in Energy and Environmental Design)[31], HQE (Haute Qualité Environnementalle)[32], etc. The certificates obtained on the basis of these methods are an important element for proving the sustainability value of a real estate project and are thus often used as a promotional and commercial tool by architects, contractors and project developers. Moreover, these certificates are also ever more required in open procurement procedures for real estate. To some extent, these assessment methods include ideas of circularity and can thus be considered to be steps towards a Circular Economy, although most of these do not explicitly embed themselves in more holistic Circular Economy thinking. Nevertheless, they are steps in the right direction and, more importantly, they prove that sustainability is an interest that the real estate sector is absolutely willing to take into account.

---

28 E.M. FOUNDATION, *Towards the Circular Economy. Economic and business rationale for an accelerated transition*, EMF, 2013, 11. See also: W. DEBACKER and S. MANSHOVE, "D1 Synthesis of the State-of-the-Art. Key Barriers and Opportunities for Materials Passports and Reversible Building Design in the current system", *Building as Material Banks* 2016, (1) 24, 75.

29 See thereon: https://www.breeam.com/ (last visited on 7 May 2018).

30 See thereon: www.dgnb.de/de/ (last visited on 7 May 2018).

31 See thereon: https://new.usgbc.org/leed (last visited on 7 May 2018).

32 See thereon: www.behqe.com/fr (last visited on 7 May 2018).

Apart from the above-mentioned measures and concepts, there are many more opportunities for circularity in the real estate sector. The Ellen MacArthur Foundation, basing itself on a Danish pilot, even considers it one of the sectors with the highest potential.[33] In general, the Foundation argues that real estate ("the built environment") (in cities) should be "designed in a modular and flexible manner, sourcing healthy materials that improve the life quality of the residents, and minimise virgin material use. It will be built using efficient construction techniques, and will be highly utilised thanks to shared, flexible and modular office spaces and housing. Components of buildings will be maintained and renewed when needed, while buildings will be used where possible to generate, rather than consume, power and food by facilitating closed loops of water, nutrients, materials, and energy, to mimic natural cycles."[34]

When we look at the contemporary real estate sector, its linear nature becomes immediately clear. A building is built by a contractor, sold to a private or professional party and used until it gets outdated and is tore down – sometimes prematurely[35] – or heavily renovated. Many of its raw materials end up as waste.[36] Admittedly, this waste is partially recycled, but mostly in asphalt for roads or similar products, which destroys a lot of the value of the original raw materials ('downcycling').[37] To quote Thomas Rau, a Dutch-German architect and one of the main proponents of a Circular Economy for the real estate sector: "In fact, waste is nothing else than material without an identity."[38] The challenge now is to change this linear way of building real estate to a circular way that fits in a Circular Economy. A first opportunity is to reduce waste, an objective that returns in many of the initiatives mentioned below and that is also the

---

33 See: E.M. FOUNDATION, *Delivering the Circular Economy. A Toolkit for Policymakers*, EMF, 2015, 111-112.

34 E.M. FOUNDATION, *Cities in the Circular Economy: an Initial Exploration*, EMF, 2017, 7. See also on this future: W. DEBACKER and S. MANSHOVE, "D1 Synthesis of the State-of-the-Art. Key Barriers and Opportunities for Materials Passports and Reversible Building Design in the current system", *Building as Material Banks* 2016, (1) 14 ff.

35 See: W. DEBACKER and S. MANSHOVE, "D1 Synthesis of the State-of-the-Art. Key Barriers and Opportunities for Materials Passports and Reversible Building Design in the current system", *Building as Material Banks* 2016, (1) 20-21.

36 See also: W. DEBACKER and S. MANSHOVE, "D1 Synthesis of the State-of-the-Art. Key Barriers and Opportunities for Materials Passports and Reversible Building Design in the current system", *Building as Material Banks* 2016, (1) 6, 16-18, 46 ff.; J.P.V. EESTEREN, "Circulariteit is route naar een écht duurzame bouwsector", *https://www.jpvaneesteren.nl/nl/circulariteit-route-naar-een-echt-duurzame-bouwsector* 2018, (1) 2.

37 See also: W. DEBACKER and S. MANSHOVE, "D1 Synthesis of the State-of-the-Art. Key Barriers and Opportunities for Materials Passports and Reversible Building Design in the current system", *Building as Material Banks* 2016, (1) 18. See on downcycling in general for instance: T. RAU and S. OBERHUBER, *Material matters. Het alternatief voor onze roofbouwmaatschappij*, Haarlem, Bertram + de Leeuw Uitgevers, 2017, 45.

38 T. RAU and S. OBERHUBER, *Material matters. Het alternatief voor onze roofbouwmaatschappij*, Haarlem, Bertram + de Leeuw Uitgevers, 2017, 12 ("Afval is immers in feite niets meer dan een verzameling grondstoffen zonder identiteitsbewijs."), 114. See also: www.rau.eu/.

focal point of RAUS work.[39] Apart from waste reduction, the Ellen MacArthur Foundation sees two other big opportunities for the real estate sector: industrialised production processes with, for instance, modularisation and 3D-printing and the sharing, multi-purposing or repurposing of buildings.[40] In this paper, I will predominantly analyse the first two opportunities. The third opportunity has already been extensively studied in other contributions on the platform economy, co-housing, the Community Land Trust (CLT), etc.[41], and therefore falls outside the scope of this paper.

Let us first look at a number of real-life initiatives in the real estate sector, based on ideas of circularity and operationalised on the basis of the lease-concept (*cf. infra*, nr. 10 ff). Subsequently, I will briefly talk about a more holistic approach for the real estate sector in a Circular Economy (*cf. infra*, nr. 17 ff). Then, the analysis of Belgian property law with regard to a Circular Economy for real estate will be started (*cf. infra*, nr. 20 ff).

3.2. REAL-LIFE CIRCULAR ECONOMY INITIATIVES IN THE REAL ESTATE SECTOR

10. RENEWABLE ENERGY – The first series of projects mentioned in this paper are all situated in the renewable energy sector.[42] Solar panels on roofs have become a familiar sight in the Belgian landscape. Many real estate owners have installed their own solar panels on their own roofs. From a Circular Economy point of view, this situation is suboptimal: a private person buys solar panels that are *made* from raw materials *taken* from nature and disposes of these panels once they do function

---

39 See for instance: T. RAU and S. OBERHUBER, *Material matters. Het alternatief voor onze roofbouwmaatschappij*, Haarlem, Bertram + de Leeuw Uitgevers, 2017, 81-83.

40 See: E.M. FOUNDATION, *Delivering the Circular Economy. A Toolkit for Policymakers*, EMF, 2015, 112 ff.

41 See from a Belgian perspective for instance: B. DEVOLDER, "Terbeschikkingstelling van kamers en woningen via een internetplatform: verboden bestemmingswijziging en onderhuur?", *TBBR* 2016, (378) 378-393; B. DEVOLDER, "Toeristische verhuur van tot privébewoning bestemde appartementen – Over het spanningsveld tussen exclusieve eigendomsrechten", *RW* 2018, (1002) 1002-1021; V. SAGAERT, "Community Land Trust: achterhaalde hippies of moderne vastgoedontwikkelaars?" in *Opening Doors. Verslagboek naar aanleiding van het nationaal notarieel congres 2017 in Gent*, Brussel, Larcier, 2017, (445) 445-471; R. TIMMERMANS, *De Community Land Trust*, Mechelen, Wolters Kluwer, 2016, 182 p. See very general from an international perspective for instance: E.M. FOUNDATION, *Cities in the Circular Economy: an Initial Exploration*, EMF, 2017, 7 (on co-housing); T. RAU and S. OBERHUBER, *Material matters. Het alternatief voor onze roofbouwmaatschappij*, Haarlem, Bertram + de Leeuw Uitgevers, 2017, 94 (on the sharing economy).

42 See also: W. DEBACKER and S. MANSHOVE, "D1 Synthesis of the State-of-the-Art. Key Barriers and Opportunities for Materials Passports and Reversible Building Design in the current system", *Building as Material Banks* 2016, (1) 14-15; E.M. FOUNDATION, *Delivering the Circular Economy. A Toolkit for Policymakers*, EMF, 2015, 113; E.M. FOUNDATION, *Cities in the Circular Economy: an Initial Exploration*, EMF, 2017, 8.

well anymore. For these solar panels, specific disposal programs are often created[43], but as mentioned above, such are just a partial solution. Equally suboptimal from a Circular Economy point of view, to my opinion, is the situation in which solar panels are leased to private persons from a mere financing perspective: this is the case, for instance, when a bank leases solar panels to a private person or a company, with a buying option at the end of the leasing period.[44]

I believe the following tendency, however, to be more circular-economy-roof: professional solar panel companies install solar panels on roofs owned by others, for instance on the roofs of farm buildings, and either lease these solar panels to the roof owner or pay a remuneration for the use of the roof, for instance by providing a free volume of electricity. The professional company knows much better than a private person how to maintain the solar panels, how to repair them and what to do with possible waste, for instance recycling the useful components. A particularly interesting initiative in this respect is a project by the Flemish Government – called Sun Sharing ('*zonnedelen*') – to invest in solar panels on the roof of building that the investor does not own.[45] Alternatives for solar panels also exist: in cities in which solar panels are not permitted – such as Bruges –, people start using solar roof tiles, which are roof tiles that are made of so-called sun cells and function similarly as solar panels.[46] Given the high cost of these solar roof tiles, leasing schemes might be even more interesting for these than for ordinary solar panels.

11. M-USE – A second example concerns the installation of elevators in real estate. Of course, a private person or – more likely – company can buy an own elevator. Mitsubishi Elevators Europe, however, offers a Circular Economy alternative to this: it offers the lease of elevators to real estate owners ('M-use') and this in combination with renewable energy ('M-Zero'). It explicitly frames this as service providing, being the use of the elevator, combined with the idea of circularity (maintaining, recycling, etc.).[47]

---

43 For instance in Flanders: https://www.vlaanderen.be/nl/bouwen-wonen-en-energie/elektriciteit-aardgas-en-verwarming/zonnepanelen-verwijderen-buiten-dienst-stellen.

44 See for instance in Belgium (a bank leasing solar panels with a buying option in the end): https://www.belfius.be/corporate/NL/OnzeProductenEnDiensten/Investeringen/Duurzame Oplossingen/Zonnepanelen/index.aspx?firstWA=no. See for instance in the Netherlands (a private company leasing solar panels with a buying option in the end): https://atama.nl/voor-particulieren/zonnepanelen-lease/.

45 See: https://www.vlaanderen.be/nl/bouwen-wonen-en-energie/elektriciteit-aardgas-en-verwarming/zonnedelen-investeer-mee-zonnepanelen-op-een-ander-dak (last visited on 3 April 2018).

46 See for instance: https://www.zonnepanelen.net/zonnepannen/. One of the best-known developers of these solar roof tiles is Tesla: https://www.tesla.com/nl_BE/solarroof.

47 See: https://www.mitsubishi-liften.nl/m-use/ (last visited on 5 April 2018). See also: H. PLOEGER *et al.*, "Circular economy and real estate: alternatives for operational lease" in *Proceedings of the International Research Conference 2017: Shaping tomorrow's built environment*, Salford (UK), 2017, (1) 7.

12. 2ND SKIN – A third initiative that must be mentioned is the so-called 2ndskin initiative.[48] In the quest for the energy-neutralisation of real estate with as little disturbance as possible for the residents, an interesting concept has been developed: why not install prefabricated façades and integrate these in existing real estate? In other words: why not give buildings a new skin?

This initiative can also be considered an example of what the Ellen MacArthur Foundation calls the modularisation of the building industry[49]: after all, the new façade is prefabricated and, in fact, constitutes a module. The use of prefabricated modules prevents on-site construction waste, because on-site assembly is limited to the bare minimum, and increases the building speed, which reduces the cost.[50] Heating, ventilation and solar panels are integrated in the new skin, in order to facilitate maintenance of the entire structure and possible future upgrades.[51]

This last aim of course rings a bell for Circular Economy proponents. In fact, this entire project could easily be fit into a Circular Economy: after all, why should the owner of the house also be the owner of the prefabricated façade? Given the explicit aim of maintaining and upgrading the façade, would it then not be much more efficient to leave the ownership of that façade with the party that is also technically capable of maintaining and upgrading that façade, *i.e.* the manufacturer? From a Circular Economy point of view, the answer is, I believe, a straightforward 'yes'. Recently, I was made aware of a Dutch project that is following the lease operationalisation model for façades: the Eneco Energy Campus in Utrecht has a façade on which the owner of the building has vested a long-lease ('*erfpacht*', or emphyteusis) in favor of the producer of the building parts of the façade, who thus remains the owner of these parts.[52] This proves that the above-sketched model is making progress I practice.

13. DESSO CARPET LEASE – Another example that fits perfectly within a Circular Economy is the leasing of fitted carpets, as offered by Desso (Desso

48 See thereon: T. KONSTANTINOU, O. GUERRA-SANTIN, J. AZCARATE-AGUERRE, T. KLEIN and S. SILVESTER, "A zero-energy refurbishment solution for residential apartment buildings by applying an integrated, prefabricated façade module", *Proceedings of the Munich Powerskin Conference (January 19th 2017)* 2017, (231) 231-240. See also: H. PLOEGER *et al.*, "Circular economy and real estate: alternatives for operational lease" in *Proceedings of the International Research Conference 2017: Shaping tomorrow's built environment*, Salford (UK), 2017, (1) 7.

49 See: E.M. FOUNDATION, *Delivering the Circular Economy. A Toolkit for Policymakers*, EMF, 2015, 112, 113 ff.

50 See: E.M. FOUNDATION, *Delivering the Circular Economy. A Toolkit for Policymakers*, EMF, 2015, 114.

51 See: T. KONSTANTINOU *et al.*, "A zero-energy refurbishment solution for residential apartment buildings by applying an integrated, prefabricated façade module", *Proceedings of the Munich Powerskin Conference (January 19th 2017)* 2017, (231) 234-235.

52 See:https://www.cobouw.nl/utiliteitsbouw/nieuws/2018/02/doorbraak-voor-circulaire-gevels-leasen-op-basis-van-erfpacht-101257661?vakmedianet-approve-cookies=1&_ga=2.176924005.1989006797.1532512804-167092041.1532512804 (last visited on 25 July 2018).

Carpet Lease).[53] Desso leases carpet tiles to users and takes these back at the end of the leasing contract, in order to reuse the tiles elsewhere or recycle the materials. Desso explicitly brands this as 'contributing to the user's sustainability aspirations' and 'a crucial step in Desso's transition to the Circular Economy'.[54] As a similar project, the Philips Lighting initiative can also be mentioned (*cf. supra*, nr. 4).

14. **Furniture lease** – Also less innovative-looking but still real estate-connected projects can be mentioned in this respect. The leasing of furniture, for instance, is by no means a total novelty.[55] Admittedly, most of these website aim at professional parties or private parties with specific characteristics – diplomates, military service, students, etc. –, but in the future this market could easily be expanded to common private parties.

This would fit perfectly within the Circular Economy, most certainly when 'furniture' is interpreted as also containing electrical equipment, kitchens, etc.

15. **Casco-sale** – As a final example, a very interesting more general concept deserves reference. In a short contribution in 2014, Van der Veen, Hulshof and Ploeger launch the idea of 'casco-sale'.[56] In fact, this concept contains all the previously mentioned initiatives. The essence of the casco-sale comes down to the following: people only buy the exterior, the 'shell' or casco, of their real estate and lease all the rest, *i.e.* the entire interior, in combination with maintenance contracts for all parts of this interior. The notion 'interior' not only contains furniture and all household equipment, but also floor and wall covering, kitchens, bathrooms and even non-supporting inner walls.[57]

---

53 See: www.desso-businesscarpets.nl/service/carpet-lease/. See also: H. PLOEGER *et al.*, "Circular economy and real estate: alternatives for operational lease" in *Proceedings of the International Research Conference 2017: Shaping tomorrow's built environment*, Salford (UK), 2017, (1) 9; T. RAU and S. OBERHUBER, *Material matters. Het alternatief voor onze roofbouwmaatschappij*, Haarlem, Bertram + de Leeuw Uitgevers, 2017, 89; M. VAN DER VEEN, M. HULSHOF and H. PLOEGER, "Cascokoop: wenkend perspectief binnen een circulaire economie", *WPNR* 2014, (857) 857.

54 See: www.desso-businesscarpets.nl/service/carpet-lease/ (under reason 1 and the picture, respectively; last visited on 5 April 2018).

55 See e.g.: https://www.alvero.be/nl/nieuws/kantoormeubelen-leasen; https://www.home-inspirations.nl/meubels-huren/meubels-leasen/; https://www.in-lease.com/nl/; https://www.rocor.be/verhuur. See also: H. PLOEGER *et al.*, "Circular economy and real estate: alternatives for operational lease" in *Proceedings of the International Research Conference 2017: Shaping tomorrow's built environment*, Salford (UK), 2017, (1) 9; M. VAN DER VEEN *et al.*, "Cascokoop: wenkend perspectief binnen een circulaire economie", *WPNR* 2014, (857) 857.

56 The authors have been inspired by the concept of 'sale-lease' that was popular in the 90s in the Netherlands: a lessee leases the exterior of a building, but buys the interior. See: M. VAN DER VEEN *et al.*, "Cascokoop: wenkend perspectief binnen een circulaire economie", *WPNR* 2014, (857) 857-859.

57 See: M. VAN DER VEEN *et al.*, "Cascokoop: wenkend perspectief binnen een circulaire economie", *WPNR* 2014, (857) 857-858.

For the authors, this is a possible key to enter the real estate sector in the so-called 'lease society'[58], which is to be considered a synonym for the Circular Economy.

16. Common characteristics – All these initiatives have in common that a movable or group of movables is leased to an owner of an immovable, who either – the solar panels, the elevator and the façade – or not – the lighting, the fitted carpet[59], the furniture, etc. – incorporates[60] that movable in his immovable.

A first question is what happens with the legal status of a movable, for instance a solar panel or an elevator, when a lessor incorporates that movable in an immovable. This first question is relevant for both the parties themselves as third parties. A second question is how third parties are treated that are confronted with – not incorporated – movables they believe to be an asset of the real estate owner, while these movables are in fact only leased. These two questions will be dealt with below (*cf. infra*, nr. 23 ff and 39 ff). In a preliminary phase, I will shortly dwell on the notion 'immovable' in Belgian law (*cf. infra*, nr. 20 ff).

3.3. TOWARDS A MORE HOLISTIC APPROACH?

17. Getting to a holistic approach? – Before getting to the legal analysis, it is worth pointing out that the above-mentioned projects by no means constitute the only possible Circular Economy concepts for the real estate sector. In fact, it is possible taking the service providing operationalisation much and much further, in order to reduce waste in the real estate sector and to further modularisation (*cf. supra*, nr. 9). For instance, why not put all raw materials used in the building sector, the bricks, steel beams, marble, wooden beams, screws, etc., in a lease scheme? And why not start applying prefabricated modules for as many building parts as possible? Both suggestions might sound like a fantasy – some would say: an utopia –, but the idea is effectively put forward in practice.

---

58 The so-called lease society is a concept that is strongly propagated by Judith Merkies, a Dutch and European politician, who sees it as the alternative to the contemporary ownership society. See also: https://www.slideshare.net/robbla/brochure-va-p-3.

59 It could be argued that lighting armatures or fitted carpet are also incorporated in the real estate. Without entering in this debate and for the sake of this paper, however, I uphold that these are not incorporated in real estate. In most cases, these lighting facilities or the fitted carpet will indeed be connected to the real estate, without being incorporated. In case the owner of the lighting instruments and the real estate would be the same, these lighting instruments would be considered immovable by destination, but not by nature on the basis of incorporation: *cf. infra*, nr. 20-21. See also: B. TILLEMAN, "De notie roerend en onroerend goed" in P. LECOCQ, B. TILLEMAN and A. VERBEKE (eds.), *Zakenrecht / Droit des biens*, Brugge, die Keure, 2005, (1) nr. 37.

60 For the exact meaning of the notion 'incorporation': *cf. infra*, nr. 20 and 26.

Some voices in the real estate sector plead effectively for a fundamental change in how buildings are built, maintained, renovated or demolished. All above-mentioned initiatives of course fit within this discourse, but what is really needed is a holistic approach.[61] This term 'holistic' means that the change is implemented in all steps of the building process: architects must keep circularity in mind when designing buildings – something that happens in the 2ndskin project, too, for instance (*cf. supra*, nr. 12) –, for instance by applying so-called Design for Change or Reversible Building Design[62], wreckers must adapt themselves even more to 'urban miners'[63] – people who collect valuable raw materials from wrecking sites specifically with the purpose to sell these to contractors to be reused as new materials – contractors must focus on using used raw materials and think of possible prefabrication of modules, for instance by 3D-printing, urban planners must provide guidance and support, etc. A combination of all this factors fully exploits the opportunities that have been identified by the Ellen MacArthur Foundation: modularisation of the production process and waste reduction (*cf. supra*, nr. 9).

18. **The Materials Passport** – In this respect, I would like to mention the so-called 'Materials Passport', invented by Rau, as a tool that might be quintessential in the process.[64] A building's Materials Passport, in its essence, numbers all the materials that have been used in that building. In the words of

---

61 This is precisely the difference between the Circular Economy as a concept and the many already existing, smaller projects: *cf. supra*, nr. 6). See also for instance: W. DEBACKER and S. MANSHOVE, "D1 Synthesis of the State-of-the-Art. Key Barriers and Opportunities for Materials Passports and Reversible Building Design in the current system", *Building as Material Banks* 2016, (1) 14 ff.; E.M. FOUNDATION, *Delivering the Circular Economy. A Toolkit for Policymakers*, EMF, 2015, 111 ff.

62 This is literally what the term means; designing buildings so that they can easily be demounted. See also: W. DEBACKER and S. MANSHOVE, "D1 Synthesis of the State-of-the-Art. Key Barriers and Opportunities for Materials Passports and Reversible Building Design in the current system", *Building as Material Banks* 2016, (1) 57-61; E.M. FOUNDATION, *Delivering the Circular Economy. A Toolkit for Policymakers*, EMF, 2015, 117-118; J.P.V. EESTEREN, "Circulariteit is route naar een écht duurzame bouwsector", *https://www.jpvaneesteren.nl/nl/circulariteit-route-naar-een-echt-duurzame-bouwsector* 2018, (1) 2. Rau uses the nice metaphor of an attraction on a fair: T. RAU and S. OBERHUBER, *Material matters. Het alternatief voor onze roofbouwmaatschappij*, Haarlem, Bertram + de Leeuw Uitgevers, 2017, 76.

63 See in particular on urban mining: J.P.V. EESTEREN, "Circulariteit is route naar een écht duurzame bouwsector", *https://www.jpvaneesteren.nl/nl/circulariteit-route-naar-een-echt-duurzame-bouwsector* 2018, (1) 2; T. RAU and S. OBERHUBER, *Material matters. Het alternatief voor onze roofbouwmaatschappij*, Haarlem, Bertram + de Leeuw Uitgevers, 2017, 114-116. See for a list of Dutch and Belgian projects that provide a map to urban miners: W. DEBACKER and S. MANSHOVE, "D1 Synthesis of the State-of-the-Art. Key Barriers and Opportunities for Materials Passports and Reversible Building Design in the current system", *Building as Material Banks* 2016, (1) 57.

64 On the Materials Passport in general, see: T. RAU and S. OBERHUBER, *Material matters. Het alternatief voor onze roofbouwmaatschappij*, Haarlem, Bertram + de Leeuw Uitgevers, 2017, 111 ff.

the Buildings as Material Banks Group: "*Material Passports are (digital) sets of data describing defined characteristics of materials and components in products and systems that give them value for present use, recovery and reuse.*"[65]

Being a digital information sheet with real estate data, the material passport is a practical example of what is called 'Building Information Modelling' (BIM): the digital collection of data on the built environment and the life-cycle of the assets therein.[66] A Materials Passport ensures that valuable components of buildings do not lose their own identity and prevents their ending up – paraphrasing RAUs above-mentioned quote – as waste.[67] As such, Materials Passports provide information on parts of buildings that can maintain their value in the future, which is of utmost importance in a Circular Economy.

Well then, once a material passports is created – or even put in an online database, the so-called Madaster (*cf. infra*, nr. 36) –, the next step is to apply a lease scheme on these materials.[68] Thus the Materials Passport might be a quintessential step in the generalisation of the lease operationalisation in a Circular Economy for real estate. It is very well possible that the (near) future of the entire real estate sector looks much more circular than we would think now.

19. THE HOLISTIC APPROACH IN PRACTICE – All this might sound rather futuristic, were it not that buildings have already been constructed or are under construction applying the above-mentioned principles. The new office of the Triodos Bank that is currently being built by J.P. van Eesteren, a contractor[69], in Driebergen-Zeist (the Netherlands) and has been designed bu RAU Architects is purposely designed demountably. This means that the raw materials used in

---

65 See on the Materials Passport also: W. DEBACKER and S. MANSHOVE, "D1 Synthesis of the State-of-the-Art. Key Barriers and Opportunities for Materials Passports and Reversible Building Design in the current system", *Building as Material Banks* 2016, (1) 54-56; E.M. FOUNDATION, *Delivering the Circular Economy. A Toolkit for Policymakers*, EMF, 2015, 119.

66 This concept is also mentioned by: H. PLOEGER *et al.*, "Circular economy and real estate: alternatives for operational lease" in *Proceedings of the International Research Conference 2017: Shaping tomorrow's built environment*, Salford (UK), 2017, (1) 6. See on BIM in general for instance: W. DEBACKER and S. MANSHOVE, "D1 Synthesis of the State-of-the-Art. Key Barriers and Opportunities for Materials Passports and Reversible Building Design in the current system", *Building as Material Banks* 2016, (1) 22-23. See also the website of the European Union Task Group on BIM: www.eubim.eu/.

67 See also: R. VAN DER ENT, "Niet uitputten, maar opnieuw inzetten", *https://www.jpvaneesteren.nl/nl/blog-niet-uitputten-maar-opnieuw-inzetten* 2017, (1) 3-4 ("Materialen krijgen een identiteit door ze te documenteren in een materialenpaspoort. […] Een goed materialenpaspoort levert geld op.").

68 See also: E.M. FOUNDATION, *Delivering the Circular Economy. A Toolkit for Policymakers*, EMF, 2015, 118, 119; J.P.V. EESTEREN, "Circulariteit is route naar een écht duurzame bouwsector", *https://www.jpvaneesteren.nl/nl/circulariteit-route-naar-een-echt-duurzame-bouwsector* 2018, (1) 2.

69 J.P. van Eesteren is a member of the TBI Group: this Dutch group of companies promotes innovative and sustainable development of the built environment. See for more information: https://www.tbi.nl/ (last visited on 10 April 2018).

the building are also easily reapplicable in other parts of the building or even in other, future building projects. For this building, a materials passport is being created, too, in combination with a 3D-model of the building.[70] In addition, the building is meant to be completely energy neutral.[71]

Other examples are the town hall in Brummen (the Netherlands)[72], also designed by RAU Architects, and Park 20/20 office building (the Netherlands), developed by the Delta Development Group, VolkerWessels, the Reggeborgh Group and designed by the American architect William McDonough.[73]

3.4. THE NOTION 'IMMOVABLE' IN BELGIAN LAW: THREE CATEGORIES

20. Immovables by incorporation – All goods are either movable or immovable (art. 516 Belgian Civil Code). The Belgian Civil Code distinguishes three sorts of immovables.[74] **The first category** is formed by immovables 'by nature' or 'by incorporation' (enumerated in articles 518-520 and 523 of the Belgian Civil Code), e.g. plots of land, houses, flats, cellars, the stairs in a house, the sewage system in a building, doors, windows, trees, etc. In short: land, buildings and fixtures. For this first category, physical attachment to the soil is required, directly or indirectly, which is called 'incorporation'.[75] Thus

---

70 For other Materials Passports existing in practice, see: W. DEBACKER and S. MANSHOVE, "D1 Synthesis of the State-of-the-Art. Key Barriers and Opportunities for Materials Passports and Reversible Building Design in the current system", *Building as Material Banks* 2016, (1) 55.

71 See: https://www.jpvaneesteren.nl/nl/triodos-bank; https://www.jpvaneesteren.nl/nl/bouw-nieuw-duurzaam-kantoor-triodos-bank-gestart. See also on the Triodos project: J.P.V. EESTEREN, "Circulariteit is route naar een écht duurzame bouwsector", *https://www.jpvaneesteren.nl/nl/circulariteit-route-naar-een-echt-duurzame-bouwsector* 2018, (1) 3; T. RAU and S. OBERHUBER, *Material matters. Het alternatief voor onze roofbouwmaatschappij*, Haarlem, Bertram + de Leeuw Uitgevers, 2017, 131.

72 See also: E.M. FOUNDATION, *Delivering the Circular Economy. A Toolkit for Policymakers*, EMF, 2015, 117; T. RAU and S. OBERHUBER, *Material matters. Het alternatief voor onze roofbouwmaatschappij*, Haarlem, Bertram + de Leeuw Uitgevers, 2017, 123.

73 The architect is also the founder of the cradle-cradle-concept, one of the first manifestations of the idea of circularity. See: www.park2020.com/. See also: E.M. FOUNDATION, *Delivering the Circular Economy. A Toolkit for Policymakers*, EMF, 2015, 117; T. RAU and S. OBERHUBER, *Material matters. Het alternatief voor onze roofbouwmaatschappij*, Haarlem, Bertram + de Leeuw Uitgevers, 2017, 82.

74 See on immovables in Belgian law: A. APERS, *Wilsautonomie bij kwalificatie van goederen*, Antwerpen, Intersentia, 2017, nr. 59 ff.; P. LECOCQ, *Manuel de droit des biens*, Brussel, Larcier, 2012, nr. 19 ff.; V. SAGAERT, *Goederenrecht*, Mechelen, Kluwer, 2014, nr. 97 ff.; B. TILLEMAN, "De notie roerend en onroerend goed" in P. LECOCQ, B. TILLEMAN and A. VERBEKE (eds.), *Zakenrecht / Droit des biens*, Brugge, die Keure, 2005, (1) nr. 1 ff; P. VAN AVERMAETE, "Het onroerend goed en zijn huidige problemen", *TPR* 1983, (1) 1-11; F. VAN NESTE, *Zakenrecht*, Brussel, E. Story-Scientia, 1990, nr. 36 ff.

75 See very clarifying on the notion 'incorporation': A. APERS, *Wilsautonomie bij kwalificatie van goederen*, Antwerpen, Intersentia, 2017, nr. 64 ff.

immovables by incorporation are an application of the unity principle (*cf. infra*, nr. 25).

'Incorporation' used to be interpreted rather strictly as what is thus connected to the soil that it cannot be removed without damaging it. Nowadays, however, this notion is interpreted more freely than it used to be: the Belgian Supreme Court stipulated that a durable and normal attachment to the soil is needed for a good to be immovable, even though (1) that good is theoretically replaceable without damaging it, but meant to stay where it is given its durable and usual connection to the soil[76], and even though (2) that good is functionally movable.[77] In fact, these extensions introduce some degree of subjectivity in the determination of the nature of a good, albeit that this subjectivity is tempered by an objective interpretation ('usual', 'commonly accepted').[78] Especially the latter extension, however, is criticised by legal doctrine for creating legal uncertainty.[79] However, as long as these notions indeed receive an objectively verifiable meaning in case law and do not give too much leanway to subjective meaning, I do not see any problem.[80] This first category will appear to be of utmost importance for this paper (*cf. infra*, nr. 26).

21. Immovables by destination – Immovables 'by destination' are the **second category** (art. 522, 524-525 Belgian Civil Code). This category contains goods that are movable by nature, but are considered *accessoria* of an immovable by nature and therefore also immovable, e.g. the ovens in a bakery, the cattle in a dairy farm (art. 522 Belgian Civil Code), etc. Thus, the legislator has created

---

76 The first decision concerned gas stations. See: Cass. 15 September 1988, *Arr.Cass.* 1988-89, 60, *RW* 1988-89, 879, *TBBR* 1990, 211, annotation J. Kokelenberg, *AFT* 1989, 78, annotation F. Laurent. See also: A. APERS, *Wilsautonomie bij kwalificatie van goederen*, Antwerpen, Intersentia, 2017, nr. 81, 100; S. BOULY, *Onroerende natrekking en horizontale eigendomssplitsingen*, Antwerpen, Intersentia, 2015, nr. 86; V. SAGAERT, *Goederenrecht*, Mechelen, Kluwer, 2014, nr. 100; B. TILLEMAN, "De notie roerend en onroerend goed" in P. LECOCQ, B. TILLEMAN and A. VERBEKE (eds.), *Zakenrecht / Droit des biens*, Brugge, die Keure, 2005, (1) nr. 10.

77 The second decision concerned cranes on rails in a harbour See: Cass. 14 February 2008, *RW* 2008-09, 456, annotation V. Sagaert, *JLMB* 2008, 1700, annotation E. Van Brustem, *TBO* 2008, 118, annotation M. Muylle, *Fisc.Koer.* 2008, 464, annotation P. Souffriau, *RCJB* 2010, 53, annotation J. Romain. This judgment hs been repeated afterwards: Cass. 15 March 2012, *Pas.* 2012, 599, *TBBR* 2013, 422, annotation A. Salvé. See also: A. APERS, *Wilsautonomie bij kwalificatie van goederen*, Antwerpen, Intersentia, 2017, nr. 81, 101; S. BOULY, *Onroerende natrekking en horizontale eigendomssplitsingen*, Antwerpen, Intersentia, 2015, nr. 87; P. LECOCQ, *Manuel de droit des biens*, Brussel, Larcier, 2012, nr. 24; V. SAGAERT, *Goederenrecht*, Mechelen, Kluwer, 2014, nr. 101.

78 See also: A. APERS, *Wilsautonomie bij kwalificatie van goederen*, Antwerpen, Intersentia, 2017, nr. 81, 105, 150.

79 See e.g.: S. BOULY, *Onroerende natrekking en horizontale eigendomssplitsingen*, Antwerpen, Intersentia, 2015, nr. 90; P. LECOCQ, *Manuel de droit des biens*, Brussel, Larcier, 2012, nr. 25; V. SAGAERT, *Goederenrecht*, Mechelen, Kluwer, 2014, nr. 101.

80 Van Vliet argues the same for the notion 'incorporation' as required for accession to an immovable: *cf. infra*, nr. 26.

a fiction. This category is an application of the *accessorium sequitur principale*-principle, that has itself an economic basis: the whole is worth more than the sum of the parts, so the whole must be maintained.[81]

A movable is an immovable by destination, if (1) this movable has the same owner as the immovable, (2) it is clear to third parties that the movable is an *accessorium* to the immovable – a matter of third party protection[82] –, either because it is objectively useful for the economic exploitation of the immovable – in French: *immobilisation par destination économique* –, either because it has been durably connected to the immovable by the owner – in French: *immobilistation par attache à perpétuelle démeure* –, e.g. mirrors on walls in a house that have been specifically designed for this purpose[83], and (3) the immovable must be specifically adapted for the movable.[84] These conditions, in particular the second one, must protect third parties: it is important for them to know what is immovable and what is not, for instance if they want to seize a good.[85]

22. Immovables because of the object – The **final category** concerns immovables because of the object they concern, in other words: immaterial rights that concern immovables and are therefore considered immovables themselves (art. 526 Belgian Civil Code), e.g. a usufruct on an immovable, a long-lease (emphyteusis), etc. This final category, however, is of less importance for this paper.

Only the above-mentioned three categories form immovables, all other goods are movables: movables are the so-called residuary category.[86]

---

81 See in this sense: V. SAGAERT, *Goederenrecht*, Mechelen, Kluwer, 2014, nr. 107, 115; B. TILLEMAN, "De notie roerend en onroerend goed" in P. LECOCQ, B. TILLEMAN and A. VERBEKE (eds.), *Zakenrecht / Droit des biens*, Brugge, die Keure, 2005, (1) nr. 12. This *rationale* is the same as one of the underlying objectives of the unity principle (*cf. infra*, nr. 25), but both – accessority and unity – may not be confused. *Accessoria* remain independent objects of property law, while the unity principle explicitly targets dependent parts of a whole. See on this distinction: S. BOULY, *Onroerende natrekking en horizontale eigendomssplitsingen*, Antwerpen, Intersentia, 2015, nr. 16, 37; K. SWINNEN, *Accessoriteit in het vermogensrecht*, Antwerpen, Intersentia, 2014, 375-376, 382 ff.

82 See also e.g.: P. LECOCQ, *Manuel de droit des biens*, Brussel, Larcier, 2012, nr. 32.

83 Without being incorporated in the wall. Otherwise, the mirror would be an immovable by nature. See on this subtle – and not very clear – distinction also: A. APERS, *Wilsautonomie bij kwalificatie van goederen*, Antwerpen, Intersentia, 2017, nr. 218 ff.; P. LECOCQ, *Manuel de droit des biens*, Brussel, Larcier, 2012, nr. 37; B. TILLEMAN, "De notie roerend en onroerend goed" in P. LECOCQ, B. TILLEMAN and A. VERBEKE (eds.), *Zakenrecht / Droit des biens*, Brugge, die Keure, 2005, (1) nr. 37.

84 See e.g.: Cass. 11 September 1980, *Ar.Cass.* 1980-81, 32, annotation, *RCJB* 1981, 173, annotation J. Hansenne, *RW* 1980-81, 1663.

85 See on this third party protection also: V. SAGAERT, *Goederenrecht*, Mechelen, Kluwer, 2014, nr. 112-113, 114, 117 (on seizure); B. TILLEMAN, "De notie roerend en onroerend goed" in P. LECOCQ, B. TILLEMAN and A. VERBEKE (eds.), *Zakenrecht / Droit des biens*, Brugge, die Keure, 2005, (1) nr. 16, 50 (on seizure).

86 See: V. SAGAERT, *Goederenrecht*, Mechelen, Kluwer, 2014, nr. 93, 127; B. TILLEMAN, "De notie roerend en onroerend goed" in P. LECOCQ, B. TILLEMAN and A. VERBEKE (eds.), *Zakenrecht / Droit des biens*, Brugge, die Keure, 2005, (1) nr. 63.

3.5. LEASING INCORPORATED BUILDING PARTS IN A CIRCULAR ECONOMY

3.5.1. Accession to immovables

23. **Introduction** – A first way in which the real estate sector is engaging is the Circular Economy is by leasing movables to a real estate owner, who subsequently incorporates these movables in his immovable. Thus these movables become immovables by nature themselves (*cf. supra*, nr. 20). An example of this is the above-mentioned leasing of solar panels or even solar roof tiles, or the leasing of an elevator or a prefabricated façade.

Apart from the movable or immovable nature of the good, the question remains what happens with the ownership of the movable once it is incorporated and has become an immovable: is the owner of the movable the lessor or the lessee? This question must be solved on the basis of so-called accession to immovables (*accessio*).

24. **Accession to immovables** – The ownership of a movable extinguishes on the very moment it is incorporated in an immovable. Thus the original owner of that movable loses his ownership and the movable becomes part of the immovable (art. 546 Belgian Civil Code). Classically, this happens for buildings on lands – already in Roman law: *superficies solo cedit* –, but logically this is also the case for goods incorporated in that immovable (fixtures). This process is called accession to immovables (art. 546, 552-553 Belgian Civil Code).[87] Some[88] claim that accession is therefore an so-called 'original' acquisition ground of property, contrary to so-called derived grounds, such as sale or inheritance.[89] However, others soundly argue that accession is only an extinction ground

---

87 See in general thereon: A. APERS, *Wilsautonomie bij kwalificatie van goederen*, Antwerpen, Intersentia, 2017, nr. 132 ff.; P. LECOCQ, *Manuel de droit des biens*, Brussel, Larcier, 2012, nr. 92, 94, 109 ff.; V. SAGAERT, *Goederenrecht*, Mechelen, Kluwer, 2014, nr. 972 ff.; F. WERDEFROY, "Beschouwingen over de onroerende natrekking, het recht van erfpacht, het recht van opstal, en het verlof tot bouwen", *TPR* 1983, (293) nr. 2 ff. See from an international perspective: L. VAN VLIET, "Accession of Movables to Land", *Edinburgh L. Rev.* 2002, (67) 67 ff. See extensively: S. BOULY, *Onroerende natrekking en horizontale eigendomssplitsingen*, Antwerpen, Intersentia, 2015, 598 p.

88 See for instance: J. HANSENNE, *Les biens. Précis*, Luik, Ed. Collection Scientifique de la Faculté de Droit de Liège, 1996, nr. 507; P. LECOCQ, *Manuel de droit des biens*, Brussel, Larcier, 2012, nr. 89, 92, 108; F. WERDEFROY, "Beschouwingen over de onroerende natrekking, het recht van erfpacht, het recht van opstal, en het verlof tot bouwen", *TPR* 1983, (293) nr. 2-3. Support for this vision can be read in art. 712 of the Belgian Civil Code. See for an overview: S. BOULY, *Onroerende natrekking en horizontale eigendomssplitsingen*, Antwerpen, Intersentia, 2015, nr. 30 ff., 104.

89 This is important, because original acquisition of property does not require that the predecessor in title has the competence to dispose of the right *in rem*, nor does it require any publicity, and, finally, possible rights *in rem* that were vested on the (object of the) real right *in rem* that is originally acquired are lost. See on the importance of this distinction for

of rights *in rem* and not an acquisition ground, because only the object of the existing right *in rem* – *in casu*: the ownership of the owner of the house – is enlarged, while no new right *in rem* is created.[90]

25. The unity principle, specificity principle and transparency principle – Accession to immovables – like immovables by incorporation (*cf. supra*, nr. 20) – is classically justified on the basis of a specific property law principle: the **unity principle** (as formulated in art. 551 Belgian Civil Code; also known as '*eenheidsbeginsel*', which is closely related to the theory of '*bestanddeelvorming*').[91] This principle means that rights *in rem* can only be vested on 'units', *i.e.* what the law considers a unity, and not on parts of that unit. Sagaert defines 'parts' (*bestanddelen*) as "all physical and legal parts [of a whole] that are not capable of independent existence according to the normal destination."[92] Those parts must have the same statute as the unit itself, because they are considered dependent themselves.

The unity principle (1) protects legal certainty of third parties, that must be able to trust their eyes, and (2) preserves the value of the immovable and its integrated parts, starting from the idea that the whole immovable is worth more than the sum of the value of its parts taken separately.[93] The value of both objectives in a Circular Economy will be dealt with below (*cf. infra*, nr. 32-33).

The unity principle is in its turn important to determine what can be the object of a right *in rem*. After all, a second property law principle, namely the

---

instance: S. BOULY, *Onroerende natrekking en horizontale eigendomssplitsingen*, Antwerpen, Intersentia, 2015, nr. 30; V. SAGAERT, *Goederenrecht*, Mechelen, Kluwer, 2014, nr. 794-795.

90 See for instance: A. APERS, *Wilsautonomie bij kwalificatie van goederen*, Antwerpen, Intersentia, 2017, nr. 133; S. BOULY, *Onroerende natrekking en horizontale eigendomssplitsingen*, Antwerpen, Intersentia, 2015, nr. 36; F. LAURENT, *Principes de droit civil, VIII*, Brussel, Bruylant, 1878, nr. 182; V. SAGAERT, *Goederenrecht*, Mechelen, Kluwer, 2014, nr. 796, 971; K. SWINNEN, *Accessoriteit in het vermogensrecht*, Antwerpen, Intersentia, 2014, nr. 380.

91 See specifically on the objectives of accession: A. APERS, *Wilsautonomie bij kwalificatie van goederen*, Antwerpen, Intersentia, 2017, nr. 142, 168; S. BOULY, *Onroerende natrekking en horizontale eigendomssplitsingen*, Antwerpen, Intersentia, 2015, nr. 19 ff.; H. PLOEGER *et al.*, "Circular economy and real estate: alternatives for operational lease" in *Proceedings of the International Research Conference 2017: Shaping tomorrow's built environment*, Salford (UK), 2017, (1) 6 (from a Dutch point of view); M. VAN DER VEEN *et al.*, "Cascokoop: wenkend perspectief binnen een circulaire economie", *WPNR* 2014, (857) 858 (from a Dutch point of view); L. VAN VLIET, "Accession of Movables to Land", *Edinburgh L. Rev.* 2002, (67) 69-71; F. WERDEFROY, "Beschouwingen over de onroerende natrekking, het recht van erfpacht, het recht van opstal, en het verlof tot bouwen", *TPR* 1983, (293) nr. 4 See on the unity principle in particular: A. APERS, *Wilsautonomie bij kwalificatie van goederen*, Antwerpen, Intersentia, 2017,142; V. SAGAERT, *Goederenrecht*, Mechelen, Kluwer, 2014, nr. 82-84; K. SWINNEN, *Accessoriteit in het vermogensrecht*, Antwerpen, Intersentia, 2014, nr. 376 ff.

92 V. SAGAERT, *Goederenrecht*, Mechelen, Kluwer, 2014, nr. 83. The author gives as an example the motor of a vehicle. I will redefine this notion below: *cf. infra*, nr. 34.

93 These objectives are similar to the objectives of the *accessorium sequitur principale*-principle: *cf. supra*, nr. 21. See also: K. SWINNEN, *Accessoriteit in het vermogensrecht*, Antwerpen, Intersentia, 2014, 376.

specificity principle, stipulates that rights *in rem* must be vested on specific goods and not on abstract values.[94] However, it must first be clear what forms part of that good, which is why the unity principle is so important.

This specificity principle forms part of the **transparency requirement** that is formulated in all legal systems for rights *in rem* to have *erga omnes*-effects, together with the *numerus clausus* principle: the existence of such right must be transparent to third parties and specificity, on the one hand, and publicity, on the other hand, make that it is.[95] Thus, the unity principle appears to be related to the justification of the very core of property law: the opposability of rights *in rem erga omnes*. Therefore, one must not look to this principle without due care. Simply claiming that some of the above-mentioned principles are a hindrance to a Circular Economy and must therefore be abolished without any reference to the objectives of these principles cannot be accepted (*cf. supra* and *infra*, nr. 8 and 32-33).

26. **Requirement of incorporation** – Accession to the immovable only happens when there is incorporation.[96] Thus, leasing movables to a person who uses those movables for the functioning of his immovable without incorporating them does not result in accession (*cf. infra*, nr. 39 ff).[97] The notion 'incorporation' is classically interpreted in the same way as the incorporation needed for immovables by nature (*cf. supra*, nr. 20).[98] However, Sagaert wonders whether this is still the case, given the gradual widening of the notion 'incorporation' for

---

94 The Belgian Supreme Court formulated this rule in a famous decision of 9 May 1947: Cass. 9 May 1947, *Arr.Cass.* 1947, 148, *Pas.* 1947, I, 193, *TBH* 1948, 208, *Rev.banque* 1948, 282. See on the specificity principle in Belgian law for instance: A. APERS, *Wilsautonomie bij kwalificatie van goederen*, Antwerpen, Intersentia, 2017, nr. 142; V. SAGAERT, *Goederenrecht*, Mechelen, Kluwer, 2014, nr. 85-90.

95 See on the transparency requirement for rights *in rem*: B. AKKERMANS, *The Principle of Numerus Clausus in European Property Law*, Antwerpen, Intersentia, 2008, 5; S. VAN ERP, "From "Classical" to Modern European Property Law?" in NATIONAL AND KAPODISTRIAN UNIVERSITY OF ATHENS (ed.), *Essays in Honour of Konstantinos D. Kerameus*, Brussel, Bruylant, 2010, (1517) 1524-1525; J.H.M. VAN ERP, "General issues: setting the scene" in J. H. M. VAN ERP (ed.), *Cases, Materials and Text on Property Law*, Oxford, Hart Publishing, 2012, (37) 52; S. VAN ERP, "Contract and Property Law: Distinct, but not Separate", *ERCL* 2013, (307) 314.

96 See: S. BOULY, *Onroerende natrekking en horizontale eigendomssplitsingen*, Antwerpen, Intersentia, 2015, nr. 77 ff.; J. HANSENNE, *Les biens. Précis*, Luik, Ed. Collection Scientifique de la Faculté de Droit de Liège, 1996, nr. 684; P. LECOCQ, *Manuel de droit des biens*, Brussel, Larcier, 2012, nr. 109; V. SAGAERT, *Goederenrecht*, Mechelen, Kluwer, 2014, nr. 978.

97 Neither do those movables become immovables by destination. After all, for movables to become immovables by destination, it is required that the same person is owner of the movable and the immovable (*cf. supra*, nr. 21).

98 See: A. APERS, *Wilsautonomie bij kwalificatie van goederen*, Antwerpen, Intersentia, 2017, nr. 167; S. BOULY, *Onroerende natrekking en horizontale eigendomssplitsingen*, Antwerpen, Intersentia, 2015, nr. 91 ff. (overview); V. SAGAERT, *Goederenrecht*, Mechelen, Kluwer, 2014, nr. 978; F. WERDEFROY, "Beschouwingen over de onroerende natrekking, het recht van erfpacht, het recht van opstal, en het verlof tot bouwen", *TPR* 1983, (293) nr. 2.

immovables by nature, and whether the notion 'incorporation' is not getting a dual interpretation, depending on whether it is used to determine the immovable nature of a good or to judge whether there accession.[99] In this respect, BOULY pleads to separate both interpretations of incorporation.[100]

Nevertheless, I uphold incorporation may still be interpreted identically in both cases, as long as it remains possible to determine its meaning on the basis of objective criteria (*cf. supra*, nr. 20); otherwise, the protective function of accession towards third parties gets lost and thus also one of the justification for accession.[101] In addition, I believe identical interpretation leads to a higher legal certainty than separate interpretation.

27. CONSEQUENCE OF INCORPORATION: TWO REFUTABLE PRESUMPTIONS – As a consequence of the incorporation, article 553 of the Belgian Civil Code creates a double refutable presumption.[102] First, it presumes that the owner of the immovable has paid for the incorporated movables that have thus become immovables. Second, it presumes that he is also the owner of those movables that have become immovables.

However, both presumptions are refutable, which is of utmost importance for this paper. The first presumption, on the one hand, can be refuted by all means: credit notes, bank accounts, etc. However, refutation of this first presumption does not prevent the accession: it only creates an obligatory claim from the financer to the owner of the immovable (*cf. infra*, nr. 38)[103], but has no effect whatsoever on the legal status of the immovable and its incorporated parts itself.[104]

---

99 See: V. SAGAERT, *Goederenrecht*, Mechelen, Kluwer, 2014, nr. 978. See also on this discussion: A. APERS, *Wilsautonomie bij kwalificatie van goederen*, Antwerpen, Intersentia, 2017, 167 ff.

100 See: S. BOULY, *Onroerende natrekking en horizontale eigendomssplitsingen*, Antwerpen, Intersentia, 2015, nr. 94-99. *Contra*: A. APERS, *Wilsautonomie bij kwalificatie van goederen*, Antwerpen, Intersentia, 2017, nr. 171, 173.

101 See also with regard to incorporation as required for accession and the objective criteria needed thereto: A. APERS, *Wilsautonomie bij kwalificatie van goederen*, Antwerpen, Intersentia, 2017, 168; M. VAN DER VEEN *et al.*, "Cascokoop: wenkend perspectief binnen een circulaire economie", *WPNR* 2014, (857) 859; L. VAN VLIET, "Accession of Movables to Land", *Edinburgh L. Rev.* 2002, (67) 214 ("*Legal systems which use objective standards for accession recognise that the rules of accession ought to protect third parties.*").

102 See: A. APERS, *Wilsautonomie bij kwalificatie van goederen*, Antwerpen, Intersentia, 2017, nr. 134; P. LECOCQ, *Manuel de droit des biens*, Brussel, Larcier, 2012, nr. 109; V. SAGAERT, *Goederenrecht*, Mechelen, Kluwer, 2014, nr. 972.

103 In this case, articles 554 and 555 Belgian Civil Code – depending upon whom has conducted the works – determine the specifics of the compensation. I will not elaborate on this in this paper. See e.g.: A. APERS, *Wilsautonomie bij kwalificatie van goederen*, Antwerpen, Intersentia, 2017, nr. 134; S. BOULY, *Onroerende natrekking en horizontale eigendomssplitsingen*, Antwerpen, Intersentia, 2015, nr. 41-42, 108 ff.; P. LECOCQ, *Manuel de droit des biens*, Brussel, Larcier, 2012, nr. 111 ff.; V. SAGAERT, *Goederenrecht*, Mechelen, Kluwer, 2014, nr. 980 e.v.; F. WERDEFROY, "Beschouwingen over de onroerende natrekking, het recht van erfpacht, het recht van opstal, en het verlof tot bouwen", *TPR* 1983, (293) nr. 6.

104 See also: V. SAGAERT, *Goederenrecht*, Mechelen, Kluwer, 2014, nr. 972, 980-986.

The second presumption, on the other hand, can be refuted in a number of ways and these are of particular importance for this paper. First, this can be done by proving that the owner of the underlying immovable has renounced to the accession. Renunciation to the accession by the owner of the immovable is in Belgian law always (!) considered the creation of a building lease (*superficies*).[105] Thus the refutation of the second presumption may first happen through the explicit or implicit creation of a building lease, which has in Belgium a maximum duration of 50 years.[106] An alternative to the creation of a building lease is the creation of an apartment condominium: in fact, this reverses the accession, because the legal status of the plot of land is adapted to the legal status of the building (strata title, art. 577-3 ff. Belgian Civil Code).[107, 108] Third, the owner of the incorporated movables may be the titular of a right *in rem*, e.g. usufruct, a long-lease (*emphyteusis*), or of a personal right of lease on the real estate, which is considered to give him the possibility to erect immovables on that real estate that remain his property: in that case, he has a so-called *accessory* building-lease[109], which prevents accession.[110]

The principles of accession being clear, it is now time to turn the eye on the effect accession may have in a Circular Economy.

---

105 See: Cass. 19 May 1988, *Arr.Cass.* 1987-88, 1230, *RW* 1988-89, 572, annotation. See also: S. BOULY, *Onroerende natrekking en horizontale eigendomssplitsingen*, Antwerpen, Intersentia, 2015, nr. 159, 216. *Contra*: P. LECOCQ, S. BOUFFLETTE en A. SALVÉ, "Les biens", *Chroniques notariales* 2008, (12) nr. 101; M.E. STORME, *Erfpacht en opstalrecht: syllabus ten behoeve van het vak notarieel zaken- en contractenrecht*, Gent, eigen uitgave, 2006, 23.

106 See: A. APERS, *Wilsautonomie bij kwalificatie van goederen*, Antwerpen, Intersentia, 2017, nr. 136; S. BOULY, *Onroerende natrekking en horizontale eigendomssplitsingen*, Antwerpen, Intersentia, 2015, nr. 186 ff.; P. LECOCQ, *Manuel de droit des biens*, Brussel, Larcier, 2012, nr. 114; V. SAGAERT, *Goederenrecht*, Mechelen, Kluwer, 2014, nr. 739-740, 972, 989; F. WERDEFROY, "Beschouwingen over de onroerende natrekking, het recht van erfpacht, het recht van opstal, en het verlof tot bouwen", *TPR* 1983, (293) nr. 4. See from a Dutch point of view: H. PLOEGER *et al.*, "Circular economy and real estate: alternatives for operational lease" in *Proceedings of the International Research Conference 2017: Shaping tomorrow's built environment*, Salford (UK), 2017, (1) 6-7. See on the creation of a building lease from an international perspective: L. VAN VLIET, "Accession of Movables to Land", *Edinburgh L. Rev.* 2002, (67) 70.

107 See: S. BOULY, *Onroerende natrekking en horizontale eigendomssplitsingen*, Antwerpen, Intersentia, 2015, nr. 145-146, 295 ff.; V. SAGAERT, *Goederenrecht*, Mechelen, Kluwer, 2014, nr. 380, 741 977; F. WERDEFROY, "Beschouwingen over de onroerende natrekking, het recht van erfpacht, het recht van opstal, en het verlof tot bouwen", *TPR* 1983, (293) nr. 4.

108 Additionally, it is also possible to create a voluntary condominium: the owner of the land, for instance, could grant half of the ownership of the land and the building to the owner of the building materials, as a remuneration for these building materials. However, this does not refute the accession. This 'solution', on the contrary, affirms the accession, because it acknowledges that the ownership of the immovable and the incorporated movables have the same legal status: both are property of the two parties together.

109 With the same duration as the right *in rem* to which it is accessory.

110 See also: S. BOULY, *Onroerende natrekking en horizontale eigendomssplitsingen*, Antwerpen, Intersentia, 2015, nr. 262 ff.; V. SAGAERT, *Goederenrecht*, Mechelen, Kluwer, 2014, nr. 741, 745; F. WERDEFROY, "Beschouwingen over de onroerende natrekking, het recht van erfpacht, het recht van opstal, en het verlof tot bouwen", *TPR* 1983, (293) nr. 4.

3.5.2. *Accession to immovables in a Circular Economy: a hindrance*

28. Accession to immovables in a Circular Economy as a hindrance – Accession may have an important effect in many instances of building projects in a Circular Economy. Let us for instance think of the example of the solar panels that the lessor places on the roof of the house of the lessee. These solar panels are incorporated in the roof, so they will become an immovable by nature themselves and the lessor will, in principle, lose the ownership of the solar panels to the lessee on the basis of accession. The same is true for the M-Use elevators: these are necessarily incorporated in the immovable.[111]

It is needless to say that the lessor will not be in favor of this consequence: he loses his real entitlement to the incorporated movable. Of course, he will have a claim for compensation, but this personal claim is not worth much in case of insolvency of the lessee or sale of the immovable. In other words: it is dangerous for a lessor to lease movables to a lessee that are incorporated in that lessee's real estate.

However, above I have mentioned three exceptions to accession (*cf. supra*, nr. 27). Would it then not be possible for the lessor to invoke one of these three to remain the owner of his incorporated movables and thus escape the problematic situation sketched above? The exceptions sounded rather straightforward, but the question is whether these three exceptions to accession are possible for **all** incorporated goods.

29. Exceptions 1 and 2: independent and dependent building lease – First of all, there is the opportunity to – explicitly or implicitly – create a building lease in favor of the lessor of the incorporated movable. This is the perfect solution for, for instance, solar panels on a roof. In fact, article 1 of the Belgian Building Lease Act has recently been amended in order to make explicitly clear that building lease may also be created on top of another building and need not necessarily be on a plot of land.[112] Before this amendment, too, this solution was defended, but some authors maintained that incorporation in the soil remained necessary.[113] Now, it is without any doubt possible for the owner of real estate to grant a building lease to someone to put solar panels on his roof, without accession being a problem.[114] This solution is also possible, I believe, for elevators.

An important warning must be made here with regard to building leases. A building lease is an immovable right *in rem* and as such it must be registered in

---

111 See explicitly e.g.: F. VAN NESTE, *Zakenrecht*, Brussel, E. Story-Scientia, 1990, nr. 41.43(B).

112 Article 124 of the Act of 25 April 2014 containing various measures on Justice amended article 1 of the Act of 10 January 1824 on building lease to this extent.

113 See for an overview: S. BOULY, *Onroerende natrekking en horizontale eigendomssplitsingen*, Antwerpen, Intersentia, 2015, nr. 237; P. LECOCQ, *Manuel de droit des biens*, Brussel, Larcier, 2012, nr. 110, footnote 1322; V. SAGAERT, *Goederenrecht*, Mechelen, Kluwer, 2014, nr. 759.

114 See for the example of the solar panels: S. BOULY, *Onroerende natrekking en horizontale eigendomssplitsingen*, Antwerpen, Intersentia, 2015, nr. 238.

the Belgian land register, in order to be opposable to third parties in good faith (article 1 of the Belgian Mortgage Act).[115] Especially implicit building leases – for instance, the real estate owner simply saying 'I renounce to accession' –, however, are more likely not to be registered, which creates a dangerous situation for the building lessee, who is the lessor of the movables incorporated in the immovable. After all, third parties in good faith – including the concurring creditors of an insolvent real estate owner, as long as at least one of them is in good faith[116] – can neglect the not registered building lease. As far as they are concerned, the incorporated movables belong to the owner of the real estate itself and they will be able to seize this real estate, including the incorporated movables, to the detriment of the lessor of these movables, who is the lessee of the not registered building lease.

Secondly, it could be a solution to grant the lessor of the incorporated movables another right – *in rem* or personal – that is considered to create an accessory building lease (*cf. supra*, nr. 27). The duration of that accessory building lease then is the same as the duration of the main right that is granted.[117] To give an example: the real estate owner can lease his roof to a solar panel owner and thus grant him an accessory building lease on that roof to put his solar panels. This solution has as an advantage that a lease – a personal right – can be more flexible than a building lease

For both an independent and an accessory building lease, however, an **important restriction** remains concerning the construction that can be built on the basis of a building lease, what I here call the object of that building lease.[118] Essentially, a building lease can only be granted in order to build *independent* constructions and not to construct mere 'ameliorations or repairs'.[119] For a

---

115 This is the rule when the building lease is created explicitly by a deed *inter vivos* or implicitly *inter vivos*. Registration is not required in case the building lease is acquired following mere facts, such as acquisitive prescription. However, I will not dwell on this exception in this paper. See also: S. BOULY, *Onroerende natrekking en horizontale eigendomssplitsingen*, Antwerpen, Intersentia, 2015, nr. 232.

116 See: Cass. 5 July 1901, *Pas.* 1901, 314; Cass. 5 March 1982, *Arr.Cass.* 1981-82, 837; Cass. 13 November 2003, *Arr.Cass.* 2003, 2003, 2098; Luik 8 November 1993, *JLMB* 1994, 326, annotation J. HANSENNE. See also e.g.: F. BAUDONCQ, "Dubbele verkoop", *NjW* 2004, (1126) 1127; K. BYTTEBIER, *Voorrechten en hypotheken*, Antwerpen, Maklu, 2005, nr. 124; M. DE CLERCQ, "Commentaar bij artikel 1 Hyp.W.", *Comm. Voorr. en Hyp.* 2017, (1) 38; J. DEL CORRAL, *De leveringsplicht bij de overdracht van roerende lichamelijke goederen*, Antwerpen, Intersentia, 2013, 480; W. DELVA, *Voorrechten en hypotheken*, Antwerpen, E. Story-Scientia, 1985 (1977), 11; H. DE PAGE, *Traité élémentaire de droit civil belge, VII*, Brussel, Bruylant, 1957, 970; A. VERBEKE and I. PEETERS, *Vijf jaar voorechten, hypotheken en andere zekerheden. 1991-1995*, Gent, Mys & Breesch, 1997, 155, 336-337.

117 See also: S. BOULY, *Onroerende natrekking en horizontale eigendomssplitsingen*, Antwerpen, Intersentia, 2015, nr. 265; V. SAGAERT, *Goederenrecht*, Mechelen, Kluwer, 2014, nr. 747; F. WERDEFROY, "Beschouwingen over de onroerende natrekking, het recht van erfpacht, het recht van opstal, en het verlof tot bouwen", *TPR* 1983, (293) nr. 16.

118 See on the discussion on what is precisely the object of a building lease: S. BOULY, *Onroerende natrekking en horizontale eigendomssplitsingen*, Antwerpen, Intersentia, 2015, nr. 188.

119 See for instance in case law: Luik 7 June 1989, *Fisc.Koer.* 1990, 214, annotation J.P. NEMERY DE BELLEVAUX; Tribunal of First Instance Brussels 26 October 2001, *T.Not.* 2003, 488, *TFR* 2002,

construction to qualify as independent, it is required that that construction can lead an independent life, *i.e.* that it can be used or activated separately from the real estate on which it is built.[120] This is the independence requirement. For a leased façade, however, I cannot see how the façade could be used separately from the real estate itself. Indeed, it is possible, I believe, to attach solar panels, plants, etc. on an existing façade and grant a building lease for these, but not for the façade itself. For solar roof tiles, too, I wonder whether these could be installed on real estate on the basis of a building lease. Again, I do not believe that solar roof tiles can be considered to be an independent construction. Admittedly, the tiles can exist separately from the building, but the roof cannot. This means that we need another solution for these initiatives to prevent accession to the real estate.

In fact, the independence requirement is again an affirmation of the unity principle and its objectives: the building lease as an exception to accession and thus to the unity principle is allowed, but only if the object of the building lease can be qualified as an independent construction in order to safeguard the objectives pursued by the unity principle. However, this unveils a bit of a paradox. On the one hand, building lease is an exception to accession and thus also to the unity principle. On the other hand, the unity principle still plays a role in determining the extent of this exception. This means, to my opinion, that the unity principle is more a gradual concept than an absolute rule: only if the value of an object and legal certainty of third parties regarding the legal status of that object are safeguarded – as is the case for, for instance, a building erected on the basis of a building lease –, it is possible to create a building lease on inherent parts as an exception to the unity principle. I will elaborate on this issue below (*cf. infra*, nr. 34).

30. Exception 3: apartment condominium – Thirdly, we might wonder whether it could be possible to create a strata title or so-called apartment condominium for Circular Economy initiatives in the real estate sector for which a building lease is impossible. Thus, the question is whether apartment condominium could be the solution for, for instance, the prefabricated façade or the solar roof tiles.

For this specific legal system to be applicable, conform articles 599-2, § 9 and 577-3 ff. of the Belgian Civil Code, it is required that (1) the real estate concerned is a building or group of buildings, (2) owned by various persons that each own a

---

421, annotation J. Van In. See also: A. APERS, *Wilsautonomie bij kwalificatie van goederen*, Antwerpen, Intersentia, 2017, nr. 138; S. BOULY, *Onroerende natrekking en horizontale eigendomssplitsingen*, Antwerpen, Intersentia, 2015, nr. 190; V. SAGAERT, *Goederenrecht*, Mechelen, Kluwer, 2014, nr. 746, 761. See on the same restriction in Dutch law and the problem it constitutes for a Circular Economy: H. PLOEGER *et al.*, "Circular economy and real estate: alternatives for operational lease" in *Proceedings of the International Research Conference 2017: Shaping tomorrow's built environment*, Salford (UK), 2017, (1) 6-7.

120 See for this modern definition: V. SAGAERT, *Goederenrecht*, Mechelen, Kluwer, 2014, nr. 761.

parcel, (3) composed of a private part and a share in the shared part(s).[121] Applied to the example of the prefabricated façade in a private house, this regime could have the following result: the house is the private parcel of the house owner, the façade the private parcel of the lessor of that façade and the plot of land is the shared part in which both the owner of the house and the lessor of the façade own a share.

However, although parties enjoy much freedom to determine the private and shared parcels, SAGAERT specifies that two restrictions must always be obeyed: (1) essential building parts must always be shared and (2) the plot of land must always be shared.[122] Well then, first of all, I do not believe many private real estate owners will be willing to share the ownership of their plot of land with the lessor of the façade. Secondly, the façade appears to me to be an essential part of any building and should therefore be a shared part in an apartment condominium. Consequently I believe it is impossible to turn that façade itself in a private parcel of the apartment condominium, even if real estate owner(s) would want to share the ownership of the plot of land with the lessor of the façade. In addition, given the stringent effects of apartment condominium[123], I think it very unlikely that the real estate owner and the façade lessor would want to opt for apartment condominium to be the legal framework governing their relationship. The same is true, as far as I am concerned, for all other essential parts of buildings, such as solar roof tiles, that can be leased and subsequently incorporated in the building itself. Thus I do not see many opportunities for apartment condominium in this respect.

In the cases where accession to the immovable of the leased movable cannot be refuted, accession – or better: the underlying unity principle – forms a hindrance to the further development of a Circular Economy (*cf. supra*, nr. 8). The question now remains whether this is a problem that can be solved and, if yes, how.

3.5.3. Alternative solutions to prevent accession to immovables?

31. ALTERNATIVE SOLUTIONS? – A straightforward solution to mitigate the negative effects of accession on the Circular Economy for real estate could be to simply abolish accession to immovables. However, this comes down to sacrificing the unity principle – for immovables, at least – and thus the interests of legal certainty and value protection – as strived for by the unity principle (*cf. supra*, nr. 25) – to the interest of sustainability. Such sacrifice cannot be undertaken lightly and requires much more thought than possible within the limited scope of this paper, as I have also already argued above (*cf. supra*, nr. 8).

---

121 See also: S. BOULY, *Onroerende natrekking en horizontale eigendomssplitsingen*, Antwerpen, Intersentia, 2015, nr. 297; P. LECOCQ, *Manuel de droit des biens*, Brussel, Larcier, 2012, nr. 172 ff.; V. SAGAERT, *Goederenrecht*, Mechelen, Kluwer, 2014, nr. 381 ff.

122 See: V. SAGAERT, *Goederenrecht*, Mechelen, Kluwer, 2014, nr. 385.

123 See for instance: S. BOULY, *Onroerende natrekking en horizontale eigendomssplitsingen*, Antwerpen, Intersentia, 2015, nr. 311 ff.

However, perhaps this sacrifice is unnecessary, if the interests protected by accession and the unity principle would prove to be outdated or could also be protected by other means. In other words: why undertake the (difficult) search for a balance of interests, if all these interests can be served at the same time by one particular solution?

32. **Preservation of value argument** – Let us first look at the economic argument for accession and the unity principle: the preservation of value (*cf. supra*, nr. 25). This argument is not as strong as it might seem, for various reasons. First of all, Werdefroy argues that, although this economic objective being the official objectives of accession, accession in fact only solves a private conflict between two private owners and has nothing to do with economic value.[124] Other authors rightfully point at the various exceptions to the accession to prove that the value argument is not as absolute as one might think.[125]

The strongest argument against the preservation of value argument is put forward by Circular Economy proponents. They argue that the economic justification for accession has become obsolete: in a Circular Economy, it is precisely the aim to corroborate to the value of things by keeping the ownership of the parts separated from each other.[126] This last argument constitutes a particularly strong one. In a Circular Economy, parts that are integrated in a building do maintain their value to a higher degree than in a linear economy, even at the end of their use. This is precisely the aim of the Circular Economy paradigm (*cf. supra*, nr. 3). Thus the value preservation-argument for accession and the unity principle loses – at least part of – its value in a Circular Economy.

33. **Legal certainty argument** – Circular Economy proponents often apply a similar argumentation for the legal certainty justification of accession. However, as far as legal certainty is concerned, I do not believe things are so straightforward as some authors suggest. For instance, for their concept of casco-sale Van der Veen, Hulshof and Ploeger seem to argue that legal certainty for third parties, in particular creditors of the real estate owner, is of minor importance compared to sustainability, once the real estate sector has fully entered the Circular Economy. After all, to their opinion, third parties will then be used to the situation in which the incorporated movables do not belong in ownership to

124 See: F. WERDEFROY, "Beschouwingen over de onroerende natrekking, het recht van erfpacht, het recht van opstal, en het verlof tot bouwen", *TPR* 1983, (293) nr. 4.

125 See for instance: S. BOULY, *Onroerende natrekking en horizontale eigendomssplitsingen*, Antwerpen, Intersentia, 2015, nr. 22.

126 See: H. PLOEGER *et al.*, "Circular economy and real estate: alternatives for operational lease" in *Proceedings of the International Research Conference 2017: Shaping tomorrow's built environment*, Salford (UK), 2017, (1) 6; M. VAN DER VEEN *et al.*, "Cascokoop: wenkend perspectief binnen een circulaire economie", *WPNR* 2014, (857) 858.

the real estate owner himself and thus their legal certainty would not be damaged anymore by the lack of accession.[127] I cannot agree with this argument.

First of all, this argument supposes that a Circular Economy for real estate is already fully into force and does not provide any transitional measures. This is clearly not the case. Nevertheless, even in a fully established Circular Economy, secondly, accession cannot simply be abolished without any measure taking its place to guarantee legal certainty. After all, the principle of accession has as an advantage that *all* incorporated parts are considered property of the owner of the real estate itself. If this is not the case, then this must be registered in the land register in order to be opposable to third parties in good faith: both a building lease as an apartment condominium must be registered (article 1 of the Belgian Mortgage Act).[128] Thus third parties always have certainty regarding the legal status of the incorporated movables. This registration requirement is precisely what justifies the exceptions to accession and to the unity principle: the legal certainty that is normally achieved by accession is now achieved by registration.[129] Abolishing accession without any additional measures would mean that third parties can never be sure regarding the legal status of the incorporated movables: these could or could not belong to the real estate owner. This situation goes directly against the transparency requirement for rights *in rem*, which is particularly strong for immovables (*cf. supra*, nr. 25): the real right of the owner-lessor of the incorporated movable is by no means transparent to third parties, such as creditors of the real estate owner. Those creditors would therefore be imposed with the heavy burden of ascertaining which incorporated movables belong to the real estate owner and which do not. This constitutes a hindrance to efficient legal circulation of real estate.

Thus accession to immovables cannot be simply abolished without sacrificing legal certainty of third parties, which is one of the objectives pursued by the unity principle. An alternative, however, could be to create an additional exception or a more lenient interpretation of an existing exception to accession. This is justified, if it happens with an accompanying measure that does protect

---

127 See: M. VAN DER VEEN *et al.*, "Cascokoop: wenkend perspectief binnen een circulaire economie", *WPNR* 2014, (857) 859.

128 Even the accessory building lease on the basis of an ordinary, personal lease will be known to third parties. First, all leases need a so-called 'fixed date' (article 1328 of the Belgian Civil Code) in order to be opposable to third parties (article 1743 of the Belgian Civil Code). The most common way to obtain this fixed date is the registration of the lease agreement with the Registration Office, a tax authority, which is obligatory within 4 months of the conclusion of the agreement. Second, a lease for longer than 9 years needs to be registered in the land register or is reduced to 9 years (article 1 of the Belgian Mortgage Act). Thus a third party that is not aware of that lease may ignore it. The accessory building lease follows the right on which it is based and thus a third party also ignore the accessory building lease, if the personal lease has not been registered. See explicitly: S. BOULY, *Onroerende natrekking en horizontale eigendomssplitsingen*, Antwerpen, Intersentia, 2015, nr. 267.

129 See for instance: S. BOULY, *Onroerende natrekking en horizontale eigendomssplitsingen*, Antwerpen, Intersentia, 2015, nr. 23-24.

the legal certainty for third parties. It is to such alternative that I now turn my attention.

34. Alternative solution – The alternative solution is quite easy: allow an independent building lease between the lessor and the lessee of the movables to be constituted on the real estate of the lessee without taking into account the independence requirement (*cf. supra*, nr. 29), but *only* insofar an additional requirement is met.

The additional requirement that immediately comes into mind to protect legal certainty of third parties is, of course, the registration of the building lease with as an object the leased incorporated movables in a register that is accessible to interested third parties, for instance the land register.[130] After all, land registers have explicitly the objective of contributing to legal certainty: they protect both the interests of the titular of the registered right and the interests of third parties that might be affected by that right.[131] Thus, registering that building lease also

130 See also very briefly on this solution: H. PLOEGER *et al.*, "Circular economy and real estate: alternatives for operational lease" in *Proceedings of the International Research Conference 2017: Shaping tomorrow's built environment*, Salford (UK), 2017, (1) 6 ('Building Information Management').

131 See for instance on protection of the legal certainty of the titular of the right *in rem*: F.F.K. BYAMUGISHA, *The Effects of Land Registration on Financial Development and Economic Growth*, Washington D.C., The World Bank, 1999, 6 e.v.; P. DALE and J. MCLAUGHLIN, *Land Administration*, Oxford, Oxford University Press, 1999, 2-3, 34; K. DEININGER and G. FEDER, "Land Registration, Governance, and Development: Evidence and Implications for Policy", *The World Bank Research Observer* 2009, (233) 247 e.v.; G. FEDER and A. NISHIO, "The benefits of land registration and titling: economic and social perspectives", *Land Use Policy* 1999, (25) 27; G. LARSSON, *Land registration and cadastral systems*, Harlow, Longman Scientific and Technical, 1991, 11-12; J. MOERKERKE, *The use of the IMOLA template in deed systems*, Brussel, ELRA, 2016, 5; UNECE, *Land administration in the UNECE region. Development trends and main principles*, New York / Genève, United Nations, 2005, 18, 22, 48; UNECE, *Social and Economic Benefits of Good Land Administration*, London, HM Land Registry on behalf of the UNECE Working Party on Land Administration, 2005, 6, 8-9; J. ZEVENBERGEN, *Systems of Land Registration. Aspects and Effects*, Delft, Nederlandse Commissie voor Geodetie, 2002, 3, 10, 98. See on the protection of the legal certainty of interested third parties: B. AKKERMANS, *The Principle of Numerus Clausus in European Property Law*, Antwerpen, Intersentia, 2008, 5; E. COOKE, *The new law of land registration*, Londen, Hart Publishing, 2003, 3; P. DALE and J. MCLAUGHLIN, *Land Administration*, Oxford, Oxford University Press, 1999, 2-3, 4-7, 34-35; K. DEININGER, H. SELOD and A. BURNS, *The Land Governance Assessment Framework*, Washington D.C., The World Bank, 2012, 34-35; K. DEININGER and G. FEDER, "Land Registration, Governance, and Development: Evidence and Implications for Policy", *The World Bank Research Observer* 2009, (233) 236-237, 247 e.v.; G. FEDER and A. NISHIO, "The benefits of land registration and titling: economic and social perspectives", *Land Use Policy* 1999, (25) 27; G. LARSSON, *Land registration and cadastral systems*, Harlow, Longman Scientific and Technical, 1991, 11-12; J. MOERKERKE, *The use of the IMOLA template in deed systems*, Brussel, ELRA, 2016, 5; UNECE, *Land administration in the UNECE region. Development trends and main principles*, New York / Genève, United Nations, 2005, 18; UNECE, *Social and Economic Benefits of Good Land Administration*, London, HM Land Registry on behalf of the UNECE Working Party on Land Administration, 2005, 6; P. VAN OOSTEROM and C. LEMMEN,

immediately makes clear to third parties that the ownership of certain parts of the home remains with the lessor on the basis of that building lease!

The quintessential question is whether this does not mean that the unity principle is abolished or undermined too absolutely. To my opinion, it is by no means. The existing exceptions to accession, after all, make clear that the unity principle is not absolute: even though incorporated buildings are an inherent part of the soil and thus form a unit with the soil, they can be the object of a building lease. It is therefore my suggestion to interpret the building lease in a more lenient way, abolishing the independence requirement. In the suggested solution, a lessor gets the right to own inherent parts of the lessee's real estate, which constitutes an exception to accession. As such, these inherent parts can be considered the object of a building lease, *if* we put aside the requirement that the object of the building lease is an independent construction (*cf. supra*, nr. 29).

What is needed instead is that the object of that building lease is clearly identifiable for third parties as a unit, which is guaranteed by the registration requirement: as soon as an object is identifiable as a unit, it may be the object of a building lease. This solution does not mean that the unity principle is undermined, even though the independence requirement for the object of a building lease – which is an outing of the unity principle (*cf. supra*, nr. 25) – is put aside. It only means that the unity principle is interpreted in a more lenient and more functional way – some might say a more modern way – in this solution, taking fully into account its objectives: as long as these objectives are still protected, the unity principle exists, albeit in a different way than before. At the same time, the road is cleared for a fully functional Circular Economy for the real estate sector with all the beneficial consequences thereof, including sustainability.

35. **Accession as a subsidiary rule** – Nevertheless, I would suggest to maintain accession as a subsidiary rule: if the lessor has not registered his ownership of some parts of the house *or* in case the lease agreement ends without the incorporated movables being reclaimed by the lessor within due time, then accession can fully play. This is very logical: if the incorporated movable is not identifiable for third parties as having a separate property law status, then legal certainty requires that third parties may consider it to have the same status as the immovable itself. This is exactly the same solution as for an existing building lease that is not opposable to third parties in good faith.

"The Land Administration Domain Model (LADM): Motivation, standardisation, application and further development", *Land Use Policy* 2015, (527) 527; A. WUDARSKI, "Das Grundbuch in der Registerwelt – Eine rechtsvergleichende Untersuchung zum deutschen und polnischen Grundbuch im europäischen Kontext" in A. WUDARSKI (ed.), *Das Grundbuch im Europa des 21. Jahrhunderts*, Berlijn, Duncker & Humblot, 2016, (23) 23, 26-27; J. ZEVENBERGEN, *Systems of Land Registration. Aspects and Effects*, Delft, Nederlandse Commissie voor Geodetie, 2002, 3, 10, 98. See from a Belgian perspective for instance: H. DE PAGE, *Traité élémentaire de droit civil belge, I*, Brussel, Bruylant, 1962, nr. 123.

36. **Madaster** – A practical matter is in which register this broader interpreted building lease must be registered. The logical answer would be the land register, just like all immovable rights *in rem* (article 1 of the Belgian Mortgage Act). Nevertheless, I wonder whether a different kind of register could not offer more legal certainty to third parties, because it is better suited for making clear that smaller parts of real estate also have a separate property law status.

In this respect, it is interesting to mention a concept that is specifically adapted to all the needs of circular real estate sector: the 'Madaster'. The Madaster is a creation of Thomas Rau. In essence, a Madaster is a cadaster for (building) materials: it is a 'public online library of materials in the built environment.'[132] Private and professional parties can upload data on their building project to the library, which enhances the management of their portfolio, but at the same time contributes to the Circular Economy proofness of the building. The website also automatically gives a circularity score to the project. In fact, the Madaster project is the online collection of all so-called 'Materials Passports' (*cf. supra*, nr. 18), building per building. Such Materials Passport can also name the owner of the specific incorporated movable.

Well then, the Madaster could function perfectly as the source of real estate information in a Circular Economy.[133] The owners of all parts of a building are mentioned in it, which gives third parties all the information they might need. Of course, a basic registration of the building lease in the existing land register remains obligatory as well, but for the exact object of that building lease, the registered deed could – perhaps digitally (?) – refer to the Materials Passport of the building in the Madaster. Therefore, ideally, the Madaster is linked with the existing land register and possibly also with the pledge register (*cf. infra*, nr. 37). Thus third parties have easy access to all the relevant information.

37. **Additional argument** – An additional argument for the above-mentioned solution can be deduced from article 19 and article 71 of the new Belgian Pledge Act, that finally entered into force on 1 January 2018.[134] In this paper, I will focus on article 71, because it resembles the position of a lessor the

---

132 See for the Madaster project: https://www.madaster.com/nl. See also on the Madaster: J.P.V. EESTEREN, "Circulariteit is route naar een écht duurzame bouwsector", *https://www.jpvaneesteren.nl/nl/circulariteit-route-naar-een-echt-duurzame-bouwsector* 2018, (1) 3; R. VAN DER ENT, "Niet uitputten, maar opnieuw inzetten", *https://www.jpvaneesteren.nl/nl/blog-niet-uitputten-maar-opnieuw-inzetten* 2017, (1) 3; H. PLOEGER *et al.*, "Circular economy and real estate: alternatives for operational lease" in *Proceedings of the International Research Conference 2017: Shaping tomorrow's built environment*, Salford (UK), 2017, (1) 6, footnote 8.

133 See also: H. PLOEGER *et al.*, "Circular economy and real estate: alternatives for operational lease" in *Proceedings of the International Research Conference 2017: Shaping tomorrow's built environment*, Salford (UK), 2017, (1) 6.

134 Act of 11 July 2013 amending the Civil Code concerning the real securities on movables and disestablishing certain provisions in that respect, *Belgian Official Gazette* 2 August 2013, amended by the Act of 26 November 2014, *Belgian Official Gazette* 1 December 2014.

most.[135] This article stipulates – contrary to the previous rule under Belgian law[136] – that the retention of title in a sale contract remains in existence, even although the movables that have been sold are incorporated in an immovable, on the condition that that retention of title has been registered in the pledge register.[137] So, despite the incorporation of the good sold under retention of title, the retention of title clause remains valid. To give an example with striking similarity to a Circular Economy lease situation: a contractor selling a wooden beam under retention of title who registers that retention of title, remains the owner of that beam, even if that beam is incorporated in an immovable.[138]

It is unclear whether article 71 is to be interpreted thus that the seller only receives a privileged position in case of insolvency proceedings – similar to the position of the unpaid seller under article 20, 5°, sixth paragraph of the Belgian Mortgage Act[139] – or whether he may really revindicate the incorporated movable, insofar it is possible to remove that incorporated movable without damage[140], but that discussion falls outside the scope of this paper. The important thing to remember is that the seller under retention of title is protected in case of incorporation of that good. The condition for that protection is precisely registration. Thus an additional exception to accession and to the strictly interpreted unity principle is created[141], or in other words: the unity

135 Article 19 basically stipulates the same as article 71, but for the pledgee of a movable that is afterwards incorporated in an immovable.

136 The former article 101 of the Belgian Insolvency Act required that the good sold under retention of title still exists *in natura* in order for the seller to revindicate the sold movable. Accession of that movable to an immovable meant that this was no longer the case. See for instance in case law: Ghent 11 March 2013, *RW* 2012-13, 1627. See also for instance: A. APERS, *Wilsautonomie bij kwalificatie van goederen*, Antwerpen, Intersentia, 2017, nr. 137; S. BOULY, *Onroerende natrekking en horizontale eigendomssplitsingen*, Antwerpen, Intersentia, 2015, nr. 92, 95; F. HELSEN, "Pand en eigendomsvoorbehoud voorbij de onroerendmaking. De Nieuwe Pandwet en het notariaat", *Not.Fisc.M.* 2018, (17) 18-19.

137 See also: A. APERS, *Wilsautonomie bij kwalificatie van goederen*, Antwerpen, Intersentia, 2017, 140; S. BOULY, *Onroerende natrekking en horizontale eigendomssplitsingen*, Antwerpen, Intersentia, 2015, nr. 95; F. HELSEN, "Pand en eigendomsvoorbehoud voorbij de onroerendmaking. De Nieuwe Pandwet en het notariaat", *Not.Fisc.M.* 2018, (17) 17 ff.; V. SAGAERT, *Goederenrecht*, Mechelen, Kluwer, 2014, nr. 971.

138 See for this example: F. HELSEN, "Pand en eigendomsvoorbehoud voorbij de onroerendmaking. De Nieuwe Pandwet en het notariaat", *Not.Fisc.M.* 2018, (17) 17.

139 In this sense for instance: E. DIRIX, *De hervorming van de roerende zakelijke zekerheden*, Mechelen, Kluwer, 2013, nr. 72.

140 In this sense for instance: A. APERS, *Wilsautonomie bij kwalificatie van goederen*, Antwerpen, Intersentia, 2017, nr. 140; F. HELSEN, "Pand en eigendomsvoorbehoud voorbij de onroerendmaking. De Nieuwe Pandwet en het notariaat", *Not.Fisc.M.* 2018, (17) 21-22; R. JANSEN, "Eigendomsvoorbehoud" in J. BAECK and M. KRUITHOF (eds.), *Het nieuwe zekerheidsrecht*, Antwerpen, Intersentia, 2014, (139) nr. 37; V. SAGAERT and J. DEL CORRAL, *Eigendomsvoorbehoud*, Mechelen, Kluwer, 2015, nr. 225.

141 According to HELSEN, its is the specificity principle that is interpreted in a more lenient way: F. HELSEN, "Pand en eigendomsvoorbehoud voorbij de onroerendmaking. De Nieuwe Pandwet en het notariaat", *Not.Fisc.M.* 2018, (17) 19. To my opinion, however, this is not directly the case: the rule that a right *in rem* must have one object is not altered. The more

principle is interpreted in a more lenient way, which can be justified on the basis of the registration requirement.

This proves that the above-mentioned solution is worth consideration. Otherwise, a seller under retention of title of a movable that is incorporated would be better off than the lessor of that same good, who *ipso facto* remains the owner of that good. As a matter of fact, that is now the case and constitutes, to my view, a completely illogical solution. Thus the suggested more lenient interpretation of the unity principle in case of building lease restores the logic.

38. Parties that benefit from this solution – The above-sketched solution is beneficial to a number of parties. First of all, of course, the lessor of movables that are incorporated in the immovable benefits from the fact that he is no longer harmed by accession. He does not longer lose his ownership of those goods, which gives him a stronger position towards the lessee and the lessee's creditors: would the lessee be bankrupt, then the lessor can revindicate his incorporated movable, as long as his immovable right *in rem*, the building lease, is opposable to third parties in good faith on the basis of its registration (*cf. supra*, nr. 29).[142] As a right *in rem* holder, he escapes the *concursus creditorum*.[143] In a slightly adapted solution, inspired by the Belgian Pledge Act (*cf. supra*, nr. 37), he may only revindicate the incorporated movable, if that can be removed without damaging the immovable, and otherwise gets a privilege in the insolvency proceedings. However, in a circular real estate sector, it is precisely the aim to make it possible to separate parts from buildings without causing any damage (*cf. supra*, nr. 17). In that respect, revindication should be possible in most instances. Evidently, also the creditors of that lessor benefit from this stronger position of the lessor.

Secondly, third parties with an interest in the real estate benefit strongly from the above-mentioned solution, especially because their legal certainty is served by the registration requirement. This is no surprise, because the solution was specifically designed to guarantee legal certainty towards third parties. Third parties interested in buying real estate or obtaining another right *in rem* on it will always be sure whether the incorporated movables are also part of the

lenient interpretation is to be situated at the level of the determination of that object, *i.e.* on the level of the unity principle.

142 Under Belgian law, it is already commonly accepted that article 1 of the Mortgage Act also plays in the relation between the concurring creditors in case of insolvency of a debtor and third parties. See for instance: H. DE PAGE, *Traité élémentaire de droit civil belge, VII*, Brussel, Bruylant, 1957, 953 e.v., especially 955-956 and 959-961; R. JANSEN and V. SAGAERT, "Overzicht van rechtspraak. Zakelijke zekerheden (2004-2010)", *TPR* 2012, (1223) 1232-1234; M.E. STORME, "Eigendomsvoorbehoud en samenloop buiten faillissement: Hof van Cassatie lijdt aan fantoompijn", *RW* 2011-12, (254) 255.

143 See also in general: E. DIRIX and K. BROECKX, *Beslag*, Mechelen, Kluwer, 2010, nr. 646; J. HANSENNE, *Les biens. Précis*, Luik, Ed. Collection Scientifique de la Faculté de Droit de Liège, 1996, nr. 25; V. SAGAERT, *Goederenrecht*, Mechelen, Kluwer, 2014, nr. 32 ff.

immovable object or whether a separate building lease has been created in that regard. This is also true for the creditors of the lessee. Admittedly, they would have had a larger object to execute their claims, if accession had still been fully into play, but thanks to the registration requirement, they are fully aware of what is part of their execution object and what is not.

The only actual party, third, whose position remains to be analysed is the lessee of the movable, who is the owner of the immovable. Under positive law, on the one hand, the lessee would become the real owner of the incorporated movables on the property law level. On the contractual level, however, he would owe a compensation to the lessor (*cf. supra*, nr. 27). If the constructions qualify as independent constructions, for instance solar panels – in the hypothesis that a building lease cannot be considered to have been created –, then the owner of the immovable can require the constructions to be removed – with as restriction abuse of law – or refund the value of the materials and labour: article 555 of the Belgian Civil Code applies, because the lessor knows that he is building with movables on the immovable of another owner and is thus in bad faith.[144] If the constructions qualify as dependent constructions, however, article 555 of the Belgian Civil Code is not applicable and the so-called 'theory of costs' (*kostenleer*) must be applied: the lessee must then fully refund the necessary costs insofar they have established a plus-value for the immovable.[145] Of course, parties can also agree upon a different compensation. Under the above-sketched solution *de lege ferenda*, on the contrary, such compensation would not be necessary anymore, because the ownership of the incorporated movables is not transferred to the owner of the immovable, if parties agree on that. Only when accession subsidiarily comes into play again (*cf. supra*, nr. 35), then a compensation would become necessary again. Parties obtain more freedom to determine their relation, without this freedom harming third parties.

A different question is what happens to the lessee, if the lessor goes bankrupt and cannot fulfill his obligations from the lease contract anymore. Of course, the ongoing performance of the contract also has value and could thus be considered an asset for the creditors.[146] This solution would be beneficial to the lessee, because the lease agreement will still be executed, albeit by a different lessor. This solution is, however, by no means the only possible one and depends on the specific matters of the case and in particular the going concern value of the lease

---

144 See also for instance: V. SAGAERT, *Goederenrecht*, Mechelen, Kluwer, 2014, nr. 982.

145 See in case law for instance: Cass. 18 April 1991, *Arr. Cass.* 1990-91, 839, *RW* 1993-94, 1065. See also e.g.: V. SAGAERT, *Goederenrecht*, Mechelen, Kluwer, 2014, nr. 985.

146 See e.g.: H. PLOEGER *et al.*, "Circular economy and real estate: alternatives for operational lease" in *Proceedings of the International Research Conference 2017: Shaping tomorrow's built environment*, Salford (UK), 2017, (1) 7; V. SAGAERT and S. BAEYENS, "De beëindiging van overeenkomsten in geval van insolventie van de partijen: loopt het insolventierecht uit de pas van het verbintenissenrecht?" in N. CARETTE and B. WEYTS (eds.), *Verantwoord aansprakelijkheidsrecht. Liber amicorum Aloïs Van Oevelen*, Antwerpen, Intersentia, 2017, (479) 488 ff.

agreement. Article XX.130 of the Belgian Economic Law Code (former article 46 of the Insolvency Act) stipulates that the curator has the power to end agreements unilaterally.[147] In case the creditors of the lessor – represented by the curator – would subsequently simply revindicate all leased goods to sell these, the lessee is clearly worse off under the solution in which he has not become the owner of the incorporated movables than under positive law under which accession fully plays. Under positive law, after all, he can simply pay the above-mentioned compensation to the creditors and remain the owner of the incorporated movables and thus also maintain the function these fulfill in his real estate. If he is not considered to be the owner, however, as is the case under the above-mentioned solution *de lege ferenda*, things do not look well for the lessee: he might just 'lose' parts of his real estate, despite their being essential to its functioning, because of the termination of the lease agreement following the bankruptcy of the lessor. In that respect, it might be useful to take additional measures to protect the lessee in that case. A possible solution might be to give the lessee a right to buy the incorporated movables after all and thus obtain ownership; this would constitute a so-called *Anwartschaftsrecht* in Belgian law. Nevertheless, I believe this question deserves deeper research than possible in this paper.

Finally, of course, sustainability itself benefits from the fact that a Circular Economy on the basis of the lease operationalisation becomes fully possible for the real estate sector. As such, the above-mentioned solution is beneficial to society as a whole.

3.6. LEASING OF MOVABLES USED IN AN IMMOVABLE, WITHOUT BEING INCORPORATED

3.6.1. Risks connected to leasing movables in a Circular Economy

39. Introduction – As mentioned above, not all movables that are leased to a real estate owner will be incorporated in his real estate. Examples of this category are the leased furniture or the leased not incorporated lamps (*cf. supra*, nr. 14).

Such leased movables will not become immovables themselves. First of all, there is no incorporation, so they are no immovables by incorporation (*cf. supra*, nr. 20). Second, they do not have the same owner as the immovable, so they cannot be considered immovables by destination (*cf. supra*, nr. 21).

---

147 See the Act of 11 August 2017 inserting book XX "Insolvency of businesses" in the Economic Law Code, *Belgian Official Gazette* 11 September 2017. See on the relation between contract law and insolvency law in Belgium for instance: V. SAGAERT and S. BAEYENS, "De beëindiging van overeenkomsten in geval van insolventie van de partijen: loopt het insolventierecht uit de pas van het verbintenissenrecht?" in N. CARETTE and B. WEYTS (eds.), *Verantwoord aansprakelijkheidsrecht. Liber amicorum Aloïs Van Oevelen*, Antwerpen, Intersentia, 2017, (479) 479-496.

40. **Risks for lessor and lessee** – Even with the lease of movables, however, the lessor and lessee will be confronted with some dangers during the performance of the lease agreement. First of all – and quite important from a property law point of view –, it is a risk for the lessor that the lessee is a rogue and sells the movables that are leased to him to a third party. The lessee might sell the movable either separately or together with the immovable itself.

Second, the risk of bankruptcy of the lessee or the lessor also exists in this case. Both risks are analysed below. This is a risk for both the lessor and the lessee.

Third, I would also like to speak of the risk of the lessor being confronted with third parties-creditors of the lessee that have a privilege on the leased goods, in particular the lessor of real estate (article 20, 1° of the Belgian Mortgage Act).

All three risks are briefly analysed below (*cf. infra*, nr. 41-42, 43, 44).

3.6.2. The rogue lessee

41. **The rogue lessee** – A first risk that the lessor is confronted with is of course, as in any lease agreement, the risk that the lessee simply sells the leased movables to a third party who presumes that the lessee is the owner of these goods. It is of course possible that the lessee sells these goods separately, but we can also easily imagine the situation in which the owner of the real estate sells his real estate with its content, for instance some furniture (lamps, a washing machine, a refrigerator, etc.). In practice, this happens very often. However, in case that furniture is leased, the real estate owner may very well sell his real estate, but not its leased content. In other words: the lessee is a mere detentor of the leased movables and has a duty to restitute the leased goods to the lessor. Yet the detentor sells the movables. The question now is how Belgian law deals with this situation.

42. **Belgian solution** – First of all, it is important to determine the nature of the goods that are sold. These goods are movables (*cf. supra*, nr. 20-22 *a contrario*), despite the buyer perhaps believing that they are immovables by destination. This means that the third party protection rules for movables are of the essence here: articles 2279 and 2280 of the Belgian Civil Code in their substantial function.[148]

These provisions provide protection for the third acquirer of movables, if certain requirements are met.[149] In order for this provision to be applicable, it

---

148 The substantial function is to be distinguished from the procedural function. See very clearly on this distinction in Belgian law: R. JANSEN, "Soms geldt bezit als vermoeden van titel, soms als termijn (noot onder Cass. 24 september 2007)", *RW* 2008-09, (826) 826-829.

149 See in general on this provision in Belgian law: J. DEL CORRAL, *De leveringsplicht bij de overdracht van roerende lichamelijke goederen*, Antwerpen, Intersentia, 2013, nr. 423 ff.; R. DEKKERS and E. DIRIX, *Handboek Burgerlijk Recht, II*, Antwerpen, Intersentia, 2005, 93 ff.; R. JANSEN, "Soms geldt bezit als vermoeden van titel, soms als termijn (noot onder Cass. 24 september 2007)", *RW* 2008-09, (826) 826-829; V. SAGAERT, *Goederenrecht*, Mechelen, Kluwer, 2014, nr. 856 ff.

is – essentially – required that (1) the third party has lawful possession of the good (articles 2228-2229 of the Belgian Civil Code), (2) the third party is in good faith – which is presumed (article 2268 of the Belgian Civil Code) –, and (3) the third party has acquired the movable on the basis of a valid title.[150] If these requirements are met, then the third acquirer is considered the owner of the movable, either immediately, if it concerns a movable of which the real owner voluntarily transferred possession (article 2279, paragraph 1 of the Belgian Civil Code), or after three years, if it concerns a movable of which the real owner involuntarily transferred possession (article 2279, paragraph 2, and 2280 of the Belgian Civil Code). For leased movables, the former will be the case, because the lessor voluntarily transfers possession of the movable to the lessee.

Thus, if the third acquirer of a movable that is sold by its lessee is in good faith, has a valid title (the sale agreement) and takes possession of the movable, then he becomes the owner of that good. The lessor will lose his ownership and only a personal claim for restitution remains. There is, however, a rather straightforward solution for this problem for the lessor and one that we already regularly see in practice, for instance on cars. The lessor could simply put a tag on the leased good, saying "Owned by X and leased to Y". Thus the good faith of the third acquirer will turn in bad faith and he will not be able to invoke articles 2279-2280 of the Belgian Civil Code. Secondly, the duty of scrutiny of the (professional) buyer could also be interpreted to the extent that it includes the duty to ask the seller for a proof of his ownership, for instance by showing the invoice.

What, however, one might say, if the lessee has removed that tag or has falsified an invoice, or if the third acquirer has not seen that tag or invoice, because he has not seen the good in real life or asked for the invoice, for instance because he acquired it on an online auction site? Well, in the second case, we might answer that such third party does not deserve protection, because he has not scrutinised the good as he should have: had he done this thoroughly, he would have seen the tag or asked for the invoice and therefore he is not considered to be in good faith. In the first case, we cannot blame the third party. The only way obtain absolute security for the lessee would be to put all leased movables in a register, of which third parties are *ipso facto* considered to be aware. However, I doubt whether this is not using a sledgehammer to crack nuts. Perhaps many lessors would prefer risking being confronted with a tag removing

[150] This last requirement has been under discussion. In a decision of 1974, the Belgian Supreme Court stipulated that this was not a requirement (Cass. 20 december 1974, *Arr.Cass.* 1975, 478, *RCJB* 1976, noot C. Renard, *RW* 1974-75, 1835). However, most recent authors do see it, very logically validly as far as I am concerned, as a requirement for the substantial functioning of article 2279 of the Belgian Civil Code: R. DEKKERS and E. DIRIX, *Handboek Burgerlijk Recht, II*, Antwerpen, Intersentia, 2005, 96-97; J. DEL CORRAL, *De leveringsplicht bij de overdracht van roerende lichamelijke goederen*, Antwerpen, Intersentia, 2013, nr. 542-543; R. JANSEN, "Soms geldt bezit als vermoeden van titel, soms als termijn (noot onder Cass. 24 september 2007)", *RW* 2008-09, (826) 827-829; V. SAGAERT, *Goederenrecht*, Mechelen, Kluwer, 2014, nr. 872.

or invoice falsifying lessee to incurring the administrative burdens of putting all their lease agreements in a public register.

3.6.3. *Bankruptcy*

43. Bankruptcy – Like in case of incorporated movables, bankruptcy of the lessor or the lessee is a thread in case of non-incorporated leased movables, too. If the lessor goes bankrupt, the situation is quite similar to the situation sketched above (*cf. supra*, nr. 38). I therefore do not repeat that here. More interesting, however, is the situation in which the lessee goes bankrupt. The lessor will, of course, be willing to revindicate the leased movables, but the question is whether his ownership on these goods is opposable to the other concurring creditors who believed these movables to be owned by the insolvent lessee.

Conform article XX.194 of the Economic Law Code (former article 101 of the Belgian Insolvency Act), the owner of a good can revindicate that good from the concurring creditors of the insolvent detentor of that good.[151] In this hypothesis, the concurring creditors cannot invoke article 2279 of the Belgian Civil Code.[152] Thus the lessor of movables in a Circular Economy does not need to worry that he will be harmed by the bankruptcy of the lessee.

3.6.4. *Privilege of the real estate lessor*

44. Privilege of the real estate lessor – Article 20, 1° of the Belgian Mortgage Act grants a specific movable privilege to the lessor of real estate: the

151 Article XX.196 of the Economic Law Code (former article 103 of the Insolvency Act) confirms this with regard to the consignor of movables to an insolvent consignee. See in case law for instance: Cass. 27 November 1981, *Arr.Cass.* 1981-82, 431 (case of lease with a purchase option for the lessee). See also e.g.: J. DEL CORRAL, *De leveringsplicht bij de overdracht van roerende lichamelijke goederen*, Antwerpen, Intersentia, 2013, 417, 419; E. DIRIX, "Actuele trends in de zakelijke zekerheidsrechten" in *Het zakenrecht. Absoluut niet een rustig bezit – XVIII° Postuniversitaire Cyclus Willy Delva 1991-1992*, Antwerpen, Kluwert, 1992, (1) 6; V. SAGAERT, *Goederenrecht*, Mechelen, Kluwer, 2014, 677-678; V. SAGAERT and J. DEL CORRAL, *Eigendomsvoorbehoud*, Mechelen, Kluwer, 2015, 16.

152 Admittedly, a minority of legal doctrine defends that the concurring creditors can invoke article 1141 and article 2279 of the Belgian Civil Cod on their own, but the cited case law concerns the hypothesis in which the insolvent party has sold but not yet delivered a movable, which is a completely different situation. See: R. DEKKERS and E. DIRIX, *Handboek Burgerlijk Recht, II*, Antwerpen, Intersentia, 2005, 162-163; E. DIRIX, "Actuele trends in de zakelijke zekerheidsrechten" in *Het zakenrecht. Absoluut niet een rustig bezit – XVIII° Postuniversitaire Cyclus Willy Delva 1991-1992*, Antwerpen, Kluwert, 1992, (1) 6-7; E. DIRIX, "Faillissement en lopende overeenkomsten", *RW* 2003-2004, (201) 208; V. SAGAERT, *Zakelijke subrogatie*, Antwerpen, Intersentia, 2003, 318-319; M.E. STORME, "Overdracht van roerende goederen, vestiging van pandrecht, eigendomsvoorbehoud: een poging tot systematisatie" in *Het zakenrecht. Absoluut niet een rustig bezit – XVIII° Postuniversitaire Cyclus Willy Delva 1991-1992*, Antwerpen, Kluwer, 1992, (403) 494 e.v. This does lead to the paradox that a buyer of a movable from an insolvent seller is less protected than the lessor of that movable to an insolvent lessee.

lessor of real estate has a privilege on the furniture (*sensu lato*) in that real estate for claims[153] from the lease contract he has on the lessee of that real estate.[154] In a Circular Economy, however, (part of) the furniture is not owned by the lessee of the real estate, because he leases it himself from another lessor. Does this mean that the real estate lessor's privilege becomes worthless or does this mean that the furniture lessor cannot revindicate the furniture anymore, because the real estate lessor's privilege trumps his ownership?

In Belgian law, article 2279 of the Civil Code (*cf. supra*, nr. 42) is applied *per analogiam*: if the lessor of the real estate believes in good faith that the furniture is owned by the lessee of the real estate, on the moment that furniture is brought into the house, then the privilege trumps the ownership of a third party.[155] Thus the privilege of the real estate lessor constitutes a risk for the furniture lessor. However, since, in fact, article 2279 of the Belgian Code is applied, I can refer to the solutions for that risk that have been mentioned above (*cf. supra*, nr. 42). In addition, the lessor of furniture could also simply warn the lessor of the real estate, for instance by a letter, that the lessee of the real estate does not own that furniture. According to 'T KINT, this happens regularly in practice for valuable objects, such as pianos, televisions, etc.[156]

4. CONCLUSION

45. TO A CIRCULAR ECONOMY FOR REAL ESTATE: THE FUTURE IS NEAR – Sustainability is a factor that is to be taken into account both in society and in law, that is for sure. This is true for the many separate projects striving for sustainability, but also for a more holistic approach that has recently been put forward: the Circular Economy. To my opinion, the Circular Economy has a huge potential and it is therefore quintessential to study how the law currently deals and in the future could and should deal with this. After all, taking into account the many ongoing initiatives, I believe that the future is very near. This has exactly been the purpose of this paper.

---

153 The exact kind of privileged claims depends upon the situation, an issue on which I will not dwell in this paper. See for instance: K. BYTTEBIER, *Voorrechten en hypotheken*, Antwerpen, Maklu, 2005, nr. 389; F. 'T KINT, *Sûretés et principes généraux du droit de poursuite des créanciers*, Brussel, Larcier, 2004, nr. 429 ff.

154 See in general on this privilege: K. BYTTEBIER, *Voorrechten en hypotheken*, Antwerpen, Maklu, 2005, nr. 383 ff.; F. 'T KINT, *Sûretés et principes généraux du droit de poursuite des créanciers*, Brussel, Larcier, 2004, nr. 422 ff.

155 See: K. BYTTEBIER, *Voorrechten en hypotheken*, Antwerpen, Maklu, 2005, nr. 391; F. 'T KINT, *Sûretés et principes généraux du droit de poursuite des créanciers*, Brussel, Larcier, 2004, nr. 440-441 (the author considers this rule unjust).

156 See: F. 'T KINT, *Sûretés et principes généraux du droit de poursuite des créanciers*, Brussel, Larcier, 2004, nr. 441(a).

The operationalisation of the idea of circularity that has been granted most attention in this paper is the lease operationalisation, because of its huge potential in the real estate sector, as proved by the ongoing initiatives. An owner of a movable can lease that movable to the owner of an immovable, who can use that movable or even incorporate it in his real estate. This leads to two hypotheses: the lease of incorporated movables and the lease of not incorporated movables. In order for that operationalisation to work, however, it is necessary that the lessor of the movable can effectively remain the owner of that movable and oppose his ownership to third parties.

46. **Lease of incorporated movables** – First, for movables that are incorporated in an immovable, the principle of accession constitutes a hindrance to the development of a Circular Economy in the real estate sector, because it makes the lease operationalisation impossible. Nevertheless, exceptions to accession exist in Belgian law. In that respect, the existing building lease in Belgian is already a good instrument for certain Circular Economy projects in the real estate sector, for instance in the situation of solar panels on a roof that are leased to an owner of a building, who grants a building lease to the lessor of those solar panels to own these panels, despite their being incorporated in the the building. The building lease ensures that accession does not happen.

This is, however, impossible for incorporated movables that do not qualify as an independent construction, for instance solar roof tiles. The most eminent hindrance to the Circular Economy in the real estate sector is therefore formed by the independence requirement that is now in force with regard to the building lease. To solve that problem, I have argued how this requirement can be abolished, without the objectives of the unity principle being not pursued anymore. First, the value preservation objective for the unity principle is in a Circular Economy better served by *not* holding on to the unity principle. Second, the legal certainty objective of the unity principle can be perfectly pursued by registering the fact that the lessor of an incorporated movable remains the owner of that incorporated movable on the basis of a building lease, despite that movable not qualifying as an independent construction. In that respect, Raus idea of a Madaster might be a great opportunity, in connection with the existing land register. An additional argument for this interpretation is to be found in the new Belgian Pledge Act, that protects the seller under retention of title of movables, even if those movables are incorporated in an immovable, on the condition that that retention of title has been registered in the pledge register.

47. **Lease of not incorporated movables** – Second, as far as the leasing of not incorporated movables used in real estate, for instance furniture, is concerned, the most eminent danger for the lessor is that a third party would acquire a right on the leased movable to the detriment of the lessor. However,

such third party is only protected by Belgian property law, if he is in good faith. The lessor can prevent that by making absolutely clear that the lessee is not the owner of the leased movable, for instance by putting a tag on that movable. Thus Belgian property law does not form a hindrance in this second hypothesis.

48. **Sustainable property law** – Summarising, the Circular Economy, in particular the lease operationalisation, for the real estate sector appears to fit rather well in the existing Belgian property law framework. The only necessary amendment would be that the unity principle is interpreted in a slightly more lenient way. That interpretation, however, does not lead to its objectives being sacrificed. In other words, sustainability and value preservation and legal certainty can go hand in hand.

This being clear, I hope that case law and legal doctrine will embrace this more lenient interpretation of the unity principle. To some extent, in the new Pledge Act, the Belgian legislator is already doing so. This could certainly lead to a more sustainability-oriented property law.

I am most curious what the future will bring.

GERMAN PROPERTY LAW AND THE CIRCULAR ECONOMY

Challenges and Opportunities for Real Estate

Klaus TONNER*

1. INTRODUCTION

This paper will analyse German law, whether it includes provisions facilitating a circular economy in the field of real estate law. There is no systematic approach in German law insofar; many of the provisions we will scrutinize do not distinguish movables and real estate, and nearly all of them are not limited to consumers. Quite the opposite: the main goal of the most provisions is not consumer protection, but promoting sustainability, in particular energy saving. This is not necessarily a contradiction, as sustainable consumption is an important component of consumer policy.[1]

We will try to identify who should be the addressee of provisions supporting a circular economy in particular and sustainability in general: Sustainability is not limited to b 2 c relations; therefore the question arises, whether all users should be addressed, be it the consumer, be it users who use goods within the course of their business, because they have the most influence how to behave with the good. We will consider the step from consumer to user and ascertain that the user, not only the consumer, is in the focus of the law. And even more: In the focus of the law is not contract law, directed to the user – business relation, but öffentliches Recht (public law) imposing obligations to business this is to say to the producer or supplier of goods and services with regard to standards of sustainability. We will then ask, whether necessary legal instruments should

* Dr. jur., Professor em. for Private Law and European Law at the University of Rostock, Germany.

1 Communication from the Commission, A European Consumer Agenda – Boosting confidence and growth, COM(2012) 225 of 22.5.2012; Bundesregierung, Nationales Programm für nachhaltigen Konsum, 2016. Both documents, however, do not mention specifically real estate.

be addressed to the user – contrary to present law -, or if there are reasons to abstain from that in the field of real estate and instead address legal instruments to the owner of land.

With regard to real estate there is a severe obstacle to address the user: Legal orders based on Roman law do not allow a split between ownership of the land and ownership of a building erected on the land. This is also the case for German law. Therefore we will have to examine, whether nevertheless the legislator has some discretion to put obligations on the user of a building or parts of it, even if he is not the owner of the land, or if all such obligations have to be addressed to the owner of the land. We also will analyse if the provisions about the tenancy contract allow imposing obligations on the tenant with regard to sustainability, or if it is again the owner of the building, not the user, who must be addressed. Therefore we will draw a brief outline of the relevant provisions of the Bürgerliches Gesetzbuch (BGB, Civil Code), which draw the distinction between real estate and movables. This is important to identify whether the owner of the estate or the owner of movables, which. e.g., he has brought as a tenant into the apartment, is responsible.

Circular economy in the strict sense of the word means recycling. But the relevant law does not distinguish recycling of movables and recycling in the field of real estate. Only general rules apply, be it the Waste Frame Directive[2], be it the German transposition by the Kreislaufwirtschaftsgesetz (Circular Economy Act).[3] Regulations on recycling in the field of real estate mean recycling of building materials. There is no hard law, but a government proposal of an Ersatzbaustoffverordnung (Replacement Building Material Regulation)[4] is discussed, and soft law of the industry exists, according to which certificates are granted. Recycling of such materials is not backed by specific European legislation, contrary to recycling of movables.

The goal of recycling is energy saving. For that reason we will consider another field of law about sustainability, dealing with energy saving to compare it with recycling. There is a lot of European legislation which applies to movables and real estate. We will sort out, which role energy savings regulation plays for real estate, in particular for buildings, and whether the user or the owner of buildings is addressed by such legislation. Thermal insulation and heating play

---

2 Directive 2008/98/EC of the European Parliament and of the Council of 19 November 2008 on waste, OJ L 312 of 22.11.2008, p. 3; amended by Directive (EU) 2018/851 of the European Parliament and of the Council of 30 May 2018 amending Directive 2008/98/EC on waste, OJ L 150 of 14.6.2018, p. 109.

3 Gesetz zur Förderung der Kreislaufwirtschaft und Sicherung der umweltverträglichen Bewirtschaftung von Abfällen (Kreislaufwirtschaftsgesetz, KrWG) of 24.2.2012, Bundesgesetzblatt (BGBl., Federal Law Gazette) 2012 I, p. 212.

4 Bundesregierung, Verordnung zur Einführung einer Ersatzbaustoffverordnung, zur Neufassung der Bundes-Bodenschutz- und Altlastenverordnung und zur Änderung der Deponieverordnung und der Gewerbeabfallverordnung, Bundesrats-Drucksache (BR-Drucks., Bundesrat printed paper) 566/17. It was still not adopted by the Bundesrat (May 2019).

a big role. Many of the obligations with regard to energy savings are imposed to the constructor and the owner, but also regulatory contract law, especially in the landlord – tenant relation, is relevant.

2. ADDRESSEES OF CE RELATED LEGAL INSTRUMENTS

2.1. FROM CONSUMER TO USER

Traditional consumer law instruments refer to the b 2 c relation; the term of consumer is in the centre of the consumer law, especially in consumer contract law. E.g., according to Art 2 (1) of the Consumer Rights Directive consumer means "any natural person who, in contracts covered by this Directive, is acting for purposes which are outside his trade, business, craft or profession."

Contrary to that approach, the legal instruments which are in place in the field discussed here, refer to the user, this is to say that there is no distinction whether the goods or services are used for a private purpose or within the course of the business of a trader. The Internal Market in Electricity Directive distinguishes five different terms of customers (Art 2 (7) – (11)), among them the term of final customer.[5] In German law they are transposed by the Energiewirtschaftsgesetz (EnWG). The term of "final customer" is also used in the Energy Efficiency Directive.[6]

In the transport sector the term of "consumer" does not apply, but "passenger". Passenger transport plays a role within the circular economy, especially when we look to the replacement of cars by carsharing[7] or business models like Uber.[8] We cannot go to details insofar, as cars are movables, and the subject of this paper is real estate.

But not only the user or "final customer" is addressed. Other Directives impose obligations to the supplier or producer of goods or services and not on the user.[9] So the Energy Performance of Buildings Directive (EPBD) includes only technical definitions, but no definition of a person, to whom the Directive

5 Directive 2009/72/EC of the European Parliament and the Council of 13 July 2009 concerning common rules for the internal market in electricity, OJ L 211 of 14.8.2009, p. 55.

6 Directive 2012/27/EU of the European Parliament and of the Council on energy efficiency, OJ L 315 of 14.11.2012, p. 1.

7 Cf. *W. Kluth*, Das Carsharinggesetz des Bundes und seine Umsetzung auf kommunaler Ebene, Landes- und Kommunalverwaltung (LKV; legal journal) 2018, 112.

8 For Uber cf. CJEU 20.12.2017, C-434/15 – Association professional Élite Taxi v Uber Systems Spain, ECLI:EU:C:2017:98 and *M. Schaub*, Why Uber is an information society service, Journal of European Consumer and Market Law (EuMCL) 2018, p. 109.

9 Directive 2012/27/EU of the European Parliament and of the Council on energy efficiency, OJ L 315 of 14.11.2012, p. 1.

imposes obligations.[10] The Waste Frame Directive is directed to the waste producer. These three legal instruments will be discussed later (*supra* I 2).

Norbert Reich had raised the question, whether there is a development from consumer to user.[11] In our view, the traditional role of the term of consumer should be maintained, because the need of protection should be determined from the perspective of a consumer and not be weakened by a mixture of consumer and small business interests, but the legislator should not be prevented from extending the scope of legal instruments in suitable cases to other final customers.[12]

With regard to tenancy law, which is not backed by European legislation, things are a bit different. German tenancy law is a subtitle in the Vertragliche Schuldverhältnisse (Contractual Obligations) of the second book (Schuldrecht, Law of Obligations) of the BGB. It distinguishes between tenancy law in general, which includes not only b 2 b contracts of real estate (commercial rents), but also rents of movables, e.g. a car, and residential rents (Wohnungsmiete), which provides for protection of the tenant of an apartment or a house as a residence. This tenant is a consumer in the traditional sense, this is to say in the sense of the definition of the CRD as quoted above. The provisions of the BGB dealing with energy saving apply only to the residential rents not to other forms of rents. We will examine whether obligations with regard to sustainability should be imposed to the landlord or the tenant.

2.2. FROM CONTRACT LAW TO PUBLIC LAW

As mentioned, many of the regulations we will examine here, do not directly refer to the consumer or the user, but to someone who is in a position to influence the amount of consumption, e.g. of energy, or the composition of the material, which is used for consumption so that it is recyclable, e.g. building materials. The Internal Market in Electricity Directive, relevant for energy saving, shows, that it is not necessarily the user, whose behaviour shall be influenced. In this Directive we find a "household customer", that "means a customer purchasing electricity for his own household consumption, excluding commercial or professional activities" (Art 2 [10]). This is the consumer in the sense of the traditional consumer protection Directives. But we also find the user as discussed above. He is a "final customer", that "means a customer purchasing electricity for his own use" (Art 2 [9]). This could be a shop keeper, who rents a shop in a building. But even more: There is a "whole sale customer", who purchases electricity for

---

10 Directive 2010/31/EU of the European Parliament and of the Council of 19 May 2010 on the Energy Performance of Buildings (recast), OJ L 153 of 18.6.2010, p. 13.

11 *N. Reich/H.W. Micklitz*, in: *N. Reich*, European Consumer Law, 2nd ed. 2014, p. 52 et seq.

12 *K. Tonner*, Europäisches Verbraucherrecht, in: *M. Tamm/K. Tonner*, Verbraucherrecht – Beraterhandbuch, 3rd. ed. 2019, forthcoming.

resale of electricity (Art 2 [8], and a "non household customer", who purchases electricity, which is not for his/her own household use and includes producers and wholesale customers (Art 2 [11]). The Internal Market in Electricity Directive refers to contracts between producers, customers, and other members of the distribution network, and provides for different standards in these contracts, e.g., the "final customer" needs less protection than the "household customer", but at least some protection. This has not necessarily to do with energy saving, but shows that different terms can be used to establish different standards of obligations how to behave. The simple use of the term of "consumer" would not be sufficient.

The Waste Frame Directive does not provide for such terms. It is based on the polluter pays principle, this is to say the polluter is responsible for waste management and disposal. It is only the polluter who is addressed by this Directive; regulatory contract law[13] does not play a role. The Directive does not overcome the public/private law divide.[14] The amendment of 2018 mentions for the first time construction and demolition waste and so clarifies, that real estate contributes to waste, which is under the scope of the Directive.

The Ersatzbaustoffverordnung also addresses the producers of such materials and traders, who put them into circulation, and would be if adopted a mere public law instrument. Recycled construction material is only one of a long list of Ersatzbaustoffen. We mention that limitation to public law instruments, as in the present debate about a circular economy regulatory contract law, which "nudges"[15] people to behave in a direction which is intended by the legislator, plays a role. This is ignored by instruments of proposed legislation as the Ersatzbaustoffverordnung. An example, how public law and contract law could be combined, is the debate about a life span guarantee for technical consumer products, which tries to combine elements of the Ecodesign Directive[16] and consumer sales law.[17] We cannot discuss that here, because it concerns movables, not real estate.[18]

---

13 For regulatory contract law cf. *H.W. Micklitz*, The visible hand of European regulatory private law, Yearbook of European Law 28 (2009), p. 3 et seq.

14 For the public/private law divide with regard to enforcement cf. *J. Stuyck*, Public and private enforcement in consumer protection: General comparison EU – USA, in: *F. Cafaggi/H. W. Micklitz*, New frontiers of consumer protection – the interplay between private and public enforcement, 2009, p. 63 et seq.

15 *C. R. Sunstein*, Nudging: a very short guide, Journal of Consumer Policy 37 (2014) p. 583 et seq.

16 Directive 2009/125/EC of the European Parliament and the Council of 21 October 2009 establishing a framework for the setting of ecodesign requirements for energy related products, OJ L 284 of 31.10.2009, p. 10.

17 *K. Tonner/R. Malcolm*, How an EU lifespan guarantee model could be implemented across the European Union, Study for the European Parliament, 2017, PE583.121.

18 Cf. *E. Terryn/S. Vandemaele*, The contracting stage: legal and commercial guarantees and the right to repair in the EU and the US, in this volume p. #.

3. LEGAL FRAMEWORK OF THE BGB

3.1. NO SPLIT OF OWNERSHIP – PROPERTY LAW

To decide whether a legal instrument shall influence the behaviour of the owner or the user (= tenant) of a building or a part of it, requires to examine, for which part of the building the owner remains responsible after the conclusion of the tenancy contract. Of course, this does not play a role, when the owner uses the building himself. This is the case not only, when he owns and uses the whole building, but also when he is Wohnungseigentümer, this is to say the owner of an apartment within a building. There is an act in Germany, which regulates Wohnungseigentum in detail, the Wohnungseigentumsgesetz (WEG, Condominium Act).

But the majority of Germans – a higher percentage than in other countries – rents their residences. So the question in which cases the owner, who is not the user, is responsible, is of importance. This is a question of Sachenrecht (property law), which is mandatory and represents basic principles of private law, which cannot easily be changed. Sachenrecht is book no. 3 of the BGB. Ownership of the building cannot be separated from the ownership of the property, in other words, the owner of the property always is owner of a building, which is built on the property, whoever erects the building: No split of ownership, a principle known in private law systems based on Roman law.

This principle is expressed in the general part of the BGB (book no. 1). According to §93 BGB „[können] Bestandteile einer Sache, die nicht voneinander getrennt werden können, ohne dass der eine oder andere zerstört oder in seinem Wesen verändert wird (wesentliche Bestandteile), [...]nicht Gegenstand besonderer Rechte sein.“[19] („Parts of a thing which cannot be separated without one or the other thing being destroyed or undergoing a change of nature (essential parts) cannot be the subject of separate rights.“). §94 subpara 1 BGB provides for that „zu den wesentlichen Bestandteilen eines Grundstücks die mit dem Grundstück fest verbundenen Sachen gehören, insbesondere Gebäude ...“ (“The essential parts of a plot of land include the things firmly attached to the land, in particular buildings ...”).[20]

The result is that construction materials, which are inserted into the building, become property of the owner of the estate only because of the installation, notwithstanding who the original owner of the construction material was and whether the owner is entitled, e.g. by a valid contract, to claim for the transfer

---

[19] Cf. for the Netherlands in the same context as here *H. Ploeger/M. Prins/A. Straub/F. van den Brink*, Circular economy and real estate: alternatives for operational lease, in: Salford University, Shaping tomorrow's built environment – Proceedings of the International Research Conference, 2017.

[20] Translation according to www.gesetze-im-internet.de.

of ownership. §946 BGB expresses this principle: "Wird eine bewegliche Sache dergestalt mit einem Grundstück verbunden, dass sie wesentlicher Bestandteil des Grundstücks wird, so erstreckt sich das Eigentum an dem Grundstück auf die Sache." ("If a movable thing is combined with a plot of land in such a way that it becomes an essential part of the plot of land, the ownership of the plot of land extends to this movable thing.")

There is much case law with regard to the question what is an essential part. Essential parts are the components which are necessary to construct the buildings, but also heating systems[21], bathroom equipment (hot water boiler)[22] or in-built kitchen if designed especially for the building.[23] It is decisive whether the building is not regarded as complete without these things, even if the things can be removed or replaced without destroying the building.

No essential parts are standard designed built-in kitchens[24], machinery in a factory[25] or a bowling alley.[26] As a result of this case law a split of ownership is possible for, e.g., electric household equipment, but not for the heating system. This means that the parties to the contract may decide whether the owner provides for household equipment or leaves it to the tenant. But in any case the owner is responsible for the heating. It does not make sense to "nudge" the tenant by legislation to save heating energy by modern heating technology, because he cannot influence how the heating system works in the residence. He has no right for installation of energy saving technology; he only may save energy by less consumption of the heating and wearing warm clothes.

3.2. PAY FOR USE – ELEMENTS OF TENANCY LAW

Not only the analysis of property law indicates, that the "user" (tenant) of a residence is no appropriate addressee for legal instruments which try to promote "circular economy" in the field of real estate. It is also the law of obligations (book 2 of the BGB), which includes provisions for the tenancy contract. There are obligations for the landlord, to which obligations supporting "circular economy" could be connected, but not for the tenant.

The basic provision with regard to obligations of the parties to the tenancy contract is §535 BGB. It reads: "Durch den Mietvertrag wird der Vermieter verpflichtet, dem Mieter den Gebrauch der Mietsache während der Mietzeit zu

21 Bundesgerichtshof (BGH), 13.3.1970, V ZR 71/67, BGHZ (official collection of judgments of the BGH in civil law cases) vol. 53, p. 324; BGH, 19.10.2012, V ZR 263/11, Neue Juristische Wochenschrift Rechtsprechungsreport (NJW-RR) 2013, p. 625.

22 BGH, 31.10.1963, VII 285/61, BGHZ 40, 272.

23 BGH, 12.12.1989, VI ZR 311/88, NJW-RR 1990, 914.

24 OLG Nürnberg 2.4.2002, 3 U 4158/01, NJW-RR 2002, 1485.

25 BGH 31.10.1986, V ZR 166/85, Wertpapier-Mitteilungen – Zeitschrift für Wirtschafts- und Bankrecht (WM) 1987, p. 47.

26 BGH 26.9.2006, XI ZR 156/05, Neue Juristische Wochenschrift (NJW) 2007, p. 216.

gewähren. Der Vermieter hat die Mietsache in einem zum vertragsgemäßen Gebrauch geeigneten Zustand zu überlassen und sie während der Mietzeit in diesem Zustand zu erhalten. ..." (A lease agreement imposes on the lessor a duty to grant the lessee the use of the leased property for the lease period. The lessor must surrender the leased property to the lessee in a condition suitable for use in conformity with the contract and maintain it in this condition for the lease period. ...")[27]

The landlord cannot exclude in the contract a claim for damages or for a reduction of the rent of the tenant in case the property is not in conformity with the contract. So, e.g., the property must have a working heating system, for which the landlord is responsible. The landlord has to take care for the heating system; in case it does not properly work the tenant has a claim for repair against the landlord; if the landlord does not repair the heating, the tenant may reduce the rent. He is not entitled to mandate a repair service on his own. Only the landlord decides whether to modernize the heating system or not. The tenant cannot influence this decision as long as the heating system works. We can conclude that the tenant (= consumer = user) is no appropriate addressee for legal instruments with regard to a circular economy.

4. RECYCLING

In a circular economy, legal instruments to promote recycling should be in the focus. But there are no such legal instruments for real estate, this is to say for building materials. Only the general rules on waste apply. This is, as already mentioned, the Kreislaufwirtschaftsgesetz, which transposes the Waste Frame Directive into German law. It includes waste, coming from demolished building material. The 2018 amendment of the Waste Frame Directive clarifies, that such waste is included in the scope of the Directive. Nevertheless building material, coming from demolished buildings, is movable and so not subject of this contribution. By the destruction of the building it becomes a property separate from the property of the land. The owner of the land becomes the owner of this property, and he can transfer it to someone else.

Contrary to that, the draft of an Ersatzbaustoffverordnung (Substitute Building Materials Regulation) deals with material, which shall be built in technical structures like roads or railway lines, this is to say it does not cover all buildings. This draft, adopted by the Federal Government, regulates the recycling of mineral substitute building materials by treatment and installation in technical structures. The draft contains requirements for the production of these substances and regulates the process of their installation in technical

[27] The terms lease, lessor and lessee are used by www.gesetze-im-internet.de. These are the general terms used for rent of real estate and movables as well (Miete), whereas tenancy, landlord and tenant are the terms for renting a residence (Wohnungsmiete).

structures. It covers 18 individually listed building materials that incur as waste during construction works or are produced in treatment plants, including slag, ash and recycled building materials.

The substances originating from the dismantling of technical structures must be collected separately and sent to a treatment plant. The operator of the treatment plant has to perform a quality control. The builder or the user may only install mineral building materials in technical structures if no adverse effects on the groundwater or soil are to be feared.

The Bundesrat (Federal Council, 2nd chamber of the German parliament) must approve the draft regulation. Whether an approval will be made is not certain. The proposal is still debated (May 2019).

Voluntary standards exist, laid down by the BGRB – Bundesgütegemeinschaft Recycling-Baustoffe, a private association.[28] (Federal Quality Control Association Recycling Building Material). It provides for a certification, which is granted, if standards of a so called RAL-Gütesicherung (RAL Quality Control) are met.[29]

The Bundesgütegemeinschaft Recycling-Baustoffe grants a certificate for, among others, mixed mineral materials from the treatment of construction and demolition material. The certified production is controlled annually by licensed private certification agencies. In addition, daily and weekly self-checks will be carried out. This is to ensure a consistently high product quality with adherence to physical- technical and environmental standards.

It should be discussed, whether the draft should be – mutatis mutandis – extended to buildings. But quite the contrary: According to the Committees of the Bundesrat the draft is going too far. The only provision for enforcement says that infringements of the regulation are an Ordnungswidrigkeit (administrative offence). This is no effective enforcement rule. An alternative could be a right of non profit environmental protection associations to claim for injunction in case of violations of this regulation. We proposed such a right for promoting sustainable consumption in general and in particular with regard to the lifespan of technical consumer products in a study for the German Umweltbundesamt.[30] This would allow using an instrument of private law to enforce a public law regulation.

5. ENERGY SAVING

"Nudging" by legal instruments to make use of recycling should be in the centre of a discussion of a circular economy. But as we saw in the previous section,

---

28 Bundesgütegemeinschaft Recycling Baustoffe (BGRB), www.recycling-bau.de.

29 RAL is an independent association, which provides for, among others, certifications with an environmental impact.

30 For a short version cf. *S. Schlacke/K. Tonner/E. Gawel*, Nachhaltiger Konsum – integrierte Beiträge von Zivilrecht, öffentlichem Recht und Rechtsökonomie zur Steuerung nachhaltiger Produktnutzung, Juristenzeitung (JZ) 2016, p. 1030 et seq.

the results of the review of the relevant German legislation are very poor, at least when it is restricted to real estate. Therefore we will extend our analysis to a subject, which is not exactly "circular economy", but has the same goal to save resources: energy saving. We will discuss three topics with regard to real estate, thermal insulation, energy certification and heating. All the three have a European background, only the regulation about heating goes beyond the applicable Directive.

5.1. THERMAL INSULATION

The European background of thermal insulations of buildings is the Energy Performance of Buildings Directive (EPBD). The original Directive was adopted in 2002.[31] After a recast in 2010[32], the 2010 Directive was amended in 2018.[33] The amendments came into force at 9th July 2018 and have to be transposed to national law within 20 months.

Subject of the EPBD is to promote the improvement of the energy performance of buildings within the Union. The Directive distinguishes minimum requirements to the energy performance of new and of existing buildings. The 2018 amendment obliges Member States to establish a "long term renovation strategy" facilitating the cost effective transformation of existing buildings into nearly zero energy buildings by 2050. For new buildings, this standard shall come into force in 2021.

The German transposition of the EPBD is the Energieeinspargesetz (EnEG, Energy Saving Act), which leaves all the details to an Energieeinsparverordnung (EnEV, Energy Saving Regulation), so that we have to examine here the EnEV only. Following the EPBD, the EnEV contains specifications not only for the heating technology of a building, but also for the thermal insulation. The current version came into force on May 1, 2014 already containing stricter standards, which have to be applied since 2016.[34] Most of the regulation deals with new buildings. The aim is to reduce the primary energy requirements for heating and hot water preparation. Not only the quantitative amount of energy is considered, but renewable energies are specifically assessed. The currently valid requirements are an intermediate step to the so-called "almost zero – energy

31 Directive 2002/91/EC of the European Parliament and of the Council of 16 December 2002 on the energy performance of buildings, OJ L 1 of 4.1.2003, p. 65.

32 Directive 2010/31/EU of the European Parliament and of the Council of 19 May 2010 on the energy performance of buildings (recast), OJ L 153 of 18.6.2010, p. 13.

33 Directive (EU) 2018/844 of the European Parliament and of the Council of 30 May 2018 amending Directive 2010/31/EU on the energy performance of buildings and Directive 2012/27/EU on energy efficiency, OJ L 156 of 19.6.2018, p. 75.

34 For details cf. *J. Nusser*, Die EnEV 2014 – Wesentliche Neuerungen, offene Rechtsfragen und praktische Auswirkungen, Zeitschrift für Umweltrecht (ZUR) 2014, p. 67 et seq.

building", which shall become a new standard in Europe from 2021 onwards, as already mentioned.

There are also replacement and refit obligations for existing buildings. For example, boilers older than 30 years may no longer be operated. Heating and hot water pipes in unheated rooms must be insulated. Top floor ceilings for unheated rooms had to be refitted until 2015 if they had no so-called minimum thermal protection. In case of a voluntary modernization of the building stricter standards have to be observed.

5.2. ENERGY CERTIFICATION

According to the EPBD an energy certification has to be handed in to the buyer of a building and a tenant before concluding the tenancy contract. The Directive is transposed in Germany by the already mentioned Energieeinsparungsverordnung. For all heated buildings that are to be sold or rented, an energy certificate is required. It allows potential tenants and buyers an insight into the energetic quality and helps to estimate the future energy costs. The energy certificate must be shown to the interested party without being requested at the latest at the viewing date. Existing tenants, on the other hand, have no right to inspect. New energy certificates issued since May 2014 must contain an efficiency class. Efficiency class and energy value must already be published in the advertisement.

5.3. HEATING

Heating has as a European background the Directive on energy efficiency. We will not deal here with this Directive in detail, because it is a general Directive on energy saving and not restricted to real estate, and because subject of this contribution is not European but national law. But it can be shown, that a national regulation, the Heizkostenverordnung (HeizKV, Heating Cost Regulation)[35], is for some parts a transposition of a European Directive, and for some parts original German law, which goes beyond the transposition of the Directive. The Directive obliges the owner to install a metering system for energy consumption and for billing information of the tenant. It requires individual consumption meters for each unit of a multi-apartment building. The costs have to be allocated separately for hot water, heat for the common areas of the building and heat for the apartments. Further details are left to national legislation, as the Directive is a minimum standard Directive. Billing of heating

---

35 Verordnung über Heizkostenabrechnung in der Fassung der Bekanntmachung vom 5. Oktober 2009, BGBl. 2009 I, p. 3250.

costs shall be carried out on a non-profit basis, but the owner is allowed to assign billing to a third party. The costs of this assignment may be passed to the final customer. For electricity, there are more detailed provisions.

The German HeizKV transposes in its first sections the provisions about the metering system, but is more advanced than the Directive providing for details how to spread the costs between the tenants.

The aim of the HeizKV is to induce the user to an energy saving conduct. Therefore a heat billing is required, which is based on the individual energy consumption of the user and loads the energy costs onto the user. It is a pay for use principle. Addressee is the owner; he is responsible for installing a metering system and for billing the user. The owner is obliged, to bill the users according to their individual energy consumption. This does not only mean transparency for the tenant, it is also an incentive for him to save energy, because he saves his own money.

According to German tenancy law, the parties to the contract may agree on an "inclusive rent", which includes the operating costs and among them the costs for heating. The landlord is responsible for operating and heating, but the costs are not separately billed. The disadvantage of this model for the landlord is that it is difficult for him to allocate increases of the operating costs to the tenants.[36] Therefore this model is seldom used, but instead a model, according to which a net rent (often called Kaltmiete, cold rent) is agreed, to which the operation costs are added and billed separately. The addition of the net rent and the operating costs is the gross rent (Warmmiete, warm rent). The law describes the details of the operating costs in a Betriebskostenverordnung (BetrKV, operating costs regulation)[37] and the distribution of the operating costs in highly complicated sections of the tenancy law of the BGB (§§556, 556a BGB). Heating costs are one item of the operating costs as enumerated in the BetrKV. The BetrKV refers to the HeizKV insofar.

The HeizKV is mandatory law; landlord and tenant must not arrange another form of heating billing. The regulation not only imposes obligations on the owner, it also interferes with the contractual relationship between landlord and tenant. The tenant has a right under the rental agreement for a form of billing that follows the regulations of the HeizKV.

The law provides for exact methods how to spread the total costs to the users. Not only the individual consumption has to be taken into account, but also the space of the flat. This makes a correct billing complicated and to a matter for specialists. The consumption-based share is 70%; a higher proportion may be agreed in the tenancy contract. The reasons given for the proportion of space are that the operation of the heating system results in costs, which are independent

[36] Cf. A. *Saxinger*, Rechtliche Aspekte der „Flatratemiete", Neue Zeitschrift für Mietrecht (NZM) 2018, p. 849.

[37] Betriebskostenverordnung vom 25. November 2003 (BetrKV), BGBl. 2003 I, p. 2346.

of the individual consumption. It arises that the transposition beyond the directive does not necessarily serve the goal of energy saving. The consumer may save energy by cooling down the heating, but there is no incentive for a more efficent heating system.

5.4. HEAT SUPPLY BY A THIRD PARTY

Heat supply by a third party (contractor) is regulated by a special provision of the tenancy law of the BGB, §556c BGB, which reads:

> "Hat der Mieter die Betriebskosten für Wärme oder Warmwasser zu tragen und stellt der Vermieter die Versorgung von der Eigenversorgung auf die eigenständige gewerbliche Lieferung durch einen Wärmelieferanten (Wärmelieferung) um, so hat der Mieter die Kosten der Wärmelieferung als Betriebskosten zu tragen, wenn
> 1. die Wärme mit verbesserter Effizienz entweder aus einer vom Wärmelieferanten errichteten neuen Anlage oder aus einem Wärmenetz geliefert wird und
> 2. die Kosten der Wärmelieferung die Betriebskosten für die bisherige Eigenversorgung mit Wärme oder Warmwasser nicht übersteigen."
>
> "If the lessee must pay the operating costs for heat or hot water and if the lessor converts the supply from internal supply to an independent commercial supply from a heat supplier (heat supply), the lessee must meet the costs of heat supply as operational costs, if
> 1. the heat is supplied more efficiently either form a new system constructed by the heat supplier or by a heat network, and
> 2. the costs of heat supply do not exceed the operating costs for the previous internal supply of heat or hot water."

Details are regulated by a Wärmelieferverordnung (WärmeLV, heat supply regulation).[38] §556c and the Regulation came into force in 2013 and tried to intend to be a contribution to energy saving according to the official explanatory statement of the government.[39] The statement refers to the energy concept of the government[40] and intends to adapt the provisions about modernization of residences to the needs of ecological energy supply.

The new provisions mean that the landlord is free to change the heating system from internal supply to supply by Wärme contracting, without asking the tenant, if the tenant is obliged according to the tenancy contract to bear the operating costs (Betriebskosten) of the residence. This is usually the case.

---

38 BGBl. 2013 I, p. 1509. Overview by *D. Beyer*, Der neue Rechtsrahmen für die gewerbliche Wärmelieferung, Contracting und Recht (CuR) 2014, 5.

39 Regierungsentwurf, BT-Drucks. 17/10485, p. 23.

40 Energiekonzept für eine umweltschonende, zuverlässige und bezahlbare Energieversorgung vom 28. September 2010, BT-Drucks. 17/3049.

There are two prerequisites: The new construction must be more effective than the previous one, and there is a principle of cost neutrality (Kostenneutralität) compared between the costs of Wärme contracting and the previous costs.

Wärme Contracting existed already before the adoption of §556c BGB as a service between an owner and an energy supplier or a heating constructor to construct or to modernise the heating system, to supply energy for 10–15 years, to maintain the heating system in this period and to bill directly the users. As the contractor calculates his original investment as part of his costs, the users have to pay for the additional costs. So the tenants have to pay for the modernisation of the heating system. This was regarded as a circumvention of the provisions about modernisation, which provide for exact standards and limitations how to allocate modernisation costs to tenants. This model may still be practised under the new law, but only, when the two prerequisites (more effectiveness, cost neutrality) are fulfilled.

In or view the incentive to install a new more efficient heating system is low. The landlord does not save money, because he can allocate the costs to the tenant before and after the modernization. The only effect of the new provision is to protect the tenant against higher costs due to Wärme Contracting, but not, as the official explanatory statement of the government says, energy saving.

6. CONCLUSION

1. Most of the legal instruments discussed here do not address the consumer, but the user or final customer, in particular those with a European background. An exemption is "Wohnungsmietrecht" (law of tenancy of residences). The tenant is a consumer. Nevertheless the interests of a "final customer" should be defined from the point of view as a consumer; the term of consumer is not out of date.

Much of the law considered here is public law. It does not address a contractual relation, be it b 2 c, be it b 2 b, but imposes obligations to the person or entity, which produces or supplies goods or renders services. A remarkable exemption is the HeizKV, which is for a great part tenancy law and so contract law.

2. The principles of property law of the BGB do not allow a split of ownership between the owner of the land and of the building. Therefore the tenant is no appropriate addressee of legal instruments to support a circular economy with regard to real estate. The same is true for the tenancy contract, which is regulated in the Law of Obligations of the BGB: The landlord (= owner of the building) remains responsible for the heating system.

3. With regard to recycling, German law does not distinguish movables and real estate. The transposition of the Waste Frame Directive, the Kreislaufwirtschaftsgesetz applies. There is only a very specific draft of a Regulation, which deals with recycling of building materials, and a private certificate for environmental friendly recycling of building materials. Unfortunately, the draft regulation is limited to technical structures. An extension to all kind of buildings and better enforcement rules should be considered.

4. German law includes specific provisions dealing with energy savings in buildings. They are transpositions of European Directives and impose obligations to the owner of the building. They are no contract law. Only the HeizKV is going one step further: on the one side it is also a transposition of an EU Directive, but on the other side it provides for more detailed provisions how to spread the heating costs to the tenant. But it arises that there is no incentive to install more effective heating systems. However, the HeizKV is partly contract law, as it provides for a claim of the tenant against the landlord to bill him for the heating costs according to the provisions of the HeizKV.

5. The development to promote a circular economy in the field of real estate is driven by European law. National provisions which are not transpositions of EU Directives, play only a subordinate role. Most of the law does not distinguish movables and real estate and is applicable to both. There is no reason why to insist on more national or more specific real estate law.

Also the focus on public law will remain. But the HeizKV is an example that a bridge between public law and private law may be helpful for enforcement. The consumer's right for being billed according to the provisions of the HeizKV enforces the proper billing by the landlord and thus supports the goal of the regulation to save energy by transparency of consumption for the individual consumer. The consumer is able to save his own money when he individually consumes less and so contributes to energy saving.

The discussion about recycling shows, that another way of overcoming the public/private law divide should be possible. In that case it does not make sense to grant individual rights to the user against the producer. But enforcement by collective rights of non-profit associations is a way to promote legal standards.

THE CIRCULAR ECONOMY IN THE REAL ESTATE SECTOR

Challenges and Opportunities in Spain

Francisco de Elizalde*

1. INTRODUCTION

The environmental and economic rationale behind the circular economy[1] justifies the existing and prospective initiatives in the real estate sector. This area of the economy not only includes the construction of immovable property (buildings, houses, etc.) but also its use, maintenance, functioning and demolition. The activities related to it generate more than 10 per cent of greenhouse gases in the EU (35 per cent in Spain)[2] and 30 per cent of the total waste (40 per cent in Spain).[3] Furthermore, the construction and use of buildings in the EU account for half of the extracted materials and energy

---

* IE University
I would like to thank Professor Matan Mayer for his insights into the circular economy. I am also grateful to Sebastian Arnold and Bárbara Gómez Cortés for their research assistance. Usual disclaimer applies. The author can be contacted at francisco.deelizalde@ie.edu.

1 The Ellen MacArthur Foundation, "Towards the Circular Economy", 2013, 63 et seq., accessible: https://www.ellenmacarthurfoundation.org/assets/downloads/publications/Ellen-MacArthur-Foundation-Towards-the-Circular-Economy-vol.1.pdf (last visited 12 July 2018). The Ellen Mac Arthur Foundation, "Growth within: A Circular Economy Vision for a Competitive Europe", 2015, 12 et seq., accessible: https://www.ellenmacarthurfoundation.org/assets/downloads/publications/EllenMacArthurFoundation_Growth-Within_July15.pdf (last visited 12 July 2018). Communication from the Commission to the European Parliament, the Council, the European Economic and Social Committee and the Committee of the Regions of 2 December 2015, "Closing the loop – An EU action plan for the Circular Economy", COM (2015) 614 final, 2.

2 For the EU, http://ec.europa.eu/eurostat/statisticsexplained/index.php/Greenhouse_gas_emission_statistics_air_emissions_accounts#Analysis_by_economic_activity. For Spain, Ministerio de Agricultura y Pesca, Alimentación y Medio Ambiente and Ministerio de Economía, Industria y Competitividad, "España Circular 2030. Estrategia española de economía circular" (borrador), febrero 2018, 39, accessible: www.mapama.gob.es/es/calidad-y-evaluacion-ambiental/participacion-publica/180206economiacircular_tcm30-440922.pdf (last visited 16 July 2018).

3 For the EU, http://ec.europa.eu/environment/waste/construction_demolition.htm (last visited 12 July 2018). For Spain, "España Circular 2030" (n 2), 39.

consumption.[4] The concern of the EU institutions for the environmental impact of real estate is therefore comprehensible and not new.[5]

However, the circular economy is starting to offer innovative solutions to the real estate sector. As a result, new business models, which are environmental and economically sounder, challenge established legal frameworks. The circular economy would foster a shift in finance[6] and an increase in B2C and B2B services vis-à-vis purchases – the former being better suited for recycling and reuse, which are core values to the circular economy.

The new scenario is particularly interesting from a private law perspective. The provision of services in real estate touches upon traditional principles and rules of property law, an area that is largely mandatory and that remains mostly an issue of national law. Property law determines the ownership of the goods deployed in the service, which on occasion leads to a non-consented transfer to the customer. If the supplier were to lose ownership, it would also affect its financer's security rights over the goods. This risk would create a serious barrier to the circular economy in those countries that adopt this rule while fostering it in others – an outcome that would depend on each specific property law. Besides, the new business models would challenge consumer protection laws which, in key aspects, and notoriously as regards quality, have been designed for sales and not services. Hence, the circular economy would foreseeably require a reform of consumer contract rules.

The purpose of this chapter is to analyse the legal challenges that arise from private law in Spain, which is the fourth economy in the Eurozone. The chapter will first assess the legal relationship that the service creates between the supplier and the consumer. This relationship establishes a contractual bond in which the quality of performance is at stake. Next, the chapter moves on to the complex proprietary consequences of the service, an issue that is aggravated in the context of real estate. The *erga omnes* effects of property rights justify the chapter's focus on the supplier-customer relationship but also on the interaction of third parties with the goods deployed in the service. Lastly, the chapter addresses an issue that affects both the contracting parties and third parties: non-performance and insolvency.

---

4 Communication from the Commission to the European Parliament, the Council, the European Economic and Social Committee and the Committee of the Regions of 1 July 2014, "On Resource Efficiency Opportunities in the Building Sector", COM (2014) 445 final, 2.

5 Among many, Directive 2008/98/EC of the European Parliament and of the Council of 19 November 2008, on waste and repealing certain Directives, OJ 2008 L 312/3.

6 ING, "Rethinking finance in a circular economy. Financial implications of circular business models", May 2015, accessible: https://drive.google.com/file/d/1hZCKSe0-LxSq4d7x0zPBJkiUvlKyGkTc/view (last visited 12 July 2018).

2. THE CONSUMER-SUPPLIER RELATIONSHIP

It is common for the circular economy to embrace service contracts as the legal support for its business model. Consumers (and other service recipients) would cease to be buyers of products, which makes them the final users of objects. Sales complicate at least two of the stated aims of the circular economy: recycling and reuse. Instead, in the circular economy, businesspersons would provide services, at the end of which, the goods should revert to the business for recycling and reuse.

Therefore, the analysis of the consumer-supplier relationship should take into account the main contractual obligations arising from the service contract. Additionally, it should reflect on the proprietary consequences that may derive from the transfer of possession (albeit designed to be temporary in nature) of the goods deployed under the service, with a special focus on accession. I will address both matters in that order.

2.1. QUALITY OF THE SERVICE

2.1.1. Dichotomy between obligations of means and obligations to achieve a result

The quality of services in Spanish law is dominated by the distinction between the obligations of means or skill and care (*obligaciones de medios*) and the obligations to achieve a result (*obligaciones de resultado*).[7] Despite the antiquity of this dichotomy (it can be traced back to Demogue in France and some scholars go as far back as Roman law)[8], it continues to be relevant. Moreover, it still[9] provokes discussions over its usefulness in many of the legal systems

---

7 For a detailed discussion, see F de Elizalde, "Las obligaciones de medios y de resultado en la Propuesta de Código Mercantil", *InDret* 3/2014, 1–40, accessible: https://papers.ssrn.com/sol3/papers.cfm?abstract_id=2501005. Important (but not definitive) provisions in this discussion are Article 1104 (negligence) and Articles 1589–91 (work contract) of the Spanish Civil code.

8 R Demogue, *Traité des obligations en général*, V, Librairie Arthur Rousseau, 1925, §1237 (pp. 536–544)] and R Demogue, *Traité des obligations en général*, VI, Librairie Arthur Rousseau, 1931, §599 (p. 644). For the Roman origins of the dichotomy, H Mazeaud, L Mazeaud and A Tunc, *Tratado teórico y práctico de la responsabilidad civil, delictual y contractual*, I-1, Ejea, 1961, §103–2 (p. 127). Against, J Frossard, *La distinction des obligations de moyens et des obligations de résultat*, LGDJ, 1965, pp. 12–24. In any case, the importance of Demogue in case law and scholarly writings is highlighted by R. Nerson, "Préface", in Frossard (ibid), pp. V-VII.

9 Indeed the polemics over the dichotomy are as old as the classification itself. In France, see P Esmein, "Obligations", in M Planiol and G Ripert, *Traité Pratique du Droit civil français*, VI, LGDJ, 1952, §378 ter. Also, MG Marton, "Obligations de résultat et obligations de moyens", 1935 *Revue Trimestrielle de Droit Civil* 499, 510–518. In the same vein, A Planqueel, "Obligations de moyens, obligations de résultat (Essai de classification des obligations en function de la charge de la prevue en cas d'inexécution)", 1972 *Revue Trimestrielle de Droit Civil* 334, 336.

that have adopted it.[10] However, the dichotomy seems to experience a '*nouvelle jeunesse*' in Spanish law and in the harmonization of European contract law, following its recognition by the Draft Common Frame of Reference (DCFR) and the Regulation Proposal on a Common European Sales Law (CESL), and it seems to have survived the reform of the French Civil code.[11]

Demogue classified the obligations in those of means and those to achieve a result (*obligations de moyens/obligations de résultat*) when assessing the burden of proof in the event of non-performance[12] and, according to the majority in French legal doctrine[13], this is the main effect of the dichotomy. The classification of obligations in this way sought to resolve the contradictions that stemmed from the wording of the original Arts 1137 and 1147 of the French Civil code (currently, but not identically, Arts 1197 and 1231-1 of the *Code*).[14] The former referred to the diligence of the reasonable person[15] in the duty to guard a thing; the latter admitted the exoneration of the debtor from non-performance or delay in performance of an obligation if it proved force majeure. The *summa divisio* introduced by Demogue intended to harmonize both rules by linking Art 1137 to the obligations of means and Art 1147 to the obligations to achieve a result.[16]

In this way, the obligations to achieve a result would presume the debtor's fault in the event of a breach. The debtor should thus prove force majeure to be exempted from the liability arising from non-performance. In the obligations of means, on the other hand, it would be up to the creditor to prove the negligence of the debtor to make the latter responsible for the breach.[17]

---

10 See the debate that is taking place in Italy, F Piraino, "Obbligazioni di resultato e obbligazioni di mezzi overo dell'inadempimento incontovertibile e dell' inadempimento controvertibile", 2008 *Europa e Diritto Privato* 83, 95–104; and A Nicolussi, "Il commiato della giuirisprudenza dalla distinzione tra obbligazioni di risultato e obbligazioni di mezzi", 2006 *Europa e Diritto Privato* 797, 797–823.

11 C von Bar and H Schulte-Nölke (eds), *Principles, Definitions and Model Rules on European Private Law: Draft Common Frame of Reference* (DCFR), Sellier, 2009, Arts IV. C. 2: 105 and IV. C. 2: 106; Art 148 of the Proposal for a Regulation of the European Parliament and of the Council on a common European Sales Law, COM (2011) 635 final (CESL). In respect of French law, see P Jourdain, "Quel avenir pour la distinction des obligations de résultat et des moyens?", 2016 *JCP* 36, 1557. Cfr. D. Mazeaud, "La distinction obligation de résultat – obligation de moyens: le saut dans le vide?", D. 2017, 198.

12 Demogue (n 8, 1925), §1237 (pp. 536–537).

13 Mazeaud, Mazeaud and Tunc (n 8), §103-5 (pp. 132–133). Also, A Weill and F Terré, *Droit civil. Les obligations*, Dalloz, 1986 §396 (pp. 399–403); and J Carbonnier, *Droit Civil*, IV, PUF, 1994, §156 (pp. 261–263).

14 Table des articles 1100 à 1381-1 au JO du 11/02/2016, accessible: https://www.legifrance.gouv.fr/Droit-francais/Codification/Tables-de-concordance/Code-civil/Table-des-articles-1100-a-1386-1-au-JO-du-11-02-2016-ancienne-nouvelle-reference (last visited 18 July 2018).

15 In its ultimate version, after the reform introduced by Art 26 of Loi n° 2014-873 du 4 août 2014 pour l'égalité réelle entre les femmes et les hommes, JORF n° 179, du 5 août. Previously, the parameter of diligence was set by reference to the "*bon père de famille*".

16 See (n 13) and Demogue (n 8, 1931) §600 (pp. 644–645).

17 Mazeaud, Mazeaud and Tunc (n 8), §103-5 (pp. 132–133).

The evidentiary consequence (the burden of proof, *onus probandi*) that may result from the distinction between obligations of means and obligations to achieve a result is not the main utility that this dichotomy has in Spanish law. In fact, legislation[18] and case law[19] recognize cases (the liability of architects, for example) in which the burden of proof does not follow the aforementioned distinction.[20] For example, an architect is bound by an obligation of means (skill and care) but case law and legislation presume its liability in the event of damage – the typical burden of proof applied to obligations to achieve a result.

The division introduced by Demogue seems better suited (at least in Spanish law) to determine the allocation of risks between the parties. In the obligations of means, the debtor does not guarantee the purpose of the contract (healing a patient, winning a lawsuit, etc.). It only undertakes to perform an activity as promised and, in the absence of agreement, with due skill and care. Instead, in the obligations to achieve a result, the debtor guarantees the purpose of the contract, which forms part of the terms, whether agreed or as default rules.[21]

That is why despite following the French terminology of obligations of means and obligations to achieve a result, it can be argued that Spanish law is more consistent with the approach in German law, which distinguishes between a service contract (*Dienstvertag*) and a work contract (*Werkvertrag*).[22] The distinction is done in the terms of the contract, not as regards the burden of proof. In a service contract the debtor promises a certain activity whereas in a work contract it is bound to a result – that agreed to or what is customary and meets the expectations of the customer in view of the type of work.[23] The same outcomes apply in Spanish law, correspondingly, to the obligations of means and the obligations to achieve a result.

2.1.2. The dichotomy in the circular economy

The contractual arrangements used in the provision of services in the circular economy would probably fall under obligations to achieve a result. The business

---

18 E.g. Ley 38/1999, de 5 de noviembre, de Ordenación de la Edificación, BOE nr 266 of 6.11.1999.

19 SSTS (1ª) 7.11.1989, ES:TS:1989:9434; 27.6.1994, ES: TS: 1994:22422; 29.5.1997, ES: TS:1997:3772; and 19.10.1998, ES:TS:1998:5986. M Jiménez Horwitz, "La distinción entre los contratos de obras y servicios en el Derecho español (estudio comparativo con el Derecho alemán), 2012 *Anuario de Derecho Civil* 551, 563.

20 A Cabanillas Sánchez, *Las obligaciones de actividad y de resultado*, Bosch, 1993, pp. 155–173.

21 Cfr. challenging the use of the dichotomy, AM Morales Moreno, "Problemas que plantea la unificación del concepto de incumplimiento de contrato. Respuesta a Enrique Barros", in E Barros Bourie, MP García Rubio and AM Morales Moreno, *Derecho de Daños*, Fundación Coloquio Europeo, Madrid, 2009, pp. 215–220.

22 §611 BGB and §§631 and 633 BGB, respectively.

23 W Fikenstcher and A Heinemann, *Schuldrecht*, de Grutyer, Berlin, 2006, paras. 1129–31.

is expected to provide a service that meets the ultimate purpose of the customer (e.g. a lightning system that works) and not just an activity.

However, the definition of the obligations of the parties in service contracts remains in the realms of agreement. The dichotomy 'obligations to achieve a result/obligations of means' is just a default rule. It could therefore occur that the business, most probably using standard terms, could reduce its commitment to an obligation of means (skill and care), thus assigning the risk of the result to the customer.

At present, legislation on the quality of the subject matter of the contract in EU consumer law does not cover all types of contracts. It is mostly restricted to sales.[24] As regards services, EU law only addresses the quality of some particular ones, such as package travel.[25] In both cases, the standard required from the product or service is benchmarked by the principle of conformity, which is mandatory law. According to it, the business must deliver an object or provide a service that is fit for purpose. However, in the absence of harmonization, the quality requirements of other services is left to national law. Spain has implemented the principle of conformity in accordance with EU law but has not extended it to other (not envisaged) contracts. Therefore, the quality of the services that could foreseeably be provided in a circular economy are currently not covered by the (mandatory) principle of conformity.

Taking advantage of this, a business could define the subject matter of the contract to fit the less demanding category of obligations of means. In the absence of mandatory law, this would be valid. Moreover, as it would concern the definition of the subject matter of the contract, it could not be challenged as unfair (if transparent), even though its likelihood of being a standard term (Art 4(2) Unfair Contract Terms Directive, UCTD).[26] However, this would not be the case if the term did not define the subject matter of the contract but, instead, limited the liability of the business (Annex, 1(b) UCTD).

Overall, EU consumer law should probably adapt to the changing scenario that a circular economy would imply, in order to reinforce the quality of the service that a consumer is entitled to demand – an objective to which the requirement of conformity seems appropriate.[27]

---

24 Directive 1999/44/EC of the European Parliament and of the Council of 25 May 1999 on certain aspects of the sale of consumer goods and associated guarantees, OJ 1999 L 171/12, Art 2.

25 Directive (EU) 2015/2302 of the European Parliament and of the Council of 25 November 2015 on package travel and linked travel arrangements, amending Regulation (EC) No 2006/2004 and Directive 2011/83/EU of the European Parliament and of the Council and repealing Council Directive 90/314/EEC, OJ 2015 L 326/1, Art 13.

26 Council Directive 93/13/EEC of 5 April 1993 on unfair terms in consumer contracts, OJ 1993 L 95/29.

27 However, the principle of conformity would be unsuitable for certain kinds of services, as claimed in F de Elizalde, "Should the implied term concerning quality be generalized? Present and future of the principle of conformity in Europe", 2017 *European Review of Private Law* 71, 96.

2.2. PROPRIETARY EFFECTS OF THE SERVICE. ACCESSION?

The move from buying products to hiring services, the natural contractual infrastructure of the circular economy, could face a major challenge in real estate from the rules on accession (*accessio*). Because of accession, under certain circumstances the supplier of the service could lose ownership over the objects it incorporates in the immovable of the customer (e.g. the air conditioning equipment in a 'pay-per-use' service). This would represent a major drawback to the circular economy, through undermining strategic interests of the supplier – the retention of ownership and the financing opportunities that derive therefrom.

The rules on accession, in those jurisdictions that recognize it, aim at the preservation of value, as accession prevents the destruction of the enlarged main object (after the incorporation of another one). This seems to have been the rationale for this institution since at least the Roman Law of the Twelve Tables, in which it was decided that the owner of a beam which was introduced in an alien building (*tignum iunctum*) could not recover it.[28]

Additionally, accession intimately relates to two important principles of property law: specificity of the object (which should exist and be certain, as well as the rights over it) and publicity of the proprietary right over the object, a requirement for the right to have *erga omnes* effects.[29] To them, civil law jurisdictions include, when it comes to accession, the unitary character of ownership.[30] Accession relates to specificity when it permanently enlarges an object (the building with the movable incorporated into it). It relates to publicity as third parties are, in principle, entitled to rely on the physical appearance of that 'enlarged object' and on the presumed ownership of the owner of the building over it. Lastly, the unitary character of ownership is, in principle, against the existence of more than one owner over the same space.

From this common core, jurisdictions diverge as to the content and extent of the rationale (the preservation of value) and the principles mentioned, with a different degree of flexibility in the application of accession. In the most rigid systems (Germany among them), accession is treated as an original acquisition of ownership. Because of accession, the owner of the movable loses ownership if the object becomes an essential component ('*wesentlicher Bestandteil*' in German law)[31] of the building. This rule, being mandatory law, cannot be altered

28 Tab. 6.7 and 6.8. According to A Guzmán Brito, *Derecho Privado Romano*, I, Editorial Jurídica de Chile, 1996, p. 561, the *ratio legis* of the rule was to keep the integrity of the city, preventing the destruction of buildings (*ne urbs ruinis deformetur*; D. 43.8.2.17). G Melillo, *Tignum Iunctum*, Jovene, 1964, pp. 2–3.

29 For a comparative overview, see van S van Erp and B Akkermans (ed.), *Cases, materials and text on Property Law*, Hart, 2012, pp. 75 et seq. As regards Spanish law, L Díez-Picazo, *Fundamentos del Derecho Civil Patrimonial*, III, Thomson Civitas, 2008, pp. 155–156.

30 Van Erp and Akkermans (n 29), pp. 224–226.

31 §§93, 94, 946 and 947 BGB.

by agreement. In contrast, other legal systems, including Spanish law, take a more flexible approach while adhering to the common principles of property law (specificity and publicity). Accession is treated as a rule to solve conflicts rather than an institution of mandatory character. This approach prevents accession in a great variety of situations, especially when the parties agree otherwise, while meeting the principle of specificity and, in respect of third parties, the principle of publicity. Therefore, the way in which accession works in Spanish law does not normally affect the supplier's right of ownership.

Under the heading 'Right of Accession' (Book II, Title II, Chapter II) the Spanish Civil code (CC) regulates a variety of situations that imply a change in the composition of objects (movable and immovable) and, consequently, on the property law relations that exist over them.[32] Under this broad regulation, accession in the CC comprises the incorporation of a movable into an immovable[33] or into another movable[34] (in both cases, an accession *stricto sensu*) but also the combination of movables (commingling)[35], the creation of new objects (*specificatio*)[36], and the acquisition of fruits (natural, civil and industrial) by its owner.[37]

If we focus on accession *stricto sensu,* as the most relevant to services provided in the real estate sector, it is a fact ("*accedere*" in Roman law would have had a vague meaning of physical change, production or augmentation of things)[38] that it would lead to the acquisition of a right of ownership only in certain circumstances.[39] For that to occur the incorporation of a movable object into an immovable (or into another movable) should be irreversible and one of the objects should be ancillary to the other one.[40] Moreover, the incorporation of the movable into the immovable (we restrict our analysis to real estate) should be done on a fixed basis, so that it cannot be separated therefrom without breaking the material or impairing the object (Art 334.3 CC).[41] Whether the incorporation meets this requirement necessarily has to be decided on a case-by-case basis.[42]

---

32 L Díez-Picazo, "La modificación de las relaciones jurídico-reales y la teoría de la accesión", 1966 *Revista Crítica de Derecho Inmobiliario* 829, 840.

33 Arts 358 CC et seq.

34 Arts 375 CC et seq.

35 Arts 381 and 382 CC.

36 Art 383 CC.

37 Art 354 CC et seq.

38 D. 41.1.56; D. 6.2.11.6 and 7. A Carrasco Perera, *Ius aedificandi y accesión*, Montecorvo, Madrid, 1986, p. 59. Díez-Picazo (n 29), p. 278.

39 Díez Picazo (n 29), p. 281. Against, see G Cerdeira Bravo de Mansilla, "El automatismo en la accesión inmobiliaria", 2012 *Revista Crítica de Derecho Inmobiliario* 43, 53.

40 Carrasco Perera (n 38), p. 67. M de los D Núñez Boluda, *La accesión en las edificaciones*, Bosch, Barcelona, 1994, p. 28.

41 As regards the relationship between the classification of immovable objects (Art 334 CC) and accession, Carrasco Perera (n 38), pp. 181–183.

42 Núñez Boluda (n 40), p. 32.

2.2.1. *Accession as a source of non-mandatory rules*

The difficulties and risks involved in deciding when a movable becomes irreversibly incorporated into an immovable, in a way that could lead to accession, are overcome by the possibility that the parties have to agree against accession. A mainstream position in Spanish law understands that the owner of the movable can agree with the owner of the immovable that despite factual incorporation accession does not occur. In this way, each party maintains its property right over its respective object. The contractual relationship is sufficient to impede accession.[43]

According to this prevailing understanding, the rules on accession would be non-mandatory. They would operate in the event of an unlawful interference with an alien property (to solve a conflict of interests), but not when the incorporation resulted from agreement. This has led some scholars to include the lack of a contractual relationship as a fundamental requirement for accession to occur.[44] In contrast, others consider that the legal regulation of accession should supplement the contract.[45]

The possibility to agree against accession is coherent with the consideration of property rights in Spanish law as *numerus apertus* – a minority stand in the comparative arena. Freedom of contract allows for the creation of new property rights (with limitations) and grants the parties the possibility to shape the content of existing ones.[46] Additionally, it is consistent with the principle of specificity as the parties identify the distinct ownership of the immovable and the goods.

As an example of the non-mandatory character of accession, the Spanish Supreme Court (*Tribunal Supremo*) decided that the rules on accession did not apply in a case in which one party had constructed an industrial building over its counterparty's land to pursue a joint poultry business, as the contract impeded accession.[47]

2.2.2. *The classification of immovable property. Case law*

The existence of a contractual relationship between the owner of the immovable (customer of the service) and the supplier of the movable that excludes accession is certainly the most convenient scenario for the latter, as it retains ownership.

---

43 Núñez Boluda (n 40), pp. 38–43. Carrasco Perera (n 38), pp. 392–395. M Alonso Pérez, "Art 358", in M Albaladejo and S Díaz Alabart (ed), *Comentarios al Código Civil y compilaciones forales*, V-1, Edersa, 1986, pp. 264–265. STS (1ª) 14.3.1983, ES:TS:1983:45.

44 Núñez Boluda (n 40), p. 28.

45 Díez-Picazo (n 29), p. 298.

46 Diez-Picazo (n 29), pp. 133 et seq. This has allowed for the creation of new rights such as *superficie* (even before the actual existence of a statute allowing it) or concepts such as *medianería horizontal* (DGRN 5.4.2002 and 24.2.2007).

47 STS (1ª) 18.4.1986, ES:TS:1986:1919.

However, a behavioural analysis proves that incompleteness of contracts is customary. It is important, therefore, to address accession in the absence of agreement.

On this, it can be recalled that accession only takes place (in real estate) when a movable becomes irreversibly incorporated into an immovable, in the sense that it cannot be separated therefrom without breaking the material or impairing the object (Art 334.3 CC).

This does not always follow the attachment of a movable to an immovable. In fact, the Spanish civil code provides for a classification of immovable objects (Art 334.1–10 CC) and only one category leads to accession. Scholars agree about organizing that classification into four: (i) immovable by nature (land); (ii) immovable by incorporation (movable incorporated into an immovable); (iii) immovable by destination (movable destined to serve the functioning of an immovable, which is to be decided by the owner of both objects); and (iv) immovable by analogy (including property rights over real estate).[48] The rules on accession only apply to an immovable by incorporation.[49]

This gives a second chance to suppliers of movable objects that are attached to an immovable (in the absence of agreement) as the loss of ownership that follows accession only occurs if the physical attachment is classified as an immovable by incorporation. This depends on whether the union is irreversible and on the possibility of separating the movable without impairing the object (it is unclear if the law refers to the movable or to the immovable). Despite the factual elements at stake, the issue of classification has been deemed one of law.[50]

It is therefore interesting to analyse case law to consider in which situations the Spanish Supreme Court has decided that a good became irreversibly attached to a building, thus classifying the outcome as an immovable property by incorporation to which the rules on accession apply. Even before the introduction of circular economy elements, the Spanish Supreme Court has had the opportunity to classify immovable objects, and thus directly or indirectly decide upon accession. On this point, it is worth mentioning case law in which the objects were classified either under immovable by destination or immovable by incorporation.

a. Immovable by destination (i.e. impeding accession)
   - Cable that conducts electricity to a plot of land[51]
   - Artificial waterway channel for irrigating land[52]
   - Electrical appliances used in a hospital[53]

---

48 Díez-Picazo (n 29), p. 213.

49 Carrasco Perera (n 38), pp. 180–181.

50 STS (1ª) 3.7.1987, ES:TS:1987:4672.

51 STS (1ª) 19.1.1927, JC 1927, 42.

52 STS (1ª) 19.1.1927.

53 STS (1ª) 3.7.1987.

b. Immovable by incorporation (that would lead to accession)
   - Washbasin
   - Bath
   - Toilet
   - Radiators[54]

The uncertainties that arise from case law justify, for the circular economy model to work, the drafting of an agreement in which the parties reject accession.

2.2.3. Excursus. Ancillary and main. Superficie solo cedit?

A final argument against accession that a supplier could bring is that, despite accession, it and not the customer should gain ownership. The consequence of accession is that the ancillary object is incorporated into the principal (*accessorium sequitur principale*). The prevailing understanding in Spanish law is that the rule '*superficie solo cedit*' (the building accrues to the land) is just an application of the overarching rule '*accessorium sequitur principale*'.[55] Therefore, in the event of the movable goods being more valuable than the soil, ownership could revert to the supplier. It is expected that this would only occur in a large scale circular economy in which more substantial elements of construction could exceed, in value, that of the land.

3. OWNERSHIP AND THIRD PARTIES

3.1. THIRD PARTY ACQUIRERS IN GOOD FAITH

In order to escape the harsh consequences of accession it is foreseeable that suppliers in a circular economy would include in their (presumably standard) terms a 'non accession' clause. In this way, they would aim to ensure that they retain ownership over the movable objects that become attached to buildings under the contractual relationship.

However, due to the principle of relativity of contracts[56] this agreement between the customer and the supplier is not opposable to third parties. Therefore, a third party who deals with the owner of an immovable could legitimately ignore the supplier's rights over the movables attached to the building.

The physical appearance of an immovable with elements of the circular economy could lead a third party to believe, among others things:

[54] For all, STS (1ª) 18.3.1961, JC 1961, 213. Scholars heavily criticized this decision.
[55] Díez-Picazo (n 29), pp. 288–289.
[56] Art 1257 CC.

(i) that the movable is permanently incorporated into the immovable and belongs to the owner of the property (because of accession);
(ii) that the movable serves the functioning or use of the property (immovable by destination, Art 334.5 CC)[57] or
(iii) that it is a movable, owned by the customer and not the supplier.

If the third party legitimately ignores, in good faith, the supplier's rights, it could prevail in the event of conflict even though it acquired from a non-owner. This could happen in the three different scenarios described.

As regards the first scenario, if the movable is irreversibly incorporated into the immovable, accession may occur when the supplier is unable to oppose its contract, including a 'non-accession' clause, to the third party. The third party acquirer of the immovable in good faith would also acquire the incorporated movable.[58]

In the second scenario, the event of the movable serving the functioning or use of the property but not being irreversibly incorporated into it, the movable may become an immovable by destination (Art 334.5 CC). For this to occur, it requires a decision from the owner of both the movable and the immovable, who should be the same person.[59] One of the most important effects of this decision is that, after it takes place, in the event of a transfer of the immovable to a third party, the transferor is obliged to deliver not only the real estate property but also the movable ancillary to it.[60] In any case, if the owner of the immovable property does not own the movable, the latter cannot become an immovable by destination.[61] The reliance that a third party could place on the customer's possession (i.e. the movable appearing to belong to him) can be protected under the rules that govern the acquisition of movables but not those governing real estate.[62] Vis-à-vis third parties, the situation of this kind of ancillary movable is similar to that of other movables.

---

57 In relation to immovables by destination, the default rule in obligations to give (*dare*) is that the 'accessories' must be delivered together with the main object (art 1097 Spanish CC). This rule would reinforce third parties' claims. See Carrasco Perera (n 38), pp. 68 and 192. These immovables by destination (movables that serve the use or functioning of the immovable) are not contained in the subject matter of the mortgage (*hipoteca*) over the property, unless otherwise agreed (Art 111.1 Decreto de 8 de febrero de 1946). The agreement by a third party who ignores in good faith the supplier's ownership would be opposable to it.

58 Arts 334.3 and 358 CC; Arts 34 and 38 Decreto de 8 de febrero de 1946, BOE nr 58 of 27.2.1946.

59 Díez-Picazo (n 29), p 219. STS (1ª) 3.7.1987.

60 Art 1097 CC. Carrasco Perera (n 38), pp. 68 and 197. F Badosa Coll, "Art 1097" in C Paz-Ares, L Díez-Picazo, R Bercovitz and P Salvador (eds.), *Comentario del Código Civil*, II-I, Ministerio de Justicia, 1991, p. 26.

61 STS 3.7.1987.

62 Movables ancillary by function to an immovable (immovable by destination) are legally autonomous from the real estate property. See M Albaladejo, "Art 334", in Albaladejo and Díaz Alabart (n 43), p. 15.

This leads to the third and final scenario: the protection of third party acquisition of movables in good faith. On this, Spanish law is far more intricate compared to other European counterparts, such as Germany and France. Complexity arises from the wording of the applicable provisions of the Spanish civil code (especially Arts 464 and 1955 CC) and the two different readings of them – a 'Germanistic' and a 'Romanistic' one. According to Art 464 CC, '[p]ossession of movable property, acquired in good faith, is equivalent to title. Notwithstanding the foregoing, any person who has lost movable property or has been deprived of it illegally may claim it from its possessor'. In turn, Art 1955 CC establishes that '[o]wnership of movable property prescribes [in the sense of acquisitive prescription, *usucapio*] after three years of uninterrupted possession in good faith'.[63]

According to the 'Germanistic' interpretation, a third party acting in good faith acquires ownership even if the transferor is not the owner. An exception to this rule is the situation of the object being lost or stolen – the expression 'illegally' of Art 464 CC being restricted to those cases. The period of three years to acquire ownership of Art 1955 CC is only required when the elements for 'possession (…) equivalent to title' are not met (i.e. objects that are lost or stolen).

In the 'Romanistic' interpretation, a third party acting in good faith cannot acquire a property right from a non-owner – the contrary being against the rule *nemo plus iuris*, according to which no one can transfer a bigger right than its own. A defect in the title can be offset by acquisitive prescription (*usucapio*), which arises from possessing the movable during three years in good faith (Art 1955 CC, ordinary or abridged acquisitive prescription). For the ordinary *usucapio* to occur the possessor needs a 'just' title. This is a title that would be perfect, valid and sufficient to transfer ownership were it not for one vice – that the transferor was not the owner.[64] Possession would presume the existence of that just title.[65] Support for this 'Romanistic' interpretation would come from the expression 'deprived of it illegally' (Art 464 CC) which would be broader than its French or German counterparts (restricted to objects lost or stolen).[66] Any situation in which the owner does not consent to the transfer of a property right would one in which it was 'deprived of it [the object] illegally'. Therefore, the owner would be entitled to claim restitution (under an action in rem: *reivindicatio*).

The Spanish Supreme Court has been uncertain about the interpretation to follow and has alternatively opted for one and then the other.[67] The Germanistic

63 For these articles of the Civil code, I used the official translation prepared by the Ministry of Justice of the Kingdom of Spain.

64 Art 1952 CC.

65 L Díez-Picazo and A Gullón, *Sistema de Derecho Civil*, III, Tecnos, 2000, p. 211.

66 §935 BGB and Art 2276 French CC.

67 SSTS (1ª) 19.6.1945, 2.12.1999 and 22.1.2002 (Romanistic, ES:TS:1999:7706 and ES:TS:2002:280); SSTS (1ª) 15.2.1990 and 25.2.1992 (both Germanistic, ES:TS:1990:1342 and ES:TS:1992:1502).

interpretation better protects third parties while the Romanistic one is more respectful of the previous owner's rights. In the context of a circular economy, it is probably unlikely that it would be argued that the movables deployed in a service were lost or stolen. According to the Germanistic interpretation, the third party acquiring those movables from the customer would be protected, while if the Romanistic interpretation were to prevail, the supplier of the service could claim restitution under a real right action, before the third party possesses them for the three years needed for acquisitive prescription (*usucapio*).

3.2. REGISTRATION

The most efficient tool to prevent the use of the 'third party in good faith' argument is registration, which gives publicity to the ownership of the supplier and any other property right that the financer of the supplier may have over the movables used in the service. In addition to a traditional land registry, Spain has established a special registry for movable objects, under the organization of the commercial registries.[68] In it, it is possible to register any identifiable movable object as well as all property rights (and others) over it. Suppliers can therefore record their rights (and their financers their own) in order to prevent third party protection.

The closest equivalent to that of the supplier in the circular economy, in respect of registration and its effects, is that of a seller under a retention of title clause. In these early stages of the circular economy, it provides a good point of comparison. Registration of retention of title clauses in the sale of movables has long been in place in Spain, even before the creation of the Registry for movable objects. Their registration has prevented third party acquirers of an immovable from gaining protection, for example, claiming ownership over electric appliances that had been sold to the transferor of the property. Following a lack of payment, the Supreme Court established that the supplier had the right to regain ownership and prevail over the third party, precisely because of registration.[69] Under the current structure of the Registry for movable objects, the supplier can record its rights, which should prevent third party protection.

The requirement of identification of the movable in order to access registration can be an issue for certain objects (e.g. bricks or beams) of the circular economy. This is where the BIM (Building Information Model), blockchain and the internet of things can have a major role in the creation of powerful product passports.[70] They are relevant to a truly circular economy in

---

68 Created by Disposición Adicional Única, Real Decreto 1828/1999, de 3 de diciembre, por el que se aprueba el Reglamento del Registro de Condiciones Generales de la Contratación, BOE nr 306, 23.12.1999.

69 STS 3.7.1987.

70 Cfr. E Schut, M Crielaard and M Mesman, *Circular Economy in the Dutch Construction Sector. A perspective for the market and government*, RIVM, 18 December 2015, 9 and 22,

which the three 'Rs' (reduce, reuse and recycle) can be potentiated throughout the lifecycle of a building by allowing a constant and updated identification of objects. From a legal perspective, this technology could be the best way for most products to be reliably identifiable, allowing for registration and so securing property rights over movables. This innovation would provide the circular economy with endless possibilities.

4. NON-PERFORMANCE AND INSOLVENCY

The last section of this chapter deals with unhealthy situations that could affect the service: non-performance of the contract and insolvency. Although non-performance is inherently an issue of contract law, it is analysed here and not in the 'supplier-customer' section because of the remedy of termination that could involve third parties. In Spanish law, termination reverts ownership over the goods to the supplier but only in the absence of a third party that deserves protection. In turn, it is self-evident that insolvency affects the rights of third parties.

4.1. NON-PERFORMANCE

The contract might be breached by the customer, normally due to a lack of payment of the service, or by the supplier, typically in the event of a flawed service. In both cases, the remedies available to the parties are those of general contract law: specific performance, withholding performance, reduction of price, termination and damages.[71] Unlike for sales, Spanish consumer law does not envisage a specific remedial regime for a B2C service relationship.[72]

In the context of a circular economy, two of the remedies mentioned could be particularly problematic. First, the remedy of specific performance when claimed by the consumer. In modern contract law, specific performance includes repair and substitution at the creditor's choice. However, this scheme, which enhances the rights of the consumer, was designed without considering sustainability. Allowing the creditor to opt for substitution seems to be a normative decision

---

accessible: rivm.nl/dsresource?objectid=806b288e-3ae9-47f-1-a287c208f884b36&type=org&disposition=inline (last visited 16 July 2018). C Kinnaird, M Geipel and M Bew, *Blockchain technology. How the inventions behind bitcoin are enabling a network of trust for the built environment*, Arup, 2017, accessible: www.arup.com/en/perspectives/publications/Research/Section/Blockchain-Technology (last visited 16 July 2018).

71 Arts 1101 and 1124 CC. For consumer contracts, see Art 59 Real Decreto Legislativo 1/2007, de 16 de noviembre, por el que se aprueba el texto refundido de la Ley General para la Defensa de los Consumidores y Usuarios y otras leyes complementarias, BOE nr 287, of 30.11.2007.

72 The difference is a result of the transposition of Dir 99/44.

that is less sustainable than repair, even though the supplier could reincorporate the goods, on occasion, into its manufacturing or service processes.

The second problematic remedy could be termination of the contract by the business. If the customer defaults, the supplier would be entitled to an action to claim payment of the outstanding debt and another action (in rem) to claim restitution of the movables deployed in the service. While the action arising from the obligation (debt) would always be available, the action in rem would depend on the supplier actually retaining ownership. This would not be the case in the presence of a third party entitled to a property right over the goods who deserves protection or in the event of accession, as seen in the previous sections. Therefore, despite the fact that termination should revert ownership to the business, it could be impeded under the rules of third party protection and accession.

The precise procedural paths that the action for termination must follow would depend on the formalities involved in the service contract. In the current framework of Spanish procedural law, the supplier should file an action in rem (*reivindicatio*) to recover the goods, in an ordinary procedure. The claim is viable because the supplier retained ownership of the goods. For this to happen, in the event of a movable object irreversibly attached to an immovable, the parties should have agreed on a 'non-accession' clause. Repossession can involve destruction of the improvements of the immovable as long as it is not left in a worse situation than its original condition (prior to the service).[73]

It is doubtful whether the real right action admits aggregation of the claim for the debt. If not, the debt should be claimed in an autonomous declarative proceeding (verbal or ordinary, depending on the amount) or in a specific order for payment procedure (which could end up in a declarative one if the debtor opposes the claim).

Instead, if the contract is formalised in a public deed the supplier would have the option to resort to an expedited execution procedure. In it, the supplier could claim both the outstanding debt and repossession of the goods.[74] Following the reform of the Spanish Procedural Act (as a result of CJEU *Aziz*[75]), the consumer is entitled to challenge, even in this expedited procedure, any unfair term that the contract may contain.[76]

As regards retention of title clauses in the sale of goods, the law has provided for a special verbal (declarative) procedure to recover possession of the goods.[77] In the absence of a legal provision, it would not be applicable to defaults outside

73 Carrasco Perera (n 38), pp. 214 and 262.

74 Arts 517.2.4°, 572.2 and 701 LEC.

75 Case C-415/11, *Mohamed Aziz v Caixa d'Estalvis de Catalunya, Tarragona i Manresa (Catalunyacaixa)*, ECLI:EU:C:2013:164.

76 Art 557.1.7° LEC.

77 Art 250.1.11° LEC and Art 16.2.d Ley 28/1998, de 13 de julio, de Venta a Plazos de Bienes Muebles, BOE nr 167 of 14.7.1998.

that scope. However, if the circular economy were to expand, it is foreseeable that the legislator would design a similar procedure for services.

4.2. INSOLVENCY

Similar to non-performance, insolvency could affect both the consumer and the supplier, financially speaking but also in procedural terms. In fact, the Spanish Insolvency law recognizes the possibility of filing an insolvency procedure for a business but also for an individual person.[78]

Starting with the latter, if the supplier meets the conditions required to retain ownership over the goods, the insolvency of the customer should not affect its rights. The goods would not form part of the assets of the insolvent and, hence, the supplier could separate its assets from those of the insolvent and recover them.[79] During an interim period, however, there is a risk that recovery is banned, depending on the interpretation of the Insolvency Law, which establishes that similar situations (such as retention of title clauses in the sale of goods) are covered by the interim non-recovery order.[80] A restrictive interpretation of that order should prevail as it entails a limitation to the right of ownership.[81]

Lastly, the scenario could be the opposite, with the business filing for insolvency. In this case, the service contract stands, in principle, as the Insolvency Law aims for the survival of the business.[82] However, the ultimate effect would depend on the outcome of the insolvency proceedings and the actual capacity of the business to continue its activities. The insolvency managers can always seek termination of the contract. If successful, termination would include any compensation due to the consumer, which would be charged to the aggregate assets of the business and paid prior to any other non-secured claim.[83]

5. CONCLUSION

Spain is one of the largest economies in the EU and so the decisions that the country adopts have a significant weight in the fulfilment of the objectives of the Union. Therefore, it is disappointing that the draft strategy plan for a circular

---

78 Art 1 Ley 22/2003, de 9 de julio, Concursal, BOE nr 164 of 10.7.2003 (LC).

79 Art 80.1 LC.

80 Art 56 LC.

81 An additional argument is that the Insolvency Law treats retention of title clauses (in the context of sale of goods) as a pledge (e.g. Art 90.1.4° LC), granting them a privilege over the assets – but not ownership.

82 Art 61 LC.

83 Art 61 LC.

economy (*España circular* 2030)[84] lacks ambitions and mostly implements mandatory EU standards. Despite it selecting construction and demolition as priority sectors[85], the strategy basically restricts itself to waste (which is understandable, as it amounts to 40% of the total, yet insufficient).

The public sector seems to be unaware of the enormous possibilities that Spanish private law provides for the development of a top-notch circular economy. Property law offers flexible rules that restrict accession (one of the main impediments to the circular economy in real estate) as it does not operate against an agreed term in which the supplier retains ownership. The prevalence of agreement is a determinant for the circular economy to be sound from business and financial perspectives.

However, for an adequate amount of customer protection, consumer rules should be updated to meet the circular economy model of services, which is more sustainable than that of sales. This should probably be done at an EU level. In particular, a mandatory quality of services, under the requirement of the principle of conformity, should be put in place. Nevertheless, for the sake of sustainability, the new rules should ensure an innovative hierarchy of remedies that privilege repair over substitution. The circular economy would thus contribute to the ongoing reflection on consumer law that is being fostered by other technological advances such as artificial intelligence.

84 Ministerio de Agricultura y Pesca, Alimentación y Medio Ambiente and Ministerio de Economía, Industria y Competitividad (n 2).

85 Ministerio de Agricultura y Pesca, Alimentación y Medio Ambiente and Ministerio de Economía, Industria y Competitividad (n 2), 38.

PART IV

CONCLUSIONS

SQUARING THE CIRCLE? RECONCILING CONSUMER LAW AND THE CIRCULAR ECONOMY*

Hans-W. Micklitz

Disclaimer: my academic career is strongly connected to the rise of consumer law in the heydays of the welfare state in the 1970s and 1980s and the delegation of consumer law making from the Member States to the European Union. As part of the EU enlargement process, the 13 more recent Member States had to take over the consumer acquis. I was involved in many projects about the transfer of European consumer law not only to the new member states, but to the EU's neighbouring states, to the Far East, to India and China, to the Global South (particularly Africa) and to the Global West (South America). The shift from the national to the European, and then to the international, is tied to a change in perspective. At the national level, consumer law is, or at least was, connected to the building of a better, more just society; at the European level, consumer law is tied to providing and giving the Internal Market project a social face; at the international level, consumer law is to be connected to the post-war international economic order, today the Global Value Chains. My short essay intends to convey a simple message: in light of the 17 UN Sustainable Development Goals[1], the 2015 EU document on circular economy[2] and the exploding digitalisation it is time to wipe the slate clean and design a new consumer law from scratch. I will formulate 8 key issues which urgently call for an answer in order to conceptualise a sustainable consumer protection law.

---

* I would like to thank Evelyne Terryn for her incredible patience and encouragement to write that paper as well as M. Durovic, A. De Franceschi, M. Namyslowska, P. Rott, E. Terryn and Ch. Twigg-Flesner for their amazing comments which pushed me ever further and deeper. The usual disclaimer applies.

1 Https://www.un.org/sustainabledevelopment/sustainable-development-goals/.

2 COM (2015) 614 final.

1. OUT OF THE COMFORT ZONE

The title of the book is consumer protection and the circular economy. Law and consumer law play a role, but major contributions are coming from other disciplines and broaden the picture far beyond the existing corpus of European and national consumer laws. Consumer protection is the legacy of the welfare state, the regulatory response to the consumer society, the rise of consumption economically but also societally. Economically, consumption makes up the biggest chunk in the current economy; societally, consumption is part of identity building. When the EU took over consumer policy in the aftermath of the Single European Act to establish the Internal Market, consumer law was deprived of its protective role; instead, consumer protection law turned into consumer law without *protection*.[3]

So why return to consumer *protection*, and what kind of protection is needed in the circular economy? The reference to protection immediately revitalises the idea of the consumer as the weaker party. However, what we have perceived in recent decades is a differentiation of the consumer into two or three categories: the responsible consumer, the confident consumer and the vulnerable consumer. In such a perspective, the vulnerable consumer would be the primary addressee in the circular economy. This is certainly much too narrow, but it allows us to put the question on the table as to what consumer protection means, and who is in need of protection, against what and what for.[4]

But is consumer protection as it developed in the consumer society of the 1980s comparable to consumer protection in the circular economy? The political rhetoric runs the risk of reducing the linkage between the two to just another technocratic problem, an exercise of adjusting regulatory techniques to the circular economy. There is more needed than a mere adjustment of the existing body of consumer law, than sticking with familiar regulatory techniques rather than investing in the work necessary for a fundamental recasting of consumer policy and consumer protection law. Consumer protection and consumer law have to be rethought (if not redesigned altogether), if one takes the circular economy and sustainability seriously. There is an obvious tension in the contributions to this book, which can only be overcome by going back to legal theory. On one side, there are, crudely speaking, the non-lawyers who provide a broader perspective, who highlight the economic, societal, psychological

3 H.-W. Micklitz, The Expulsion of the Concept of Protection from the Consumer Law and the Return of Social Elements in the Civil Law – A Bittersweet Polemic, *Journal of Consumer Policy*, (2012),Volume 35, Issue 3, pp 283–296.

4 Th. Wilhelmsson, *Critical Studies in Private Law. A Treatise on Need-Rational Principles in Modern Law*, (Dordrecht: Kluwer Academic Publishers, 1992).

and natural sciences dimension of the concepts of circular economy and sustainability. On the other side, there are the lawyers, who tend to break down the big issues into nitty-gritty legal questions of how and by what means the circular economy and sustainability can be squeezed into the existing legal regimes. Such an exercise implies – to use fashionable EU speak – that consumer law is 'fit for purpose'[5], that consumer law as it has developed over the last 50 years is at least in principle able to handle the call for circular economy.[6]

I have my doubts. This volume makes it abundantly clear that lawyers have to leave their comfort zone. They have to actively engage with those disciplines that have been and are working for decades on what is called today sustainability and circular economy. It is the century-old debate on the law and …: law and economics, law and sociology, law and psychology, law and natural sciences etc.[7] The rise of the consumer society in the 1960s in the US, later in Europe and now in the other continents initially triggered a deep theoretical debate on what consumer law stands for, how consumer law and consumer protection could carry the social policy implications and how the legal rules should be designed so as to cope with the new economic, societal and social challenges. The political dimension has got somewhat lost over the decades.

Consumer lawyers have to leave the safe harbour of the rules that the nation states and the EU have established to give first the national economy and society, and later the Internal Market, a social face. In short, what is needed is a theoretical debate on what the role of consumer protection and consumer law could be and how a consumer law that meets the needs of a circular economy should be designed. In the 1960s/1970s, the opponents of consumer law argued that consumer policy is politics and not law. Consumer law was political law. Over time, and through the shift away from the Member States to the EU (which goes hand in hand with the decline of the welfare state), consumer law was de-politicised. The political, economic and societal recognition of consumer law ended in consumer bureaucracy and consumer technocracy. Seen in this way, theorising and politicising consumer law in the age of the circular economy requires the re-politicisation of consumer law as a necessary requirement. This is will not be possible without serious self-reflection.

---

5 This is the aim of the better regulation programme and the consumer refit initiative, https://ec.europa.eu/info/law/law-topic/consumers/review-eu-consumer-law-new-deal-consumers_en.

6 Insightful Roger Brownsword's distinction between "coherentism" and "regulatory instrumentalism" is interesting (a good summary is at R. Brownsword, After Brexit: Regulatory-Instrumentalism, Coherentism and the English Law of Contract (2017) 34 *Journal of Contract Law*, 139–164, at 142–3.

7 V. Nourse and G. Shaffer, Varieties of New Legal Realism, Can a New World Order Prompt a New Legal Theory, (2009) 95, *Cornell Law Review*, 95 (2009), p 60.

2. CIRCULAR ECONOMY AND SUSTAINABILITY

The 2015 EU Communication on the Circular Economy[8] has to be placed into the context of the 17 United Nations' Sustainable Development Goals (SDG). A brief look at the substance of the two documents suffices to make it clear that the UN's approach goes much further and asks many more fundamental and comprehensive questions about the effects on consumers, on consumer protection and consumer law. Be that as it may, the EU document is ambitious enough to trigger a deeper debate. It remains surprising though that it needed the United Nations to pressure the Global North to adjust its economy to the ever more visible effects of climate change. The EU Member States and the EU were unable to generate the necessary commitment to the urgently needed change of our economies.

The EU has to face a challenge that Ludwig Krämer put upfront as early as 1997 in the *Liber Amicorum* for Norbert Reich.[9] The event resulting in that book brought together the then leading scholars of consumer law in Europe. Backed by the newly introduced qualified majority voting rule, the EU succeeded to get a whole series of consumer law rules adopted. Looking back, the 1990s could be regarded as the heydays of European consumer law. The building of consumer law through the EU strengthened the belief that the EU could turn into more than market building, into something which could be described as building a European society, or perhaps even building a European Constitution and European Civil Law. Ludwig Krämer destroyed the festive mood with his forceful critique that consumer law had neglected the environmental dimension. Whilst each and every consumer lawyer nodded her head and admitted that there is a need to bring consumer and environmental protection into a holistic legal perspective, nothing happened. The cautious attempts to merge the two fields did not produce consistent results. In fact, consumer and environmental law developed separate rationales and have followed their own path dependency until today.

Therefore, whether the link is environmental protection, sustainability or circular economy, the question remains whether and how these three other fields could be merged into one, and then, depending on the level of abstraction, whether this could be brought into line with the consumer society and consumer law? I do not want to be misunderstood. For sure, there remained

8 COM (2015) 614 final.

9 L. Krämer, 'Vom Rechte, das mit uns geboren – Der Einzelne im gemeinschaftlichen Umweltrecht', in Krämer, L., Micklitz, H.-W. and Tonner, K. (eds.), *Law and Diffuse Interests in the European Legal Order / Recht und diffuse Interessen in der Europäischen Rechtsordnung. Liber amicorum Norbert Reich* (Baden-Baden: Nomos, 1997).

voices advocating the need for a sustainable European constitution[10] as there were doctrinal attempts to find gateways in the existing body of consumer law through which environmental protection, sustainability and circular economy implications could be channelled. Throughout the text I will refer back to the attempts to break down the grand concepts – sustainability and circular economy – into particular substantive or procedural requirements that allow for the greening of consumer law.

I see myself as having been and as being part of the group of these consumer lawyers, well-minded but all too easily ready to fall back into their/my comfort zone. These incremental attempts, however, did suppress the crucial questions lying beneath, which can now no longer been avoided if we take sustainability, circular economy and climate change seriously:

> Is consumer law as it was developed in the consumer society the problem?
> Is 'irresponsible' behaviour of consumers the problem?
> Is the consumer the problem?
> Are we the problem?

Consumer law follows the market rationale. Consumer law is intrinsically tied to the market and its relevance for the society we are living in. If the gross income in the EU results basically from consumption – 54,4%[11] – then consumption is needed for sustaining and growing the economy. The rationale of the market requires the consumer to buy ever more products and to constantly replace the old ones with new ones. The more the consumer buys, the better it is for the economy. The consumer shall not repair products but replace them immediately, she shall not tinker around to get the product going again, but get rid of it instead.[12] From a purely economic point of view, planned obsolescence makes perfect sense.[13] It keeps the economy going. Language matters. Old used products are second hand = second best products. They are waste, they are not raw material.

The critique that behavioural economics and behavioural science has to face is that they promote economic efficiency to steer consumer behaviour into one particular

---

10 A. Azmanova and M. Pallemaerts, *The European Union and Sustainable Development: Internal and External Dimensions*, (Brussels:VUB Press, 2006).

11 Https://ec.europa.eu/eurostat/statistics-explained/index.php/Household_consumption_by_purpose.

12 For an early discussion Ch. Twigg-Flesner, 'The Law on Repairs and Guarantees', in T. Cooper (ed.), *Longer Lasting Products: Alternatives to the Throwaway Society*, (Aldershot:Gower, 2010).

13 T. Brönneke and A. Wechsler (eds.), *Obsoleszenz interdisziplinär Vorzeitiger Verschleiß aus Sicht von Wissenschaft und Praxis*, VIEW Schriftenreihe Volume 37, 2015; A. De Franceschi, Editorial Planned Obsolescence: The Apple and Samsung Cases, *EuCML* (Journal of European Consumer and Market Law), 2019, 7:6, 217.

direction – the direction of increasing the efficiency of the market.[14] No doubt behavioural economics and behavioural science can also be instrumentalised to steer the consumer into sustainable behaviour, into strengthening and building the circular economy. I will come back to this point at the end of my essay. The multifunctionality of the tool points to a deeper problem, the relationship between individual autonomy and the public interest. In his breath-taking reconstruction of 500 years of consumption, Frank Trentmann[15] leaves us with a rather pessimistic assessment on how we have behaved and how we still behave today. We the consumers are longing for ever more consumption. The Europeans are following the lead given by the United States, and China is to be regarded as the culmination point for a society in which consumption becomes the politically-promoted substitute for a meaningful life. The exchange of letters between Rawls and van Parijs has not lost its significance. Here is what Rawls asked in 2003[16]:

> One question the Europeans should ask themselves ... is how far reaching they want their union to be ... The long-term result of this [the US federal union driven by market efficiency HM] ... is a civil society awash in a meaningless consumerism of some kind. I can't believe that that is what you want.

There is a huge gap between the economic importance of private consumption and the deep philosophical and societal questions that consumer law faces today. What might have worked in the 20th century in the historical compromise of the Global North between a capitalist market economy and a democratic regime, has obviously not only led to a crisis of democracies and the EU in the 21st century[17], but it has catapulted the very political and societal importance of consumption for our lives into the limelight. This exactly is the place where the relationship between the circular economy, sustainability and consumer law has to be placed.

3. TECHNOLOGY

The new consumer law I am advocating cannot be designed without taking digitalisation into account. It seems that history is repeating itself once more. The current hype about digitalisation, about machine learning, neuronal nets

14 H.-W. Micklitz, 'The Politics of Behavioural Economics of Law', in H.-W. Micklitz, A.-L. Sibony, F. Esposito, *Research Methods in Law and Consumer Law*, (Northampton: Elgar, 2018), pp 513–556.

15 F. Trentmann, *The Empire of Things, How we Became a World of Consumers, from the Fifteenth Century to the Twenty-First,* (London: Penguin Books, 2016).

16 J. Rawls and P. Van Parijs, 'Three Letters on the Law of Peoples and the European Union' (2003) 4 *Revue de philosophie économique*, pp 7–20, available at: www.uclouvain.be/cps/ucl/doc/etes/documents/RawlsVanParijs1.Rev.phil.Econ.pdf.

17 P. F. Kjaer and N. Olsen (eds.), *Critical Theories of Crisis in Europe. From Weimar to the Euro,* (London: Rowman & Littlefield, 2016).

and blockchain, about algorithms and big data analytics, has conquered the awareness of lawyers around the world, first in the US and Israel, and now, with the usual delay, also Europe. The research invested into digital consumer law or more broadly the impact of digitalisation on consumer law has triggered conferences, publications and the new EU Directive on digital content.[18] This trend of research and political action is again following its own path, and is by and large separated from the parallel claim of building a circular economy and of implementing the 17 SDGs.

The Consumer Refit exercise was a kind of stock taking effort under five major paradigms: effectiveness, efficiency, coherence, relevance and added value.[19] The European Commission set a huge machinery into motion: studies were commissioned, hearings were held, a 'New Deal for Consumers' was presented that eventually led to concrete proposals for reform of the existing body of EU consumer law rules and even the introduction of a collective compensation claim.[20] At the time of writing, it looks as if this initiative will have to be handled, if any, in the next Parliamentary session.[21] This major effort of reform which must have swallowed up millions of taxpayers' money neither links consumer law to the circular economy/sustainability nor to digitalisation. The bifurcation of consumer law, the separation between the market and the environment, has now led to a trifurcation. When it comes to consumer law, the market based consumer law, environmental law and the digital consumer law are separate silos, without much interaction. The language used in the context of the Consumer Refit uses the necessary catchwords, but the overall political exercise was not meant to review whether the existing body of consumer law is fit for the circular economy and for the challenges of the digital economy and society. The whole undertaking follows the Internal Market rationale.[22] One might even argue that out of the five parameters, economic efficiency dominates.

There is no difficulty to find academic research on the digitalisation of environmental law and of consumer law, but how are the two interconnected

---

18 Directive (EU) 2019/770 of the European Parliament and of the Council of 20 May 2019 on certain aspects concerning contracts for the supply of digital content and digital services (Text with EEA relevance.) PE/26/2019/REV/1OJ L 136, 22.5.2019, p. 1–27.

19 Https://ec.europa.eu/info/law/law-topic/consumers/review-eu-consumer-law-new-deal-consumers_en and the analysis of H.-W. Micklitz and A. Villanueva, 'Refit or Rethink – The Politics of EU research – A Grand Misunderstanding?' in E. van Schagen and St. Weatherill (eds.), *Impact Assessments in EU Contract Law: The Unfair Terms Directive after the Fitness Check*, (Oxford: Hart Publishing, 2019).

20 Website of the European Commission, COM(2018) 183 and 184 final.

21 According to the legislative observatory, Parliament has already voted on the compromise text and the Council is still to vote: https://oeil.secure.europarl.europa.eu/oeil/popups/ficheprocedure.do?reference=2018/0090(COD)&l=en.

22 Ch. Twigg.-Flesner, Editorial: From REFIT to a Rethink: Time for Fundamental EU Consumer Law Reform? (2017) 6 *EuCML*, pp 185–189.

in light of the circular economy and sustainability? The political promise of digital capitalism is that all the dysfunctionalities and failures of the old market economy will be overcome through the new technology.[23] Through 3D printing, the production is brought back home to the industrial states. Online platforms are said to promote the sharing economy far beyond Uber and Airbnb, through the joint use of do-it yourself products or the local organisation of all sorts of daily life activities. There are no limits to imagination. However, the promising land ahead of us should not be entered without a deeper understanding of the political economy behind digitalisation.[24] Digitalisation of the economy and the society could be understood as response of capitalism to the increased social costs of labour. Industrialisation replaced blue collar labour through machines, digitalisation substitutes not only the remaining rest of blue collars but now also white collar labour.[25]

It is by no means clear what the digital economy and digital society will look like in, say, 10 years from now, let alone what the role of consumption as well as that of consumer law will be.[26] Ten years is a huge time span in light of the exponential development of technology. In the business world and in academia, the feasibility of personalised law gains ground.[27] We are gradually getting accustomed to personalised advertising and personalised prices. Personalised consumer law, tailored along the lines of our alter ego in the net, responds to our behavioural preferences, both our own and those that are associated with our profile through data generated from other consumers with a similar profile.

---

23 OECD Guidelines on AI 26 May 2019 refers 8 times to SDGs, without addressing the tension: *RECOGNISING that AI has the potential to improve the welfare and well-being of people, to contribute to positive sustainable global economic activity, to increase innovation and productivity, and to help respond to key global challenges*, https://legalinstruments.oecd.org/en/instruments/OECD-LEGAL-0449#_ga=2.241625666.15407406.1559741306-1807715073.1520074357.

24 Y. Benkler, *The Role of Technology in Political Economy*, 25th July 2018, Harvard University, Berkman Klein Center, https://cyber.harvard.edu/story/2018-07/role-technology-political-economy.

25 See the publications of P. Drahos, which point into that direction, for instance, *The Global Governance of Knowledge: Patent Offices and Their Clients*, (Cambridge; New York: Cambridge University Press, 2010) and R. Süsskind, https://legal-tech-blog.de/legal-tech-book-series-tomorrows-lawyers-by-richard-susskind-part-3.

26 See the editorial of H.-W. Micklitz and Ch. Twigg-Flesner, Think Global – Towards International Consumer Law, *Journal of Consumer Law*, (2010) 33, pp 201–207.

27 A. Casey and A. Niblett, The Death of Rules and Standards,*Coase-Sandor Working Paper Series in Law and Economics*,(2015) No. 738, available at: https://chicagounbound.uchicago.edu/law_and_economics/775/; A. Porat and L. J. Strahilevitz, Personalizing Default Rules and Disclosure with Big Data, 112 Mich L. Rev. (Michigan Law Review), (2014), p 1417, available at: http://repository.law.umich.edu/mlr/vol112/iss8/2; A. Porat and O. Ben-Shahar, Personalised Mandatory Rules in Contract Law, *University of Chicago Law Review*, Forthcoming., University of Chicago Coase-Sandor Institute for Law & Economics Research Paper No. 855, U of Chicago, Public Law Working Paper No. 680, https://papers.ssrn.com/sol3/papers.cfm?abstract_id=3184095.

What might be a nightmare for some looks like the promised land for others – at last we can achieve the just society in which everybody gets the law she needs.

But where is sustainability in this personalised law and where is the circular economy? A personalised consumer law would be tailored and adjusted to the behavioural preferences taken from the net. A consumer who has no interest in sustainability would receive information on her needs and the respective remedies for undisturbed consumption, a consumer who looks for sustainable consumption would get what she needs. Personalised law, in short, favours the choice model.

4. ECONOMICS

Current consumer law is built on the premise that the same rules could, in principle, be applied to all the consumers in the European Union, and that potential differences in the capabilities of consumers can be balanced out through the triad of the responsible, the confident and the vulnerable consumer. It must be recalled that the existing body of consumer law was adopted by and large in the 1990s, largely based on predecessors elaborated within the then 15 Member States during the 1970s and 1980s.[28] The EU used the existing national rules for the development of minimum standards that left the 15 Member States with leeway for the development of higher standards of protection. The Lisbon Agenda 2000 paved the ground for the adoption of the consumer policy programme 2002–2006. Here, the Commission advocated full harmonisation, gradually replacing the minimum standards with uniform rules throughout the EU. The Consumer Refit is the latest attempt to achieve this objective.[29] Member States and large parts of the Consumer Law Community resisted full harmonisation for long. However, the recently adopted Directive on Consumer Sales provides for full harmonisation.[30] The European Commission will celebrate its adoption as a success and as an incentive to fight for full harmonisation in

---

28 This is the first wave of European consumer law, the second wave is much more vertical, introducing consumer rights into the EU rules on regulated markets. Here the EU was overall much more successful to realise full harmonisation.

29 More generally on the evaluation of EU policy making, S. Smismans, and R. Minto, Are integrated impact assessments the way forward for mainstreaming in the European Union?; *Regulation & Governance*, (2017) 11:3, pp 231–251. (10.1111/rego.12119); S. Smismans, The politicization of ex post policy evaluation in the EU, *European Journal of Law Reform*, (2017), 19:1, pp 74–96. (10.5553/EJLR/138723702017019102005); C. A. Dunlop and C. M. Radaelli (eds.), *Handbook of Regulatory Impact Assessment*, (Cheltenham, UK; Northhampton, MA: Edward Elgar Publishing, 2016).

30 Directive (EU) 2019/771 of the European Parliament and of the Council of 20 May 2019 on certain aspects concerning contracts for the sale of goods, amending Regulation (EU) 2017/2394 and Directive 2009/22/EC, and repealing Directive 1999/44/EC, OJ L 136, 22.5.2019, p. 28–50.

the remaining parts of consumer law. Full harmonisation reduces the leeway of Member States to deviate from European standards.[31]

Ten new Member States joined the EU in 2004, 2 more in 2007, with Croatia in 2013 being the latest Member State. When these countries joined the EU, the legislative standards were already set. The new Member States were obliged to take over the consumer acquis as part of the accession process. The Agreements concluded with the then candidate states did not take the socialist past and the different standards in the economy into account. Or, to put it the other way round, – the consumers in the new Member States were supposed/promised to enjoy the same level of protection as the consumers in the old Member States, independent of the differences in the economies of the established Western capitalist markets and the Eastern socialist markets in the process of change.

The approach developed by the EU in the enlargement process governs its policy towards neighbouring countries. The different agreements concluded with the Western Balkan countries, Georgia and the Ukraine contain a long list of consumer law directives which have to be implemented.[32] The EU monitors the implementation process and requires progress reports on a regular basis.[33] The ideology is identical – consumers in the neighbouring countries shall enjoy the same standards as those in the EU itself, both new and old Member States. The EU does not take potential differences in the markets and the societies into account. To give just one example: sponsored by the German Gesellschaft für Internationale Zusammenarbeit, a team of Georgian lawyers and economists produced a Regulatory Impact Assessment (RIA) of the draft consumer law – meant to implement key consumer law directives (unfair terms, unfair commercial practices, consumer sales, consumer rights) along the lines of the requirements laid down in the Association Agreement.[34] On the basis of the available quantitative and qualitative data, the RIA analyses the economic and societal impact of the EU-imposed consumer rules on the Georgian economy

---

31 I will enter the debate on the reach of full harmonisation, see N. Reich, Von der Minimal- zur Voll- zur „Halbharmonisierung" – Ein europäisches Privatrechtsdrama in fünf Akten, *ZEuP*, (2010), 7.

32 J. Stuyck and M. Durovic, 'The External Dimension of Consumer law', in H.-W. Micklitz and M. Cremona (eds.), *Private Law in the External Dimension of the EU*, (Oxford: Oxford University Press, 2016), pp 227.

33 M. Karanikic, H.-W. Micklitz and N. Reich, *Modernising Consumer Law – The Experience of the Western Balkan*, (Baden-Baden: Nomos, 2012).

34 Draft Law on Consumer Rights Protection, Regulatory Impact Assessment, May 2019 on file with the author Chapter 1 – Kety Gujaraidze (Georgian Institute of Public Affairs) Chapter 2 – Davit Maisuradze and Irakli Shakiashvili (Ilia State University) Chapter 3 – Jaba Gvelebiani (Georgian Institute of Public Affairs) Chapter 4 – Jaba Gvelebiani (Georgian Institute of Public Affairs) Chapter 5 – Liana Akhobadze (GIZ Legal Program) Chapter 6 – Ana Khurtsidze, Nata Sturua and Gaioz Japaridze (University of Georgia) Chapter 7 – Working group Chapter 8 – Working group.

and society. The key finding is the existence of two markets: the first is one for the 'rich' people who can afford to buy the same products as in the West. These products are usually imported from the old West or from the US. The other market is local, where the 'poor' people buy substandard and often counterfeited products at low prices. These products are produced locally and/or imported from China. The economists are claiming that the imposition of one and the same consumer protection standard on the two markets would squeeze the local producers out of the market and would lead to a supply shortfall.

There is no need to "Go East" in order to find two markets within one economy. The rising tension between global cities and forgotten regions and between centre and periphery[35] can be observed both in the US and in the EU itself. It suffices to travel through the old coal and steel regions in Belgium, France, Germany, Luxemburg and the UK. It seems that the phenomenon of the two markets in one country is no longer to be found in former socialist states or in the Global South. These are all variations of what S. Santos terms "localised globalisation" and "globalised localisation".[36] The next generation of European consumer law has to take the reality of the *two* markets into account, if the idea of a circular economy and sustainable consumption should remain more than a pipe dream.

5. ETHICS

The digitalisation of the economy and society has triggered a debate in the Western world about the ethics of the world in which we are already living and into which we are ever deeper drawn. Western democratic states have set up ethics commissions, the European Union just published ethics guidelines[37] and the academic debate is blossoming.[38] The German Advisory Council to the Ministry of Justice and Consumer Protection, of which I am a member, tried to launch a debate about if and eventually in what terms digitalisation requires regulatory measures in order to protect the digital sovereignty of the consumer.[39]

---

35 D. Kukovec, Law and the Periphery, (2015) 21: 3, *European Law Journal*, pp 406–428.

36 B. De Sousa Santos, Law: A Map of Misreading: Toward a Postmodern Conception of Law (1987) 14, *Journal of Law and Society*, 279–302.

37 Http://ec.europa.eu/research/participants/data/ref/h2020/grants_manual/hi/ethics/h2020_hi_ethics-data-protection_en.pdf.

38 F. Pascale, *The Black Box Society, The Secret Algorithms that Control Money and Information*, (Cambridge: Harvard University Press, 2015); S. Zuboff, *The Age of Surveillance Capitalism: The Fight for a Human Future at the New Frontier of Power*, (Public Affairs, 2019).

39 The relevant three opinions on Consumer Law 2.0 (2016), Digital Sovereignty (2017) and Consumer-Friendly Scoring (2018) are available also in English on the website of the Advisory Council, www.svr-verbraucherfragen.de/en/documents/documents/.

In practice, the states are united in a 'wait and see' approach, at the very best a 'watch and see' approach. 'Watch' and 'see' requires top level competence of computer scientists in ministries and supervisory agencies. It is plain that the reality is different. The best computer scientists are by and large working for the big four (Google, Amazon, Microsoft, Apple) and, if not for the big four, for one of the many digital start-up companies. There are two reasons: the high salaries and the creative space. The big four may pay the best salaries, which allows them to recruit the best people. The salary scales for public officials in western democracies do not offer a competitive income. However, there is more to this than salaries. The tech firms offer the most interesting jobs in a very different working environment, largely without traditional hierarchies, in a protected space where individuality and creativity are strongly promoted.[40] Salary constraints, better job opportunities, hierarchical command and control structures and the empty labour market render it difficult to establish the necessary competence within states, even if the states were ready to establish such a monitoring and surveillance unit in whatever form. 'Watch' and 'see' requires an institution similar to the national and the European Central Bank. The salaries paid for central bankers are by and large competitive. We need institutions that survey the market and the exponential development of technology. However, such institutions do not even exist, at least not in the Western World, let alone a political debate on the ethics of digitalisation. There does not seem to exist the political will and the political preparedness to take action beyond investing in research, including consumer informatics. Europe does not have a Cyber Ministry like Audrey Tang from Taiwan.[41]

What are the ethics of a circular consumer law in light of the fast moving digitalisation of the economy and the society? Strictly speaking these are two separate though interconnected discourses. The circular economy requires a human being which accepts to be steered into the politically recognised right direction, at least if we are ready to learn from the 500 years of the 'Empire of Things'. Somewhat empathically, one might argue that the circular economy needs a new human being who accepts responsibility for the environment, for sustainability and for climate change. Such a claim looks frighteningly similar to communist times which had called for the creation of the 'new individual'.[42]

---

40 One of my phd researchers Anna Maria Nowak is writing her phd on Fintechs. She has interviewed the employees at all levels in the firms. These interviews provide a deep insight into the motivations of those who decide to work for a small Fintech instead for a big bank or a public agencies.

41 The web is full of information about her commitment to building a democracy where AI is used to survey what the government does and not to control the citizens, see the passionate article in Süddeutsche Zeitung, https://www.sueddeutsche.de/digital/cyberministerin-audrey-tang-taiwan-1.4468006?reduced=true.

42 C. Milosz, *The Captive Mind*, (London: Secker & Warburg, 1953).

In the digital economy and society, the human risks turning into an appendix of technology.[43] If digitalisation is apt to contribute to the building of a circular economy the ethical question is whether technology can take over steering humans in the "right" – i.e., the politically correct and desired – direction, the building of a circular economy. I will not suggest that I have any answers to these issues. However, the new consumer law should ideally have at least a tentative, perhaps experimental answer to the triangular relationship between the ethics of the circular economy, the ethics of technology and the role of the (consumer) Law.

If the answer is to be expected from technology, then we are back to the political economy of digitalisation. Since Samuelson, since 1948, economics relies on mathematics, and, more recently, econometrics. Vogl[44] has vehemently criticised the idea, or even ideology, that man is able to forecast the future through developing mathematical models. It is only more recently that empirics have come back to economics, mainly, but not only, through behavioural economics. The political message of mainstream economics is that Law, can only work if it increases efficiency. I will not deny that the quantitative efficiency test helps to discover the unwanted distributive effects of well-meant consumer protection regulation.[45] However, law is more than what can be measured and tested in categories of economic efficiency. Law, this is the plea, cannot be reduced to numbers and statistics. The measuring of the law in allusion to the well-known book of D. Kehlmann *Measuring the World*[46] does not do justice to the societal and ethical role and function of the Law.[47]

6. BEYOND THE NATION STATE

The world we are living in is a world beyond national consumer law, whether public or private, it is a world beyond the nation state. Nation states are under pressure to adapt their rules to the needs of a globalised – many say neo-liberal[48] – economy. The credo of the Lisbon Agenda of 'transforming the EU into the most competitive economy of the world' has never been repealed or corrected. The SDGs and the 2015 EU document on the circular economy speak a different

43 There is much debate on human centred AI – see OECD Guidelines, (n. 24).

44 J. Vogl, *The Specter of Capital*, (Stanford: Stanford University Press, 2014).

45 O. Ben-Shahar, The Paradox of Access Justice, and Its Application to Mandatory Arbitration, (2016) 83, *The University of Chicago Law Review*, pp 1755–1817.

46 D. Kehlmann, *Die Vermessung der Welt*, 2005, (eng. *Measuring the World*, 2010).

47 H.-W. Micklitz, *The measuring of the law*, Manuscript, on file with the author.

48 There is a word of caution needed on the loose use of 'neo-liberal'. There is more than one concept behind, C. Crouch, *The Strange Non-Death of Neo-Liberalism*, (Cambridge: Polity Press, 2011), the same, C. Crouch, *Can Neoliberalism Be Saved from Itself?*, (Social Europe Edition, 2017).

language. One question is how to reconcile these goals and whether technology is the answer to present-day problems. The other question is WHO does it – the nation state, the EU as a regional organisation, or the community of the states within the United Nations?

The debates about the circular economy and the role consumer law and consumer policy might play more often than not address, if not explicitly then implicitly, the nation state, i.e. the state as the key regulator. This is the undercurrent of most of the contributions to this book, be they by economists, lawyers or philosophers. For more than 20 years, the market dominated the minds of politicians. Now it seems as if we can discover a revival of the nation state as the key actor, not only across the Atlantic but also within the European Union. Legally speaking, the Member States have no competence when and where the EU fully harmonised consumer law. The rather generous interpretation on the scope of EU consumer law through the ECJ has even strengthened the position of the EU.[49] Any attempt to put the Member States into the driver's seat in leading the transformation of the current linear economy into a circular economy faces strong constitutional constraints. One might argue that the concept of the circular economy remains outside the scope of the whole integration process which was based first on the Common Market and nowadays on the Internal Market. Let us assume there is a Member State, and the Nordic countries belong certainly to the group of candidates, who is willing to take drastic steps in order to set an end to the linear economy. The legal measures to be taken nationally have to be brought into line with the Treaty. There is a potential escape hatch offered by Art.114(5) TFEU and following, permitting derogation from harmonisation measures adopted on the basis of Art 114 where "a Member State deems it necessary to introduce national provisions based on new scientific evidence relating to the protection of the environment or the working environment on grounds of a problem specific to that Member State arising after the adoption of the harmonisation measure". It is not a broad exception – the criteria are very specific. It needs (i) new scientific evidence (ii) relating to the protection of the environment (iii) on grounds of a problem specific to that Member State. So it would be difficult, albeit not impossible, to use this to push through a national initiative in support of the circular economy. However, Member States could use this provision as a means of forcing the European Commission to put forward proposals for amending harmonising measures to take better account of the circular economy. Art.114(5) etc are based on a notification procedure. If the Commission was flooded with notifications from individual Member States, then that might result in some

49 ECJ case law on full harmonisation of product liability, Case C-183/00 *González Sánchez vMedicina Asturia*, [2002] ECR I-3901 or the ECJ case-law on the scope of the Unfair Commercial Practices Directive, Joined Cases C-261/07 and C-299/07 *VTB-VAB et al v Total Belgium et al*, [2009] ECR-2949, confirmed by Case C-522/08 *Telekommunikacia Polska* [2010] ECR I-2079 para 31.

kind of reaction resulting in changes to existing harmonisation directives or entirely new initiatives.[50]

Is the competence shift from the national to the European level a satisfactory answer in light of the challenges ahead of us – the 17 SDGs? Certainly not, which is why there is so much debate about the political future of the EU. Interestingly enough, even the most powerful critics like W. Streeck[51] do not put much emphasis on sustainability and circular economy. Their major concern is the decline of democracy and sovereignty in the Member States. It should not be forgotten though that the Member States, their governments and their parliaments supported and promoted the kind of market society we are living in, the one Rawls criticises forcefully. The Member States joined forces with the EU, even used and instrumentalised the EU to a point where the peoples of Europe tend to perceive the EU as the neo-liberal hegemon which destroys the national welfare state, solidarity and justice, forgetting about the complicity between the Member States and the EU. Taking the plea of sustainability and the circular economy seriously requires nothing less and nothing more than rebuilding the foundation on which the whole European project stands – the Internal Market.

Let us assume that the EU and the Member States are willing to take exactly these steps, to rethink the Internal Market project and to gradually transform the linear into a circular economy; to merge economic, social, consumer and environmental regulation, how about the role and function of the EU in the global world? So far, the EU seems to torn between two extremes – the gentle civilizer and the neo-liberal hegemon.[52] The EU exported its consumer law to the new Member States and via the Association Agreements to the neighbouring countries. However, the looser the connections between the EU and the respective third countries, the weaker becomes the role of consumer law and policy and the more dominant the free trade paradigm. The necessary consequence would be to fix the role and function of consumer law in EU law on external relations – a sustainable consumer law that takes the economic and political reality of the *two* markets into account could indeed turn into an export hit and help to justify the EU's raison d'être.[53]

---

50 I would like to thank Christian Twigg-Flesner for pointing to Art. 114 (5) TFEU.

51 W. Streeck, *How will Capitalism End? Essays on a Failing System*, (London: Verso, 2016).

52 H.-W. Micklitz, 'The Role of the EU in the External Reach of Regulatory Private Law – Gentle Civilizer or Neoliberal Hegemon? An Epilogue', in M. Cantero and H.-W. Micklitz (eds.), *The Role of the EU in Transnational Legal Ordering: Standards, Contracts and Codes*, (Edward Elgar, forthcoming 2019).

53 G. De Burca, 'Europe's Raison d'être' in D. Kochenov and F. Amtenbrink (eds.), *The European Union's Shaping of the International Legal Order*, (Cambridge University Press, 2013), p 21.

It seemed naïve to expect the decisive move to come from the international organisations. However, exactly this happened in the elaboration and the unanimous adoption of the SDGs by 193 states in the General Assembly. What remains is the need to overcome the divide between the United Nations and its institutions on the one hand, and the World Trade Organisation on the other. So far any attempt to bring together the two institutions and the rules they developed has failed. The dividing line between free trade on the one hand and environmental and consumer protection on the other seems to be even deeper than in the EU and in the Member States. The two poles reflect the distinction between product and process regulation, national product regulation shall not work as a barrier to international trade, process regulation may follow national requirements on labour, consumer and environmental protection.[54] One may wonder whether hope results from the transformation of the global economy itself. The rise of global value chains breaks down the clear distinction between product and process and makes it theoretically possible for the lead company to exercise control over the whole process, including the degree to which local, regional and national standards on labour, consumer and environment are respected.[55] Consumers could in theory be informed on the conditions under which the products are manufactured. Sustainability clauses are ever more common in global value chains. The practical problem is compliance and enforcement before courts.[56]

7. RESPONSIBILISATION

In the globalised economy and society, in the law beyond the nation state, beyond the distinction between the public and the private, private responsibilities come into sharp focus. The public attention is very much on the behaviour of European and American transnational companies in the Global South. *Kiobel* was the latest effort thus far to hold an American company liable under the Alien Tort Claims Act.[57] The US Supreme Court rejected any liability for the infringement of customary international law of the indigenous people in Niger.

---

54 For recent attempts to connect the two poles, C. Glinski, CSR and the Law of the WTO – The Impact of Tuna Dolphin II and EC–Seal Products, 2018 *NJCL* (*Nordic Journal of Commercial Law*),p 122; S. Sankari, Collective valuation of common good through consumption: What is (un)lawful in mandatory country-of-origin labelling of non-food products 'in A. do Amaral Junior, L. Klein Vieira and L. de Almeida (eds.) Sustainable Consumption: The Right to a Healthy Environment', (forthcoming: Springer International Publishing AG, 2020).

55 R. Baldwin, *The Great Convergence: Information Technology and the New Globalization*, (Cambridge: Harvard University Press, 2016).

56 On practice N. Klein, *No Logo: Taking Aim at the Brand Bullies*,(Toronto: Knopf, 2000). It would be interesting to get to know whether the situation has improved in the last 20 years.

57 US Supreme Court *Kiobel v. Royal Dutch Petroleum Co.*, 569 U.S. 108 (2013) https://www.supremecourt.gov/opinions/12pdf/10-1491_l6gn.pdf.

To my knowledge, there is no similar case which ever entered the jurisdiction of the ECJ. This type of litigation is usually decided before national courts, sometimes with promising results.[58] L. Azoulai[59] argues that *Viking* and *Laval*[60] if put upside down, allows for arguing that European companies bear the legal responsibility to respect social rights. Whether this would equally apply to their behaviour outside the European territory is open for discussion. The responsibilisation of business is at the forefront of the debate. Rightly so.

What about the responsibility of consumers, of us? The European system of consumer law is built on obligations imposed on business to the benefit of consumers. European consumers are free to decide whether they want to enforce these rights in case business has not respected them. There is no legal obligation for consumers to make use of their rights. It is for the consumers to decide whether they read the information provided to them, how they handle information and whether they are ready to translate information into action. The EU has adopted a whole set of rules which inform the consumer on the environmental implications of the product or service she intends to order. It is plain and well researched that consumers do not read standard terms and do not take notice of the information provided and that there is a mismatch between the publicly declared willingness to buy sustainable products and their actual behaviour.[61] It is also true that the decision of an individual consumer to utilise their rights is obviously also constrained by their individual capabilities and capacity The individual decision of the consumer NOT to read and NOT to bring wishful thinking and behaviour into compliance forms an integral part of individual autonomy.

Currently I can identify three ways under discussion how to overcome this mismatch. The first is through labelling. The consumer has the choice between circular and non-circular products. This is by and large the current state of affairs, provided the consumer has access to both categories of products; which is quite often not the case and provided she receives the information in

58 UK Supreme Court *Vedanta Resources PLC and another (Appellants) v Lungowe and others (Respondents)* before Lady Hale, President Lord Wilson, Lord Hodge, Lady Black, Lord Briggs, (2019), available at: https://www.supremecourt.uk/cases/docs/uksc-2017–0185-judgment.pdf; *AAA v Unilever* (2018) EWCA Civ, p 1532, and *Okpabi v Royal Dutch Shell Plc* (2018) Bussiness Law Review, p. 1022.

59 L. Azoulai, The Court of Justice and the Social Market Economy: The Emergence of an Ideal and the Conditions for its Realisation, (2008) 45 *Common Market Law Review*, pp 1335–1355.

60 ECJ Case C-341/05, *Laval un Partneri* [2007] ECR I-11767; ECJ Case C-438/05 *International Transport Workers' Federation and Finnish Seamen's Union v Viking Line ABP and OÜ Viking Line Eesti*, ECR 2007 I-10779.

61 Overview on the state of the debate by A.-L. Sibony, 'Data and Arguments: Empirical Research In Consumer Law', in H.-W. Micklitz, A.-L. Sibony and F. Esposito (eds.), *Research Methods in Law and Consumer Law*, (n. 15), p 165.

an appropriate form, eg. not only in writing by using logos and symbols. The second option would be to integrate the external costs into the price. This would probably make non-circular products more expensive. The poor consumer cannot afford the increased costs. Redistributional measures would be needed to give this option a perspective. The third is the most delicate one, but one that needs to be taken seriously in the light of 500 years of borderless consumption.[62] We need to open Pandora's box and discuss the responsibilisation of the consumer. The International Association of Consumer Law organised a conference in 2015 under the provocative title of 'virtue and consumer law'.[63] This could have been an invitation to bring the responsibility of the consumer to the fore and to rethink the consumer rights rhetoric. Unfortunately, this was only partially taken up, mainly in the keynote speeches of O. Ben-Shahar and O. Bar-Gill.

The European Union is speaking of the *consumer citizen* in quite a number of documents.[64] Similarly the worker could be called the *worker citizen* and the employer the *employer citizen*. There are good reasons why it makes sense to use such a designation in EU law, in the law beyond the nation state. The "citizen", as opposed to "the consumer", bears obligations towards a European society beyond the nation state. Taking the idea of the consumer citizen seriously eventually leads to the responsibilisation of the consumer.[65] Legally speaking, the question would be whether the consumer may lose her rights when she is not making use of them or whether the non-use or the mis-use of rights can even be sanctioned and the consumer can be held liable. The notion of responsibilisation entails that consumers should expect to be subject to a number of active duties, particularly to act in a manner which prioritises conduct in line with the circular economy. In this context, a broadening of consumer education, perhaps even at school, would be a practical step towards increasing awareness of this responsibility.

The triad of the vulnerable, the confident and the responsible consumer paves the ground for a context-sensitive solution. Whereas the vulnerable consumer should and must be exempted from any responsibility, the confident and

---

62 F. Trentmann locates the rising of the phenomenon at the beginning the Renaissance, ID., *The Empire of Things*, (n. 16).

63 Https://csecl.uva.nl/content/events/conferences/2015/06/virtues-and-consumer-law.html.

64 J. Davies, *The European Consumer Citizen in Law and Policy*, (Houndmills, Basingstoke; New York: Palgrave Macmillan, 2011); M.W. Hesselink, European Contract Law: A Matter of Consumer Protection, Citizenship, or Justice?, (2007) 15:3, *European Review of Private Law*, pp 323–348.

65 M. Dani, Assembling the Fractured European Consumer (2011) *(LEQS Paper) No. 29 LSE 'Europe in Question' Discussion Paper Series*; N. Shuibhne, The Resilience of EU Market Citizenship (2010) 47 *Common Market Law Review*, pp 1597–1628; critical M. Everson and Ch. Joerges, Consumer Citizenship in Postnational Constellations? (2006) *EUI Working Paper Law No. 47*.

the responsible consumer might very well become the addressee of legal obligations. The change would be dramatic. Individual autonomy, the legacy of the enlightenment, would be sacrificed on the altar of the public interest, the need for a circular economy. I will not downplay the tectonic shift, but this is no excuse not to address the question. The tricky question then is how non-compliance with such a duty could be tackled. Reliance on the triad begs a number of questions. First, what is the conception of vulnerability here – is it category-based or situational? Secondly, how can one define that a person was vulnerable, confident or responsible in any given context? Thirdly, why should vulnerability mean that there would be exemption from any sanction/liability for non-compliance with this duty? If sustainability/promotion of the circular economy is the goal, then should not all consumers be subject to a sanctionable duty? There is more to study.

Merging the two dimensions of the increased responsibility of the relevant actors would lead to a twin approach: (i) the lead company which has demanded/imposed these terms in its supply contracts; and (ii) consumers/customers of the lead company who could hold the lead company to claims about ethical and sustainable conduct in its supply chain. For (i), the question is what sort of consequence there might be if a supplier in the value chain was in breach of the clause – would the lead company terminate the contract or would this be outweighed by the economic disbenefit of seeking a new and more expensive supplier? Alternatively, could the contract impose penalties on the supplier? As for (ii), if goods are marketed as sustainably produced etc., then the UCPD regime should be robust enough to offer one route to enforcement (subject to the general concerns about enforcement etc), and it might in any event be a breach of contract which might entitle the consumer to a remedy. Difficulty is which remedy would be appropriate, particularly as damages are not easily available for this kind of breach if the consumer cannot demonstrate a loss, the "consumer surplus" idea?

8. CONSUMER LAW

What then are the consequences for the future of consumer law? Is the current body of consumer law fit for purpose? Is it possible within the existing body of consumer law to handle the challenges of the circular economy in the digital economy and society? I propose to distinguish between three different options – the possibilities to integrate the circular economy into the existing body of law, the possibilities to use technology and new regulatory techniques to steer the consumer into the politically needed direction, and the rethinking of consumer law from scratch.

There have been manifold efforts to integrate sustainability into European private law. It suffices to mention the notion of defect in the Consumer Sales Directive, the broad scope of application of the Unfair Commercial Practices Directive or the use of the cross-section clause in Art. 6 TFU.[66] Recitals 32 and 48 of the revised of the Consumer Sales Directive 2019/77/EU build bridges towards sustainability in the conformity test and in the choice of consumer remedies. The still rather unexplored question in the Unfair Commercial Practices Directive is whether and to what extent it provides for an obligation to inform the consumer on sustainability.[67] One might bring forward good arguments. The problem remains that there is no clear-cut case law of the ECJ that would allow to connect the set of information duties enshrined in various directives, the verdict on misleading omissions and the notion of defect into one coherent legal concept. The ECJ seems to treat the UCPD as *lex generalis* with specific obligations elsewhere sometimes displacing the UCPD requirements. The other gateway is the right to repair. It is worth recalling the battle over the hierarchy between the four remedies in consumer sales law. The first draft of the European Commission intended to leave the choice to consumers. Consumer lawyers strongly supported the model and the ideology behind. Under pressure from business and from some Member States including Germany, the finally adopted version distinguishes between two layers, first repair and replacement then price reduction and termination. A closer analysis reveals that the two remedies at the first level do not enjoy the same status. In fact, the consumer is bound to ask for repair first. Doctrinal details do not matter. In 1997 I wrote an article in which I tried to make the case for the free choice model through an interpretative route, without even considering sustainability.[68] In light of the circular economy, consumer lawyers and business lawyers seem to be walking hand in hand, united in the emphasis on repair.[69] However, replacement might be cheaper than labour

---

66 For a systematic account of European and national consumer policy: LE Europe, VVA Europe, Ipsos, ConPolicy, Trinomics, *Behavioural Study on Consumers' Engagement in the Circular Economy Final Report-ANNEXES* (October2018) Specific contract –No 2016 85 06 Implementing Framework Contract –CHAFEA/2015/CP/01/LE, pp 17, 18 and 21, available at: https://ec.europa.eu/info/sites/info/files/ec_circular_economy_final_report_0.pdf.

67 H. Schebesta, Regulating Sustainability Claims on Seafood – EU Ecolabel, Unfair Commercial Practices Directive or Seafood Information Requirements?, *Journal of European Risk Regulation* (2016) 7: 4, pp 784–788.

68 H.-W. Micklitz, Ein neues Kaufrecht für Verbraucher in Europa?, (1997) *EuZW*,pp 229–237; to the possibilities of greening consumer sales law in line with sustainability Th. Wilhelmsson, Twelve Essays on Consumer Law and Policy, *Publications of the Department of Private Law*, (1996) University of Helsinki, pp267–287; C.Glinski and P. Rott, Umweltfreundliches und ethisches Konsumverhalten im harmonisierten Kaufrecht, (2003) *EuZW*, pp 649–654; J.C. Dastis, Ethischer Konsum und Vertragsrecht, (2017) *VuR*, p 252; St. Sonde, *Das kaufrechtliche Mängelrecht als Instrument zur Verwirklichung eines nachhaltigen Konsums*, 2016; even more ambitious A. Halfmeier, *Nachhaltiges Privatrecht*, (2016) Archiv für civilistische Praxis, pp 717.

69 K. Tonner, E. Gawel, S. Schlacke, M. Alt, W. Bretschneider, Gewährleistung und Garantie als Instrumente zur Durchsetzung eines nachhaltigen Produktumgangs, (2017)

intensive repair. The answer might be that the Sales Directive is flawed in the way the proportionality test is designed by focusing on the financial impact on the trader as the determining factor. A solution might have been a rule that the threshold for proportionality should have been raised – e.g., not just significant difference in cost but that repair would "not be economically viable". Here we are back to how the products are designed and for how long, whether obsolescence is inbuilt and that manufacturers should be obliged to make spare parts available for the life span of the product.

The limited impact of a pro-circular economy reading of these prominent areas of consumer law is all too obvious. More is needed. Two options gain ground in the political debate, on the one hand regulation by design (default), on the other regulation through nudging. Both avenues deserve careful analysis. What could be the role of regulation by design in the circular economy? Is it imaginable that business takes the lead and designs the product so that they last for ten years without repair?[70] I recall the famous example discussed in the 1960s when Americans flew to the moon. If a car – that was the story – was designed with the same degree of care as the shuttle, the car could and would not have the tiniest defect in the first 100,000 kilometres. Is it thinkable that industry is ready to produce such products without a stick behind the door and without consumers who are willing to accept that they will have to keep the very same car perhaps for the rest of their lives? It seems that regulation through nudging is the more promising option. Whilst I recognise the potential nudging offers, I am not ready to accept that nudging can be introduced by the Member States and by the EU without an open political debate in the parliaments. Democratic decision is needed on where and under what conditions nudging is legitimate.[71] The downside of nudging is plain. It suffices to recall China's policy on social scoring and the way how the Chinese citizens are 'nudged' towards politically promoted behaviour through surveillance technology.[72] For those in the West who reject such a scenario it might be useful to engage with Shoshana Zuboff's surveillance capitalism.[73]

VuR, p 3; K. Tonner, E. Gawel, S. Schlacke, *Stärkung eines nachhaltigen Konsums im Bereich Produktnutzung durch Anpassungen im Zivil- und öffentlichen Recht*, Gutachten im Auftrag des Umweltbundesamtes, 2017.

70 Beyond the contributions in this volume and A. Boos, T. Brönneke, A. Wechsler (eds.), *Konsum und nachhaltige Entwicklung*, Verbraucherpolitik neu denken, 2019.

71 C. R. Sunstein and L. A. Reisch, Trusting Nudges: Toward a Bill of Rights for Nudging. (Boca Raton, Florida: CRC Press, 2019); id., A Bill of Rights for Nudging, Editorial (2019) *EuCML*, p 93.

72 M. Siems, The Chinese Social Credit System, A Model for other Countries, *EUI Working paper Law 2019/1*, available at: http://cadmus.eui.eu/bitstream/handle/1814/60424/LAW_2019_01.pdf?sequence=1&isAllowed=y.

73 S. Zuboff, Big Other: Surveillance Capitalism and the Prospects of an Information Civilization,(2015) 30:1 *Journal of Information Technology*, pp 75–89.

More is needed. The 're' in the thinking about consumer law has become prominent. Geraint Howells, Christian Twigg-Flesner and Thomas Wilhelmsson[74] have just published their book on Re-thinking consumer law. The authors aim first and foremost at the re-introduction of the social in consumer law, at revitalising the protective device, but there is not much on sustainability and digitalisation. The European Commission has occupied the 're' most prominently in the Consumer REFIT, an exercise which is caught in its path dependency. In the rhetoric unfolded, European consumer law is doomed to succeed in order to keep the Internal Market going. Against this background I am advocating a more radical approach[75]:

> Not Rethinking consumer law – but – A clean slate design for a new consumer law Thinking consumer law from scratch.

In this essay, I have tried to sketch out the broad range of questions which need to be put to the forefront, theoretically and conceptually – the 500 years of irresponsible consumption, the current belief in technology as a saver, the highly divided legal framework which carves out what belongs together, the economic and social reality in Europe, the existence of two markets and two societies which are governed by one law, the tension between global cities and forgotten regions. On the conference at the European University Institute in September 2018 '40 years Journal of Consumer Policy' Claudia Lima Marques advocates a Brundlandt-style[76] report on consumer law and policy which should set the tone for a fresh start.[77]

9. WHAT NEXT

This essay might leave the reader with the feeling, or even the conviction, that the future of consumer law and private consumption looks rather gloomy. This would indeed be correct if consumer policy and consumer law were to continue along the path taken in the 1970s – more consumption, better choice is good for the global economy, for the society and for the consumer herself. It is simply not enough to stretch the existing body of consumer law so as to be able to integrate sustainability into the notion of conformity, into the remedies under the

[74] G. Howells,, Ch. Twigg-Flesner,. and Th. Wilhelmsson, *Rethinking European Consumer Law*, (Abingdon: Routledge, 2017), but see pp 334–5, and especially the final sentence at p 335.

[75] A similar plea can be found in the book by A. Boos et al (eds.), (n. 71). The subtitle says 'Verbraucherpolitik neu denken'- hinking consumer policy afresh'. I am putting emphasis on consumer *law*.

[76] Http://netzwerk-n.org/wp-content/uploads/2017/04/0_Brundtland_Report-1987-Our_Common_Future.pdf.

[77] There will be a special issue in the Journal of Consumer Policy, scheduled for 2019/2020.

Consumer Sales Directive or into misleading omission under the Directive on Unfair Commercial Practices. I will not downgrade these attempts. They provide for a first step into the 'coherentist'[78] direction we all have to move. Courts have been reluctant so far to accept the greening of consumer law through interpretation. Policy makers, whether at the national or the European level, try to integrate sustainability into the existing economic and legal order and plead for a harmony which might be unachievable.

Inertia is the problem. There is a need to rethink the economy and the society we want to live in. For consumer lawyers and consumer activists, the turn towards the circular economy offers breath-taking theoretical and conceptual opportunities for designing a sustainable consumer law which deserves its name and which is not mere window-dressing. The starting point for such a new concept must be the notion of the consumer herself, around which the new law is to be built. The move from consumer to customer indicates the erosion of the old concept, the move from the consumer in the proper sense of the word to the citizen consumer points into the direction the new design of consumer law has to move.

Some 20 years ago Ewould Hondius invited me to a conference under the provocative title 'Has Consumer Law come to an End?'. Now, I ask: 'Is the circular economy setting an end to consumer law, at least to the consumer law as it stands after 50 years?' We should not be afraid of the question nor its possible answers, and tackle it upfront. Sustainability should be made one of the founding principles of consumer law.

---

78 See, R. Brownsword, After Brexit, (n. 7).

CONSUMER, COMPETITION & MARKET SERIES

Each book in the Consumer, Competition and Market Series brings together the results of the research activities of the INSTITUTE FOR CONSUMER, COMPETITION & MARKET of the KU Leuven, co-directed by Wouter Devroe, Bert Keirsbilck and Evelyne Terryn. Furthermore the series publishes the papers presented on the conferences organised by the Institute.

The series focuses on the legal infrastructure of the internal market of the European Union (EU) and in particular on the "four freedoms" (free movement of goods, persons, services and capital/payments) and on competition law, including EU and national antitrust law, EU merger control and EU state aid law. The series also covers the consumer acquis, and sectoral market regulation, including the EU secondary legislation that seeks to protect the economic interests of consumers and companies in the internal market.

www.ingramcontent.com/pod-product-compliance
Ingram Content Group UK Ltd.
Pitfield, Milton Keynes, MK11 3LW, UK
UKHW051040120926
8556IPUK00030B/489

9 781780 6865